D0149597

George Herbert
An Annotated Bibliography of Modern Criticism
1905–1974

WITHDRAWN
UTSA LIBRARIES

University of Missouri Studies LXVIII

GEORGE HERBERT

An Annotated Bibliography of Modern Criticism
1905–1974

John R. Roberts

University of Missouri Press
Columbia & London, 1978

LIBRARY
The University of Texas
At San Antonio

Copyright © 1978 by
The Curators of the University of Missouri
University of Missouri Press, Columbia, Missouri 65201
Library of Congress Catalog Card Number 77-25314
Printed and bound in the United States of America
All rights reserved

Library of Congress Cataloging in Publication Data

Roberts, John Richard.
  George Herbert: An Annotated Bibliography of
Modern Criticism, 1905–1974.

  Includes bibliographical references.
  1. Herbert, George, 1593–1633—Bibliography.
Z8398.3.R6   [PR3508]   016.821'3   77–25314
ISBN 0–8262–0243–8

LIBRARY
The University of Texas
At San Antonio

To the Memory
of
Milissa Jane Roberts
(1960–1973)

Yet ev'n the greatest griefs
May be reliefs,
Could he but take them right, and in their wayes.
Happie is he, whose heart
Hath found the art
To turn his double pains to double praise.

—From "Mans medley"

Contents

Preface

The primary purpose of this annotated bibliography is to provide scholars and critics of George Herbert with an aid to research. This study is the first to collect and fully annotate the criticism and scholarship written on Herbert in this century. My own work has been greatly facilitated, however, by a number of previously published bibliographical essays and checklists and is, in one sense, both an extension of, and an elaboration on portions of, these earlier studies, especially *George Herbert: A Concise Bibliography* by S. A. and D. R. Tannenbaum (New York: S. A. Tannenbaum, 1946); *Studies in Metaphysical Poetry: Two Essays and a Bibliography* by Theodore Spencer and Mark Van Doren (New York: Columbia University Press, 1939); *A Bibliography of Studies in Metaphysical Poetry, 1939–1960* by Lloyd E. Berry (Madison: University of Wisconsin Press, 1964); "George Herbert: A Recent Bibliography, 1960–1967" by Harry B. Caldwell, Edward E. Samaha, Jr., and Donna G. Fricke in *Seventeenth-Century News* 26, no. 3 (1968): 54–56, and supplemented by "A Bibliography of George Herbert, 1960–1967: Addenda" by Humphrey Tonkin in *Seventeenth-Century News* 27, no. 2 (1969): 29; "Herbert" by Margaret Bottrall in *English Poetry: Select Bibliographical Guides*, edited by A. E. Dyson (London and New York: Oxford University Press, 1971), pp. 60–75; "Recent Studies in Herbert" by Jerry Leath Mills in *English Literary Renaissance* 6, no. 1 (1976): 105–18; and the extensive bibliography in C. A. Patrides's edition of *The English Poems of George Herbert* (London: J. M. Dent & Sons, 1974; Totowa, N.J.: Rowman and Littlefield, 1975). Although I gratefully acknowledge my debt to each of these earlier studies and to varying degrees have found each of them useful in preparing the present volume, my bibliography is more comprehensive and complete and more fully annotated than any previous work.

The present bibliography begins in 1905, the date of the publication of George Herbert Palmer's three-volume edition of *The English Works of George Herbert* (Boston and New York: Houghton Mifflin and Co.). Although Palmer's edition has long been superseded by the work of F. E. Hutchinson and others, it represents, in one sense, the first major study of Herbert in this century and, therefore, seemed like a reasonable starting point. The present study ends in 1974 because more recent studies were not always available and because bibliographical aids after this year were incomplete. Since 1974 a number of important works on Herbert have appeared, of course, such as Helen Vendler's *The Poetry of George Herbert* (Cambridge: Harvard University Press, 1975), Amy M. Charles's *A Life of George Herbert* (Ithaca and London: Cornell University Press,

1977), and A *Concordance to the Complete Writings of George Herbert,* edited by Mario A. Di Cesare and Rigo Mignani (Ithaca and London: Cornell University Press, 1977) to name but a few; and in the next year or so several other significant works will appear, such as Stanley Fish's forthcoming study of the unity of *The Temple* and J. Max Patrick's and John R. Mulder's new edition of the poems. I shall want to include these works, and the many others that continue to appear, when the present bibliography is revised and updated in the next few years.

Although some of the items in this bibliography (especially some of the earlier ones) are quite obviously very minor efforts, often more inspired by Christian zeal and enthusiasm than by critical thought and reflection, others represent major contributions to our understanding and appreciation not only of the poetry and prose of Herbert but also of the art and sensibility of the early seventeenth century, of metaphysical poetry and poets as a whole, and, in some cases, even of the very nature of poetry itself and of the poetic process. During the past twenty-five years Herbert's art has engaged some of the best minds of the scholarly world, and in part through their efforts he has been fully established as one of the major poets in the English language. Today nearly all serious critics and students of English literature would agree with Joseph Summers, who called Herbert "the author of the best extended collection of religious lyrics in English, a man whose art is as unquestionable as his spiritual authenticity." No longer seen as merely one of the many followers of John Donne or as a simple, pious Anglican versifier, Herbert now occupies a permanent and central position in our understanding of the development of English poetry and is recognized as one of the chief poets of the seventeenth century.

The annotations in this bibliography are descriptive, not evaluative, because I find that what is important and/or useful to one scholar or critic is not equally significant to another. Since I have made the annotations quite detailed and often quote rather extensively from the item, the reader should be able to judge rather easily whether a particular work will be useful for his purposes. Likewise, I have listed each item chronologically, in part so that by glancing over the various entries the reader will be able to get a sense of the various shifts and developments that have occurred in Herbert criticism during this century. Such an arrangement allows the reader to observe that Herbert and his works have been run through many different critical sieves (linguistic, stylistic, biographical, psychoanalytic, bibliographical, textual, formalistic, affective, etc.) and that, in a sense, the work done on him represents a kind of microcosm of what has taken place in literary criticism as a whole in the past sixty years. By means of the three detailed indexes (author, subject, and works of Herbert cited in the annotations), the reader can easily locate individual items that interest him.

I have attempted to make the bibliography as complete and as comprehensive as possible, but even from the beginning it was clear that certain limitations had to be imposed. The basic guiding principle has been to include all books, monographs, and articles specifically on Herbert written from 1905 to 1974; but, in addition, I have also tried to include extended discussions of Herbert that appear in works not centrally concerned with him. Of course, nearly all books and many articles concerned with metaphysical poetry or individual metaphysical poets contain some comment on or reference to Herbert, but to have included all items that mention Herbert in relation to Donne, Vaughan, Crashaw, Marvell, Carew, Traherne, et al. would have extended the present bibliography far beyond manageable bounds. Since my primary intention is to list and to annotate Herbert criticism, I have not included all editions of his poetry and prose that have appeared since 1905; reprints of earlier editions that were originally published before that date have also been excluded. I have attempted to include, however, editions that contain critical discussions and/or notes or that, for one reason or another, seem to have some historical interest, such as W. H. Auden's edition of selected poems (1973). In referring to Herbert's poems, I have followed F. E. Hutchinson's revised edition (1945). Publications are listed according to the date of the edition that I used in preparing my bibliographic entry; reprints, revisions, and new editions have been recorded when known. Book reviews have been excluded, for the most part, and brief mentions of Herbert in books and articles as well as references in literary histories, encyclopedias, and anthologies have also been omitted. Unpublished doctoral dissertations have also been excluded, since the early ones were impossible to obtain in some instances and since the more recent ones are adequately annotated in *Dissertation Abstracts* or *Dissertation Abstracts International*. Many items written in languages other than English have been included (French, German, Italian, Dutch, Norwegian, Spanish, Japanese, etc.), but I have no assurance that I found all items in these languages or in lesser-known ones.

It gives me much pleasure to acknowledge and to thank all those who have been so generous and kind in assisting me in this project. I wish to thank, first of all, Douglas Collins, my research assistant, who carefully gathered materials, did much of the preliminary work that made this bibliography possible, and assisted me in translating German, French, and Italian items. I should also like to thank Mark Bassett and Michael Walker, two of my former graduate students, who, at different times, checked numerous bibliographies and helped me in sundry ways. I am indebted to Maika Takeda, Professor Dennis Mueller, Gunilla Jansson, and Professor Edward Mullen of the University of Missouri–Columbia who assisted me with foreign language items and to Jeaneice Brewer, Humanities Librarian at the University of Missouri Ellis Library, who was always helpful in locating books and articles that were unavailable in the University of Missouri library. Many Herbert scholars and critics were most kind to call my attention to lesser-known materials and to encourage me with this project, especially Professors Lloyd E. Berry, Joseph Summers, C. A. Patrides, Humphrey Tonkin, Mark Taylor, Anthony Low, William J. Scheick, Ira Clark, Vincent Leitch, Edmund Miller, Sidney Paul Gottlieb, Philip Dust, Edward C. Jacobs, Wayne T. Caldwell, Hermine J. van Nuis, Michael McCanles, Peggy Curet, and John L. Idol, Jr. I owe much to my fine colleagues and students at the University of Missouri–Columbia for their helpful suggestions, insights, and encouragement; and I wish to acknowledge the Faculty Research Council of the University of Missouri–Columbia, which gave me a grant to do research at the Houghton Library, Harvard, where I was most cordially received and allowed to search for Herbert materials. I should also like to thank the Guildhall Art Gallery, London, for allowing me to use William Dyce's imaginary historical portrait, *George Herbert at Bemerton*. And to my wife, Lorraine, I owe a very special note of thanks for having generously supported me with her love and affection throughout the years that this bibliography was in preparation.

J.R.R.
Columbia, Missouri
1 October 1977

Abbreviations of Titles
of Journals

ABR • American Benedictine Review

AL • American Literature

AN&Q • American Notes and Queries (New Haven, Conn.)

Archiv • Archiv für das Studium der Neueren Sprachen und Literaturen

ArielE • Ariel: A Review of International English Language

AWR • Anglo-Welsh Review (Pembroke Dock, Wales)

BNYPL • Bulletin of the New York Public Library

BSE • Brno Studies in English (Brünn)

BuR • Bucknell Review

CE • College English

CL • Comparative Literature

CLAJ • College Language Association Journal (Morgan State Coll., Baltimore)

CLJ • Cornell Library Journal

CLS • Comparative Literature Studies

ConnR • Connecticut Review

ContempR • Contemporary Review (London)

Costerus • Costerus: Essays in English and American Language and Literature

CP • Concerning Poetry (West Wash. State Coll.)

CQR • Church Quarterly Review

CritQ • Critical Quarterly

CSR • Christian Scholar's Review

DubR • Dublin Review

DUJ • Durham University Journal

EA • Etudes Anglaises

E&S • Essays and Studies by Members of the English Association

EIC • Essays in Criticism (Oxford)

ELH • Journal of English Literary History

ELLS • English Literature and Language (Tokyo)

ELN • English Language Notes (U. of Colorado)

ELR • English Literary Renaissance

ES • English Studies

Expl • Explicator

GorR • Gordon Review

GR • Germanic Review

HAB • Humanities Association Bulletin (Canada)

HJ • Hibbert Journal

HLB • Harvard Library Bulletin

HLQ • Huntington Library Quarterly
HSL • Hartford Studies in Literature
HudR • Hudson Review
IJES • Indian Journal of English Studies (Calcutta)
JAAC • Journal of Aesthetics and Art Criticism
JEGP • Journal of English and Germanic Philology
JHI • Journal of the History of Ideas
JWCI • Journal of the Warburg and Courtauld Institute
KR • Kenyon Review
Lang&S • Language and Style
LangQ • Language Quarterly (U. of South Florida)
LHR • Lock Haven Review (Lock Haven State Coll.)
M&H • Medievalia et Humanistica (Case Western Reserve U.)
McNR • McNeese Review (McNeese State Coll., La.)
MdF • Mercure de France
MichA • Michigan Academician
MissQ • Mississippi Quarterly
ML • Modern Languages (London)
MLN • Modern Language Notes
MLQ • Modern Language Quarterly
MLR • Modern Language Review
Mosaic • Mosaic: A Journal for the Comparative Study of Literature and Ideas
MP • Modern Philology
N&Q • Notes and Queries
Neophil • Neophilologus (Groningen)
NEQ • New England Quarterly
NRF • Nouvelle Revue Française
NYHTB • New York Herald Tribune Book Review
PAAS • Proceedings of the American Antiquarian Society
PBA • Proceedings of the British Academy
PCP • Pacific Coast Philology
PLL • Papers on Language and Literature
PMLA • Publications of the Modern Language Association of America
PoetryR • Poetry Review
PQ • Philological Quarterly
PR • Partisan Review
QQ • Queen's Quarterly
RenP • Renaissance Papers
RES • Review of English Studies
RL • Revista de Literatura
RLV • Revue des Langues Vivantes (Brussels)
RN • Renaissance News

RSH • Revue des Sciences Humaines

RUO • Revue de l'Université d'Ottawa

SAQ • South Atlantic Quarterly

SCB • South Central Bulletin

SCN • Seventeenth-Century News

SEL • Studies in English Literature, 1500–1900

SELit • Studies in English Literature (Tokyo)

ShStud • Shakespeare Studies (U. of Tokyo)

SoR • Southern Review (Louisiana State U.)

SP • Studies in Philology

SR • Sewanee Review

SRen • Studies in the Renaissance

TLS • [London] Times Literary Supplement

TSLL • Texas Studies in Literature and Language

UTQ • University of Toronto Quarterly

VP • Victorian Poetry (W. Va. U.)

WascanaR • Wascana Review (Regina, Sask.)

XUS • Xavier University Studies

YES • Yearbook of English Studies

❧ 1. HERBERT, GEORGE. *The English Works of George Herbert.* Newly Arranged and Annotated and Considered in Relation to His Life, by George Herbert Palmer. Vol. 1, *Essays and Prose*; vol. 2, *Cambridge Poems*; vol. 3, *Bemerton Poems.* Boston and New York: Houghton Mifflin and Co. xx, 429p.; xiv, 443p.; 455p.

Reprinted, London: Hodder, 1920.

Large-paper edition in six volumes limited to 150 copies, 1905.

2d ed., 1907: A few changes and several errors corrected, two additional title pages, two additional indexes, and two new indexes.

Reprinted, 1915.

One volume edition of the poems with general preface, 1916. xii, 427p.

Vol. 1: Preface (pp. xi–xx); Chronology (pp. 3–13); Outlines of the Life (pp. 17–46); Traits of the Man (pp. 49–83); The Type of Religious Poetry (pp. 87–120); The Style and Technique (pp. 123–67); The Text and Order of Poems (pp. 171–91); The Country Parson, with preface (pp. 195–328); A Treatise of Temperance and Sobriety, written by Lud. Cornarus, translated into English by Mr. George Herbert, with preface (pp. 331–57); Prefatory Letter and Notes by George Herbert, To the Divine Considerations, Treating of Those Things Which Are Most Profitable, Most Necessary and Most Perfect in Our Christian Profession, by John Valdesso, with preface (pp. 363–86); Letters of George Herbert, with preface (pp. 389–412); Herbert's Will (pp. 413–16); Notes (pp. 419–29). Contains eleven illustrations. Vol. 2: The Printers to the Reader, by Nicholas Ferrar (pp. xi–xiv); The Church-Porch, with preface (pp. 3–67); The Resolve, with preface (pp. 71–107); The Church, with preface (pp. 111–203); Meditation, with preface (pp. 207–73); The Inner Life, with preface (pp. 277–319); The Crisis, with preface (pp. 323–401); Textual Variations of the Manuscripts (pp. 405–25); indexes: Titles Alphabetically Arranged (pp. 429–31), Titles Arranged in the Order of This Edition (pp. 435–37), Index of First Lines (pp. 439–43). Contains nine illustrations. Vol. 3: The Happy Priest, with preface (pp. 3–63); Bemerton Study, with preface (pp. 67–167); Restlessness, with preface (pp. 171–239); Suffering, with preface (pp. 243–307); Death, with preface (pp. 311–43); Additional and Doubtful Poems, with preface (pp. 347–431); Textual Variations of the Manuscripts (pp. 435–38); indexes: Titles Alphabetically Arranged (pp. 441–43), Titles Arranged in the Traditional Order (pp. 445–46), Titles Arranged in the Order of This Edition (pp. 447–49), Index of First Lines (pp. 451–55). Contains nine illustrations.

❧ 2. PALMER, GEORGE H. "George Herbert As a Religious Poet." *Atlantic Monthly* 95:194–205.

Maintains that Herbert contributed to the four main varieties of sacred poetry prevalent before his time: the vision, the meditation, the paraphrase of psalms, and the hymn. Argues that his most significant and original contribution was to the development of the religious love lyric. Sees Southwell, Campion, and, to some extent, Donne, as precursors. Evaluates the piety, intellectual play, and artistic construction of Herbert's religious love lyrics.

1906

ৰঙ্গ 3. ANON. "Holy Mr. Herbert." *Saturday Review* (London) 102: 583–84.

Essentially a review of A. G. Hyde's *George Herbert and His Times* (entry 8). Comments on Herbert's life and his "elegant sanctity," which "helped to give Anglicanism that peculiar stamp of cultivation and refinement which, united to the sedate charm and quaintness, the old-world fragrance of the seventeenth century, fascinated the author of 'John Inglesant'" (p. 584).

ৰঙ্গ 4. ALLEN, A. V. G. "Palmer's Herbert." *Atlantic Monthly* 97:90–100.

Primarily a detailed, appreciative, and favorable review of George Herbert Palmer's edition of 1905 (entry 1), but also uses Palmer as a springboard for a critical estimation of Herbert the man and the poet. A commentary on Palmer's commentary. Discusses the development of the religious lyrical element in Christian literature and suggests that "what Augustine did for the old world of the Graeco-Roman Empire, Herbert has done in his measure for the modern day" (p. 99), that is, reclaim the lyric for the expression of divine love.

ৰঙ্গ 5. CLUTTON-BROCK, A. "The Fantastic School of English Poetry." In *The Cambridge Modern History*, edited by A. W. Ward, G. W. Prothero, and Stanley Leathes, 4:760–75. New York: Macmillan Co.

Contrasts metaphysical poetry (called "fantastic poetry") rather unfavorably with Elizabethan poetry, pointing out such major features as its private mode, roughness, argumentative rationality, wit, and ingenuity. Briefly discusses Herbert (pp. 765–69), commenting on his wedding of the homely and the sublime, his obscurity, his realism, and his wit. Compares Herbert to Donne: "He wrote, like Donne, to express his own individual experiences; to explain himself to himself" (p. 768). Also compares Herbert with Vaughan, Traherne, and Crashaw.

ৰঙ্গ 6. DUNCAN, FRANCES. "Life of George Herbert." In "Three Notable Biographies: Paul's Froude, Palmer's Herbert, and Traubel's Whitman." *The Critic* 49:180–87.

Reviews favorably George Herbert Palmer's edition (entry 1). Calls

Herbert a "comparatively unimportant poet" (p. 83) who may not always appeal to Americans, "with our scant supply of artistic instinct, our journalistic despatch, our matter-of-fact literalness" (p. 185). Suggests that Herbert is enjoying a revival but is more often bought than read. Finds Palmer's rearrangement of the poems effective and innovative.

◄§ 7. GRIERSON, HERBERT J. C. "English Poetry." In *The First Half of the Seventeenth Century*, pp. 135–201. Periods of European Literature, edited by George Saintsbury, vol. 7. Edinburgh and London: William Blackwood and Sons.
Brief critical evaluation of Herbert's poetry (pp. 165–66). Characterizes Herbert's verse as didactic and rhetorically quaint.

◄§ 8. HYDE, A. G. *George Herbert and His Times*. New York: G. P. Putnam's Sons; London: Methuen & Co. xiv, 327p.
Biography of Herbert that the author describes as "little more than a commentary on Walton's narrative, except when . . . an effort has been made to show the relation of its subject and his writings to his own and later times" (pp. vii–viii). Contains seventeen chapters: (1) The Poet and the Age (pp. 1–11); (2) Birthplace, Family and Childhood (pp. 12–28); (3) School and University (pp. 29–46); (4) Early Life and Writings at Cambridge (pp. 47–61); (5) Orator and Theologian (pp. 62–84); (6) Herbert As a Courtier (pp. 85–108); (7) The Lady Magdalen Herbert (pp. 109–28); (8) Friends and Contemporaries (pp. 129–50); (9) The Reordering of the Church (pp. 151–72); (10) Transitional (pp. 173–96); (11) Nicholas Ferrar and Little Gidding (pp. 197–222); (12) Bemerton: The Parson and His Cure (pp. 223–40); (13) Last Days (pp. 241–56); (14) *The Temple*. The Church-Porch (pp. 257–68); (15) *The Temple*. The Shorter Poems (pp. 269–88); (16) *The Country Parson* and Other Writings (pp. 289–308); (17) Conclusion (pp. 309–15). Index (pp. 317–27). Thirty-two illustrations.

◄§ 9. MORE, PAUL ELMER. "George Herbert." In *Shelburne Essays*, 4th ser., pp. 66–98. New York and London: G. P. Putnam's Sons.
Biographical sketch that, in part, challenges certain of George Herbert Palmer's remarks that seemingly play down Herbert's saintliness and piety. Suggests that we bring to Herbert a defective religious sensibility that does not allow us to understand Herbert's intimacy with things divine. Suggests the strong influence of Donne on Herbert.

1907

◄§ 10. ANON. "News for Bibliophiles." *The Nation* 84:586.
Gives bibliographical data on two copies of *The Temple* with undated title pages, one in the Huth library and one in the Robert Hoe library.

William Thomas Lowndes suggested that these copies were rare first editions issued by Nicholas Ferrar for presentation to Herbert's friends in 1631. Argues that this claim is invalid, that the copies were most likely printed between the first dated edition (1633) and the second dated edition (1633).

᪤ 11. HERBERT, GEORGE. *The Poems of George Herbert*. With an introduction by Arthur Waugh. Oxford edition. London, New York, Toronto: Henry Frowde, Oxford University Press. xxiii, 327p.
Reprinted, 1913.
Reprinted in The World's Classics, no. 109, 1907, 1912, 1914, 1934, 1952, 1955, 1958. (For 2d ed., see entry 457.)
Introduction reprinted in *Reticence in Literature and Other Papers* (London: J. G. Wilson, 1915), pp. 130–43.
Text based on Grosart. Introduction (pp. iii–xv); contents (pp. xvii–xxiii); The Temple (pp. 1–196); The Church Militant (pp. 197–208); Additional Sacred Poems (pp. 229–37); Parentalia (pp. 239–52); Anti-Tami-Cami-Categoria et Georgii Herberti, Angli Musae Responsoriae, ad Andreae Melvini, Scoti, Anti-Tami-Cami-Categorium (pp. 253–62); Pro Disciplina Ecclesiae Nostrae Epigrammata Apologetica (pp. 263–84); Alia Poemata Latina (pp. 285–94); Passio Discerpta. Lucus (pp. 295–318); index of first lines (pp. 319–27).

᪤ 12. SKIPTON, H. P. K. "Some Friendships of Nicholas Ferrar." In *The Life and Times of Nicholas Ferrar*, pp. 110–23. London, Oxford, New York: A. R. Mowbray & Co.
Reviews the scant information known about the friendship of Ferrar and Herbert. No record exists to prove that they ever met. They were involved in the rebuilding of the church at Leighton Bromswold. Herbert's good friend, Arthur Woodnoth, was first cousin of Ferrar.

1908

᪤ 13. HERBERT, GEORGE. A *Priest to the Temple or, The Country Parson*. His Character and Rule of Holy Life by George Herbert. With an introduction and brief notes by the bishop of North Carolina [Joseph Blount Cheshire]. New York: Thomas Whittaker, 154p.
New edition, 1915.
Introduction (pp. 5–13); The Author to the Reader (p. 15); contents (pp. 17–18); text of *The Country Parson* (pp. 19–149); Author's Prayer Before Sermon (pp. 150–53); Prayer After Sermon (p. 154). States that this is the first edition of *The Country Parson* "published in America separate from his Poems" (p. 5). Suggests that Herbert's prose "is wholly free from the faults which mar his verses" (p. 5). Praises both the style and

the sound Christian advice contained in the book: "Its simplicity and un-affectedness, its directness of purpose, the practical good sense of its rules and suggestions, its genuine humility and sympathy, it condescension to human weakness yet with loyalty to divine righteousness, its absolute fidelity to truth and duty, its heavenly wisdom, and clear vision, are embodied in that quality of English prose which we love and admire but can no longer write or speak" (p. 6). Brief notes are primarily from George Herbert Palmer's edition (entry 1). One illustration.

14. ———. *The Temple & A Priest to the Temple.* Edited by Edward Thomas. Everyman's Library, no. 309. London and Toronto: J. M. Dent & Sons; New York: E. P. Dutton & Co. xvii, 304p. Reprinted, 1927.

Introduction (pp. vii–xii); bibliography (pp. xiii–xiv); The Printers to the Reader (pp. xv–xviii); dedication (p. xix); *The Temple* (pp. 1–209); index of titles of poems (pp. 210–12); *A Priest to the Temple, or, The Country Parson* (pp. 213–93); index of words (pp. 295–301); and list of dates (pp. 302–5). Introduction is primarily a biographical sketch with general comments on the themes, tone, and techniques of Herbert's poetry. Praises in particular his ability to capture the spirit of the Anglican Church of his day: "I can believe that a century or so hence, when some of these things have grown a little dim with their own age and the dust of the velocity of progress, men poised in flying machines over continents resembling one vast Ancrlcy and Tooting will be moved by George Herbert's verse to a passing melancholy at the thought of the poet's Church, his epoch, and his country, all irrecoverable and beautiful" (p. xii).

15. SAINTSBURY, GEORGE. "Caroline Lyric, Pindaric, and Stanza." In *A History of English Prosody from the Twelfth Century to the Present Day*, 2:321–43. London: Macmillan and Co.

Briefly comments on Herbert's prosody. Maintains that although he docs not necessarily censure Herbert for using shaped verse forms, he finds "more of the mechanical in Herbert's prosody than is shown merely by the adoption of these mechanical forms; and it is only when the fire of his poetry burns hottest that inspiration takes the place of mechanism" (p. 332). Says that Herbert is "scarcely ever bad" but "he has not the rarest touch of his fellow-disciples, Crashaw and Vaughan" (p. 332).

1909

16. COOK, ALBERT S. "Notes on Milton's 'Ode on the Morning of Christ's Nativity.'" *Transactions of the Connecticut Academy of Arts and Sciences* 15:307–68.

Comments on the possible influence of Herbert on Milton, especially as reflected in certain parallels between "Christmas" and "Whitsunday" and Milton's "On the Morning of Christ's Nativity" (pp. 309–10, 334).

≈§ 17. HINCHMAN, WALTER S. "George Herbert: An Interpretation." In *Haverford Essays: Studies in Modern Literature*, pp. 69–89. Haverford, Pa.: privately printed.

Divided into three sections: (1) "The Place," a rhapsodic tourist's impressions of Salisbury and Bemerton. (2) "The Man," a brief biographical sketch with some general comments on Herbert's poetry. States that "much of Herbert's verse . . . is of a not very high order" (p. 82); not only is it dwarfed by the accomplishments of his contemporaries (especially Chapman and Jonson), but "the quaintness often renders it dull to anyone who is not particularly interested in seventeenth century lyrics" (p. 82). (3) "The Medlar-Tree," a summary in which the author poses the question that informs the whole essay: "We find it hard, under these old trees, to answer the searching question: which is it that you really like—Bemerton, or Herbert, or his verse?" (p. 86).

≈§ 18. RUDLER, MIRIAM NINA. *George Herbert: Courtier, Priest, Poet, 1593–1633*. Wilmslow, Eng.: M. Jones. 60p.

Primarily a biographical sketch that relates Herbert's poetry to his life. Says that he belongs to no specific school of poetry but that he "may be regarded as the Laureate of Religious poetry" (p. 47). Praises Herbert's metrical inventiveness and his "power to charge a few common words full to over-flowing with meaning" (p. 52).

1910

≈§ 19. BUCHANAN, E. S. *George Herbert Melodist*. London: Elliot Stock. x, 76p.

Hagiographic presentation of Herbert in which the poetry is valued only for being "the true expression of his own soul and its conflicts" (p. 9). Praises Herbert's poems for their conciseness of expression, great precision, and melody but does not rank them with hymns, since "they are too full of deep thought, too full of fancy, too delicately wrought, too intimate and personal" (p. 39). Maintains, "Only to a sensitive and suffering soul will they yield their inner meaning" (p. 39).

≈§ 20. GRIFFINHOOFE, C. G. *Celebrated Cambridge Men*. Cambridge: A. P. Dixon; London: James Nisbet & Co. 215p.

Brief biographical sketches of famous men who were students at Cambridge from 1390 to 1908. Comments on Herbert's association with the university under the mastership of Nevile and on his life after he left the university (pp. 69–70). Lists several of Herbert's associates and friends during his Cambridge days.

ᴥ§ 21. HARLAND, MARION [Mary Virginia (Hawes) Teyhune]. "Gentle George Herbert at Bemerton." In *Where Ghosts Walk: The Haunts of Familiar Characters in History and Literature*, 2d ed., pp. 237–62. New York and London: G. P. Putnam's Sons.

Personal account of the author's visit to Bemerton. Contains a hagiographic account of Herbert's life and personality. "His sacred lyrics have been for long, long years songs in the house of my pilgrimage, coming readily to my lips in moments of sudden joy or sorrow, staying my soul under the stress of homely toils and carking, belittling cares such as are known, in all their meanness and weariness, to women only" (p. 251). (The first edition of 1898 does not contain the Herbert sketch.)

ᴥ§ 22. HOLLIDAY, CARL. "George Herbert." *SR* 18:268–82.

Reprinted in *The Cavalier Poets: Their Lives, Their Day, and Their Poetry* (New York: Neale Publishing Co., 1911), pp. 61–78.

Appreciative biographical sketch that focuses on Herbert's saintly personality. Comments only briefly on *The Temple*, calling it eccentric, odd, curious, quaint, and excessively ingenuous: "Even the very forms of his most heartfelt poems are fantastic" (p. 277). Concludes, however, that "soul earnestness goes a long way in art and will cover a multitude of technical sins" (p. 278).

ᴥ§ 23. JOHN, FRANCIS, ed. "Baxter and the Herbert Family." In *An Excerpt from Reliquiae Baxterianae or Mr. Richard Baxter's Narrative of The Most Memorable Passages of His Life and Times. . .*, pp. 155–60. London: Longmans, Green, and Co.

Comments briefly on Richard Baxter's dealings with the Herbert family. Indicates Baxter's great esteem for George Herbert.

ᴥ§ 24. STEBBING, WILLIAM. "George Herbert." In *Five Centuries of Verse*, 1:79–88. London, New York, Toronto, and Melbourne: Henry Frowde and Oxford University Press.

Revised, 1913.

Calls Herbert "the model, the exemplar, the prince, of sacred poets" (p. 79) and compares him favorably with Sidney. Does not condemn Herbert entirely for his "artifices" and "fireworks of wit," but rather sees these faults "as fashion's rather than his": "A true soul breathes beneath the excrescences of style" (p. 80). Praises in particular the musical quality of Herbert's lyrics and, by quoting extensively from individual poems, surveys briefly some of Herbert's major themes and characteristics.

◢§ 25. THOMAS, EDWARD. *Feminine Influence on the Poets.* London:
   Martin Secker; New York: John Lane Co. 351p.
Biographical sketch of Magdalen Herbert and a survey of her relationship with her two sons, Edward and George (pp. 124–28). Brief comments on Jane Danvers (pp. 151–54).

1911

◢§ 26. HERBERT, GEORGE. *Gathered Rosemary from the Poems of
   George Herbert, for the Sundays and Some Holy Days of the
   Church's Year.* Edited by Mary Burn. With an introduction by the
   bishop of Hull. Heart and Life Booklets, no. 32. London: H. R.
   Allenson. 72p.
Herbert's poems arranged for each Sunday of the year and for various
feast days of the Church calendar.

◢§ 27. HUTCHINSON, F. E. "The Sacred Poets." In *The Cambridge History of English Literature,* edited by A. W. Ward and A. R.
   Waller, vol. 7, *Cavalier and Puritan,* pp. 30–54. New York: G. P.
   Putnam's Sons; Cambridge: University Press.
Biographical sketch of Herbert, claiming that the fascination of Herbert "is due as much to his character as to his writings" and that his
"personal history, therefore, is of more than ordinary moment for an understanding of his poems" (p. 30). Suggests that George Herbert Palmer's
reordering of the poems (see entry 1) is at times arbitrary and unconvincing but that "no greater service has been done towards understanding
Herbert than by this attempt to arrange his poems chronologically" (p.
34). Outlines some of the major characteristics of Herbert's poetry.
Praises his skillful craftsmanship, his experimentation with form, his concentration, and his good humor. Laments that Herbert sometimes employs the "fantastic" conceit, a "serious defect of taste he shares with the
poets whom Johnson styled 'metaphysical'" (p. 35). Suggests that Herbert's ingenuity "misleads him into what can only be called tricks" (p.
35) and frowns on Herbert's tendency "to draw from the sense of smell
and taste images which make a modern reader, rightly or wrongly, ill at
ease" (p. 36).

◢§ 28. PALMER, GEORGE HERBERT. A *Herbert bibliography being a catalogue of a collection of books relating to George Herbert, gathered
   by George Herbert Palmer.* Cambridge, Mass.: privately printed.
Consists of 142 titles and 159 volumes of books relating to Herbert:
(1) biographies; (2) manuscripts; (3) writings other than *The Temple*;
(4) editions of *The Temple* published during the first century after 1633;
(5) modern editions of *The Temple*; (6) writings of the brothers of
Herbert; (7) Nicholas Ferrar and Little Gidding; (8) other men and

books associated with Herbert; and (9) desiderata. (Seventy copies printed.)

⋙ 29. ———. *A George Herbert Bibliography.* Bibliographical Contributions of the Library of Harvard University, edited by William Coolidge Lane, no. 59. Cambridge, Mass.: Library of Harvard University. iv, 19p.
   Reprinted, Folcroft, Pa.: Folcroft Library Editions, 1973.
   Descriptive and annotated list of books relating to Herbert. Divided into nine major groups, as listed above.

⋙ 30. TIPPLE, EZRA. "Bemerton." In *Some Famous Country Parishes*, pp. 40–78. New York: Eaton & Mains; Cincinnati: Jennings & Graham.
   Discusses Wilton, Bemerton, and Salisbury and describes a visit to various Herbert shrines. Appreciative biographical sketch. Scattered comments on the poems and prose works: "The poems of 'The Temple' are as didactic and hortatory as much of Longfellow" (p. 65). Praises *The Country Parson*: "No modern book of pastoral theology is richer in the wisdom of good sense or more prolific in helpful suggestions" (p. 69). Fourteen photographs.

⋙ 31. WILLIAMS, R. VAUGHAN. *Five Mystical Songs.* Words by George Herbert set to music for baritone solo, chorus (ad lib.) and orchestra by R. Vaughan Williams. London: Strainer & Bell
   Musical settings for "Easter" (two separate settings), "Love (III)," "The Call," and "Antiphon (I)."

1912

⋙ 32. LANG, ANDREW. "Late Elizabethan and Jacobean Poets." In *History of English Literature from "Beowulf" to Swinburne*, pp. 283–302. London: Longmans, Green and Co.
   Brief biographical sketch of Herbert. Suggests that Herbert is not a truly great poet: "He never storms the cloudcapt towers, and 'flaming walls of the world,' like Crashaw" (p. 331). Considers "Easter-wings" and "The Altar" as "examples of extreme decadence" (p. 331). Laments that Herbert's poetry is filled with conceits but says, "He has not the extravagances that mar the work of Donne and Crashaw" (p. 331).

⋙ 33. REED, EDWARD BLISS. "The Jacobean and Caroline Lyric." In *English Lyrical Poetry from Its Origins to the Present Time*, pp. 233–301. New Haven: Yale University Press; London: Humphrey Milford, Oxford University Press.
   Reprinted, 1914.

Surveys briefly the works of twenty seventeenth-century poets. Suggests that Herbert created a new school of verse, the religious love lyric. Compares and contrasts Herbert and Donne and laments that many of Herbert's conceits are overly ingenious. Says that "his lyrics are rarely metrically perfect throughout" (p. 280) and that "with exceptions, the musical appeal is not an immediate one" (p. 280). Suggests that the real value of Herbert's poetry is that it reveals the inner character of the man.

◄§ 34. Tallentyre, S. G. "The Parson-Poets." *North American Review* 12:84–93.
Biographical sketches of Herrick, Herbert, and Richard Barham. Praises Herbert for his exquisite feeling for lyric style, his serenity, his word play, and his delicate humor. "As for the quips, cranks, and oddities which were the poetical characteristics of the age, one can hardly dream his poetry without them, and one loves him for them" (p. 89).

1913

◄§ 35. Bett, Henry. *The Hymns of Methodism in Their Literary Relations.* London: Charles H. Kelly. vii, 131p.
New and enlarged ed., 1920.
3d ed., revised and enlarged, 1945.
3d ed., reprinted, 1946, 1956.
Comments on several adaptations of Herbert's poems made by John Wesley. Herbert was a favorite of Susanna Wesley, mother of John and Charles. Points out that Wesley used Herbert's lines in translating German hymns into English.

◄§ 36. Rhys, Ernest. "The Later Amorists—Fashionable Lyric—The Herbert Group." In *Lyric Poetry*, pp. 210–21. London and Toronto: J. M. Dent & Sons; New York: E. P. Dutton & Co.
Brief commentary on Herbert (pp. 215–18) that praises his "unusual adaptation of the personal narrative-note to the lyric" and his "melodic forms" (p. 216). Admits that Herbert "had a sense of lyric form which is rather wanting in some of his nearer associates in poetry" but wishes that "he had never been tempted by Donne and the metaphysical versemen to be so over-ingenious" (p. 217). Compares Herbert to Vaughan (who took "every advantage of Herbert's bad example in the way of oddities and tricks of style" [p. 218]) and to Crashaw.

◄§ 37. Schelling, Felix E. "The Lyric in the Reign of the First Two Stuart Monarchs." In *The English Lyric*, pp. 73–111. Boston and New York: Houghton Mifflin Co.

Very brief comment on Herbert (pp. 95–96). Says that Herbert is "a conceittist, and delights not only in ingenious imagery but even in the puerilities of acrostics, anagrams, and shaped verses" (p. 96). In spite of "surface foam and bubbles" (p. 96), Herbert is a major devotional poet because of his deep, irresistible fervor and sincerity of feeling.

◆§ 38. SPURGEON, CAROLINE F. E. "Devotional and Religious Mystics." In *Mysticism in English Literature*, pp. 111–58. Cambridge: University Press.

Brief discussion of Richard Rolle, Julian of Norwich, Crashaw, Herbert, Christopher Harvey, Blake, and Francis Thompson as mystics. Comments on the personal tone and homely intimacy of Herbert's religious lyrics.

1914

No Entries

1915

◆§ 39. BENSON, LOUIS F. *The English Hymn: Its Development and Use in Worship*. Richmond, Va.: John Knox Press. xvii, 624p. Reprinted, 1962.

Survey of the development of the English hymn in which there are several comments about the uses made of Herbert's poetry, particularly during the late seventeenth and the eighteenth centuries, by such hymnologists as Henry Playford, Joseph Boyse, Samuel Bury, Simon Browne, Isaac Watts, and especially John Wesley, whose *Hymns and sacred Poems* (1739) contained forty-two adaptations from Herbert.

◆§ 40. CURRIER, ALBERT H. "George Herbert." In *Biographical and Literary Studies*, pp. 183–207. Boston, New York, Chicago: Pilgrim Press.

Appreciative biographical sketch of Herbert. Calls him the St. Francis of the English Church. Quotes extensively from *The Country Parson* and calls it a classic of religious literature.

◆§ 41. HEIDE, ANNA VON DER. *Das Naturgefühl in der englischen Dichtung im Zeitalter Miltons*. Anglistische Forschungen, 45. Heidelberg: Carl Winters Universitätsbuchhandlung. 131p.

Discusses the uses of nature in seventeenth-century English poetry and argues (pp. 65–69) that Herbert had a deeper understanding of the essence of nature than had most of his contemporaries. Points out, however, that Herbert always viewed nature from a theological perspective, as an expression of God's wisdom and power. Several specific poems mentioned, especially "Providence."

◄§ 42. INGE, WILLIAM RALPH. "English Religious Poetry." *Transactions of the Royal Society of Literature*, 2d ser. 33:177–203.

Surveys English religious poetry and compares and contrasts poets influenced by different religious traditions and beliefs. Calls Herbert "a typically Anglican poet" (p. 192) who might have been a greater poet had he not imitated Donne, "but this influence affects only the form of his writing" (p. 192). Praises Herbert's piety and compares him with Vaughan.

1916

◄§ 43. JACKSON, GEORGE. "The Bookshelf by the Fire: I. George Herbert's 'Country Parson.'" *Expository Times*, March, pp. 248–52.

Calls Herbert a saint and comments on *The Country Parson* as "intimate self-revelation" (p. 249). Considers the work a collection of "simple pieties and sweet charities" (p. 251), but notes two minor defects: (1) the book is "a little too suggestive of a visitant from some other sphere who comes to right the wrongs of our poor world" (p. 252) and (2) there is "an undue emphasis on asceticism" (p. 252).

1917

◄§ 44. HODGKIN, JOHN. "Luigi Cornaro and Nicholas Ferrar." *TLS*, 28 June, pp. 309–10.

Reply to Francis Hutchinson, entry 45. States that Ferrar had no part in editing or translating Lessius of Louvain's *Hygiasticon*, that Herbert translated only Cornaro's first treatise and had nothing to do with the translation of either Lessius or the anonymous Italian piece contained in the volume. Suggests that the real translator and editor of Lessius and the Italian piece is a certain Thomas Sheppard, a friend of the Ferrars.

◄§ 45. HUTCHINSON, FRANCIS. "Luigi Cornaro." *TLS*, 7 June, p. 273.

Points out that "the first of Cornaro's 'Discorsi della Vita Sobria' was introduced to English readers in a little volume of 1634 which had Nicholas Ferrar for editor, George Herbert for translator, and Richard Crashaw to commend the theme with his prefatory verses" (p. 273). States that Ferrar consulted Herbert about printing a treatise by Lessius of Louvain ("The Right Course of Preserving Health of Extream Old Age"), that Herbert approved and suggested Cornaro's tract be added. A third treatise by an anonymous Italian on dieting was added, thus making up the volume *Hygiasticon*. For a reply, see John Hodgkin, entry 44.

1918

◄§ 46. Anon. "George Herbert." *The Saturday Review* (London) 125: 47–48.
Reprinted in *The Living Age* 296 (1918):813–15.
Appreciative sketch of Herbert's life and temperament. Praises him as "the most sincere poet of . . . religious moderation" (p. 47). Calls his poetry "sweet roses of undying fragrance from the garden of his soul" (p. 48).

◄§ 47. Palmer, George Herbert. "George Herbert." In *Formative Types in English Poetry*, pp. 101–31. Boston and New York: Houghton Mifflin Co.
The Earl Lectures of 1917. Discusses Herbert as a poet of "the inner life, veracious, intellectual, individualistic, energetic" (p. 112). Biographical sketch that stresses the various conflicts in Herbert's temperament and the introspective nature of his poetry. Says that Herbert is "a conscious artist and has a strong sense of orderly poetic form" (p. 114).

◄§ 48. Quiller-Couch, Sir Arthur. "Some Seventeenth Century Poets." In *Studies in Literature*, pp. 96–167. New York: G. P. Putnam's Sons; Cambridge: University Press.
Reprinted, 1922, 1926.
Brief biographical sketch. Suggests that Donne "infected" Herbert and that few of Herbert's poems are flawless. Compares Herbert with Vaughan and argues that Vaughan is "actually more original and certainly of deeper insight as well as of ampler, more celestial range than the man he copied" (p. 141).

1919

◄§ 49. Cox, E. Marion. "Notes on Rare Books." *The Library* (London), 3d ser. 10:18–25.
"The First Edition of Herbert's 'Temple' " (pp. 23–25) challenges the assumption that the undated copies of the first edition of *The Temple* represent presentation copies printed a year or so earlier than the dated first edition. Suggests, using evidence obtained from the Huth copy, that the undated copies were printed after the dated ones, shortly before the second edition of 1633. Perhaps the printer objected that the dated title page gave no information as to where the book could be purchased; the addition of "Francis Green Stationer" crowded the type, and the date, coming last, was omitted to avoid destroying the symmetry of the page.

◄§ 50. OSMOND, PERCY H. "George Herbert, Harvey, and Quarles." In *The Mystical Poets of the English Church*, pp. 67–111. London: Society for Promoting Christian Knowledge; New York: Macmillan Co.

Anthology of mystical poets of the English Church, with a few extracts from those outside that communion. Herbert is called "the foremost of the distinctively sacred poets of England" (p. 67) and is placed among the mystics. Reviews some of the major spiritual themes of the poetry, but criticizes Herbert's use of the conceit: "This failure is the result, not always of the use of obsolete phraseology, but sometimes of the abuse of analogy and the strained ingenuity of wit, into which he was led by his admiration of Donne" (p. 75). Laments Herbert's uses of "artificial tricks of rhyme and metre, which give a suggestion of insincerity" (p. 88).

◄§ 51. W., E. W. "Donne's Puns." *TLS*, 11 December, p. 750.

Points out Herbert's use of the *sun-son* pun not only in "The Sonne" but also possibly in the last line of "Mattens" ("Then by a sunne-beam I will climb to thee").

1920

◄§ 52. ANON. [Clutton-Brock, A.]. "George Herbert." *TLS*, 1 April, pp. 205–6.

Reprinted (in part) in *More Essays on Books* (London: Methuen; New York: Dutton, 1921), pp. 14–23.

Essentially a highly complimentary review of George Herbert Palmer's edition (entry 1). Comments on some of the more salient features of Herbert's poetry and method, and laments that often he is dismissed as "Quaint Old Herbert." Briefly discusses some of Herbert's major themes, his distrust of external beauty and of love poetry, his uses of music, his mastery of form, etc. "It is never safe to reject a poem of Herbert as a failure; the failure may be in you, and with another attempt you may discover a secret beauty which seems all the more beautiful for having lain hid so long" (p. 206).

◄§ 53. CLOUGH, BENJAMIN C. "Notes on the Metaphysical Poets." *MLN* 35:115–17.

Points out that Dryden's lines in *Upon the Death of Lord Hastings* ("Each little pimple had a tear in it/ To wail the fault its rising did commit") are reminiscent of stanza 70 in *The Church-Porch*.

◄§ 54. COLBY, ELBRIDGE. *The Echo-Device in Literature*. New York: New York Public Library. 61p.

Discusses various forms and techniques of the echo-device in poetry and drama and traces briefly the development and history of the device, starting with *The Greek Anthology*. The echo-device, frequently associated with the pastoral tradition, enjoyed a revival in England from 1575 (Gascoigne) to the middle of the seventeenth century. Herbert's "Heaven" is discussed as a representative example of one technique, that of using a conversation between a speaker and an echo. Points out that Lord Herbert of Cherbury also used the device.

◄§ 55. RAYSON, ROBERT SPENCER. "The Poetry of George Herbert." *American Church Monthly* 8:132–46.

Appreciative essay and biographical sketch. Calls *The Temple* a "pleasant by-way of English poetry" (p. 146). Compares Herbert and Cowper. Comments on Herbert's High Church theology (such as his views on the Eucharist and on saints) as it is reflected in his poetry and praises his religious sensibility. Comments on the universal appeal of such a poem as "Vertue" but rejects *The Church-Porch* as lacking "the indefinable something . . . that is essential to great poetry" (p. 145). Finds Herbert least effective as a practical moralist.

1921

◄§ 56. ELIOT, THOMAS STEARNS. "The Metaphysical Poets." *TLS*, 20 October, pp. 669–70.

Reprinted in *Homage to John Dryden: Three Essays on Poetry of the Seventeenth Century* (1924); the contents of *Homage* were reprinted in *The Hogarth Essays* (1928) and in *Selected Essays, 1917–1932* (1932; 2d English ed., 1934; 2d American ed., 1950; 3d English ed., 1951).

Reprinted in *Criticism: The Major Texts*, edited by Walter Jackson Bate (New York: Harcourt, Brace, 1956), pp. 529–34; *Discussions of John Donne*, edited by Frank Kermode (Boston: D. C. Heath Co., 1962), pp. 42–47; *Seventeenth Century English Poetry: Modern Essays in Criticism*, edited by William Keast (entry 480), pp. 22–30, rev. ed., (entry 707), pp. 23–31; *John Donne's Poetry: Authoritative Texts, Criticism*, edited by A. L. Clements (New York: W. W. Norton & Co., 1966), pp. 123–30; *Perspective on Poetry*, edited by James L. Calderwood and Harold Toliver (New York: Oxford University Press, 1968), pp. 267–76.

Translated into French by Henri Fluchère in *Cahiers du Sud* 28 (1948): 487–98.

Claims, "The poets of the seventeenth century, the successors of the dramatists of the sixteenth century, possessed a mechanism of sensibility which could devour any kind of experience. . . . In the seventeenth century a dissociation of sensibility set in, from which we have never recovered; and this dissociation, as is natural, was due to the influence of the two most powerful poets of the century, Milton and Dryden" (p. 669). In contrast, the metaphysical poets were "engaged in the task of trying to find the verbal equivalent for states of mind and feeling" (p. 670). Illustrates the point by saying: "The difference is not a simple difference of degree between poets. It is something which happened to the mind of England between the time of Donne or Lord Herbert of Cherbury and the time of Tennyson and Browning; it is the difference between the intellectual poet and the reflective poet. Tennyson and Browning are poets, and they think; but they do not feel their thought as immediately as the odour of a rose. A thought to Donne was an experience; it modified his sensibility" (p. 669). Comments briefly on the simplicity of language in Herbert's poetry, "a simplicity emulated without success by numerous modern poets" (p. 669), and yet finds in Herbert a complexity of structure that reflects "a fidelity to thought and feeling" (p. 669).

᎑§ 57. ⸻. "The Metaphysical Poets." *TLS*, 3 November, p. 716.
    Reply to George Saintsbury, entry 60. "Mr. Saintsbury appears to believe that these poets represent not merely a generation, but almost a particular theory of poetry. The 'second thoughts' to which he alludes are, I think, and as I tried to point out, frequent in the work of many other poets besides, of other times and other languages. I have mentioned Chapman, and the contemporaries of Dante. I do not believe that the author of *Hamlet* and *Measure for Measure* was invariably satisfied with 'the first simple, obvious, natural thought and expression of thought.'" For a reply, see George Saintsbury, entry 61.

᎑§ 58. GRIERSON, HERBERT J. C., ed. *Metaphysical Lyrics & Poems of The Seventeenth Century: Donne to Butler.* Selected and edited, with an essay by Herbert J. C. Grierson. Oxford: Clarendon Press. lviii, 244p.
    Reprinted, 1925, 1928, 1936, 1942, 1947, 1950, 1958, 1962. First issued in Oxford Paperbacks, 1965. Galaxy, 1959.
    Introduction reprinted in *The Background of English Literature* (London: Chatto and Windus, 1925), pp. 115–66.
    Pages xiii–xxxviii reprinted in *Seventeenth Century English Poetry: Modern Essays in Criticism*, edited by William Keast (entry 480), pp. 3–21; rev. ed. (entry 707), pp. 3–22.
    Contains an important critical introduction (pp. xiii–lviii); selections from twenty-six poets divided into three major categories: love poems, divine poems, and miscellanies (pp. 1–215); notes (pp. 217–40); index of first lines (pp. 241–44). By the introduction and selection of poems, Grierson, in effect, defines the metaphysical school, although he is cautious with the term itself. Maintains, however, that the term *metaphysical* "lays stress on the right things—the survival, one might say the reaccentuation, of the metaphysical strain, the *concetti metafisici ed ideali* as Testi calls them in contrast to the imagery of classical poetry, of mediaeval

Italian poetry; the more intellectual, less verbal, character of their wit compared with the conceits of the Elizabethans; the finer psychology of which their conceits are often the expression; their learned imagery; the argumentative, subtle evolution of their lyrics; above all the peculiar blend of passion and thought, feeling and ratiocination which is their greatest achievement" (pp. xv–xvi). Considers Donne "the great master of English poetry in the seventeenth century" (p. xvi) and focuses the critical discussion on his poetry, considering the other poets primarily in contrast with or in comparison to Donne. Yet warns: "To call these poets the 'school of Donne' or 'metaphysical' poets may easily mislead if one takes either phrase in too full a sense" (p. xxx). Calls Herbert "the poet in whom the English Church of Hooker found a voice of its own" (p. xl). Comments on "the note of conflict, of personal experience, which troubles and gives life to poetry" (p. xli) and is found in Herbert's poetry, but concludes that, unlike Donne, Herbert reflects a feeling of reconciliation, joy, and peace. Maintains that Herbert learned the metaphysical manner from Donne but that, unlike his master, Herbert's interest in theology is always practical and devotional, not metaphysical. "Herbert's central theme is the psychology of his religious experiences" (p. xlii), and thus he does for religious poetry what Donne did for love poetry. Compares Herbert also with Vaughan, Crashaw, and Quarles.

⊷§ 59. MERRILL, L. R. "George Herbert's *Church Porch.*" *MLN* 36:249–50.
Suggests that the closing sentiments in *The Church-Porch* are possibly derived from Nicholas Grimald's "Musonius, the Philosopher's saiying," in *Tottel's Miscellany.* Points out that Grimald was born at Brownshold and that Herbert was later a lay prebendary in that parish.

⊷§ 60. SAINTSBURY, GEORGE. "The Metaphysical Poets." *TLS,* 27 October, p. 698.
Reply to T. S. Eliot, entry 56. Suggests that when Dryden used the term *metaphysics* in connection with Donne's poetry, he did not equate it with philosophy but rather opposed it to nature. In Greek the word means "second thoughts, things that come *after* the natural first." Suggests, "This definition would . . . fit all the poetry commonly called 'metaphysical,' whether it be amatory, religious, satirical, panegyric, or merely trifling; while 'philosophical,' though of course not seldom suitable enough, sometimes has no relevance whatever [for] these poets always 'go behind' the first, simple, obvious, natural thought and expression of thought." For a reply, see T. S. Eliot, entry 57.

⊷§ 61. ———. "The Metaphysical Poets." *TLS,* 10 November, p. 734.
Brief reply to T. S. Eliot, entry 57. "I fully agree with him that, in the great examples he quotes, and perhaps in all similar things, there *is* 'second

thought.' I might even go so far as to say—indeed I meant to hint this in my last sentence—that all true poetry must be in a way second thought, though much second thought is not in any way poetry. What I was endeavouring to point out was that, *in this period* [the seventeenth century], the quest of the second thought became direct, deliberate, a business, almost itself a *first* thought."

≈§ 62. THOMPSON, ELBERT N. S. "Mysticism in Seventeenth-Century English Literature." SP 18:170–231.
Mentions Herbert only in passing. Comments on the enormous popularity of sacred poetry during the seventeenth century and discusses the element of mysticism in a number of poets of the period as well as in a number of their predecessors. Maintains that Herbert "had little if any mysticism in his temperament" even though "his poems show an unfaltering sense of the nearness of God" (p. 182). Suggests Plato's influence on Herbert's poetry, especially evident in "Love (I)."

≈§ 63. WOODBERRY, GEORGE EDWARD. "Notes on the Seventeenth Century Poets: A College Syllabus." In *Studies of a Litterateur*, pp. 137–48. New York: Harcourt, Brace and Co.
Briefly comments on Herbert's life, personality, and poetry. Says the poetry reflects the faults of his age: "The conceits, the tastelessness in diction, the intellectual, fantastic and uneven traits are all there" (p. 142), but, at the same time, "all these things are fused, and find their artistic wholeness in his spirituality" (p. 143).

1922

≈§ 64. AULT, NORMAN, ed. *The Poets' Life of Christ*. Compiled, arranged and decorated by Norman Ault. London: Humphrey Milford, Oxford University Press. xxviii, 275p.
Reprinted, 1923.
Introduction (pp. v–x); scheme and contents (pp. xi–xxvii); a selection of poems on the life of Christ by various authors (pp. xxviii, 1–272); index of authors (pp. 273–75). The purpose of this anthology is "to reveal the extent to which the life and teaching of Christ have inspired the poets of the English-speaking race . . . as well as to illustrate that wonderful life itself by the poems thus inspired" (p. v). Nearly four hundred poems arranged in twelve main sections to illustrate chronologically Christ's life and teaching. Includes eleven of Herbert's poems. No notes and no commentary. Illustrations.

≈§ 65. NETHERCOT, ARTHUR H. "The Term 'Metaphysical Poets' before Johnson." MLN 37:11–17.
Points out, "The use of the term 'metaphysical' in connection with

certain poets or with certain types of poetry was far from uncommon in the seventeenth and eighteenth centuries, and that therefore there were various sources from which Johnson might have got the suggestion for his phrase, altho probably the responsibility was mainly Dryden's" (pp. 12–13).

1923

◆§ 66. BUTTERWORTH, S. "Wordsworth and George Herbert." *N&Q*, 12th ser. 12:113.
Partly a reply to G. C. Moore Smith, entry 69. Suggests that Wordsworth's indebtedness to Herbert's "Constancie" in "Character of a Happy Warrior" is apparent, but that the resemblances between Herbert's "Mans medley" and Wordsworth's "Ode on Immortality" are less apparent. Points out Alice Meynell's borrowing from Herbert's "Christmas" for several of her lines in "Shepherdess."

◆§ 67. FAUSSET, HUGH I'ANSON. "Idealism and Puritanism." In *Studies in Idealism*, pp. 87–116. London and Toronto: J. M. Dent & Sons; New York: E. P. Dutton & Co.
Reprinted, Port Washington, N.Y.: Kennikat Press, 1965.
Calls Herbert a mystical poet and considers him one of the first to attempt reconciling "a natural ecstasy with Christian devotion" (p. 87). Compares Herbert's view of the world with that of Vaughan: "In Herbert the sense of eternity, of infinite existence, is translated into a principle, that of Love. The translation is direct and logical. He who loves the Infinite loves every embodiment of it which he presupposes in the Finite. He does not criticise the Finite, or venture the opinion that in this creature the Infinite is less apparent than in that. He sees the Infinite in all things, and loves accordingly" (pp. 105–6). Comments on Herbert's vision of reality, his finer religious sensibilities, and his view of sin.

◆§ 68. GOSSE, EDMUND. "Metaphysical Poetry." In *More Books on the Table*, pp. 307–13. London: William Heinemann.
Essentially a review of *Metaphysical Lyrics & Poems*, edited by Herbert J. C. Grierson (entry 58). First appeared in the *Sunday Times* (London). Suggests that the common purpose of poets from Donne to Cowley "was an application of the psychological method to the passions" (p. 309). Maintains that Donne's greatest gift to his followers (and Herbert is included as a disciple) was the intellectual intensity of his expression: "He taught the poets to regard mellifluousness with suspicion, if it concealed poverty of thought, and to be more anxious to find words, even stumbling and harsh words, for their personal emotions, than to slip over the surface of language in a conventional sweetness" (pp. 311–12). Herbert is mentioned only in passing.

69. MOORE SMITH, G. C. "Wordsworth and George Herbert." *N&Q*, 12th ser. 12:30.

Suggests that Wordsworth was familiar with Herbert's poetry, as evidenced in his sonnet "Seathwaite Chapel" ("Such as the heaven-taught skill of Herbert drew"). Agrees with F. Haverfield (*N&Q*, 6th ser. 8 [1883]:206) that Herbert's "Mans medley" suggested some lines near the beginning of "Ode on Immortality" and sees Herbert's "Constancie" as a possible source for Wordsworth's "Character of a Happy Warrior." For a reply, see S. Butterworth, entry 66.

70. READ, HERBERT. "The Nature of Metaphysical Poetry." *Criterion* (London) 1:246–66.

Reprinted in *Reason and Romanticism: Essays in Literary Criticism* (London: Faber and Gwyer, 1926), pp. 31–58; *Collected Essays in Literary Criticism* (London: Faber and Faber, 1938), pp. 69–88; and *The Nature of Literature* (New York: Horizon Press, 1956), pp. 69–88, rpt. (1970).

Defines the essential nature of metaphysical poetry "as the emotional apprehension of thought—or, to use words suggested by Dante, as thought transmuted into vision" (p. 249). An elaboration on T. S. Eliot's theory of dissociation of sensibility. Singles out Milton as having done more than any other poet to destroy the metaphysical tradition. No specific references to Herbert. Donne and Chapman are used to illustrate the general concepts.

1924

71. BERESFORD, JOHN. "Holy Mr. Herbert." In *Gossip of the Seventeenth and Eighteenth Centuries*, pp. 195–208. London: Richard Cobden-Sanderson.

Reprinted, Freeport, N.Y.: Books for Libraries Press, 1968.

Praises Walton's biography and chides Herbert J. C. Grierson for being a "little patronizing to George Herbert" (p. 197) in his anthology of 1921 (entry 58). Brief appreciative biographical sketch with numerous quotations from Walton and from the poems to illustrate Herbert's inner life and spirit. Suggests that Herbert's real genius can be appreciated only by reading the whole of *The Temple*, not by simply reading selected poems.

72. DAVIDSON, M. B. "George Herbert and his Poetry." *Canadian Journal of Religious Thought*, July, pp. 290–99.

Appreciative biographical sketch. Believes that "it is not difficult to recount Herbert's sins as a poet" (p. 299): the poems are marred by being "overloaded with fantastic figures of speech, with strange conceits, with a love of complicated ornament, with a play on words" (p. 292), by striving for "prettiness rather than beauty" (pp. 292–93). Forgives Herbert for his lack of taste and praises his poems for their "uniformly religious character" (p. 294).

◄§ 73. FAUSSET, HUGH I'ANSON. *John Donne: A Study in Discord*. London: Jonathan Cape. 318p.
    Reprinted, New York: Russell and Russell, 1967.
    Brief comparison of the personalities and religious sensibilities of Herbert and Donne. Herbert "was essentially a cultivated, a fastidious spirit, alike in his worldliness and his mysticism, and thus incapable of the barbarism to which Donne descended in search of reality, or of the obscene and violent depths over which he hung" (p. 269). Suggests that in Herbert "the artist predominated, in Donne the scientist; in the one the saint, in the other the seer" (p. 269). Comments briefly on the relationship between the two poets.

◄§ 74. HULLEY, LINCOLN. *Sonnets on The Immortal Bards*. n.p. 31p.
    Original poem on Herbert (p. 13).

◄§ 75. NETHERCOT, ARTHUR H. "The Reputation of the 'Metaphysical Poets' During the Seventeenth Century." *JEGP* 23:173–98.
    Considers separately the reputations of Donne, Cowley, Cleveland, Carew, Herbert, Crashaw, Vaughan, and Quarles during the seventeenth century. Maintains that although throughout the century "Herbert's admirers and imitators were almost legion" (p. 186), the critics emphasized his piety rather than his poetry. Reproduces the comments of such men as Lord Herbert of Cherbury, Barnabas Oley, Wood, the anonymous writer of the preface to Crashaw's *Steps to the Temple*, Vaughan, Pestil, Fuller, Walton, Dean Duport of Peterborough, Samuel Woodford, Charles Cotton, Edward Phillips, Winstanley, and Richard Baxter. Lists several imitators, such as Dr. Bryan, Archbishop Leighton, John Dunton, and others. Discusses Dryden's critical comments on the metaphysicals and gives a brief account of the shifting literary tastes of the Restoration, which account, in part, for the decline of interest in the metaphysical poets.

◄§ 76. WHITING, BARTLETT J., comp. *Poems of Carew, Suckling, Lovelace and Herbert*. With biographical introductions by Bartlett J. Whiting. Little Blue Book, edited by E. Haldeman-Julius, no. 501. Girard, Kans.: Haldeman-Julius Co. [ca. 1924]. 64p.
    Contains a general introduction to Herbert's poetry, a biographical sketch, and ten poems from *The Temple*. Praises Herbert for his piety but says, "All the faults of the metaphysical school are to be found upon his pages; and there as well, we may discover their sturdy and whimsical virtues" (p. 59).

1925

◄§ 77. LEA, KATHLEEN M. "Conceits." *MLR* 20:389–406.

Discusses the nature and development of the conceit and contrasts the Elizabethans and the metaphysicals: "For the most part we may say that the besetting sin of the Elizabethans was the over-emphasis of the simile, the tendency to digress upon the comparison. This fault was to be corrected by the next generation. The 'metaphysical' poet regarded the simile as useful, not as an ornamental device: and the conceits of their poetry were due to under-emphasis" (p. 398). Contrasts Herbert and Donne: "Herbert was arguing from the physical to the spiritual: Donne, certain of the spiritual experience, was searching for the clearest illustration by which he could communicate it. Where Donne found poetry too difficult, Herbert found it too easy" (p. 401). Contrasts also Herbert and Vaughan: "Herbert is a moralist, weaving parables: Vaughan is a mystic" (p. 402). Briefly comments on Herbert's simplicity and uses of allegory.

◄§ 78. LEGOUIS, ÉMILE. "George Herbert." In *Dans les sentiers de la renaissance anglaise*, pp. 86–91. Paris: Société anonyme d'édition «Les Belles-Lettres».

Comments on the "alliance singulière de sincerité et de bizarrerie" (p. 86) in Herbert's poetry. Translates into French "The Quip," "The Elixir," and "Death."

◄§ 79. NETHERCOT, ARTHUR H. "The Reputation of the 'Metaphysical Poets' During the Age of Johnson and the 'Romantic Revival.' " *SP* 22:81–132.

Surveys critical attitudes toward the metaphysical poets (especially Donne, Carew, Cowley, Cleveland, Crashaw, Herbert, Vaughan, and Quarles) during the eighteenth century (1744–1800) and the early nineteenth century. In the eighteenth century, the center of discussion was Cowley, rather than Donne or Herbert. The notion of a "school of metaphysical poets" was not generally recognized before Johnson. Points out that Johnson does not classify Herbert and Crashaw as metaphysical poets. Surveys Johnson's comments and discusses his importance in shaping critical opinion during the remainder of the eighteenth century. Treats very briefly the interest of the early romantics in the metaphysical poets.

◄§ 80. ———. "The Reputation of the 'Metaphysical Poets' During the Age of Pope." *PQ* 4:161–79.

Suggests in this brief summary of early eighteenth-century attitudes toward the metaphysical poets that "in spite of the wide and continued diffusion of the Metaphysical taste through the early decades of the eighteenth century, readers and critics soon developed the reaction which had been indicated by the later seventeenth century, so that before many years scarcely any one dared admit himself an unswerving admirer of the Metaphysical writers. Many of these were becoming neglected or else forgotten, although the more important ones still retained a reputation for certain qualities or types of work" (p. 176). Three editions of Herbert appeared during the period (1703, 1709, 1711), and Herbert still was admired by many, primarily for his piety. Refers to the comments of Giles Jacobs, John Dunton, Joseph Warton, Pope, and Addison on Herbert. Points out that Cowley was the best known of the metaphysical poets, "thus showing that the populace does not always follow the verdict of the professional critics" (p. 177).

≈§ 81. PRAZ, MARIO. *Secentismo e Marinismo in Inghilterra: John Donne—Richard Crashaw.* Florence: La Voce. xii, 294p.
Contains a brief contrast between Herbert's rendition of Psalm 23 and Crashaw's paraphrase (pp. 252–53).

≈§ 82. STENBERG, THEODORE T. "Wordsworth's *Happy Warrior* and Herbert's 'Constancy.' " *MLN* 40:252–53.
Points out that both Emerson in his *Journals* and E. K. Chambers in his edition of *Poems of Henry Vaughan* note that Wordsworth's "Character of a Happy Warrior" is possibly indebted to Herbert's "Constancie," but argues that Wordsworth borrowed only the form, not the subject matter, from Herbert. Disagrees with Chambers's suggestion that Wordsworth also had Vaughan's "Righteousness" in mind.

1926

≈§ 83. INGE, WILLIAM RALPH. *The Platonic Tradition in English Religious Thought.* New York: Longmans, Green and Co. vii, 124p.
Comments on Herbert reprinted in an expanded version in "English Religious Poetry." In *More Lay Thoughts of a Dean* (New York and London: Putnam, 1932), pp. 225–54.
Briefly comments on Herbert as the typically Anglican poet: "Refinement, good taste, culture and reserve, with a foundation of devout feeling and pure living, are the qualities which we recognize as belonging to this type" (pp. 91–92).

≈§ 84. LEGOUIS, ÉMILE. *A History of English Literature,* translated by Helen Douglas Irvine. Vol. 1: *The Middle Ages & the Renascence (650–1660).* New York: Macmillan Co. xii, 387p.
Revised and reprinted many times, most recently in 1971.
Praises *The Country Parson* for its simple, smooth prose and says that it is "most characteristic of the prose writing of the time" (p. 337). Discusses briefly *The Temple,* the "most popular of Anglican poems" (p. 351), praising Herbert's fervor, sincerity, and subtlety while criticizing his obscurity, fantastic uses of imagery, and lack of taste. "His poetry con-

stantly offends taste, but often gives the impression of a sort of sublimity"
(p. 352). Suggests that Herbert is "of all Donne's disciples the one most
like him" (p. 352).

◄§ 85. NEWBOLT, HENRY. "Some Devotional Poets of the Seventeenth
Century." In *Studies in Green and Gray*, pp. 277–88. London,
Edinburgh, New York: Thomas Nelson and Sons.
Very general essay on devotional poetry of the seventeenth century.
Contrasts Herbert and Donne and comments on Herbert's influence on
Crashaw and Vaughan. Unlike Donne, Herbert's "aim is not so much
to discover, as to exhibit in new ways what he had long known. He has
no need to invent a new kind of verse: and his concepts are above all designed to be intelligible—they are examples chosen from familiar life but
used with a dexterous twist which makes them attractive and memorable"
(p. 280).

1927

◄§ 86. GILLMAN, FREDERICK JOHN. *The Evolution of the English Hymn:
An Historical Survey of the Origins and Development of the Hymns
of the Christian Church*. Foreward by Sir H. Walford Davies. London: George Allen & Unwin. 312p.
Briefly discusses the "Herbert group, a family party, linked together by
ties of blood or friendship or literary tastes, and presided over by the
genial and kindly fisherman, Izaak Walton" (p. 164). Includes Donne,
Wotton, Crashaw, Henry King, Nicholas Ferrar, Thomas Ken, Vaughan,
and Richard Baxter. Calls Herbert the typical poet of the Anglican
Church and refers to his version of Psalm 23 as "a perfect gem" (p. 152).
Briefly compares Adam of Brito, a twelfth-century hymnist, to Herbert.
Suggests that "Antiphon" is the best hymn among Herbert's lyrics. Comments also on Henry Playford's *Divine Companion* (1701) and John
Wesley's *Charlestown Hymn Book* (1737), both of which contain adap-
tations from Herbert.

◄§ 87. HERBERT, GEORGE. *George Herbert*. Edited by Humbert Wolfe.
The Augustan Books of English Poetry, 2d ser., no. 2. London:
Ernest Benn. 31p.
Anthology that contains thirty-three poems with no notes or com-
mentary. Brief introduction stresses Herbert's concept of God as a friend.
Says that Herbert's poetry "is cool, it is silver, it is the hautbois in that
celestial orchestra" (p. iii).

◄§ 88. ———. *The Temple. Sacred Poems & Private Ejaculations*.
Edited by Francis Meynell. London: Nonesuch Press. x, 213p.
Prefatory note on the text, the portrait, etc. (pp. v–viii); contents (pp.

viii–x); text of the poems (pp. 1–194); bibliographical note by Geoffrey Keynes (pp. 197–202); textual notes with variant readings (pp. 203–13). Limited to 1,500 copies. Prints "for the first time the text of the Bodleian MS., on the ground that it is without doubt the nearest to Herbert's own, if it is not indeed Herbert's own" (p. v). Describes the manuscript and comments on a portrait of Herbert (reproduced) originally in the possession of George Young of Salisbury.

◄§ 89. JUDSON, ALEXANDER CORBIN, ed. *Seventeenth-Century Lyrics.* Edited with short biographies, bibliographies, and notes. Chicago: University of Chicago Press. xix, 412p.

Anthology of fourteen seventcenth-century lyric poets containing 275 poems with modernized spellings. Herbert is represented by 17 poems (pp. 90–102). Brief biographical sketch provides a setting for each of the poems represented (pp. 302–3), a highly selective bibliography (pp. 303–4), and notes on individual poems (pp. 305–10).

◄§ 90. MANN, CAMERON. A *Concordance to the English Poems of George Herbert.* Boston and New York: Houghton Mifflin. xii, 277p.

Reprinted, Ann Arbor: University Microfilms, 1970; Folcroft, Pa.: Folcroft Press, 1970; St. Clair Shores, Mich.: Scholarly Press, 1972.

Based on George Herbert Palmer's three-volume edition (entry 1). Covers all the English poems and some of doubtful authorship. Modern spellings. Contains abbreviations for the titles of the poems and a list of words that occur only in titles. In cases of words that can have various grammatical functions, no distinctions are made, but the use of the words is obvious. Does not include all references to articles, prepositions, conjunctions, interjections, and auxiliary verbs, but select passages are given to illustrate each, and the number of times each appears is indicated in parentheses. Example: *bubble*

earthly job is but a b.	Van. I, 18
do end in b. s	E. S., I, 14
my soul will turn to b. s Nat. 9	

◄§ 91. SCHELLING, FELIX E. "Devotional Poetry in the Reign of Charles I." In *Shakespeare and "Demi-Science": Papers on Elizabethan Topics*, pp. 138–57. Philadelphia: University of Pennsylvania Press.

Briefly contrasts the moral poetry of the Elizabethans with the devotional poetry of the Caroline period and surveys the religious verse of Quarles, Wither, Herbert, Sandys, Crashaw, Herrick, Marvell, and Vaughan. Praises Herbert for "his sincerity, his piety, his rhetorical if somewhat artificial and 'conceited' style and his originality of figure" (p. 146). Contrasts Herbert with Crashaw: "Crashaw turns the passion of earth to worship and identifies the spiritual and material in his devotion;

Herbert with all his love of ritual, has somewhat of the Puritan spirit in him, which is troubled in the contemplation of earthly vanities and struggles to rise above and beyond them" (p. 149). Points out that Herbert is more restrained than Crashaw, more of the craftsman: "But if Herbert has never fallen into Crashaw's extravagances, he is equally incapable of his inspired, rhapsodic flights" (p. 149).

◄§ 92. WELBY, T. EARLE. "George Herbert at Bemerton." *The Saturday Review of Politics, Literature, Science and Art* 144:538–39.
Recalls a visit to Salisbury and Bemerton. Comments briefly on Herbert's religious sensibilities and art: "He is very unequal, and in part of his work he forgets that if poetry is to witness to God it can be only through success in an ambition proper to it; but from time to time he writes, perhaps no more than a stanza, never more than a short poem, in which the passion for unity with God is a poetic no less than a religious passion" (p. 539).

1928

◄§ 93. EMPEROR, JOHN BERNARD. *The Catullian Influence in English Lyric Poetry, Circa 1600–1650.* University of Missouri Studies, vol. 3, no. 3. Columbia: University of Missouri. 133p.
Attempts to show that during the first half of the seventeenth century Catullus became one of the most important molding forces in English poetry. Points out that, in contrast to Donne and many others, "no trace of a Catullian influence appears in the poems of George Herbert" (p. 42). Attributes this phenomenon to the wholly religious nature of Herbert's poetry.

◄§ 94. KELLER, WOLFGANG, and FEHR, BERNHARD. *Die Englische Literatur von der Renaissance bis zur Aufklärung.* Wildpark-Potsdam: Akademische Verlagsgesellschaft Athenaion M.B.H. 282p.
Biographical sketch of Herbert with some generally negative comments on *The Temple*: "Der Verse sind nur selten schlackenrein. Donnes 'metaphysical Witz' und leidige Concetti trüben allzu oft den Ausdruck" (p. 136).

◄§ 95. KEMP, VIOLET I. "Mystic Utterance in Certain English Poets." *HJ* 26:474–83.
Discusses the nature of mysticism and the methods of the poet mystics. "Poetry can only be mystical to a certain degree. Pure mysticism, when the state of union is reached, is mute" (p. 475). Comments briefly on "The Collar" as reflecting the "anguished conflict and discouragement as well as the unavoidable obligation to follow on, in one who has once

seen the way" (p. 476). Sees Vaughan and Traherne, among the seventeenth-century poets, as true mystics; Herbert is excluded because "he was too orthodox and good a churchman to be one of the mystics" (p. 481).

◄§ 96. LUCAS, F. L. "George Herbert." *Life and Letters* 1:548–61.
Reprinted as "The Poet of Anglicanism," in *Studies French and English* (London: Cassell and Co., 1934), pp. 138–50.
Discusses Herbert as a poet of the Church of England. Brief biographical sketch and character study, based primarily on Herbert's works and on Walton. Familiar, appreciative essay. Fully agrees with Coleridge's statement concerning *The Temple*: "To appreciate this volume, it is not enough that the reader possess a cultivated judgement, classical taste, or even poetic sensibility, unless he be likewise a *Christian*, and both a zealous and orthodox, both a devout and *devotional*, Christian. But even this will not suffice. He must be an affectionate and dutiful child of the Church."

◄§ 97. NAYLOR, E. W. "Three Seventeenth Century Poet-Parsons and Music." *Proceedings of the Musical Association* (London) 54:93–113.
Reprinted in *The Poets and Music* (New York: E. P. Dutton & Co., 1928), pp. 71–83.
Discusses Herbert, Herrick, and Traherne. Comments on Herbert's musical abilities and briefly explicates possible musical allusions and references in "The Pearl," "Easter," and "Prayer." Wonders if Herbert knew the sequences of Notker Balbulus of St. Gall (ninth century), which closely echo Herbert's famous line, "Let all the world in every corner sing, My God and King."

◄§ 98. READ, HERBERT. "Poetry and Religion." In *Phases of English Poetry*, pp. 57–82. Hogarth Lectures on Literature. London: Hogarth Press.
Reprinted, London: Faber and Faber, 1950.
Suggests that Herbert more than any other of the metaphysical poets "shows how the poetry of metaphysical wit can be transmuted into the poetry of religious experience" (p. 68). Comments on Herbert's uses of domestic imagery and praises his masculine strength. Contrasts him with Crashaw and Vaughan.

◄§ 99. ROBBIE, H. J. L. "George Herbert." *CQR* 105:359–64.
Biographical account of Herbert, stressing his piety and dedication to the Anglican communion. Sees the poetry as spiritual autobiography. Comments on Herbert's complex uses of form, "his making the form of

it symbol of his thought" (p. 363). Praises Herbert for ridding
of "fine phrases, glittering metaphors and the classical decorative allusion of his predecessors" (p. 363) and points out his simple diction, love for common things, and his successful musical metaphors.

⋘ 100. ROBERTS, R[ICHARD] ELLIS. "George Herbert." In *Reading for*
    Pleasure and Other Essays, pp. 170–74. London: Methuen & Co.
    2d ed., 1931.
Comments on Herbert's intellectual affinities with Donne: "It is no
exaggeration to say that it is to Donne's startling personality that we owe
the poetry of Herbert, of Vaughan, of Traherne, of Crashaw, and of Marvell; and while none of them can fetch so dangerous a course as Donne,
nor bring to earth with quite a certain power the very glow and sunshine
of eternity, Herbert, in some ways, remains nearest to his master's mind"
(pp. 170–71). Calls Herbert "the one poet whose work has done most to
make something passionate and extreme out of the religion of the middle
way" (p. 172).

1929

⋘ 101. FLETCHER, J. M. J. *George Herbert, A. D. 1593–1633*. A Ser-
    mon preached in St. John's Church, Bemerton [on 3 March 1929].
    Salisbury: Bennett Brothers. 8p.
Comments favorably on Herbert's saintly life. Calls him "your special
Bemerton saint" (p. 2).

⋘ 102. GRIERSON, H. J. C. "Humanism and the Churches." In *Cross*
    Currents in English Literature of the XVIIth Century, pp. 166–231.
    London: Chatto & Windus.
Reprinted, New York: Harper Torchbooks, 1959; Gloucester, Mass.:
Peter Smith, 1965.
Comments briefly on the note of Christian humanism struck in Herbert's poetry (pp. 214–18). Calls Herbert the "most characteristic Anglican" of the period, "not in virtue of his doctrine . . . but of his feeling"
(p. 215). Points out that Herbert's theme is "Christ's sacrifice, not as a
doctrine of substitution and imputed righteousness, but as a history of
human goodness and suffering, of how a man who was also God gave his
life for erring, ungrateful humanity" (p. 215). Suggests that love in Herbert's poetry is "the centre and circumference of his Christianity . . . the
tempered, disciplined, pure and deep yet gentle passion which the spirit
in and behind nature awoke in Wordsworth" (p. 215). Argues that Herbert is more like Petrarch and Shakespeare than has been usually noticed
in that *The Temple* is "the record of God's wooing of the soul of Herbert
recorded in the Christian story and the seasons and symbols of the

Church, and Herbert's wooing of God, a record of conflict and fluctuating moods" (p. 216). Compares and contrasts Herbert briefly with Vaughan, Donne, Crashaw, Milton, and Bunyan.

◄§ 103. NEWBOLT, SIR HENRY, ed. *Devotional Poets of the XVIIth Century*. London & Edinburgh: Thomas Nelson. xxi, 293p.

Compares the aims, temperament, and methods of Herbert with those of Donne. States that Donne tried "to find that which seems to him beyond discovery, to express that which was never yet expressed" (p. xiv), whereas Herbert's aim was not so much to discover as it was to exhibit in a new way what he had long known. Contrasts Herbert's simplicity with Donne's more violent temperament: "Herbert, with a less chaotic experience, and less strength of every kind, came nearer to success within his own chosen limits" (p. xiv). Includes thirty-eight of Herbert's poems.

◄§ 104. TAGGARD, GENEVIEVE, ed. *Circumference: Varieties of Metaphysical Verse, 1456–1928*. New York: Covici Friede. xiii, 236p.

Anthology of metaphysical poems that includes six poems by Herbert. In part 1 (pp. 3–13) the editor broadly defines metaphysical poetry as primarily reflecting a "state of mind." No specific comments on Herbert. Suggests that Donne and Emily Dickinson are the most genuine metaphysical poets in English and that Keats is "the clearest example of what a metaphysical poet is not" (p. 7). Limited to 1,050 copies.

1930

◄§ 105. COFFIN, ROBERT P. TRISTRAM. *Laud: Storm Center of Stuart England*. New York: Brentano's. 331p.

Biographical study of William Laud and his times. Herbert is mentioned throughout, primarily in contrasts between the archbishop and the pastor of Bemerton. Views both men as champions of the Anglican cause, each in his own way.

◄§ 106. ELIOT, T. S. "Thinking in Verse: A Survey of Early Seventeenth Century Poetry." *The Listener* 3:441–43.

No specific mention of Herbert. Suggests that the "profoundest thought and feeling" of the Elizabethan age "went into its dramatic blank verse" (p. 441), and thus maintains that "the Elizabethans in their drama are forerunners of the Jacobean and Caroline poets in their lyrical verses" (p. 442). Argues that playwrights, like Chapman, "*think* in verse, rather than *sing* in verse" (p. 441). Comments on the religious sensibility of the seventeenth century, and calls that period "the third most interesting period in the history of Christianity; the others being

the early period which saw the development of dogma in the Greek and
Latin churches, and the thirteenth century" (p. 442). Comments on the
influence of the Counter-Reformation on the arts and literature, especially the importance of St. Ignatius Loyola and the Jesuits, as well as of
St. Teresa of Avila and St. John of the Cross.

◄§ 107. ————. "The Devotional Poets of the Seventeenth Century:
    Donne, Herbert, Crashaw." *The Listener* 3:552–53.
    Distinguishes between religious poetry and devotional poetry: "I call
'religious' what is inspired by religious feeling of some kind; and 'devotional' that which is directly about some subject connected with revealed religion" (p. 552). Calls Herbert and Crashaw "devotional" poets
and Vaughan "religious." Comments briefly on the wit and the uses of
the conceit in "Prayer (I)." Compares and contrasts Herbert with Donne
and Crashaw. Remarks about Donne and Herbert: "And if I set myself
to imitate either, I think that Herbert might be the more difficult model
of the two. There remains his personal quality, and the necessity for
saturating oneself in his verse to get it" (p. 553).

◄§ 108. EMPSON, WILLIAM. *Seven Types of Ambiguity*. London: Chat-
    to & Windus. 325p.
    Reprinted, New York: Harcourt Brace and Co., 1931; Meridian Paper-
back, 1936.
    2d ed., London: Chatto & Windus, 1947; New York: New Directions,
1947.
    3d ed., London: Chatto & Windus, 1953; Norfolk, Conn.: New Di-
rections, 1953; New York: Noonday Press (Meridian Books), 1957; New
York: New Directions, 1966; Harmondsworth: Penguin Books, 1961;
London: Chatto & Windus, 1963; Cleveland: World Publishing Co.
(Meridian Books), 1964; New York: New Directions, 1974.
    Italian edition: *Sette tipi di ambiguità. Edizione italiana a cura de
Giorgio Melchiori* (Turin: Einaudi, 1965).
    Defines ambiguity as that which "adds some nuance to the direct
statement of prose" (p. 1). Later revises the definition and maintains
that ambiguity is "any verbal nuance, however slight, which gives room
for alternative reactions to the same piece of language" (p. 1, 2d ed.). In
his discussion of the "third type of ambiguity" (when two apparently
unconnected meanings are given at the same time), Empson comments
on Herbert's use of symbols in "Hope" (pp. 150–58) and discusses "The
Pilgrimage" (pp. 163–65), suggesting that it anticipates Bunyan's *Pilgrim's Progress* and "contains both special and general ambiguity of the
third type, both pun, allegory, and variety of feeling" (p. 163). In his
discussion of the "sixth type of ambiguity" ("when a statement says
nothing, by tautology, by contradiction, or by irrelevant statements, if
any; so that the reader is forced to invent statements of his own and they

are liable to conflict with one another" [p. 223]), Empson briefly comments on the last stanza of "Affliction (I)" (pp. 232–33) and calls the last line of the poem an example of "an ambiguity of tautology." Comments rather extensively on the double meanings and apparent contradictions in "The Sacrifice" (pp. 286–95) as an example of the "seventh type of ambiguity" (when one finds complete contradiction, suggesting a division in the author's mind). Empson's comments on the poem provoked a number of rebuttals, most notably by Rosemond Tuve in "On Herbert's 'Sacrifice'" (entry 310). In his preface to the third edition, Empson somewhat qualifies some of his earlier comments and regrets his "rather distracting leap into Depth Psychology" (p. xvi) but maintains his original point that in "The Sacrifice" Herbert "felt the paradox of the vengeful God of Love to be an extremely severe strain" and that "in treating a traditional theme, he had to heighten the paradoxes till a reader is forced to wonder whether they will manage to balance" (p. xvi). Firmly maintains, in spite of adverse criticism, that lines 202–3 of "The Sacrifice" ("Man stole the fruit, but I must climb the tree;/ The tree of life to all, but onely me") "carry the usual homely quality of Herbert, but present Christ in torment, with ghastly pathos, as an adventurous boy" (p. xvi).

109. HAMER, ENID. *The Metres of English Poetry*. New York: Macmillan Co. xi, 340p.
Brief comments on Herbert's experimentation with trochaic verse in "Discipline" (pp. 238–39).

110. NETHERCOT, ARTHUR H. "The Reputation of Native Versus Foreign 'Metaphysical Poets' in England." *MLR* 25:152–64.
Discusses the reputation of Marino, du Bartas, and Góngora in England: "In the early seventeenth century all three continental poets had considerable weight and authority. They were read, translated, and imitated. By the Restoration all were being severely attacked for excesses of style—whereas the English metaphysicals were yet fairly well entrenched in popular regard. During the age of Pope the foreigners were held in even more contempt than the English, for whom some readers and critics still had a good word to say. During the age of Johnson that dictator's criticisms of the English would seem fulsome encomiums compared to what was being generally said about the foreigners. There was a revival of interest in the English Metaphysicals as a minor aspect of the Romantic Revival. But there was not such a revival for Marino, Du Bartas, and Góngora" (p. 164). Herbert is not specifically mentioned.

111. WILLIAMSON, GEORGE. *The Donne Tradition: A Study in English Poetry from Donne to the Death of Cowley*. Cambridge, Mass.: Harvard University Press; Oxford: University Press. x, 264p.

Reprinted, New York: Noonday Press, 1958 (paperback) and 1961;
New York: Noonday Press, ed. bound by Peter Smith, 1958.

States that, while the metaphysical poets did not regard themselves as
belonging to a particular school of poetry, there was a Donne tradition,
although perhaps not sharply defined: "There was no sealed tribe of
Donne," but "his influence was the most profound and pervasive of any
in the first half of his century" (p. 229). Traces the influence of Donne
to the death of Cowley. Chapter 1 presents a general biographical
sketch of Donne. Chapter 2 outlines certain major characteristics of the
poetry of the Donne tradition: intellectual intensity, unified sensibility,
wit, the conceit, analysis, technical features, particular uses of language,
erudition, and difficulty. Concludes that the tradition can best be defined as "complex, sensuous, and intellectual as opposed to the simple,
sensuous, and passionate tradition" (p. 57). Chapter 3 presents a comparison of Donne and Chapman. Chapter 4 discusses two major aspects
of the tradition: the conceit and *metaphysical shudder*, a term used to
describe the emotional quality of the poems. Concludes, "The line of
Metaphysicals in the seventeenth century becomes distinct in the influence of poet upon poet, deriving more or less directly from Donne, but
remaining a thing of individuals rather than a school, till it attains
something like critical consciousness in the mind of Dryden" (p. 75).
Chapter 5 traces the sacred line of the tradition in the poetry of Herbert,
Crashaw, and Vaughan. Suggests, "Of all the Metaphysicals, Herbert is
in some ways most like Donne" (p. 99). Recognizes the individual talent
of Herbert, and outlines some of the major features of the Donne tradition that shaped Herbert's sensibility and manner. Challenges George
Herbert Palmer's assertion that Herbert "devised the religious love-lyric"
and "introduced structure into the short poem" (p. 103): "Rather than
give Herbert the emphasis of a pioneer, it is more exact to say that Herbert simply carried on the sacred side of the Donne tradition and developed it in certain ways" (p. 110). Thus, it is "through *The Temple*
that the religious side of Donne passed to other poets who reflected his
manner of praise even when they forgot his name" (p. 110). Chapter 6
traces the profane line in the poetry of Lord Herbert of Cherbury, Henry
King, Marvell, and Aurelian Townshend. Chapter 7 comments on the
chief offenders of the tradition, namely, Cleveland, Benlowes, and Cowley. Chapter 8 compares Donne and Jonson and concludes that Donne
was the chief influence on the Cavalier poets. Chapter 9 surveys Dyrden's
critical position toward the Donne tradition and briefly accounts for the
reaction that set in during the Restoration. The final chapter is entitled
"A Short View of the Tradition." Appendix A (pp. 251–52) is "A Chronology of Inheritance." Appendix B (p. 253) lists seventeenth-century
editions of Donne's poems. Appendix C (pp. 254–57) is a collection of
conceits from Chapman's poems. Appendix D (pp. 258–64) is a selective
bibliography.

1931

≈§ 112. BEACHCROFT, T. O. "Mysticism as Criticism." *The Symposium: A Critical Review* 2:208–25.

Dialogue between two fictitious disputants, "Sophister" and "Senior," about the nature of mystical poetry. Briefly mentions Herbert's use of emblems (p. 219). Contrasts the emblematic with the romantic imaginative symbol.

≈§ 113. ———. "Quarles—and the Emblem Habit." *DubR* 188:80–96.

Discusses the nature and function of the emblem and the symbolic habit of mind that it produced and reflected. Suggests that Quarles "was perhaps the first writer of the Theological School to introduce those multiplied images in illustration of a single thought that are so freely used in Crashaw, Herbert, and Donne" (p. 94). Comments briefly on Herbert's various uses of the emblem and suggests, "His basing a whole poem on the chequered floor of his church is as perfect a bodying forth of the emblem habit as could be found, while only the presence of emblems in an acute form could account for the attack of typographical topiary fever even in such a poem of Herbert's as 'Easter Wings' " (pp. 95-96). Mentions also "The Collar," "The Pulley," and "Clasping of hands."

≈§ 114. KITCHIN, GEORGE. "Jacobean and Later Seventeenth Century Parody and Burlesque." In *A Survey of Burlesque and Parody in English*, pp. 68–98. Edinburgh and London: Oliver and Boyd.

Comments on Herbert's "A Parodie" (pp. 76–77). Suggests inaccurately that the poem is a Christian parody of Donne; it is actually a parody of "Song" ("Soules joy, now I am gone"), which is now attributed to William Herbert, 3d earl of Pembroke (see Rosemond Tuve, entry 467). Also reproduces a "genuine parody of Herbert's eccentric manner" (p. 77), a poem entitled "Confusion." Calls such an exercise "saint-baiting."

≈§ 115. MACAULAY, ROSE. "Anglican and Puritan." In *Some Religious Elements in English Literature*, pp. 84–126. Hogarth Lectures on Literature Series, no. 14. London: Leonard and Virginia Woolf at The Hogarth Press.

Contrasts the Anglican spirit of reserve, dignity, and restraint exemplified by Herbert with the voluptuousness of Catholic devotional poetry of the period. Calls Herbert "the first of the Anglican poets; coloured by and confined within the walls of his Church" (p. 96). Suggests that "The H. Communion" "breathes the very spirit of the Anglican catechism" (p. 98).

➳§ 116. Wolfe, Humbert. "George Herbert." In *Snow: Poems by Humbert Wolfe*. London: Victor Gollancz.
Original poem on Herbert (p. 49).

1932

➳§ 117. Bald, R. C. *Donne's Influence in English Literature*. Morpeth, Eng.: St. John's College Press. 62p.
Reprinted, Gloucester, Mass.: Peter Smith, 1965.
Traces the influence of Donne from his own time to the twentieth century. Discusses Donne's influence on Herbert (pp. 24–28). Calls Herbert "the religious poet whose work was most directly influenced by Donne and whose life presents a certain parallel to his" (p. 24), yet recognizes certain differences as well: "Herbert's wit plays quaintly with the homeliest images, and expresses emotions originally complex in terms that are essentially simple, instead of refining them with Donne's subtle reasonings" (p. 26). Comments on Herbert's serenity, simplicity, subtlety, and especially on his uses of "images more homely even than that of the parables" (p. 25).

➳§ 118. Beachcroft, T. O. "Nicholas Ferrar and George Herbert." *Criterion* 12:24–42.
Discusses Herbert's friendship with Nicholas Ferrar. Calls Herbert a mystical poet and contrasts him with Wordsworth. In Herbert's poetry "the images are not chosen for their emotional so much as for their reasonable equivalence" (p. 38). Contrasts Herbert's sense of a personal God with the more vague position of Wordsworth: "The mind accustomed to speak of religious issues in vague and pretentious generalities will find itself on unfamiliar ground with Herbert: ground where God is not collective unseen forces, spiritual principle, or the power that makes for good" (p. 39). Defends Herbert's style and witty use of words and devices. Suggests that Herbert's simplicity "is the *outcome*, not the lack of a critical and cultured mind, and of a poet's sensibility" (p. 40).

➳§ 119. Browne-Wilkinson, Arthur Rupert. "The Catechism and Children's Worship." In *Liturgy and Worship: A Companion to the Prayer Books of the Anglican Communion*, edited by W. K. Lowther Clarke, with the assistance of Charles Harris, pp. 429–42. New York: Macmillan Co.
Comments on the insistence of Anglican bishops and divines in the seventeenth century on the necessity of catechizing children in preparation for confirmation, a practice in fact very often neglected. The Puritans, who opposed confirmation, "had the effect, no doubt quite unintentionally, of weakening this system of instruction simply because it

was, by the rubrics, devised as a preparation for that rite" (pp. 433–34).
Comments briefly on Herbert's endorsement of the practice in *The Country Parson*.

◆§ 120. ELIOT, T. S. "Studies in Sanctity: VIII—George Herbert."
    Spectator 148:360–61.
    Reprinted in *Spectator's Gallery: Essays, Sketches, Short Stories &
Poems from The Spectator 1932*, edited by Peter Fleming and Derek
Verschoyle (London: Jonathan Cape, 1933), pp. 286–90.
    Laments that Herbert has been generally neglected and often misunderstood: "Whatever Herbert was, he was not the prototype of the clergyman of Dickens' Christmas at Dingley Dell" (p. 361). Suggests, "Of all the 'metaphysical' poets Herbert has suffered the most from being read only in anthologies" (p. 361). Comments on the spiritual stamina of *The Temple*: "Throughout there is brain work, and a very high level of intensity; his poetry is definitely an *oeuvre*, to be studied entire" (p. 361). Suggests that only religion could have evoked Herbert's full genius: "It is very rare to find a poet of whom one may say, that his poetic gift would have remained dormant or unfulfilled but for his religious vocation" (p. 361). Compares Herbert to Christina Rossetti and to Donne.

◆§ 121. ELTON, OLIVER. "Poetry, 1600–1660." In *The English Muse: A
    Sketch*, pp. 202–31. London: G. Bell and Sons.
    Reprinted, 1937.
    Brief survey of Herbert (pp. 217–19) in which he is called "an inveterate quibbler, a too hard driver of his metaphors" (p. 218). Seen as a poet who "has refreshed generations of devout Anglicans" (p. 218), Herbert is considered quaint and overly ingenious.

◆§ 122. FRIEDERICK, WERNER P. *Spiritualismus und Sensualismus in
    der englischen Barocklyrik*. Weiner Beitrage zur englischen Philo-
    logie, vol. 57. Vienna and Leipzig: Wilhelm Braumüller. 303p.
    Shows that the term *baroque* is applicable to the English lyrics of the seventeenth century. Views the age as one of polarization, disharmony, and contrasts. Comments on the sensuality and spirituality of the period and on the effects of the conflicts between the two. Comments on specific baroque themes and features of Herbert's poetry, especially the intensity of religious feeling, the theme of the conflict of the soul suspended between hope and despair, the theme of death, the theme of renunciation of the world and of worldly goods, and the theme of the discrepancy between man and God. Considers certain baroque stylistic traits in Herbert's poetry, especially his use of exotic vocabulary in "The Odour" and his playful uses of rhymes in "Paradise."

⤙§ 123. HALL, BERNARD G. "The 'Jacula Prudentum.' " *TLS*, 21 April, p. 291.

Argues that there is no solid evidence for attributing *Jacula Prudentum* to Herbert, finds the work incompatible with Herbert's wit, and suggests that it be dropped from the canon of his works.

⤙§ 124. MITCHELL, W. FRASER. *English Pulpit Oratory from Andrewes to Tillotson: A Study of Its Literary Aspects*. London: Society for Promoting Christian Knowledge; New York and Toronto: Macmillan Co. xii, 516p.

Comments on Herbert's objections to the then-fashionable "metaphysical" style of preaching, to "the total break up of anything approaching a connected prose style and the multiplying of endless divisions, due not to the careful working out of a sound rhetorical plan, but to the caprice and ingenuity of the preachers" (p. 362) as well as to a delight in Latin words and rhetorical ostentation. In the seventh chapter of *The Country Parson*, Herbert rejects what he calls this "crumbling a text into small parts" (p. 362). Brief comments on Herbert's popularity among Anglican churchmen; his works, like those of Jeremy Taylor, "have always ranked high among Anglican works of devotion" (p. 242).

⤙§ 125. PALMER, G. H. "E. C. Lowe's Edition of George Herbert's *Church Porch*." *N&Q* 162:442.

George Herbert Palmer, then ninety years old, asks for assistance in obtaining a copy of E. C. Lowe's edition of Herbert's *The Church-Porch*. Lowe, headmaster at Hurstpierpoint School, reportedly required all boys who entered St. John's School to memorize *The Church-Porch*. Palmer suggests that this edition is the only Herbert item that he has been unable to locate. Comments on Herbert collection at Harvard, which he amassed: "No collection of Herbert equals it in size."

⤙§ 126. SHARP, THOMAS. "The George Herbert Medlar." *The Gardner's Chronicle* 91:117, 119.

Describes a medlar tree planted by Herbert in 1632 in the garden at Bemerton rectory. Two photographs. "A good many pieces of the dead trunk have been taken to America by literary pilgrims" (p. 119).

⤙§ 127. SMITH, CHARD POWERS. *Pattern and Variation in Poetry*. New York: Charles Scribner's Sons. xv, 408p.

Brief comparison of "The Collar" with Coventry Patmore's "Farewell" (pp. 192–94). Praises Herbert's poem for its "flashes of greatness" but says that it "is irritating for its lack of technical control" (p. 192). States that Herbert "never ordered his life, and he never disciplined his talent. When he blunders into art, he writes greatly. But he seldom does" (p. 193).

◄§ 128. YOUNG, G. M. "Cock-sure." *TLS*, 29 December, p. 989.

Discusses the possible meanings of the term *cocksure* and suggests that it may mean "(objectively) the state of the hay, (subjectively) the state of the mind of the farmer when there is no sign of any break of weather before the hay is cocked." Illustrates this usage with a passage from *The Country Parson*, chap. 30.

1933

◄§ 129. ANON. "George Herbert, 1593–1633." *Cambridge Review* 54: 291–93.

Defends Herbert's simplicity, sincerity, unpoetic plainness, uses of puns, and, in particular, his ability to make proverbs, allegories, and myths. "This ability to make myths, even little ones, is the gift which is most lacking in the metaphysicals; and the danger of a too exclusive admiration of their kind of poetry is that it leads to a neglect of this essential part of poetic creation—narrative on a mythological level is the primary, oldest, and most profound poetry" (p. 293). Challenges Dr. Johnson's negative comments about religious poetry and briefly contrasts Herbert with Vaughan and Crashaw. Suggests that Herbert's poems contain "an artlessness which make them more fit for the study of the religious than for the more objective student of poetry" (p. 291).

◄§ 130. ANON. "George Herbert." *TLS*, 2 March, pp. 133–34.

Asks for a reassessment of Herbert as a poet and suggests that he is much less conventional than is popularly thought: "There is not one of our poets whose style is less easy-going, whose sweetness is less mild" (p. 133). Appreciative critical essay that comments briefly on Herbert's major themes, his obscurity and originality, his uses of music and diction, etc. "But we do not read 'The Temple' to-day because it explains the world to us and justifies Providence. We read it because, in spite of Herbert's belief that he possessed an explanation, he passed through the strenuous and ultimate internal struggle which is imposed on every man, whether religion comes to him as a singular or as a universal mystery" (p. 134). For a reply, see H. Ince Anderton, entry 132.

◄§ 131. ANON. "Parson Herbert: The Saint of Bemerton." *Times* (London), 3 March, pp. 15–16.

Praises Herbert's genuine saintliness: "To follow him through his short life is to discern a character much less simple than the conventional saint, much less melodramatic than the disappointed courtier, and much more worthy than either to be honoured by his Church and his country" (p. 15). Brief biographical sketch with only general comments on the poetry. Maintains that "it is in the parsonage at Bemerton rather than in

'The Temple' that we must look for George Herbert the Churchman"
(p. 16).

◄§ 132. ANDERTON, H. INCE. "George Herbert." *TLS*, 9 March, p. 167.
   In part, a reply to an anonymous article in *TLS* (entry 130). Disagrees
with Walton's statement (repeated in the article) that the king gave
Herbert a sinecure "which fell into his disposal, I think, by the death of
the Bishop of St. Aspah. It was the same that Queen Elizabeth had
formerly given to her favourite, Sir Philip Sidney." Traces various ecclesiastical benefices and appointments held by Herbert.

◄§ 133. BARRATT, KATHLEEN I. "George Herbert." *TLS*, 2 March, p.
   147.
   Asks for information on Herbert manuscripts, private letters, early musical settings, etc.

◄§ 134. DEARMER, PERCY, comp. *Songs of Praise Discussed: A Hand-
   book to the Best-Known Hymns and to Others Recently Intro-
   duced*. Compiled by Percy Dearmer with notes on the music by
   Archibald Jacob. London: Humphrey Milford, Oxford University
   Press. xxxii, 559p.
   Reprinted, London and New York: Oxford University Press, 1952.
   Comments briefly on the following hymns adapted from Herbert's
poems: (1) "Enrich, Lord, heart, mouth, hands in me" from "Trinitie
Sunday" (pp. 219–20); (2) "Come, my way, my truth, my life" from
"The Call" (p. 253); (3) "King of glory, King of Peace" from "L'En-
voy" (p. 294); (4) "Let all the world in every corner sing" from "Anti-
phon (I)" (pp. 296–97); (5) "Sweet day, so cool, so calm, so bright" from
"Vertue" (p. 345); (6) "Teach me, my God and King" from "The
Elixir," giving John Wesley's adaptation (p. 346); (7) "The God of love
my shepherd is" from "The 23rd Psalme" (p. 347). Comments on
music for each hymn, mostly eighteenth-, nineteenth-, and early twentieth-century versions. Contains biographical and historical notes on
authors, composers, sources (pp. 376–532).

◄§ 135. FLETCHER, J. M. J. *Herbert of Bemerton: Poet and Saint*. n.p.
   14p.
   Notes from a lecture given on 23 February 1933 at the opening of the
George Herbert Exhibition held in Salisbury. First published in the
Salisbury and Winchester Journal on Friday, 24 February 1933. Primarily
an appreciative biographical sketch of Herbert with very brief comments
on his poetry. Mentions Wesley's adaptations of Herbert's verse and
quotes Phillip Brooks on New England knowledge of Herbert's poems:
"I think his lesson is one that we in America need greatly."

◄§ 136. HALL, BERNARD G. "The Text of George Herbert." *TLS*, 26 October, p. 731.

Describes and compares the Bodleian and Williams manuscripts. Suggests that the former is the work of the ladies of Little Gidding and that the printers never had Herbert's own manuscript to work from. Argues that the 1633 text is faulty in many respects, shows the difficulties of reconstructing the true text, and suggests several major emendations, based primarily on calligraphy. For a reply, see John Sparrow, entry 144.

◄§ 137. HUTCHINSON, F. E. "George Herbert: A Tercentenary." *The Nineteenth Century and After* 113:358–68.

Succinct but comprehensive biographical sketch of Herbert. Describes in some detail Herbert's death (1 March 1633) and his burial on Quinquagesima Sunday, 3 March. Suggests that "Holy Mr. Herbert" was not an invention of Walton but can be authenticated by contemporary accounts. Sees Herbert's prolonged struggle toward saintliness as the main clue to understanding *The Temple*.

◄§ 138. HUXLEY, ALDOUS. *Texts and Pretexts: An Anthology with Commentaries*. New York and London: Harper & Brothers. vii, 322p.

References to Herbert throughout. Calls Herbert "the poet of inner weather": "Accurately, in a score of lyrics unexcelled for flawless purity of diction and appositeness of imagery, he has described its changes and interpreted, in terms of a mystical philosophy, their significance. Within his limits he achieves a real perfection" (p. 13). Calls "The Collar" "one of the finest [poems] he ever wrote and among the most moving, to my mind, in all our literature" (p. 90). Argues that the real power of the poem is that Herbert's reply, "My Lord," is from "an intimate conviction . . . that the Being who had summoned him was a projection of his most real, his essential self" (p. 90). For a reply, see Mary Butts, entry 176.

◄§ 139. ORANGE, U. M. D. "The Poetry of George Herbert." *PoetryR* 24:118–27.

Suggests that Herbert, unlike Donne and Marvell, has been generally neglected by modern readers and critics because he is "very much out of temper with the twentieth century" (p. 118). Comments rather unfavorably on some of the general characteristics of metaphysical poetry, especially its uses of conceits, its introspective nature, its strong individuality. Herbert, in spite of some lapses, "is really out of place in this group" (p. 125). Suggests that Herbert is most successful when he is less ambitious and less under the influence of Donne. Herbert is a great poet in small things. "Repose, commonsense, sanity, a delicate if not profound perception, an instinct both for the fitting and for the dramatic—these are not characteristics which make for great poetry perhaps, but they are associated in the minds of Herbert's readers with comfort and wisdom" (pp. 126–27).

◄§ 140. PHILIP, ADAM. *George Herbert: A Tercentenary Appreciation.* Lutterworth Papers, no. 18. London: Lutterworth Press. 16p.

Biographical sketch of Herbert that stresses his piety and his pastoral virtues. Criticizes the modern tendency "to disparage the virtues of men of high talent and outstanding Christian character," such as Gladstone and General Gordon. Even Herbert was said to have chosen "to hide his disappointed ambitions under the canonical coat." Very superficial discussion of Herbert's poetry and prose.

◄§141. PINTO, VIVIAN DE SOLA. "George Herbert After Three Hundred Years." *Wessex: An Annual Record of the Movement for a University of Wessex* 2:33–39.

General appreciative account of Herbert's life and works. Calls him "one of the most original, one of the most intensely personal, and one of the most passionate of English poets" (p. 37). Says that *The Temple* and *The Country Parson*, taken together, "may be said to contain the finest expression of seventeenth century Anglicanism" (p. 37). Announces a memorial service in Herbert's honor held at Bemerton in February 1933 and says that in June of the same year the poet laureate will visit Bemerton to deliver an address.

◄§ 142. SLADE, HILDA M. "The George Herbert Tercentenary." *PoetryR* 24:115–17.

Short biographical sketch with some very general comments on the poetry. Calls *The Temple* a collection of "simple verses."

◄§ 143. SMITH, JAMES. "On Metaphysical Poetry." *Scrutiny* 2:222–39.

Reprinted in *Determinations*, edited by F. R. Leavis (London: Chatto & Windus, 1934), rpt. 1970; and *Shakespearian and Other Essays* (Cambridge: University Press, 1974), pp. 262–78.

Extended definition of metaphysical poetry that attempts to show precisely how it differs from other kinds of poetry that are sometimes closely associated with it. States that the "verse properly called metaphysical is that to which the impulse is given by an overwhelming concern with metaphysical problems; with problems either deriving from, or closely resembling in the nature of their difficulty, the problem of the Many and the One" (p. 228). Discusses the nature of metaphysical poetry primarily in terms of Donne's poetry and contrasts Donne with Dante, Lucretius, Chapman, and others, poets who "wrote metaphysics in poetry, rather than metaphysical poetry" (p. 237). Argues that a distinguishing feature of metaphysical poetry is its particular use of the conceit. In the metaphysical conceit "tension between the elements continues" (p. 234), yet the two elements "can enter into a solid union and, at the same time maintain their separate and warring identity" (p. 234), thereby effecting a union "of things that, though hostile, in reality cry out for association with each other" (p. 235). Mentions Herbert only in passing, but, in the light of his definition, calls Herbert a true metaphysical poet. Suggests that Herbert has much in common with Calderón.

⊸§ 144. Sparrow, John. "The Text of George Herbert." *TLS*, 14 December, p. 896.
Reply to Bernard G. Hall, entry 136. Questions Hall's method of correcting the 1633 text and disagrees with six of his suggested emendations.

⊸§ 145. Squarey, Newell P., and Offer, Peter. "George Herbert at Bemerton." *Times* (London), 3 March, p. 10.
On the occasion of the tercentenary of Herbert's death the church-wardens at Bemerton ask for financial assistance for the parish.

⊸§ 146. Thomas, Gilbert. "George Herbert." *ContempR* 143:706–13.
Reprinted (in revised form) in *Builders and Makers: Occasional Studies* (London: Epworth Press, 1944), pp. 17–24.
Appreciative essay on Herbert the man praising his religious sensibility and piety. Suggests that Herbert's hard-won piety is more worthy of remembrance than his art: "His work is not only narrow in artistic range, but is marred by unconscious awkwardness as well as by the deliberate mannerisms which . . . he borrowed from the conventions of the hour. He has his small, assured place in the best anthologies; but his main appeal is not, in the strict sense, literary" (p. 707).

1934

⊸§ 147. Bennett, Joan. *Four Metaphysical Poets: Donne, Herbert, Vaughan, Crashaw*. Cambridge: University Press. 135p.
2d ed., 1953; rpt. with corrections, 1957.
3d ed., with a new chapter on Marvell and title changed to *Five Metaphysical Poets*, 1963; rpt., 1966.
First edition contains seven chapters: (1) Introduction, (2) John Donne, 1573–1631, (3) Donne's Technical Originality, (4) George Herbert, 1593–1633, (5) Henry Vaughan, 1622–1695, (6) Richard Crashaw, 1613?–1647, and (7) Religious Poetry, a Postscript. Short bibliography. Summarizes in the introduction the major characteristics of metaphysical poetry and maintains, "The word 'metaphysical' refers to style, not to subject matter; but style reflects an attitude to experience" (p. 3). Suggests, "The peculiarity of the metaphysical poets is not that they relate, but that the relations they perceive are more often logical than sensuous or emotional, and that they constantly connect the abstract with the concrete, the remote with the near, and the sublime with the common-

place" (p. 4). Presents a brief biographical sketch of Herbert and comments on the autobiographical nature of his poetry: "All his poetry is spiritual autobiography" (p. 58). Surveys the major characteristics of Herbert's individual talent: his uses of dialectic structure, concrete imagery, familiar diction, sound patterns that imitate the rhythms of speech, and his metrical ingenuity and experimentation. Comments on his precision, intellectuality, simplicity and restraint, and playfulness. Suggests, "Herbert, like Donne, was capable of clear thought in conjunction with vehement feeling" (p. 61).

148. BLUNDEN, EDMUND. "George Herbert's Latin Poems." *E&S* (for 1933) 19:29–39.
Comments on the general neglect given to the Latin poetry of English poets and singles out Herbert's Latin poems as worthy of critical attention. Translates several into English, commenting briefly on their interesting features. Particularly likes Herbert's "In Honorem Illustr. D.D. Verulamij, Sti Albani." For a reply, see A. Brulé, entry 149.

149. BRULÉ, A. "Un Poème latin de George Herbert." *Revue Anglo-Américaine* 12:49–51.
Reply to Edmund Blunden, entry 148. Disagrees with Blunden's translation of a Latin poem from *Parentalia* ("Ah Mater, quo te deplorem fonte?"). Blunden claims the poem contains "the oddest figure of a man being mixed with a river to produce ink that ever was contrived." Brulé paraphrases the controversial lines and argues that they make perfect sense. Challenges the notion that Herbert's imagery is bizarre; its spirit, he maintains, is simply different from the modern: "Mais il était aristocratiquement intelligent, son esprit suit toujours une marche parfaitement ordonnée; il n'aurait jamais condescendu à présenter, comme on le fait de nos jours, une image uniquement pour son étrangeté" (p. 51).

150. BUTT, JOHN. "Izaak Walton's Methods in Biography." *E&S* (for 1933) 19:67–84.
Surveys Walton's methods and varying aims in *The Lives*. Points out that Walton obtained information on Herbert from Arthur Woodnoth, a friend of both Herbert and Nicholas Ferrar. Calls *The Life of Herbert* Walton's "nearest approach to hagiography" (p. 71) and sees the influence of Barnabas Oley. Walton's intention was "to recall the country clergy to a sense of their duty" (p. 71), thus he keeps his eye always on Herbert's life of holiness at Bemerton. Walton points out some of Herbert's weaknesses "because they are part of the truth, but he does not think them important" (p. 84). Comments on Walton's use of *The Temple* and *The Country Parson* as source books, explaining Walton's method of constructing conversations and commenting on episodes of Herbert's life by paraphrasing Herbert's work.

◆§ 151. LEISHMAN, J. B. *The Metaphysical Poets: Donne, Herbert, Vaughan, Traherne.* Oxford: Clarendon Press. 232p.

Reprinted, Ann Arbor and London: University Microfilms, 1962; New York: Russell and Russell, 1963.

Introduction to the four poets for the general reader. Virtually an anthology of poems with a running critical commentary. Discusses Herbert's poetry (pp. 99–144) within a biographical framework, quoting generously from Walton, *The Country Parson,* and the letters. Praises Herbert's faith ("the extraordinarily intimate and personal nature of his attitude to God" [p. 136]), his general common sense and humor, his technical excellence and originality, his control of form and rhythms ("He is a poet of poems and not, like so many of his contemporaries and predecessors, of passages" [p. 120]), and his impassioned conversational tone. Contrasts Herbert and Donne: "He has not Donne's curious detached interest in ideas for their own sakes, and although there are exceptions, his similes are on the whole less ingenious and remote than Donne's" (p. 120). Sees Herbert as the poet of religious faith and submission and Donne as the poet of religious tension.

◆§ 152. PRAZ, MARIO. *Studi sul concettismo.* Milan: Soc. Ed. La Cultura. viii, 168p.

English version (with revisions and new appendix): *Studies in Seventeenth-Century Imagery,* vol. 1 (entry 200).

2d Italian ed., Florence: G. S. Sansoni, 1946. vi, 321p.

Discusses the importance of emblem books and devices in seventeenth-century literature. See also "The English Emblem Literature" (entry 153).

◆§ 153. ———. "The English Emblem Literature." *ES* 16:129–40.

Discusses English emblem books and compares Herbert's and Quarles's uses of the emblem: "Quarles's wit is all on the surface, gaudy and provincial, without a breath of that devotional spirit which animates the mute emblems of Herbert's *Temple,* or even the *Parthenia Sacra* . . . of the Jesuit Henry Hawkins" (p. 139). This discussion of the emblem is reprinted in *Studi sul concettismo* (entry 152), and in the English version, *Studies in Seventeenth-Century Imagery,* vol. 1 (entry 200).

◆§ 154. SHARP, ROBERT LATHROP. "The Pejorative Use of *Metaphysical.*" *MLN* 49:503–5.

Traces the changing connotation of the word *metaphysical* from its simple meaning of "above the material world, supersensible, and hence above nature" (p. 504) to its pejorative meaning of "non-sensical." Suggests that both Dryden and Johnson chose the term because they were aware of its pejorative possibilities, "thereby suggesting to their readers not only that Donne, Cowley, and the rest were thoughtful, speculative, and abstract, but that they dealt in notions which, to a neo-classical mind, were incomprehensible, vague, and repugnant to common sense" (p. 505). No specific references to Herbert.

◆§ 155. Smith, W. Bradford. "What Is Metaphysical Poetry?" *SR* 42: 261–72.

"Metaphysical Poetry is a paradoxical inquiry, imaginative and intellectual, which exhausts, by its use of antithesis and contradiction and unusual imagery, all the possibilities of a given idea. This idea will predominantly be a psychological probing of love, death, or religion as the more important matters of experience in the life of the poet, and will be embodied in striking metaphorical utterance or in the use of the common (familiar) or scientific word" (p. 263). Uses Donne, primarily, to exemplify the definition and only briefly mentions Herbert. Suggests that Marvell's "To his Coy Mistress" is the perfect example of metaphysical poetry. Mentions Emily Dickinson several times as one who "more than any other except Donne, has faithfully followed the metaphysical muse" (p. 267).

1935

◆§ 156. Brooks, Cleanth. "Three Revolutions in Poetry: I. Metaphor and the Tradition." *SoR* 1 (1935–1936):151–63.

First in a series of three articles on modern poetry (see also entries 157, 158). Challenges certain modern conservative critics who maintain "the division of the world into poetic and nonpoetic, and the segregation of the intellect from the emotions" (p. 152). Views the modern conceit in a historical perspective. Argues that modern poets are "the restorers of orthodoxy, attempting to bring back into poetry some of the virtues of the School of Donne" (p. 162): "The relation of our moderns to the School of Donne is of the same type as the relation of Wordsworth and Coleridge to the folk ballad. Just as an appreciation of the folk ballad went hand in hand with appreciation of Romantic poetry, so an appreciation of our own radicals demands an ability to enjoy the metaphysicals, and involves a revision of our whole conception of poetry, a revision certainly no less radical than that sponsored by the *Lyrical Ballads* in 1798" (pp. 162–63). Stresses in particular the importance of the so-called radical metaphor and argues that Donne's images (such as the compass) are functional, whereas Milton's metaphors and similes are primarily decorative. No specific mention of Herbert.

◆§ 157. ———. "Three Revolutions in Poetry: II. Wit and High Seriousness." *SoR* 1 (1935–1936):328–38.

Second in a series of three essays on modern poetry (see also entries 156, 158). Argues, "The play of the intellect and the play of wit are not intrinsically incompatible with the poet's seriousness, or with his sincerity in implying to the reader that he means to be taken seriously" (p. 329). Points out that Herbert and Crashaw, "even when they fail, always impress the reader as being serious. And they succeed often enough to make their poetry, with that of Donne and Vaughan, the greatest religious poetry which England can claim" (p. 331). States that much metaphysical poetry "occupies this shadowy borderline between frankly playful *vers de société* and deeply serious lyric poetry. It is most important to notice that the deepening seriousness, when it occurs, is not accompanied by a correspondent lessening of the play of wit" (p. 330). Illustrations are drawn primarily from Donne, but Herbert is briefly mentioned.

◅§ 158. ———. "Three Revolutions in Poetry: III. Metaphysical Poetry and the Ivory Tower." *SoR* 1 (1935–1936):568–83.

Third in a series of three essays on modern poetry (see also entries 156, 157). Defines metaphysical poetry as "a poetry in which the heterogeneity of the materials and the opposition of the impulses united are extreme. Or if one prefers to base himself directly on Coleridge: it is a poetry in which the poet attempts the reconciliation of opposite or discordant qualities" (p. 570). Challenges those who insist on the didactic function of poetry or on the scientific validity of the poetic statement, especially the Marxists. Agrees with I. A. Richards that "it is never what a poem says that matters, but what it is" (p. 573). Sees a number of modern poets returning to the orthodoxy of the past, especially to the seventeenth century, in an attempt to repair the damage caused by the Age of Reason and the Romantic Movement. Considers Eliot, Tate, Ransom, Crane, Warren, and even Hardy and Yeats in this light. No specific mention of Herbert.

◅§ 159. SHARP, ROBERT LATHROP. "Observations on Metaphysical Imagery." *SR* 43:464–78.

Stresses the "organic growth of figurative language and the capacity of poets to adjust their imaginations to the resultant new levels of the poetic idiom" (p. 464) and cautions that "the delights of poetry for Donne and the metaphysicals were not wholly what they are for us" (p. 465). Argues, "No other metaphysical possessed Donne's genius, but they all agreed with Donne that a faster, more efficient rhetoric should be used and that the rhetoric merely of periphrasis and adornment was exhausted" (p. 478). Points out, "Because the poetic idiom of the Elizabethans was already a welter of metaphors, with countless variations of the same notion, the poetic necessity of being new and different led the metaphysicals to sensitize their perceptions. . . . Whereas the Elizabethans began with the figures of Shakespeare" (p. 470). No specific mention of Herbert.

◄§ 160. SMITH, CHARD POWERS. *Annals of the Poets: Their Origins, Backgrounds, Private Lives, Habits of Composition, Characters, and Personal Peculiarities.* New York and London: Charles Scribner's Sons. xxv, 523p.

Catalogues miscellaneous information about English poets—their hobbies, pets, friendships, formal education, early domestic attachments, looks and manners, etc. Herbert is mentioned in sixteen places. For example, under hobbies, Herbert is listed as enjoying music; he appears in a list of poets who died between the ages of thirty-one and sixty-one.

◄§ 161. THOMPSON, W. MEREDITH. *Der Tod in der englischen Lyrik des siebzehnten Jahrhunderts.* Sprache und kultur der germanischen und romanischen völker . . . A Anglistische reihe . . . , vol. 20. Breslau: Priebatsch. viii, 97p.

Discusses various attitudes toward death as they are reflected in the works of selected seventeenth-century poets. Contrasts and compares Herbert's orthodox Christian position on death with the positions of Herrick, Donne, and Vaughan. Suggests that the only element of fear in Herbert's view is the possibility of the soul's exclusion from God as a result of sin.

◄§ 162. WILD, FRIEDRICH. "Zum Problem des Barocks in der englischen Dichtung." *Anglia* 59:414–22.

Defines the concept of the baroque for English literature and gives examples of poets and aspects of poetry that might be called baroque. Comments on Herbert's use of the "fantastic conceit" (for example, in "The Pulley") and calls this a baroque feature. Also remarks on Herbert's interior tension ("innere zerrissenheit") as seen in "The Pearl," "The Collar," and "Aaron."

◄§ 163. WRIGHT, HERBERT G. "Was George Herbert the Author of *Jacula Prudentum?*" *RES* 11:139–44.

Reviews various arguments in the debate surrounding the authorship of *Jacula Prudentum* and argues that the collection is the authentic work of Herbert. Presents an account of MS 5301 E at the National Library of Wales as part of the proof.

1936

◄§ 164. BLACKSTONE, BERNARD. "A Paper by George Herbert." *TLS*, 15 August, p. 664.

Reproduces a heretofore unpublished paper by Herbert found among the manuscripts in Magdalene College Library and bearing the inscription, written in a Ferrar hand: "Mr Herberts reasons for Arth. Woodenoths Liuing wth Sr Jhon Da[n]uers." The paper itself is in Herbert's hand and bears no date. Arthur Woodnoth, cousin of Nicholas Ferrar and close friend of Herbert, was apparently at the time in the service of Sir John Danvers, Herbert's stepfather. For a reply, see F. E. Hutchinson, entry 169.

⊲§ 165. BRITTIN, NORMAN A. "Emerson and the Metaphysical Poets." *AL* 8:1–21.
Discusses the possible influence of the metaphysicals on Emerson and Emerson's appreciation of these poets. Points out Emerson's particular admiration for Herbert. Herbert is mentioned in the *Journals* many times, is listed among Emerson's favorite poets (ahead of Shakespeare), is mentioned frequently in speeches, and is quoted in *Nature*. Concludes that Emerson's poetry, "not in general, but in numerous individual passages, resembles slightly that of Donne and Cowley, and strongly, that of Herbert and Marvell" (pp. 20–21).

⊲§ 166. COLERIDGE, SAMUEL TAYLOR. "Herbert's 'Temple' and Harvey's 'Synagogue.' " In *Coleridge's Miscellaneous Criticism*, edited by Thomas Middleton Raysor, pp. 244–51. Cambridge, Mass.: Harvard University Press.
Reproduces Coleridge's various comments on Herbert and Harvey. Calls Herbert a "true poet," but argues that unless the reader "be likewise a *Christian*, and both a zealous and an orthodox, both a devout and a *devotional* Christian" (p. 244) he cannot fully appreciate Herbert's poetry. States that the reader "must be an affectionate and dutiful child of the Church, and from habit, conviction, and a constitutional predisposition to ceremoniousness, in piety as in manners, find her forms and ordinances aids to religion, not sources of formality; for religion is the element in which he [Herbert] lives, and the region in which he moves" (p. 244). Reproduces a letter of December 1818 to Collins in which Coleridge recommends most highly *The Temple*: "I find more substantial comfort now in pious George Herbert's *Temple*, which I used to read to amuse myself with his quaintness, in short, only to laugh at, than in all poetry since the poems of Milton" (p. 250). Singles out "The Flower" as particularly impressive.

⊲§ 167. HARPER, GEORGE MCLEAN. "George Herbert's Poems." *QR* 267: 58–73.
Reprinted in *Literary Appreciations* (New York and Indianapolis: Bobbs-Merrill Co., 1937), pp. 19–45.
Rejects the term *metaphysical poets*, disagrees with the notion of a school of Donne, and suggests that Donne is perhaps overrated in the twentieth century. Praises the excellences of Herbert's verses and sensi-

bility: "The music, the pictorial power, the play of imagination that makes us sharers of his thought and feeling" (p. 62). Calls "The Flower" "the loveliest of Herbert's poems" (p. 67).

168. HUTCHINSON, F. E. "John Wesley and George Herbert." *London Quarterly and Holborn Review* 161:439–55.

Surveys the extent and nature of John Wesley's attraction to Herbert and, in particular, his adaptations of Herbert's poems for use as hymns. States that during the eighteenth century Wesley "did more than any man to keep alive the knowledge of Herbert's poems" (p. 439). Points out that in adapting Herbert, Wesley not only revised Herbert's intricate metrical schemes to suit existing tunes, but he also eliminated obscurities, conceits, certain phraseology, remote allusions, and much of the humor. "The thought is Herbert's thought, but the voice is Wesley's voice; . . . sometimes we are surprised to find how completely the language and tone of the eighteenth century have imposed themselves on Herbert's verse" (p. 453).

169. ———. "A Paper by George Herbert." *TLS*, 22 August, p. 680.

Reply to Bernard Blackstone (entry 164), who announced the discovery of an unpublished paper in Herbert's hand addressed to Arthur Woodnoth. Points out that the paper clarifies a reference in Walton that Woodnoth "was a useful Friend of Mr. Herberts Father." The reference is to Herbert's stepfather, Sir John Danvers, not to his natural father. Marshals support for Blackstone's suggestion that the paper was written after 1628 and points out characteristics that are typical of Herbert.

170. OLIVERO, FEDERICO. "Scuola Metafisica." In *Lirica Religiosa Inglese*, pp. 230–78. Turin: S. Lattes & Co.

Expanded version, Turin: Società Editrice Internazionale, 1941, 2: 111–207.

Biographical sketch followed by general critical evaluation of Herbert's poetry. Calls *The Temple* "la descrizione simbolica di una chiesa" (p. 242) and comments on its emblematic imagery: "Questo emblematismo ci ricorda poeti medievali; supremo in Dante" (p. 242). Says that Herbert "ricerca e scruta i più profondi recessi della coscienza, percorre le vie sotterranee del cuore; ne risulta una poesia analitica, concentrata in immagini che sono sintesi di stati d'animo e di sentimenti. Tuttavia le sue figure hanno una certa freddezza, un intellecttualismo che le irrigidisce; mancano dell'ardore di quelle del Crashaw, sono pensate con sottigliezza, non *viste* come apparizioni eterne nell'esaltazione mistica del poeta cattolico. In lui, come nel Donne, impreviste associazioni di idee sono la base della sua arte. È curioso il contrasto, in tutta la sua opera, fra un linguaggio semplice e bizzarri tropi,—una dizione sottile e cavillosa ed una limpida grazia,—una strana ingegnosità di fantasia ed una semplicita spontanea del sentire" (p. 242).

❧ 171. PICKEL, MARGARET BARNARD. "Other Royal Poets." In *Charles I as Patron of Poetry and Drama*, pp. 69–94. London: Frederick Muller.
Surveys Charles I's patronage of various poets and dramatists and mentions Herbert briefly (pp. 74–75). Points out that Herbert's poems were part of the well-used library that consoled the king at Carisbrooke.

❧ 172. WARREN, AUSTIN. "George Herbert." *American Review* 7:249–71.
Reprinted in revised form in *Rage for Order: Essays in Criticism* (Chicago: University of Chicago Press, 1948; rpt.: London and Ann Arbor: University of Michigan Press, 1959), pp. 19–36.
Critical evaluation of Herbert's poetry with a biographical sketch. Explores Herbert's Anglican spirit, his sensibility, and his themes. Comments on Herbert's use of shaped verse and stanzaic experimentation: "Herbert's ingenuities proceed from a principle which is analogous to onomatopoeia and as readily apprehended: that adaptation of form to sense, or structure to theme" (p. 263). And again, "In Herbert's stanzaic invention and precision of craftsmanship he shows the survival of his temperamental fastidiousness; he also, wittingly or not, creates that tension between inner struggle and outer neatness which gives living distinction to his poetry" (p. 264). Discusses the revival of metaphysical poetry and suggests that Donne's influence on Herbert was more personal than literary: "Herbert's nature had neither the complexity nor the intensity of Donne's, and these temperamental differences, together with Herbert's artistic sincerity, make difficult any attempt to trace palpable derivations" (p. 271).

❧ 173. WATKINS, W. B. C. "Spenser to the Restoration (1579–1660)." In *Johnson and English Poetry Before 1660*, pp. 58–84. Princeton Studies in English, no. 13. Princeton: Princeton University Press.
Comments on Dr. Johnson's slight acquaintance with Herbert's poetry. Johnson quotes Herbert only five times in the *Dictionary*.

❧ 174. WHITE, HELEN C. *The Metaphysical Poets: A Study in Religious Experience*. New York: Macmillan Co. ix, 444p.
Reprinted, 1962 (Collier Books).
Studies Donne, Herbert, Crashaw, Vaughan, and Traherne. Discusses in the introduction how mysticism and poetry are alike and how they differ. Concludes that, although none of the poets discussed are genuine mystics in the strict sense of the word, all, to varying degrees, evidence

elements of mysticism in their poetry. Chapter 1, "The Intellectual Climate"; chapter 2, "The Religious Climate"; and chapter 3, "Metaphysical Poetry," set up the necessary background and generalities as a framework for the discussion of the individual poets (two chapters to each poet). Chapter 6, "George Herbert and the Road to Bemerton" (pp. 150–75), presents a sketch of Herbert's life and a discussion of his religious temperament and intellectual sensibilities. Suggests that Herbert's essentially mystical aspiration gave to his ministry "its distinctive character and accounts for the peculiar effect it has exercised upon all who have come in contact with it, whether by actual experience or by report" (p. 165). Sees Herbert's poems as primarily reflections of his inner life, as "intensely and fully self-revelatory verse" (p. 166). Challenges George Herbert Palmer's arrangement of the poems in his edition (entry 1) and concludes that the organization of the 1633 edition is metaphysical and that the symbol of the temple is capable of several references. Chapter 7, "George Herbert and *The Temple*" (pp. 176–210), discusses in some detail the particulars of Herbert's religious sensibilities and attitudes as reflected in his poetry, such as the nature of his faith, his conception of God, the note of intimacy of feeling in his poetry, and his quiet confidence. Calls this last quality "the most persistent and central thing in Herbert's religious consciousness and the source of the peculiar power of his verse" (p. 189). Contrasts Herbert with Donne. Presents in the conclusion a series of contrasts and comparisons among the five poets.

⊸§ 175. WILLIAMSON, GEORGE. "Senecan Style in the Seventeenth Century." *PQ* 15:321–51.

Traces the development of Senecan prose style during the seventeenth century and reproduces two brief comments on preaching style from *The Country Parson*. Points out that Herbert disliked the method of "crumbling the text into small parts" and therefore he "anticipates the method of Tillotson and condemns that of Andrewes, in which Donne was a lesser offender" (p. 335). Suggests that, although Herbert criticized witty preaching, he "reveals the profit to be derived from Senecan brevity" (p. 335).

1937

⊸§ 176. BUTTS, MARY. "The Heresy Game." *The Spectator* 158:466–67.

Reply to Aldous Huxley, who, in *Texts and Pretexts: An Anthology with Commentaries* (entry 138), suggested that "The Collar" has great appeal to the modern reader primarily because "the tragedy of the poem lay in Herbert's self-deception: that he was calling out when there was none to hear; that the tragedy meets out tragedy" (p. 466). Says that Huxley's interpretation "is as pure a specimen of wish-fulfillment as one could hope to find" (p. 467).

᪣ 177. Harrison, Archibald W. "Arminianism in England." In *Arminianism*, pp. 122–56. London: Duckworth.

Outlines the Arminian controversy that began in England after the visit of Grotius to London in 1613. Comments briefly on Herbert's allegiance in the controversy. Suggests that both Herbert and Nicholas Ferrar "would be classed as Arminians in the phraseology of the period" (p. 142). Comments also on Herbert's loyalty to the Church of England and points out, "The breadth of his charity could not be confined to the formulas of Geneva" (p. 143).

᪣ 178. Johnson, Thomas H. "Edward Taylor: A Puritan 'Sacred Poet.' " *NEQ* 10:290–322.

Comments on the influence of Herbert on the poetry of Edward Taylor and maintains, "Herbert's example and influence was paramount" (p. 319). Several of Taylor's poems reproduce exact stanzaic patterns found in *The Temple*; especially noteworthy is Taylor's use of the six-line iambic pentameter rhyming ababcc, the form of Herbert's *The Church-Porch*. Suggests that the example of Herbert is also seen in Taylor's "holy aspiration, his devotional rather than mystical qualities, his homely comparisons, his intimate appeal to the person of Christ" (p. 318). Both Taylor and Herbert employ many of "the same rhetorical devices of question, refrain, apostrophe, and direct address; there is especially an observable correspondence in the length of their songs" (p. 318).

᪣ 179. Jones, Thomas S., Jr. *Shadow of the Perfect Rose: Collected Poems of Thomas S. Jones, Jr.* With a memoir and notes by John L. Foley. New York: Farrar & Rinehart. xxix, 239p.

Original sonnet on Herbert (p. 147).

᪣ 180. Luke, Stanley. "An Old Handbook on the Pastoral Office." *The London Quarterly and Holborn Review* 162:198–206.

Appreciative essay on various themes in *The Country Parson*, consisting primarily of many quotations from the work with an approving commentary. Presents the book as a manual of devotion appropriate for modern clergymen: "It has not a little which is of practical positive value for the conduct of a ministry in this day and a minister who absorbs its spirit and captures its mood will work not only with better heart but to better purpose" (p. 206).

᪣ 181. Marks, Harvey B. "English Psalmody and Early English Hymnody." In *The Rise and Growth of English Hymnody*, pp. 77–92. New York: Fleming H. Revell Co.

Brief comments on Herbert's life and his contribution to the development of the sacred lyric. Points out that the Canadian Presbyterian Book of Praise contains "Throw away Thy rod," an adaptation of "Discipline." Praises in particular "The Pilgrimage," "having but six stanzas, with its lines so full of thought that it contains the whole substance of Bunyan's 'Pilgrim's Progress' " (p. 88).

⚜§ 182. N., C. L. "Mr. Woodnot." N&Q 172:32.
Asks if the Mr. Woodnot who Walton says attended Herbert on his deathbed was Theophilius Woodnote (d. 1662). For a reply, see Wasey Sterry, entry 185.

⚜§ 183. PHILLIPS, C. S. Hymnody Past and Present. London: Society for Promoting Christian Knowledge; New York: Macmillan Co. x, 300p.
Laments that most of Herbert's poems were not written to be sung in church: "Most of them are unsuited to the purpose by reason of the elaborate and fantastic imagery which Herbert shared with the other poets of his time, and also on account of their peculiar metres" (p. 156). Points out that Herbert "perfectly expresses the characteristic Anglican mentality at its best" (p. 156) and lists several of his poems that have come into use as hymns. Comments briefly on Henry Playford's The Divine Companion (1701), which contained some hymns by Herbert, and on John Wesley's Collection of Psalms and Hymns (1737), which also contained adaptations from The Temple.

⚜§ 184. ROBERTS, MICHAEL. "The Seventeenth Century—Metaphysical Poets and the Cambridge Platonists." In The Modern Mind, pp. 88–117. New York: Macmillan Co.
Very general treatment of Herbert's attitude toward science. Points out that Herbert's poetry contains a number of images drawn from contemporary scientific discoveries and from the new astronomy and new mechanics, but maintains that in Herbert's poetry there is no real conflict with science. Suggests that Herbert's process in his poetry is exactly the opposite of that of science. For example, "Prayer (I)" is "a simile in which the feelings, not the measurements, are asserted to be congruent, and it deliberately uses a method which is not the method of science" (pp. 91–92).

⚜§ 185. STERRY, WASEY. "Mr. Woodnot." N&Q 172:105.
Reply to C.L.N., entry 182. Suggests that the Mr. Woodnot who Walton says attended Herbert on his deathbed is Theophilius Woodnote (d. 1662). Woodnote was first cousin of Nicholas Ferrar.

1938

⚜§ 186. ANON. "Devotional Poetry: Donne to Wesley: The Search for an Unknown Eden." TLS, 24 December, pp. 814, 816.
Maintains, "Religious verse is seldom the statement of assured belief

but more often the passionate protestation of a mind that wishes to believe and believes and doubts again. [Therefore,] the periods most prolific of devotional masterpieces are those in which a certain body of religious faith is counterbalanced by a definite strain of inquietude" (p. 814). Contrasts Donne's "turbulent mysticism" with Herbert's "calm and collected piety" and suggests that Herbert is "a more accomplished technician though a lesser poet" (p. 814). "For Donne, God is the stern taskmaster, the supreme enigma; for Herbert, the welcome guest and familiar friend, a projection of the subtlety and charm of his own intelligence" (p. 814).

187. BLACK, MATTHEW W., ed. "The Devotional Lyricists." In *Elizabethan and Seventeenth-Century Lyrics*, pp. 479–530. Chicago: J. B. Lippincott Co.

General introduction to the devotional lyric of the seventeenth century. Sees Herbert as Donne's disciple and suggests that "like Donne he can unite strong feeling with clarity of thought; but his mind is far less complex and his conceits are neither extended nor subtle" (p. 482). Calls Herbert's use of acrostics, anagrams, and shaped verse naive and puerile. Briefly compares Herbert to Crashaw, Vaughan, and Traherne and anthologizes fourteen of Herbert's poems (pp. 494–503).

188. BLACKSTONE, BERNARD, ed. *The Ferrar Papers; containing a life of Nicholas Ferrar; the Winding-sheet, an ascetic dialogue; a collection of short moral histories; a collection of family letters.* Cambridge: University Press. xxii, 323p.

Many references throughout to Herbert. The *Life of Nicholas Ferrar* here presented is "a composite of the surviving manuscript accounts, each of which derives ultimately from the original *Life* by John Ferrar" (p. xvii). The *Life* contains many references to Herbert: notes Herbert's approval of the night watches established at Little Gidding (p. 55); recounts the friendship of Ferrar and Herbert (pp. 58–60); and reproduces two letters of Herbert to Ferrar (pp. 77–79). Also reproduces two letters about Herbert written by Arthur Woodnoth to Ferrar (pp. 266–69, 276–77) and prints a new Herbert document (pp. 269–70), including a facsimile reproduction in Herbert's own hand of the first page (reduced) of the paper. This document is entitled "Mr Herberts reasons for Arth. Woodenoths Liuing wth Sr Ihon Da[n]uers," and was first published by Blackstone in *TLS* (entry 164).

189. FORD, FORD MADOX. *The March of Literature: From Confucius' Day to Our Own.* New York: Dial Press. vii, 878p.

Scattered references to Herbert throughout. Calls Herbert, Donne, Crashaw, Marvell, Vaughan, and Dryden "the most English of all writers" and suggests, "If there is any sustained beauty in the Anglo-Saxon soul it was they who proved its existence" (p. 477). Suggests that the last two lines of "Love (III)" "enshrine the very essence . . . of that so-called metaphysical poetic age" (p. 482). Says that Herbert strikes a "Petrarchist-Christist" note not sounded again until Christina Rossetti.

≈§ 190. HAYES, ALBERT McHARG. "Counterpoint in Herbert." SP 35: 43–60.

Comments in detail on Herbert's technical excellence and stanzaic experimentation: "The cause of this great variety in stanzas lies partly in Herbert's desire to make the outward form of each poem representative of its inner meaning" (p. 44). Discusses Herbert's theory and practice of versification: "Clearness and exactness were his aims; simplicity, his art" (p. 46). Discusses "counterpoint," his term for Herbert's major device for focusing attention on the sense of a poem rather than on its sound by constructing the pattern of line lengths independently of the pattern of rhymes and thus defeating "the excessive expectation of rime by making its position unpredictable" (p. 48). Suggests that Herbert may have gotten the idea of counterpoint from Donne and/or Puttenham's *Arte of English Poesie*. Divides Herbert's 127 stanzaic poems into seven major types: (1) harmonic stanzas, (2) approximately harmonic stanzas, (3) isometrical stanzas, (4) approximately contrapuntal stanzas, (5) contrapuntal stanzas, (6) off-balance stanzas, and (7) irregular stanzas. Points out, "Half the poems (63) fall into the first three classifications, which are the normal pattern of English lyrics, and half (64) into the last four, the experimental types" (pp. 53–54). Comments on Herbert's love of and knowledge of music. Contains two tables of stanzaic types in order to compare Herbert with other major poets.

≈§ 191. HUTCHINSON, F. E. "George Herbert." In *Seventeenth Century Studies Presented to Sir Herbert Grierson*, pp. 148–60. Oxford: Clarendon Press.

Reprinted, New York: Octagon Books, 1967.

Comments on Herbert's fluctuating reputation during the past three centuries. Surveys the manuscript tradition of the poems and seriously questions the assumptions of George Herbert Palmer in his edition of the poems (entry 1), especially his attempt to arrange the poems in a chronological order based on his biographical interpretations. Presents a brief character sketch of Herbert, based partly on early biographical accounts and partly on themes and attitudes found in the poetry. Suggests that Herbert's principal temptation was ambition but that out of his many spiritual conflicts "he made music" (p. 155). Sees the tension and conflict in Herbert's soul "as exceptionally good material for a religious poet" and suggests that they are "the staple elements of the larger part of *The Temple*" (p. 156). Comments on Herbert's art and suggests that his imagery "grows naturally out of the idea of a poem and can therefore be developed without giving a sense of artificiality" (p. 156). Discusses Herbert's skill in choosing verse forms that match his subject, his ability to use plain words found in ordinary speech with natural dignity, his love for homely and proverbial material, and his complex simplicity of diction. Discusses in particular "The Agonie" as an example of Herbert's artistry, to show how "out of familiar material, as old as the Christian religion, Herbert builds up a closely knit poem and makes his points with surprising freshness and force" (p. 159). Argues that although Herbert did not invent the English religious lyric, "in his hands the religious lyric has travelled far beyond the dreary Scriptural paraphrases and obvious moralizings of the Elizabethan versifiers" (p. 160).

᪲§ 192. MAY, G. L. *George Herbert*. Little Books on Religion, no. 141. London: Society for Promoting Christian Knowledge. 32p.
Brief biographical survey that stresses Herbert's sanctity. Comments on the poems as autobiographical statements. Suggests, "It is a pity that much of Herbert's poetry loses its charm for us through the artificiality—so loved by his age" (p. 15), but believes that the piety of his poetry more than atones for his faults as a poet.

᪲§ 193. MAYCOCK, A. L. *Nicholas Ferrar of Little Gidding*. London: Society for Promoting Christian Knowledge. xiii, 322p.
Reprinted, 1963 (paperback).
Many references to Herbert throughout. Briefly surveys the friendship of Herbert and Ferrar (pp. 233–35). "It was a friendship springing from complete spiritual harmony" (p. 233), and it "set its mark upon English spirituality for a hundred years or more" (p. 234). Notes that Herbert was consulted in the planning of the night watches at Little Gidding and that his opinion was sought in drawing up the famous inscription that was hung in the parlor at Little Gidding. Although the two met as undergraduates at Cambridge, they apparently never met thereafter, but sustained their friendship through correspondence and mutual friends, especially Arthur Woodnoth and Edmund Duncon.

᪲§ 194. MEYER, GERARD PREVIN. "The Blackmoor and Her Love." *PQ* 17:371–76.
Argues that Henry Rainold's famous poem, "A Black-moor Maid wooing a fair Boy," is a capricious translation of Herbert's Latin poem, "Aethiopissa ambit Cestum Diversi Coloris Virum," which the author calls Herbert's "only poem of human love." Rainold's poem first appeared in an edition of Bishop Henry King's poems (1647) and occasioned a reply by King entitled "The Boys Answer to the Blackmoor." Suggests that Herbert's poem also inspired a poem by John Cleveland entitled "A Fair Nymph Scorning a Black Boy Courtin Her." For a reply, see Cornelia C. Coulter, entry 197.

◆§ 195. UNTERMEYER, LOUIS. "The Religious Conceit: Play for God's Sake." In *Play in Poetry*, pp. 27–51. New York: Harcourt, Brace & Co.

Comments on the variety and seriousness of play in Herbert's poetry: "It is not an irresponsible playfulness, but a mixture of play and passion which allows Herbert to embody his most profound thoughts in anagrams and acrostics, shaped whimsies and puns" (p. 28). Comments specifically on the wit of "Jesu," "Anagram of the Virgin Marie," "The Altar," "Coloss. iii. 3. *Our life is hid with Christ in God*," "Paradise," "Heaven," "Man," "Aaron," "Artillerie," "Discipline," "The Collar," and "The Pulley." Contrasts Herbert's playfulness with Crashaw's: "Crashaw pushed his comparisons further than they could bear to go, and thus made his metaphors not only incongruous, but unpleasantly comic" (p. 38). Suggests that the poetry of Emily Dickinson represents "the continuation, possibly the culmination, of the strain begun by Donne and Herbert: the mingling of rapture and irreverence which makes death a playmate and God a playfellow" (p. 51).

1939

◆§ 196. BROWN, B. GOULDING. "Place." *TLS*, 8 July, p. 406.

Response to R. F. Rattray's query in *TLS* (entry 201) on Herbert's use of the phrase *great places* in *The Church-Porch* (line 327). See also J. Middleton Murry, entry 199.

◆§ 197. COULTER, CORNELIA C. "A Possible Classical Source for The Blackamoor Maid." *PQ* 18:409–10.

In part a reply to Gerard Previn Meyer, entry 194. Suggests that the theme of the blackamoor maid in Herbert's "Aethiopissa ambit Cestum Diversi Coloris Virum" may have been anticipated in two passages in Vergil's *Eclogues* (2, vv. 14–18 and 100, vv. 33–41), where the Latin poet carries on the motif of the despised lovers developed by Theocritus. Concludes, "It is quite conceivable that these two Vergilian passages, coupled with a hint from the Song of Songs, may have suggested to George Herbert the idea of featuring an Ethiopian maid in the rôle of the despised lover" (p. 410).

◆§ 198. HUTCHINSON, F. E. "Missing Herbert Manuscripts." *TLS*, 15 July, p. 421.

Hutchinson announces that while preparing his edition of Herbert's poems he has been unsuccessful in locating five Herbert manuscripts and asks for information about these items.

◆§ 199. MURRY, J. MIDDLETON. "A Herbert Query." *TLS*, 1 July, p. 390.

Reply to R. F. Rattray, entry 201. Suggests that *great places* in *The*

Church-Porch (line 327) means "positions of consequence in society, whether high offices under the Crown (which is the primary meaning of the phrase) or influential stations in the social order." Suggests also that the whole poem is "a treatise on the practical Christian education of an aristocrat." See also B. Goulding Brown, entry 196.

☙ 200. Praz, Mario. Studies in Seventeenth-Century Imagery. 2 vols. Studies of the Warburg Institute, edited by Fritz Saxl, 3. London: Warburg Institute, 1939–1947. 233p.; xi, 209p.
2d ed. (considerably enlarged), Rome: Edizione di Storia e Lettera-tura, pt. 1, 1964; pt. 2, 1974.
Vol. 1 (1939) is an English version (with revisions and a new ap-pendix) of Studi sul concettismo (entry 152). Comments on the exten-sive use of emblem books and devices in seventeenth-century literature. Contrasts Herbert and Quarles: "Quarles' wit is all on the surface, gaudy and provincial, without a single breath of that devotional spirit which animates the mute emblems of Herbert's Temple, or even the Parthenia Sacra" (p. 150). Calls The Temple "a conspicuous case of a mute em-blem-book (i.e. wanting only the plates)" (p. 205). Vol. 2 (1947) is a bibliography of emblem books.

☙ 201. Rattray, R. F. "A Herbert Query." TLS, 24 June, p. 374.
Asks the meaning of places in The Church-Porch (line 327): "Kind-nesse, good parts, great places are the way/ To compasse this." For a reply, see J. Middleton Murry, entry 199, and B. Gould Brown, entry 196.

☙ 202. Spencer, Theodore, and Van Doren, Mark. Studies in Meta-physical Poetry: Two Essays and a Bibliography. New York: Colum-bia University Press. 88p.
Reprinted, Port Washington, N.Y.: Kennikat Press, 1964.
Part 1 consists of two essays. (1) "Recent Scholarship in Metaphysical Poetry" (pp. 3–18), by Spencer, in which some of the major develop-ments in metaphysical criticism and scholarship are briefly outlined, especially Donne scholarship, which is called "a kind of microcosm of scholarship relating to metaphysical poetry in general" (p. 14). (2) "Seventeenth-Century Poets and Twentieth-Century Critics" (pp. 21–29) by Van Doren, in which various notions of metaphysical poetry are reviewed, especially T. S. Eliot's concept of "unified sensibility." Main-tains, however, that the outstanding feature of metaphysical poetry is its humor: "Humor is the life of their poetry; wit is its language" (p. 28). Part 2 presents an unannotated bibliography of studies in metaphysical poetry from 1912 to 1938 (pp. 33–83). Items are arranged chronologically by author with an additional section entitled "General Studies." There are 44 items listed under Herbert, as compared to 199 for Donne.

✒ 203. TAKETOMO, SOFU. "Metaphysical Poetry of George Herbert."
    SELit 19:155–72.
General introduction to Herbert's life and art for a Japanese audience.
Presents a biographical sketch and analyzes Herbert's temperament and
personality. Finds two opposing traits that account for much of the tension in the poetry, Herbert's saintly character and his aristocratic sensibility, the former emerging gradually through a life of asceticism and
evidenced in such works as "The Collar" and the "Affliction" poems.
Outlines Herbert's major religious themes and comments on his devotion to Anglicanism. Compares Herbert with Donne and suggests that
the differences in their poetry are primarily reflections of differences in
their personalities. Sees a number of similarities between Herbert and
Spenser, especially their uses of allegory.

✒ 204. THOMPSON, ELBERT N. S. "*The Temple* and *The Christian
    Year.*" *PMLA* 54:1018–25.
Compares and contrasts *The Temple* with John Keble's *The Christian
Year.* Sees Herbert as introspective, self-analytic, individualistic, personal,
—a Renaissance man, "caring less than Keble for the Church as a divine
institution" (p. 1021). In contrast, *The Christian Year* more fully and
more adequately represents Anglican theology: "Its author's main purpose was to present the 'sound rule of faith' and the 'sober standard of
feeling in matters of practical religion' that are offered in the Book of
Prayer" (p. 1022). Comments on Herbert's great condensation, his uses
of conceit, his vigor of expression, his intellectual energy, and "his close
fusion of mind and Heart" (p. 1025). Suggests that the modern reader
will find in Herbert's poetry "a touch of freshness not found in *The
Christian Year*" (p. 1025).

1940

✒ 205. BRADNER, LEICESTER. *Musae Anglicanae: A History of Anglo-
    Latin Poetry,* 1500–1925. New York: Modern Language Association
    of America; London: Oxford University Press. xii, 383p.
Comments favorably on Herbert's Latin poems, mentioning in particular the series of poems defending the Anglican Church against
Andrew Melville's attacks in *Anti-Tami-Cami-Categoria,* especially "De
Musicâ Sacrâ"; the short poems on Christ's passion in *Passio Discerpta;*
the poems on moral and religious themes in *Lucus;* and the short meditations on the death of his mother, the latter being called early examples
of sacred epigram. Suggests that Herbert's poems, combining genuine
religious sentiment and a high degree of polish, may be favorably compared to Crashaw's Latin epigrams. Points out that the seventeenth-
century movement toward experimental forms in Latin poetry may have
influenced Herbert's experimentations in English. Points out in particu-

lar the similarity between the mixed ode in English (exemplified in such poems as "The Collar," "The Church-floore," "An Offering," and "Vanitie") and the Latin mixed ode (exemplified by Herbert's "In Sacram Anchoram Piscatoris"). Contrasts Herbert also with Peter Du Moulin. Contains a chronological list of Anglo-Latin poetry (pp. 346–73).

◄§ 206. CECIL, LORD DAVID, ed. *The Oxford Book of Christian Verse.* Oxford: Clarendon Press. xxxiii, 560p.
Introduction (pp. xi–xxxiii) comments on the nature and limitations of religious poetry and briefly traces the history of English religious verse from Richard Rolle to T. S. Eliot. Compares Herbert favorably with Donne, Crashaw, and Vaughan and calls him "the most complete exponent in our poetry of the peculiar genius of the English Church" (p. xx). Selections from Herbert (pp. 136–55). No notes or commentary on individual poems.

◄§ 207. DANIELS, R. BALFOUR. "George Herbert's Literary Executor." In *Some Seventeenth-Century Worthies in a Twentieth-Century Mirror*, pp. 80–90. Chapel Hill: University of North Carolina Press. Reprinted, 1971.
Brief sketch of the life of Nicholas Ferrar and of the friendship between Ferrar and Herbert.

◄§ 208. HERBERT, THOMAS WALTER. *John Wesley as Editor and Author.* Princeton Studies in English, no. 17. Princeton: Princeton University Press; London: Humphrey Milford, Oxford University Press. vii, 146p.
Comments on John Wesley's attempts to adapt Herbert's verse for congregational singing. Suggests that these paraphrases were ultimately less successful as hymns than were Wesley's translations from German hymns: "They were not written as songs; their thought required too many lines to come to a comprehensible point" (p. 57). Thus, very soon the adaptations from Herbert were "relegated to the single function of providing poetry for Methodists" (p. 58). Comments also on Wesley's admiration of Herbert as reflected in his publication of a pamphlet in 1773 containing twenty-three poems from *The Temple* and in his frequent quotations from Herbert in his journals and letters.

◄§ 209. HUTCHINSON, F. E. "The First Edition of Herbert's *Temple.*" *Oxford Bibliographical Society: Proceedings and Papers* (for 1939) 5:187–97.
Presents evidence to challenge the assumption (made as early as 1859 by William Thomas Lowndes) that the few copies of the first edition of *The Temple* that are undated were printed before the dated copies of 1633. Argues that a fair copy of Herbert's original manuscript (such as

MS Tanner 307 in the Bodleian) was used by the printer; the Bodleian manuscript bears strong resemblances to many examples of Gidding writing. Discusses possible reasons for the first edition having alternative title pages and for there being some slight variations in different copies. Accounts for the numerous, but mostly unimportant, differences between the Bodleian manuscript and the printed text of the first edition. Comments also on the date of Herbert's death: Friday, 1 March 1632–1633.

210. JONAS, LEAH. "George Herbert, Richard Crashaw, and Henry Vaughan." In *The Divine Science: The Aesthetic of Some Representative Seventeenth-Century English Poets*, pp. 211–27. Columbia University Studies in English and Comparative Literature, no. 151. New York: Columbia University Press.

Comments on the principles informing Herbert's poetic creed and on how, under the influence of Donne, he converted the techniques of the secular lyricists to the service of religion, "using them as a model for his own greater design" (p. 219). Discusses the tension between, and the resolution of, Herbert's desire to express his spiritual temper in the simplest and most direct manner and his equally genuine delight in the perfection and mastery of complex artistic forms, always striving for "an eloquence proper to divine poetry" (p. 222). Comments on Herbert's influence on Crashaw and Vaughan and compares the three poets: "It was their aim to divert some of the beauty of poetry to the praise of its great Creator" (p. 227). Views such a theory and practice as ultimately constrictive and limiting: "The divine poet assumes more the role of a priest" (p. 227).

211. REESE, HAROLD. "A Borrower from Quarles and Herbert." *MLN* 55:50–52.

Comments on *Miscellanea; or, a mixture of choyce observations and institutions, moral and divine, composed for private use. Being the product of spare hours, and the meditations of J. H. . . .* London, printed for Thomas Helder, at the Sign of the Angel in Little-Brittain, 1669. Sixty-four of its ninety-two chapters are taken wholly or partially from Quarles's *Enchiridion*. The compiler also made unacknowledged use of Herbert's "Providence." The poem, without title, appears in a prose chapter; the compiler rearranged stanzas and omitted a number of stanzas.

212. SHARP, ROBERT LATHROP. *From Donne to Dryden: The Revolt Against Metaphysical Poetry.* Chapel Hill: University of North Carolina Press. xiii, 221p.

Traces the revolution in taste in the seventeenth century from poetry that the author calls extravagant, obscure, and harsh (the three elements he chooses to emphasize) to poetry that exalts the standards and practice of propriety, clarity, and harmony. Examines both literary and non-literary forces that set up a reaction to metaphysical poetry. "The revolt was not a silent one; it was articulate in criticism as well as in poetry. Thoroughgoing, it reached to the root of poetry and affected the experience underlying literary creation. By following it, the reader should get a clearer notion of what happened to English poetry between 1600 and 1700" (p. xii). In addition to a general preface and an introduction, there are seven main chapters: (1) Donne and the Elizabethan Poets, (2) The Course of Metaphysical Poetry, (3) The Faith of the Critics, (4) The Protest of the Poets, (5) The Return to Nature, (6) New Standards, and (7) John Dryden. Several references to Herbert.

ี้§ 213. SHUSTER, GEORGE N. "Milton and the Metaphysical Poets." In *The Ode from Milton to Keats*, pp. 64–92. Columbia University Studies in English and Comparative Literature, no. 150. New York: Columbia University Press.
Several references to Herbert. Calls him "a mystic and a humanist" but points out that "his was a classicism not of Pindar and Horace but of Ambrose and Prudentius" (p. 86). Points out also Herbert's use of Horatian meters in his Latin verses but notes that "the waters of Arethusa are not in them" (p. 86). Compares Herbert briefly to Donne, Vaughan, Joseph Beaumont, and Crashaw.

ี้§ 214. WELLS, HENRY W. *New Poets from Old: A Study of Literary Genetics.* New York: Columbia University Press. x, 356p.
Studies the indebtedness of certain modern poets to earlier ones. Refers to Herbert in several places and in particular suggests his possible influence on Genevieve Taggard, Elinor Wylie, and W. H. Davies.

1941

ี้§ 215. ANON. "From Court to Sanctuary: George Herbert's Songs, An Emancipated Spirit." *TLS*, 12 July, pp. 334, 337.
Primarily a review of F. E. Hutchinson's edition of Herbert's poems (entry 223). Comments on the religious sensibility of Herbert's poems while warning against a too-literal autobiographical reading. Comments on Herbert's analogies and metaphors: "Scripture, gardens, trees, herbs, stars, fencing, bowl, card games, medicine, anatomy, everything serves his purpose" (p. 334). Discusses briefly Herbert's "disciplined intellectual energy and conviction" (p. 334) and particularly the implications of music in his poetry: "The word 'music', indeed, supplies the key to his dominant thought as the word 'light' supplies the key to Vaughan" (p. 337). Defends Herbert's uses of shaped verse and suggests that there are Herbertian echoes in Coleridge. For a reply, see H. S. Curr, entry 217.

216. BENNETT, JOAN. Review of *The Works of George Herbert*, edited by F. E. Hutchinson. *RES* 17:348–52.

Essentially a review of F. E. Hutchinson's edition (entry 223). "Biography, critical apparatus, text and commentary are alike excellent" (p. 348). Agrees strongly with Hutchinson's decision to retain the traditional ordering of the poems in *The Temple*. Finds Herbert's obscurity, though different, no less challenging than Donne's, especially those difficulties that arise from Herbert's simple diction.

217. CURR, H. S. "George Herbert." *TLS*, 2 August, p. 371.

Reply to an anonymous article in *TLS*, entry 215. Suggests that the sentence: "There is mirth as well as seemliness in right living./All things are big with jest: nothing that's plain,/ But may be wittie, if thou hast the vein" (p. 334, entry 215) recalls a line from the metrical version of Psalm 100.

218. DANIELS, EARL. The Art of Reading Poetry. New York: Farrar & Rinehart. vii, 519p.

Brief explication of "Prayer (I)" (pp. 202–5). Comments primarily on the uses of paradox in the poem. Comments also on "The Pulley" (pp. 206–10) and contrasts it with a hymn by Isaac Watts. Presents a series of critical questions designed for students on "Vertue" (p. 381) and "The Collar" (pp. 472–73).

219. DE SELINCOURT, ERNEST. "George Herbert." *HJ* 39:389–97.

Praises F. E. Hutchinson's edition (entry 223). Presents a biographical sketch of Herbert's life and personality. Calls *The Temple* "Herbert's intimate autobiography, a kind of diary in which he set down from day to day the fluctuations of his inner experience" (p. 392), but agrees with Hutchinson that the order of the poems is not chronological. Suggests that Herbert's prevalent mood, "his besetting sin . . . was deep dejection, in which he doubted not merely his fitness for the priesthood, but even his right to be numbered among the children of God" (p. 392). Praises "Love (III)" as an "exquisite lyric" (p. 395), but dislikes many features of Herbert's "metaphysical" style, such as his delight in anagrams, acrostics, and puns and his use of the farfetched conceit: "Such extravagances are little to our taste; yet they express clearly enough the ideas he wishes to convey, and expresses them in a manner which his age approved" (p. 396). Says that Herbert is consistently the artist but that he is not "the greatest of our sacred lyricists" (p. 396): "He lacks the passion and majesty of Donne; he never rises to the ecstasy of Crashaw; Vaughan surpasses him both in flashes of imaginative vision, and in delicate response to the beauty and wonder of the natural world" (p. 396).

ᵛᵍ§ 220. F., R. "George Herbert's 'A Parodie.'" *N&Q* 180:334.
Asks the meaning of the word *parody* in Herbert's title.

ᵛᵍ§ 221. FREEMAN, ROSEMARY. "George Herbert and the Emblem Books." *RES* 17:150–65.
Reprinted in revised and expanded form in *English Emblem Books* (entry 284), pp. 148–72.
Maintains that, although emblem books exercised considerable influence on scores of minor and major writers of the sixteenth and seventeenth centuries, Herbert's poetry "comes nearest to that of the emblem writers, while at the same time being infinitely more distinguished" (p. 150). Shows "how a convention which in itself produced only mediocre writing was modified to suit the purposes of a great poet" (p. 150). Briefly outlines the history of the emblem convention and comments on the chief characteristics of emblem books. Shows how Herbert transformed the convention and its methods into poetry. Discusses in particular the visual aspects of Herbert's imagery ("Herbert's images remain emblems and nowhere encroach on the province of symbol" [p. 159]), his uses of patterned forms, the emblematic function of many of his titles, the liturgical roots of his poetry, and his special uses of personifications. Herbert's poetry is characterized "by a simplicity of image, an extreme unobtrusiveness, and a concentration of meaning in which the complexity becomes only gradually apparent" (p. 157).

ᵛᵍ§ 222. H., C. E. "A Query from Herbert." *N&Q* 181:246.
Asks the meaning of the figure in line 30 of "The H. Communion" ("And all our lump to leaven"). Wonders if this is a reference to the "leaven of malice and wickedness."

ᵛᵍ§ 223. HERBERT, GEORGE. *The Works of George Herbert*. Edited with a commentary by F. E. Hutchinson. Oxford: Clarendon Press. lxxvii, 619p.
Revised, 1945.
Reprinted, 1964.
Preface (pp. iv–viii) in which the editor states that his main object is to establish the text for *The Temple*. Contents (pp. ix–xvii); list of illustrations (p. xix). Introduction includes: (1) biography of Herbert (pp. xxi–xxxix), (2) contemporary and later reputation (pp. xxxix–l), (3) manuscripts of *The Temple* poems (pp. l–lvi), (4) early editions of *The Temple* (pp. lvi–lxii), (5) editions of *A Priest to the Temple* and other writings (pp. lxiii–lxv), (6) modern editions of Herbert's works (pp. lxv–lxx), (7) the text of *The Temple* (pp. lxx–lxxvii). *The Temple* (pp. 1–199). English poems in the Williams manuscript not included in *The Temple* (pp. 200–205). Poems from Walton's *Lives* (pp. 206–7). Doubt-

ful poems (pp. 208–22). A *Priest to the Temple* (pp. 223–90). Herbert's
translation of Cornaro, A *Treatise of Temperance and Sobrietie* (pp. 291–
303). *Briefe Notes on Valdesso's "Considerations"* (pp. 304–20). *Outlandish Proverbs* (pp. 321–55). Proverbs in *Jacula Prudentum* not included in *Outlandish Proverbs* (pp. 356–62). Letters (pp. 363–81).
Herbert's will (pp. 382–83). *Musae Responsoriae* (pp. 383–403). *Passio
Discerpta* (pp. 404–9). *Lucus* (pp. 410–21). *Memoriae Matris Sacrum*
(pp. 422–31). Alia Poemata Latina (pp. 432–39). Orationes (pp. 440–
55). Epistolae (pp. 456–73). Commentary (pp. 475–608). Appendix:
Pro Svpplici Evangelicorum Ministrorum in Anglia (pp. 609–14). Index
of first lines (pp. 615–19).

⋙ 224. Matthiessen, F. O. *American Renaissance: Art and Expression
in the Age of Emerson and Whitman*. London, Toronto, New
York: Oxford University Press. xxiv, 678p.
Mentions Herbert in several places. Comments on Emerson's and
Thoreau's admiration of Herbert and the seventeenth century: "The
seventeenth-century frame is of greatest relevance for the practice of their
art. In reading Herbert or Browne they were affected not only by ideas,
or by form as an abstract pattern, but also by qualities of their own language which the eighteenth century had allowed to decay, and which
they were determined to renew" (p. 102). Specifically mentions Emerson's delight in Herbert's "Man" and that Emerson's poem "Grace"
was mistaken for one by Herbert. "Herbert's face was turned upward;
Emerson's and Thoreau's faces inward. Herbert pleads with God for
vision; Emerson and Thoreau only pricked themselves perpetually on to
further spiritual discoveries" (p. 113).

⋙ 225. Mortimer, Raymond. "Books in General." *New Statesman and
Nation* 21:534.
Appreciative review of F. E. Hutchinson's edition (entry 223) but primarily a general critical essay on Herbert's poetry: "I have tried to
summarize my sense of Herbert's poetry by illustration rather than by
comment." Praises Herbert's variety of feeling, experimentation with
prosodic forms, and musicality. Evidences much distrust of the modern
enthusiasm for metaphysical poetry and suggests that it is not in the
mainstream of English verse. Calls it "a backwater exuberant with rare
flowers, and not unconnected with certain little-visited Continental
creeks named Gongora and Marini [sic]."

⋙ 226. Potter, George Reuben. "A Protest Against the Term *Conceit*." In *Renaissance Studies in Honor of Hardin Craig*, edited by
Baldwin Maxwell et al., pp. 282–91. Stanford: Stanford University Press.
Reprinted in *PQ* 20 (1941):474–83.

Surveys the various denotative and connotative meanings of the word *conceit* from the medieval period to modern times and urges that it be discontinued as a critical term. Comments specifically on the confusion that the term has caused when applied to the metaphysical poets. No specific mention of Herbert.

227. SHEWRING, WALTER. Review of *The Works of George Herbert*, edited by F. E. Hutchinson. *DubR* 20:213–14.
Uses the review of F. E. Hutchinson's edition (entry 223) as a way of commenting on Herbert. Rejoices that, unlike Donne, Herbert has not become fashionable in the modern age: "His spirit has proved too tranquil, his real conflicts of soul are resolved too well, to make him in any sense an idol of our times; he is one who saw too clearly the differing values of motion and rest" (p. 213). Comments on Herbert's traditional moral theology, which "Catholics have a particular interest in observing" (p. 213). Praises the Latin poetry, especially "In Angelos," "which is in the true Scholastic tradition" (p. 214).

1942

228. BRADBROOK, M. C. "The Liturgical Tradition in English Verse: Herbert and Eliot." *Theology* (London) 45:13–23.
Compares and contrasts Herbert and Eliot to "show how in Mr. Eliot a symbolic technique has been adapted to a less congenial age; Herbert's successes throw light on Eliot's difficulties and help to an understanding of what he has achieved" (p. 13). Suggests that Eliot's essay on Lancelot Andrewes is also applicable to Herbert: "Herbert analysed and split up the Church building or the service, as Andrewes divided and subdivided his text, and upon this fixed and literal basis each will play those variations suggested by his learned and intellectual interests, his natural and simple tastes, and his deep devotional fervour" (p. 13). Sees Herbert as "one of those few English poets who relies upon liturgy not for its emotional effects, but for its power to concentrate dogma" (p. 14). Recognizes some flaws in Herbert's verse, especially in its excessive intellectuality and idiosyncrasy, but concludes: "In Herbert may be seen a mind sensitive and controlled presenting the *vie intérieure* in terms of liturgy and ritual, recording the widest emotional reverberations in terms of perpetual struggle and self-conquest with a flawless precision, honesty, and grace of statement" (p. 17).

229. BRANDENBURG, ALICE STAYERT. "The Dynamic Image in Metaphysical Poetry." *PMLA* 57:1039–45.
Suggests that the underlying quality that connects many of the seemingly unrelated features of metaphysical poetry might be called "the dynamic image." Distinguishes between two types of images: the static

image, which "describes the appearance, taste, smell, feel, or sound of an object—the qualities in short, which mediaeval philosophers called accidents" (p. 1039), and the dynamic image, which "describes the way in which objects act or interact" (p. 1039). Comments primarily on the nature and function of Donne's dynamic images. Points out that Donne's followers, including Herbert, continued the use of dynamic images but "did not turn so frequently to science for their material or neutralize their images so thoroughly" (p. 1044). Mentions Herbert's "Artillerie."

᧥ 230. GRIERSON, H. J. C. Review of *The Works of George Herbert*, edited by F. E. Hutchinson. *MLR* 37:207–14.

Essentially a detailed review of F. E. Hutchinson's edition (entry 223), but also includes Grierson's critical comments on Herbert. Finds Herbert, on the whole, more difficult than Donne and feels that as religious poets "they are poles asunder" (p. 208). Contrasts Herbert and Donne and concludes that there is "a closer link between Herbert and the Emblem writers, Quarles and his sources, than between the tormented Dean and the pastor of Bemerton" (p. 208). Laments that Hutchinson does not devote more space to commentary and critical analysis.

᧥ 231. ROWSE, A. L. "The Caroline Country Parson: George Herbert's Ideal." *Country Life*, 6 February, pp. 252–55.

Reprinted in *The English Spirit* (New York: Macmillan Co., 1945), pp. 148–53; rev. ed., 1966.

General and popular account of Herbert's life and works with several photographs of places associated with him. Calls Herbert's poetry "the most perfect, the ideal, expression of it [the Caroline world], if not the most complete, because of its unworldliness" (p. 252). Most remarkable about Herbert "is his combination of great common-sense, his feeling for the plain country people, with the rigorous standards of a saint" (p. 254), which is manifested, for example, in *The Country Parson*. Contrasts Herbert and Herrick: "Almost all of Herbert's poetry is concerned with this inner world of experience, as against his contemporary Herrick's frank acceptance of the good things of this world" (p. 255). Yet, "they had so much in common: their love of music, so true to Caroline England, of flowers and birds and church-bells, of the old country customs and the country people, their devotion to the English church they served and by which they are remembered" (p. 255).

᧥ 232. TUVE, ROSEMOND. "Imagery and Logic: Ramus and Metaphysical Poetics." *JHI* 3:365–400.

Discusses Renaissance imagery in the light of rhetorical training, especially Ramist logic. Suggests that much confusion and uncertainty about the nature and function of Renaissance images results from "an insufficient understanding of the relation of the origin and function of images in sixteenth- and seventeenth-century practice to the poetic theory of their creators" (p. 369). No specific references to Herbert. See also A. J. Smith, entry 396, and George Watson, entry 420.

1943

233. L., E. W. "Herbert's 'The Collar.' " *Expl* 2:question 16.
Asks for an explanation of the interrelation of the images in "The Collar," specifically "cordial fruit," "cage," "good cable," and "death's-head." For a reply, see Dan S. Norton, entry 250.

234. McLuhan, Herbert Marshall. "Herbert's 'Virtue.' " *Expl* 2: item 4.
Reprinted in *Readings for Liberal Education*, edited by Louis G. Locke, William M. Gibson, and George Arms (New York: Rinehart, 1948), 2:534–35.
Points out that each stanza of "Vertue" is a paradox and that the last stanza "is a paradox of religious faith which is intended to exalt over the melancholy contradictions of the other three." Suggests that the Church Fathers (as well as their baroque imitators) used the paradox not only to excite wonder and enthusiasm but also as a means of exegesis.

235. Miles, Josephine. "Some Major Poetic Words." *University of California Publications in English* 14:233–39.
Presents various comparisons and generalizations based on lists of the ten words (excluding prepositions, conjunctions, etc.) most frequently used by each of twenty-one poets from Chaucer to Housman (based on concordance data existing at the time of writing). For Herbert the list includes *make* (200), *God* (150), *man* (150), *heart* (130), *love* (130), *death* (120), *good* (120), *know* (120), *give* (120), *sin* (110), *life* (100), *thing* (100).

236. Purcell, Henry. "With Sick & Famished Eyes." A song by Henry Purcell, the words by George Herbert. For voice, with piano (or harpsichord) and violoncello. Edited by Ina Boyle. 2 parts. London: Oxford University Press. Part 1, 3p.; part 2, 8p.
First published in Henry Playford's *Harmonia Sacra* (1688). Musical setting for Herbert's "Longing" (with some verses and words omitted).

237. Wilson, F. P. "A Note on George Herbert's 'Quidditie.' " *RES* 19:398–99.
Explains that the last line of "The Quidditie" ("I am with thee, and *most take all*") is based on a rare proverb. *Most* is used in the sense of "the most powerful." Suggests that the poem is called "The Quidditie"

"because in it the poet distinguishes the essence or quiddity of the spiritual life from the accidents of the world" (p. 399). As Herbert writes his verses, "dedicated not to the mundane activities, pleasures, and accomplishments enumerated in the poem but to the service of God, the poet is with God, and God the all-powerful takes complete possession of him ('Most take all')" (p. 399).

1944

238. AGATHA, MOTHER, O.S.U. "George Herbert: Poet of Right Intention." *Ave Maria* 59:327–30.
Hagiographic sketch of Herbert's life. Suggests that the poems "are not in any sense great. There is much that is artificial, cold and in spots ugly. Their technical and literary faults are largely atoned for by their spiritual content" (p. 329). States that the predominant theme in Herbert's poetry is death.

239. ALLEN, DON CAMERON. "George Herbert's *Sycomore*." *MLN* 59:493–95.
Explains Herbert's use of *sycomore* in "The World" ("Then enter'd *Sinne*, and with that Sycomore,/ Whose leaves first sheltred man from drought & dew/ . . . The inward walls and sommers cleft and tore"). Suggests that Herbert is referring to the fig tree of Genesis. Explains the origin and extent of the confusion caused by various early translations of the Bible.

240. CLOKEY, JOSEPH WADDELL. *The Temple, a Cycle of Poems by George Herbert (1593–1633)*. Set for soli, chorus and orchestra with optional parts for singing by members of audience or congregation. With a foreword by Howard D. McKinney. New York: J. Fischer & Bro. 58p.
An oratorio based on Herbert's poems.

241. D., G. H. "George Herbert and Dante." *N&Q* 187:81.
No. 553 of Herbert's *Outlandish Proverbs* ("We cannot come in honour under a Couerlet") reminds the author of Vergil's words to Dante in the *Inferno* (24:47–48). Wonders if the proverb comes from Dante or if Dante was quoting the proverb.

242. DOUDS, J. B. "George Herbert's Use of the Transferred Verb: A Study in the Structure of Poetic Imagery." *MLQ* 5:163–74.
Defines the "transferred verb" as a verb that "is transferred from its ordinary, literal, concrete meaning to an abstract and figurative one" (as in "See how spite *cankers* things" from "The Sacrifice") (p. 163). Calls this "one of the numerous grammatical devices used for fusing the

terms of a metaphor" (p. 163). Discusses many poems to illustra
wide range of effects that Herbert achieves through this device. "Because
it is the most dynamic part of speech and because it offers one of the
most compact ways of expressing a metaphor, the transferred verb is
capable of great poetic force; and Herbert's extensive use of it is probably responsible in part for the impression of energy which his style produces" (p. 174).

ᴇᵍ 243. ELIOT, T. S. "What Is Minor Poetry?" *Welsh Review* 3:256–67.
Reprinted in *On Poetry and Poets* (New York: Farrar, Straus, and
Cudahy, 1957), pp. 34–51.
Discusses the nature and kinds of so-called minor poetry. Points out
that "we mean different things at different times" by the term, and attempts to dispel "any derogatory association connected with the term"
(p. 256). Comments on the various uses of different kinds of anthologies
of poetry. Uses Herbert to illustrate that a poet who writes "a work
which consists of a number of short poems, even of poems which, taken
individually, may appear rather slight, may, if it has a unity of underlying pattern, be the equivalent of a first-rate long poem in establishing an
author's claim to be a 'major' poet" (p. 263). Points out that if we read
through the whole of *The Temple* we are "surprised to find how many
of the poems strike us as just as good as those we have met with in anthologies" (p. 261). Maintains that *The Temple* is not simply "a number of religious poems by one author" but rather "a book constructed
according to a plan; and as we get to know Herbert's poems better, we
come to find that there is something we get from the whole book,
which is more than a sum of its parts" (p. 261). Sees *The Temple* as "a
continued religious meditation with an intellectual framework," as a
book that "as a whole discloses to us the Anglican devotional spirit of
the first half of the seventeenth century" (p. 261). Concludes that Herbert cannot be called a minor poet "for it is not of a few favorite poems
that I am reminded when I think of him, but of the whole work" (p.
262). Briefly contrasts Herbert with Herrick and Thomas Campion.

ᴇᵍ 244. GARDNER, W. H. *Gerard Manley Hopkins (1844–1889): A Study
of Poetic Idiosyncrasy in Relation to Poetic Tradition.* London:
Martin Secker & Warburg, 1944–1949. 2 vols. Vol. 1: 1944; 2d rev.
ed., 1948; reissued by Oxford University Press, 1958. xvi, 304p. Vol.
2:1949; reissued by Oxford University Press, 1958. xiv, 415p.
Numerous references to Herbert and a number of specific comparisons
between Hopkins and Herbert. Points out Hopkins's admiration of Herbert: "Herbert's frank avowal of Christ; his passionate yet restrained
colloquies with God; his vigorous and subtle exposition of doctrine; his
significant quaintness and happy conceits—all of these elements are
found, in duly modified form, in the later Hopkins" (2:73–74). Argues,

"In the delicacy, ingenuity, and almost fantastic wit of many of his images, Hopkins continues the tradition of Donne, Herbert, Crashaw, Vaughan, and Marvell" (1:189). Suggests several direct borrowings from Herbert as well as less obvious echoes. For example, points out that in "The Storm" one finds "a concise statement of the central ethical theme of Hopkins's two poems of shipwreck" (1:171), that the image of the soul hunted by God in *The Deutschland* is anticipated by Herbert's "Affliction (IV)" (stanza one), that the image of the sloes in *The Deutschland* may have been suggested by either "Bitter-sweet" or "Paradise," and that there are echoes of Herbert's "The Flower" in "Carrion Comfort" and similarities between *The Church-Porch* and Hopkins's "The Starlight Night." Suggests, "The most patently Herbertian of all his verse is a poem of 1864 with the characteristic title *New Readings*" (2:74).

❧ 245. GRIERSON, H. J. C., and SMITH, J. C. "The Carolines." In *A Critical History of English Poetry*, pp. 158–71. London: Chatto and Windus.
1st American ed., 1946.
2d rev. ed., 1947.
Reprinted, 1950, 1956, 1962.
Comments briefly on Donne's influence on Herbert. Praises Herbert's loving and reasonable temper in *The Temple*, thus "making us excuse, even find pleasure in, his metrical flourishes . . . and his innumerable conceits" (p. 164). Suggests that Herbert's conceits "are sometimes penetrating by their homely quaintness, never electrifying like those of Donne; they are the products of Fancy not Passion and Imagination, 'emblems' in the manner of Quarles" (p. 164).

❧ 246. HOWARTH, R. G. "George Herbert." N&Q 187:122.
Sees possible echoes of Kyd's *Spanish Tragedy* (act 4, scene 4, lines 90–92) in the third and fourth stanzas of "The Pilgrimage."

❧ 247. KNIGHTS, L. C. "George Herbert." Scrutiny 12:171–86.
Reprinted in *Explorations: Essays in Criticism Mainly on the Literature of the Seventeenth Century* (London: Chatto and Windus, 1946; 1st American ed., New York: George W. Stewart, 1947).
Proposes to discuss the human value, as opposed to the specifically Christian, in Herbert's poetry and to show how Herbert's poetry "is an integral part of the great English tradition" (p. 171). Comments on Herbert's craftsmanship and sees it as "one with the moral effort to know himself, to bring his conflicts into the daylight and, as far as possible, to resolve them" (p. 172). Points out that, although Herbert's poetry clearly reflects his refined and cultivated background, it is, at the same time, generally informed by the homely manner of the popular

preacher and contains much humor, mimicry, sarcasm, and common Elizabethan speech and homely illustration. "It is the artist's feeling for *all* the resources of 'our language' that gives to the greater poems of spiritual conflict their disturbing immediacy" (p. 175). Comments also on Herbert's use of allegory and symbol to tie together the natural and supernatural order of things. Sees the conflicts presented in Herbert's poetry as only partially caused by the temptation of ambition and suggests that his dejection of spirit, caused by his tendency to regard his life as worthless and unprofitable, likewise shaped his poetry. Thinks that this despondency, in part, accounts for Herbert's preoccupation with time and death and reflects his feeling that "life, real life, is going on elsewhere, where he happens not to be himself" (p. 180). Illustrates through a discussion of several poems, especially "Affliction (I)," "The Collar," "Love (III)," and "The Flower," the mature and complex process of Herbert's "acceptance." Suggests that the poems "are important human documents because they handle with honesty and insight questions that, in one form or another, we all have to meet if we wish to come to terms with life" (p. 186).

◄§ 248. MABBOTT, T. O. "Herbert's 'The Collar.' " *Expl* 3:item 12.
    Comments briefly on Herbert's use of *rope of sands* in "The Collar." " 'What is impossible with man is possible with God' is the implication; and He can redeem the otherwise helpful human soul, as He can make sand serve to make a rope if He will." See also Dan Norton, entry 259.

◄§ 249. MOLONEY, MICHAEL FRANCIS. *John Donne: His Flight from Mediaevalism*. Illinois Studies in Language and Literature, vol. 29, nos. 2–3. Urbana: University of Illinois Press. 223p.
    Comments on the rationalizing strain in Herbert's poetry and suggests that his poetry reflects some elements of the dissociation of sensibility: "Too often in Herbert, the sensuous imagery disappears before a plodding rationalism" (p. 205). Points out the "over-logicality" in *The Church-Porch*, "The Thanksgiving," and "Discipline." Comments on Herbert's general suspicion of the flesh and of women. Compares and contrasts Herbert with both Donne and Crashaw.

◄§ 250. NORTON, DAN S. "Herbert's 'The Collar.' " *Expl* 2:item 41.
    In part a reply to E. W. L., entry 233. Points out that the images in "The Collar," especially "cordial fruit," "cage," "good cable," and "death's head," "contrast the fertility and freedom of worldly life with the sterility and constrictions of the Christian discipline, and the reality of things of the senses with the illusion of religious faith and scruple." Paraphrases the main argument of the poem and sees the conclusion as a complete reversal that "creates a powerful irony by which all the values of the images are changed, as if a positive print were instantly made from

a photographic negative." Suggests that this reversal compels the reader "to review the imagery and to see it reinterpreted in Christian terms."

◄§ 251. SYPHER, WYLIE. "The Metaphysicals and the Baroque." *PR* 11:3–17.

Argues that our modern admiration for Donne "is in a sense hollow and affected, and our depreciation of Milton wilful" (p. 4). Argues that Milton "is more characteristic of his century than Donne. . . . If we understand the baroque, it is a questionable tactic to elevate Donne at the expense of Milton" (p. 4). Proceeds to survey baroque "manners" in sculpture, painting, architecture, and principally poetry. Refers to "the amazing profusion of freakish imagery in George Herbert" (p. 9).

1945

◄§ 252. BUSH, DOUGLAS. *English Literature in the Earlier Seventeenth Century, 1600–1660.* Oxford History of English Literature, edited by F. P. Wilson and Bonamy Dobrée, vol. 5. Oxford: Clarendon Press. vi, 621p.

Reprinted, 1946, 1948, 1952, 1956.

Rev. ed., 1962; reprinted with corrections, 1966.

First issued as an Oxford University Press paperback, 1973 (with omission of chronological tables and bibliography).

General critical and historical survey in which Herbert is mentioned throughout. Herbert's poetry is discussed primarily in chapter 4 (pp. 104–69, esp. 136–39). Comments on the inner tensions of Herbert's poetry, his principal themes of sin and love, his exquisite sense of metaphor, his peculiar intimacy and honesty, his uses of everyday images or of images drawn from nature, the liturgy, and the Bible (in contrast to the scholastic and scientific imagery of Donne). Sees many of Herbert's poems as "allegorical anecdotes and transfigured emblems" (p. 139). Praises Herbert's technical mastery and metrical experimentation, his "functional sense of metre and rhythm" (p. 138). Points out that Herbert avoided the surface classicism of his age but "had muscular density, precision, deceptive simplicity, and a dynamic sense of form" (p. 139). Suggests that one can distinguish essentially two poets in Herbert: (1) the affectionate son of the Church of England to whom "we owe much of our picture of the order, strength, and beauty of seventeenth-century Anglicanism at its best" (p. 138) and (2) "the very human saint who gives fresh and moving utterance to the aspirations and failures of the spiritual life" (p. 138). Presents a brief biographical sketch. Compares and contrasts Herbert with Donne, Quarles, Crashaw, Traherne, Marvell, and (in the revised edition) Sir Philip Sidney. Comments on Walton's life of Herbert (pp. 222–24). Bibliography (pp. 548–49).

◄§ 253. GARROD, H. W. "Donne and Mrs. Herbert." *RES* 21:161–73.

Examines the relationship between Donne and Magdalen Herbert and other members of the Herbert family, especially Edward, Lord Herbert of Cherbury. Attempts to date several of Donne's poems that have been often associated with Mrs. Herbert and questions the evidence of some of those believed by Grierson and others to have been written to her. George Herbert is mentioned only briefly.

◄§ 254. KNIGHTS, L. C. "On the Social Background of Metaphysical Poetry." *Scrutiny* 13:37–52.

Reprinted in *Further Explorations* (Stanford: Stanford University Press, 1965), pp. 99–120.

Examines "only a very few of the ways in which it is possible to work out *from* literature—from Metaphysical poetry—to 'the life of the time' in the early seventeenth century" (p. 39). Maintains that it is "much more likely that the distinctive note of Metaphysical poetry—the implicit recognition of the many-sidedness of man's nature—is in some ways socially supported; that—to borrow some phrases from a suggestive passage in Yeats' criticism—'unity of being' has some relation to a certain 'unity of culture' " (p. 42). Refers to Herbert to illustrate the social and cultural milieu of his time. For example, states that Herbert's "homely imagery is not simply a form of expression; it is an index of habitul modes of thought and feeling in which the different aspects and different levels of his personal experience are brought into intimate relation to each other" (p. 40). Calls Herbert "courtly" and "metaphysical" and says he possessed "a mechanism of sensibility that could devour any kind of experience" (p. 41). Comments on the vital, enriching religious tradition that informs Herbert's poetry and contrasts it with the tradition expressed by Dryden.

◄§ 255. McCUTCHAN, ROBERT GUY. *Hymns in the Lives of Men.* New York and Nashville: Abingdon-Cokesbury Press. 208p.

Several comments on Herbert's contribution to the development of the English hymn. Points out that Susanna Wesley was devoted to Herbert's poetry and that "The Elixir" and "Antiphon" were adapted for use as hymns (pp. 142–43).

◄§ 256. MEAD, D. S. "Herbert's 'The Pulley.' " *Expl* 4:item 17.

Explains the visual conceit of a pulley that informs the whole poem: "To make use of the pulley in the poem, God must be thought of as threading the rope through the wheel. On one side he lets down man and from his 'glass of blessings' he gives man strength, beauty, wisdom, honor, pleasure—all the rest. Rest He witholds in his glass so that man without it will experience restlessness. Man can climb up the rope to

God by virtue of his goodness, but in case he does not, and, spurning his earthly riches yearns in his weariness for peace, God need but release His rest on the other side of the pulley and its weight, greater than man's unburdened soul, will hoist or 'toss' man to His level."

◈§ 257. MILES, JOSEPHINE. "From *Good* to *Bright*: A Note in Poetic History." *PMLA* 60:766–74.

Traces the "developing relation of the standard epithets *good* and *bad* to the qualities epithets *bright* and *dark* through the work and the concordance listing of four or five poets on either side of 1740" (p. 866). Although Herbert is mentioned, Donne is discussed as a pre-1740 representative.

◈§ 258. NELSON, LAWRENCE E. "Altar and Angel Wings." In *Our Roving Bible: Tracking Its Influence Through English and American Literature*, pp. 64–72. New York and Nashville: Abingdon-Cokesbury Press.

Brief comments on "The Altar" and on "Easter-wings." Quotes (with comment) W. S. Walsh, who, in his *Hand-book of Literary Curiosities* (1925) says: "Heading the list of English word-torturers stands so good and great a man as George Herbert. We quote two specimens and then pass on with our eyes veiled, to avoid gazing too intently on a good man's shame" (p. 65). Calls emblem poems and metaphysical poems "rather harmless eccentricities which sometimes served as the channels for deep piety" (p. 72).

◈§ 259. NORTON, DAN. "Herbert's 'The Collar.' " *Expl* 3:item 46.

Points out the play on the words *collar* and *choler* in the title of the poem: "Until God speaks to him, Herbert is in a choler because he wears the collar of religious discipline; and galling restraint has caused his rage." Supports T. O. Mabbott's reading (entry 248) of *rope of sands*: "To make a rope of sands ... is a symbol of futile or impossible industry." See also Dan S. Norton, entry 250, and Jack M. Bickham, entry 317.

◈§ 260. OLIVER, PETER. "George Herbert (1593–1633)." *Action*, 5 December, pp. 9–12.

Short biographical sketch in which Herbert's piety and dedication to the Church of England are emphasized. Calls the seventeenth-century religious poets "missionaries of civilization" who "regarded the arts, not as pleasant pursuits, but as allies in the battle for a nobler future" (p. 9).

◈§ 261. SCOTT, WALTER SIDNEY. *The Fantasticks: Donne, Herbert, Crashaw, Vaughan*. London: John Westhouse. 170p.

General introduction to the four poets. The introduction to Herbert (pp. 55–60) presents a brief biographical sketch and comments very generally on Herbert's use of conceits, his "loveliness," and his "near approach to integration" in life. Selections from Herbert's poems (pp. 61–93).

◄§ 262. TODD, MABEL LOOMIS, and BINGHAM, MILLICENT TODD, eds. *Bolts of Melody: New Poems by Emily Dickinson*. New York and London: Harper & Brothers. xxix, 352p.
Reproduces stanzas 1 and 2 of Herbert's "Mattens" and attributes them to Dickinson (p. 125). In the third printing the error is corrected. See also William White, "Dickinson and Dover Publications," *AN&Q* 11 (1972): 7.

◄§ 263. WILSON, F. P. *Elizabethan and Jacobean*. Oxford: Clarendon Press. vi, 144p.
Reprinted, 1946.
Points out some of the major differences between Elizabethan and Jacobean literature. Mentions Herbert in several places and compares him briefly with Donne. Comments on Herbert's use of close-knit, dialectical argumentation: "It is this 'sequaciousness', this following through of logic and passion, which make it possible to say that George Herbert and Marvell (with all their many differences from Donne) belong to the same 'school' of poetry as Donne, and that Southwell and Crashaw do not" (p. 58).

1946

◄§ 264. CHURCH, MARGARET. "The First English Pattern Poems." *PMLA* 61:636–50.
Discusses the origins and history of the pattern poem and comments on the earliest English poets who wrote shaped verse, among them Herbert. Suggests that the idea of pattern poems probably originated in Asia Minor and was transmitted to the Western World through *The Greek Anthology*. The first English pattern poem was written by Stephen Hawes in *The Convercyon of Swerers* (1509). Comments briefly on and discusses the tradition out of which such poems as "The Altar" and "Easter-wings" arose.

◄§ 265. DANIELLS, ROY. "English Baroque and Deliberate Obscurity." *JAAC* 5:115–21.
Attempts to define the baroque as it is applied to English literature: "Baroque may be regarded as the logical continuation and extension of High Renaissance art, with conscious accentuation and 'deformation' of the regular stock of techniques. These become more dynamic and (in both good and bad senses of the word) theatrical. Baroque is developed as a complete art form of wide influence and application, the expression

of a specific artistic sensibility of which some of the marks are well known: a sense of triumph and splendour, a strenuous effort to unify opposite terms of paradoxes, a high regard for technical virtuosity" (p. 117). Suggests that the English baroque appears as early as 1590. Brief mention of Herbert as evidencing a baroque sensibility that "has lost the fragile unity and tentative balance of the best Elizabethans" (p. 117). Specifically comments on poetical uses of obscurity as "a cult of significant darkness" (p. 119).

◄§ 266. MILCH, WERNER J. "Metaphysical Poetry and the German 'Barocklyrik.' " *Comparative Literature Studies* (Cardiff) 23–24: 16–22.

Comments on various possible areas for comparative studies between the German *barock* poets and the English metaphysicals as well as between the larger aspects of each movement. Sees the *barock* poets and the metaphysicals as "the last great European attempt to bring about a unified world of thought since the rift between contemplative and active life, between unquestioned faith and scientific urge had become the central feature of all philosophy" (p. 20). Suggests that Herbert "should be considered in connection with Fleming and Gryphius, in order to study the motive of resignation and self-denial in seventeenth century religious poetry" (p. 21).

◄§ 267. MILES, JOSEPHINE. "Major Adjectives in English Poetry from Wyatt to Auden." In *The Vocabulary of Poetry, Three Studies*, pp. 305–426. University of California Publications in English, vol. 12 (1942–1946). Berkeley and Los Angeles: University of California Press.

Presents various statistical tabulations of the number of major adjectives used by twenty-five representative poets, including Herbert. Based on concordance data. Table 1 (pp. 314–15) lists the following adjectives most used by Herbert: *good* (120), *great* (70), *poor* (55), *dear* (40), *full* (35), *old* (30), *sweet* (30). Table 2 (pp. 316–18) lists major words most used by Herbert: *make* (200), *God* (150), *man* (150), *heart* (130), *love* (130), *death* (120), *give* (120), *good* (120), *know* (120), *sin* (110), *life* (100), *thing* (100). Presents an extended critical and comparative discourse on the language of selected major poets (excluding Herbert) based on the statistical data collected.

◄§ 268. PRAZ, MARIO. "Poesia Metafisica Inglese del Seicento." *Poesia* 3–4:232–41, 283–89.

Brief summary of modern critical reaction to metaphysical poetry. In a brief sketch of Herbert (pp. 236–37), the author relates Herbert to Donne: "Con lui la maniera metafisica si fa parrocchiale, discende all' emblematica spicciola, rasenta in modo pericoloso il concetto predicabile"

(p. 237). Points out the sources of Herbert's inspiration and concludes, "Ogni sia pur umile occasione vien trasportata al morale, ma la spontanea freschezza, il candore del poeta, e il suo fermo fervore devoto ricscono ad avvivare la materia spesso artificiosa e didattica" (p. 237). Translates "Church-monuments," "The Windows," "Vertue," "The Collar," and "Easter-wings" into Italian.

❧ 269. TANNENBAUM, SAMUEL A., and TANNENBAUM, DOROTHY R. *George Herbert: A Concise Bibliography*. Elizabethan Bibliographies, no. 35. New York: Samuel A. Tannenbaum. 52p.
Unannotated listing of Herbertiana. Divided into nine major sections: (1) poetical works (54 entries), (2) prose works (37 entries), (3) collected editions (41 entries), (4) selections (172 entries), (5) songs and hymns with music (53 entries), (6) biography and criticism (382 entries), (7) bibliography (7 entries), (8) addenda (21 entries), and (9) index of names and subjects.

❧ 270. WELLEK, RENÉ. "The Concept of Baroque in Literary Scholarship." *JAAC* 5:77–109.
Reprinted in *Concepts of Criticism* (New Haven: Yale University Press, 1963), pp. 69–127.
Surveys the various uses of the term *baroque*, particularly as it is applied to the literature of several countries. Although Herbert is not cited, the metaphysical poets, especially Donne and Crashaw, are mentioned throughout. Bibliography of writings on the baroque in literary scholarship (pp. 97–109).

❧ 271. WILSON, F. P. "English Proverbs and Dictionaries of Proverbs." *The Library* (London), 4th ser. 26:51–71.
Discusses "the value of an interest in proverbs for the student of literature, and especially to a student in the literature of the sixteenth and seventeenth centuries" (pp. 51–52). Several comments on *Outlandish Proverbs*. Calls Herbert "the only poet of the seventeenth century who made a collection of proverbs" (p. 56). Explicates the last line of "The Quidditie" ("I am with thee, and *most take all*") by referring to a proverb. Presents a short-title list of books containing collections of proverbs from 1640 to 1670. See also Wilson, entry 237.

1947

❧ 272. ADDISON, WILLIAM. *The English Country Parson*. London: J. M. Dent & Sons.
Reprinted, 1948.
Brief comments throughout on Herbert as the ideal parson: "In the long record of faithful ministry in the Church of England there is no name the passage of time has tarnished less than his" (p. 39). Number

of references to *The Country Parson*. Calls John Keble a latter-day Herbert but points out that "as a poet he fell short of Herbert" (p. 152).

◄§ 273. DAY-LEWIS, CECIL. *The Poetic Image*. New York: Oxford University Press. 157p.

Reprinted (pages 80–81) in *Reading for Liberal Education* (New York: Rinehart & Co., rev. ed., 1952), pp. 39–40.

Defines the nature and limits of the image and surveys various types of imagery as well as differing views of imagery from English poetry and literary criticism during the past four hundred years. Mentions Herbert and the metaphysical poets in several places. Calls "The Collar" "an example of the strictly functional use of images; their use, that is, to point a theme already defined" (p. 80). Suggests that the central image of the poem is "the spiritual rope by which the Christian is tied to his God" (p. 80) and sees the poem as a dialogue between Christ and the devil.

◄§ 274. DELATTRE, FLORIS. "De la Chanson Élizabéthaine au Poème Métaphysique." *ML* 28:91–96.

Points out that, in contrast to the Elizabethan lyricists, who stressed musicality, generalized emotional experience, and exquisite form, the metaphysical poets, especially Donne, rejected traditional views of beauty and classical allusion, stressed muscular tone, revolted against rhythmical regularity in their search for individual consciousness, and retained music in a privileged position. No specific comments on Herbert.

◄§ 275. FERGUSON, F. S. "The Temple." *TLS*, 3 May, p. 211.

Comments on the undated title page of some copies of the first edition of *The Temple*. Argues that the title page was not entirely reset (as suggested by Marion Cox [entry 49] and F. E. Hutchinson [entry 209]) but is rather a variant altered from the standing type of the dated title page (as suggested by William A. Jackson). "There is no doubt that when it was decided to make the change in the dated title-page all the type of the first signature, with the exception of that title, had already been distributed."

◄§ 276. MILCH, WERNER. "Deutsche Barocklyrik und 'Metaphysical Poetry.'" *Trivium* 5:65–73.

Comments on the contemporaneity of the metaphysical poets and certain German baroque poets. States that German baroque poetry was without a real leader whereas the English had Donne. Comments on various religious, political, and philosophical conditions in both Germany and England that were favorable to the development of baroque poetry. Suggests that a comparison of Herbert with Fleming and Gryphius would show the place of the idea of renunciation in the two parallel movements.

⊷§ 277. Ross, MALCOLM MACKENZIE. "George Herbert and the Humanist Tradition." *UTQ* 16:169–82.
Reprinted in *Poetry and Dogma* (entry 368), pp. 135–53.
Maintains that Herbert occupies a "unique place in a moment of cultural metamorphosis" (p. 170); inheriting the tradition of the Elizabethan humanists (especially Hooker), Herbert "alters the tradition and imparts to it a new direction" (p. 170). Suggests that Herbert's work "reveals a significant interaction between the intellectual tradition as such and the disturbing pressures of Caroline society" (p. 181). Sees in Herbert a crucial conflict between worldly and otherworldly values that is not dominant in his immediate predecessors: "A very un-Elizabethan world comes through in the texture of Herbert's poetry" (p. 173). Discusses Herbert's attitude toward the court, as revealed in his poetry, as an example of "one aspect of the break-down of the Elizabethan synthesis" (p. 173). Although never antiroyalist, Herbert's references to the court are fundamentally negative, as are his references to commerce, wealth, and trade: "Only once is Christ expressed in the metaphor of gold" (p. 177). Maintains that Herbert kept an inner balance between various and sometimes conflicting demands: "In this inner synthesis of awareness and withdrawal, crisis is never fully resolved nor is synthesis ever quite destroyed" (p. 182). Concludes that this synthesis "is almost mystical, almost Romanist, almost free of social conscience or concern— but never entirely any one of these. A quality and habit of mind steeped in a great tradition turns from an outer tangible world upon which it can make no impress and in which it can no longer 'its own resemblance find,' to the construction of an inner world where conflicts can be at least tentatively resolved" (p. 182).

⊷§ 278. Rossi, MARIO M. *La Vita, Le Opere, I Tempi di Edoardo Herbert di Chirbury.* 3 vols. Biblioteca Storica Sansoni, n.s. 14. Florence: G. C. Sansoni. ix, 599p.; 544p.; 598p.
Numerous references to George Herbert. In particular compares George Herbert and Lord Herbert of Cherbury. Comments on their relationship with their mother, Magdalen Herbert. Portrays George as the dutiful son. Briefly discusses George's influence on his brother's poetry and the influence of Donne on both. Stresses George's Christian mysticism and Protestant piety. Detailed discussion of the Herbert family.

⊷§ 279. TUVE, ROSEMOND. *Elizabethan and Metaphysical Imagery: Renaissance Poetic and Twentieth-Century Critics.* Chicago: University of Chicago Press. xiv, 442p.
Reprinted, University of Chicago Press (Phoenix Books), 1961.
Extracts appear in *Discussions of John Donne*, edited by Frank Kermode (Boston: D. C. Heath & Co., 1962), pp. 106–17.
Reconsiders Elizabethan and metaphysical modes of expression in

terms of the contemporary habits of thought, principally in terms of Renaissance theories of rhetoric and logic. An inquiry into the nature and function of imagery and a corrective evaluation of twentieth-century critical approaches to Renaissance poetry. Many of the so-called unorthodox and new qualities of metaphysical poetry are viewed as much less novel than many contemporary critics suggest and are seen as part of a large and consistent tradition. Mentions Herbert throughout, primarily as a vehicle for explaining generic critical points. See especially pp. 217–20, 225, 303, and apps. L, O.

◄§ 280. WASSERMAN, EARL R. *Elizabethan Poetry in the Eighteenth Century.* Illinois Studies in Language and Literature, vol. 32, no. 3. Urbana: University of Illinois Press. 291p.

Comments on various eighteenth-century revisions of Herbert's "Vertue," especially one found in *Universal Harmony* (1745), in which the poem is so "thoroughly refashioned to Augustan taste that it becomes a praise, not of the virtuous soul, but of wedded love" (p. 180) and one in the *Universal Magazine* (83 [1788]: 159) by W. H. Reid who "removes the metaphysical wit, and turning Herbert's theme upside down, concludes with a *carpe diem*" (p. 180). Calls these adaptations of Herbert "the most astonishing revisions of a pre-Restoration poem" (p. 179).

1948

◄§ 281. ADDLESHAW, G. W. O., and ETCHELLS, FREDERICK. *The Architectural Setting of Anglican Worship: An Inquiry into the arrangement for Public Worship in the Church of England from the Reformation to the present day.* London: Faber and Faber. 288p.

Brief comments on various architectural features of the church at Leighton Bromswold, Huntingdonshire, which Herbert helped restore. Suggests that Herbert "set the fashion of making both reading pew and pulpit the same height and size" (p. 76), thus emphasizing the equal importance of preaching and prayer. Comments also on the positioning of the reading pew in the church (facing the congregation). Plan of the church at Leighton Bromswold (p. 79).

◄§ 282. BETHELL, S. L. "Two Streams from Helicon." In *Essays on Literary Criticism and the English Tradition*, pp. 53–87. London: Dennis Dobson.

Contrasts two principal traditions in English poetry, one represented by Shakespeare and Donne and the other by Spenser, Milton, and Tennyson. Contrasts the uses of language, rhythms, imagery, and subject matter in each tradition and challenges F. R. Leavis and the *Scrutiny* critics for their assumptions about the superiority of the first group. Points out briefly Herbert's use of proverbial phrases and folk idioms. Claims that Herbert "owes nothing directly to mediaeval writers and little to the contemporary ballad, but as a conscientious parson he was familiar with the way his parishioners thought and spoke; from his prose treatise, A *Priest to the Temple,* we know how he studied the rural mind in order to be 'understanded of the people' and it is this which is reflected in his verse" (p. 66). Suggests that there is no trace of folk tradition in Donne, Crashaw, Vaughan, or Marvell. (First published in *New English Weekly* during the winter and spring of 1945–1946.)

283. CLARKE, GEORGE HERBERT. "Christ and the English Poets." QQ 55:292–307.
Comments on Herbert's deep, personal feelings for Christ as expressed in his poetry and praises his excellences as a writer of hymns.

284. FREEMAN, ROSEMARY. *English Emblem Books.* London: Chatto and Windus. xiv, 256p.
Reprinted, 1967.
Broad study of the emblem book in the sixteenth and seventeenth centuries. Chapter 6, "George Herbert" (pp. 148–72), is a revised and expanded form of "George Herbert and the Emblem Books," entry 221. In this chapter the author attempts "to work out the relation of the poetry of George Herbert to the fashion, since, apart from some poems in which even the material of the emblem books is used, there is much in his writing that is generally emblematic, and the conventions seem to provide an approach by which his real merits can be estimated and in which his peculiarities appear natural" (p. 7). Argues that Herbert transformed the emblem into poetry of the first order: "It is only in the ordered and controlled treatment of George Herbert that the potentialities of the convention for the expression of devotional and psychological themes were fully realised" (p. 147). Suggests, "To apply the same method to the work of other metaphysical poets would be lacking in a sense of perspective: for, although the emblem books were at hand for any writer to draw upon, Herbert's poetry is primarily and consistently emblematic where theirs is only spasmodically so" (p. 7). Compares Herbert briefly with Spenser, Christopher Harvey, and Bunyan.

285. FUSON, BENJAMIN WILLIS. *Browning and His English Predecessors in the Dramatic Monolog.* State University of Iowa Humanistic Studies, edited by Franklin H. Potter, vol. 8. Iowa City: State University of Iowa. 96p.
Comments briefly on how the metaphysical poets' handling of emotional shifts in their subjective religious monologues was in effect an

adaptation of Donne. Suggests that Herbert's "only overt objective monolog is the formalized but moving plaint of Jesus in the *quia amore langueo*
tradition, 'The Sacrifice' " (p. 59, n. 131). Points out also certain dramatic shifts in mood and tone to be found in "Affliction," "Dialogue,"
"Assurance," "A Parodie," and "Conscience."

◄§ 286. HUSAIN, ITRAT. *The Mystical Element in the Metaphysical Poets
   of the Seventeenth Century*. With a Foreword by Evelyn Under-
   hill. Edinburgh and London: Oliver and Boyd. 351p.

   Contains an introduction on the general characteristics of mysticism,
followed by individual studies of Donne, Herbert, Crashaw, Henry and
Thomas Vaughan, and Traherne. Attempts "to establish the amount of
personal spiritual experience which lies behind the work of these poets"
(foreword). Tries "to estimate the *content* of the religious thought of
these poets in order to determine the nature and significance of the mystical element in their poetry" (p. 13). Chapter 3, "The Mystical Element
in the Poetry of George Herbert" (pp. 120–58), surveys Herbert's religious attitudes and personal sensibilities. Points out the main concerns of Herbert's verse: personal sin and the problems of sin, salvation,
and grace. Comments on Herbert's love of Christ, the Church, the Bible,
and music. Stresses the specifically Anglican dimension of his theology
and piety. Divides Herbert's religious life into two main divisions: (1)
awakening of the self and purgation, and (2) illumination. Suggests
that the higher levels of the mystical life (the dark night of the soul and
the unitive experience) are not found in Herbert's poetry. "Though he
has not the intensity and passion of a great mystic, his poetry is rich in
mystical content. He is the poet who has known God and has felt the
peace and joy of His presence and also the pain and agony of His absence
in a manner peculiar to the mystics, and he has communicated his experience to us with the complexity and richness characteristic of a sensitive
and sincere artist" (p. 158).

◄§ 287. MILES, JOSEPHINE. *The Primary Language of Poetry in the
   1640's*. University of California Publications in English, vol. 19, no.
   1. Berkeley and Los Angeles: University of California Press; London: Cambridge University Press. 160p.

   Incorporated into *The Continuity of Poetic Language: Studies in
English Poetry from the 1540's to the 1940's* (Berkeley and Los Angeles:
University of California Press; London: Cambridge University Press,
1951).

   Distinguishes the major poetic vocabularly of the 1640s from the
language that preceded and followed it. Although there is no extended
discussion of Herbert, he is mentioned in several places. Descriptive
evaluations of the vocabulary of Donne and other metaphysical poets,
and a discussion of Donne's influence on the vocabulary of his followers.

✍§ 288. Mims, Edwin. "George Herbert: Holy Shepherd." In *The Christ of the Poets*, pp. 65–75. New York and Nashville: Abingdon-Cokesbury Press.

Reprinted, Ann Arbor: University Microfilms, 1970.

Discusses various attitudes toward Christ expressed by poets from Spenser to certain modern American Negro poets. Biographical sketch of Herbert. Comments on Herbert's devotional life and piety as reflected in *The Temple*, noting that "of the 169 poems that make up the volume, fully one half suggest some aspect of the Saviour's life or some evidence of his actual presence" (p. 70). Compares Herbert briefly with Donne.

✍§ 289. O'Connor, William Van. "The Influence of the Metaphysicals on Modern Poetry." *CE* 9:180–87.

In revised form, this essay appears in *Sense and Sensibility in Modern Poetry* (Chicago: University of Chicago Press, 1948), pp. 81–92.

Surveys the importance and the extent of the modern revival of interest in seventeenth-century metaphysical poetry, especially the poetry of Donne, and comments on the influence of this renewed interest on the poetry of certain modern poets, especially Eliot, Stevens, Yeats, Aiken, Edith Sitwell, the Fugitive Poets, Robert Lowell, and Elinor Wylie. No specific mention of Herbert but a number of references by implication.

1949

✍§ 290. Boase, Alan M. "Poètes Anglais et Français de l'Époque Baroque." *RSH* 55–56:155–84.

Suggests that there is a poetry comparable to English metaphysical poetry in France during the late sixteenth and early seventeenth centuries. Uses Donne primarily as the touchstone of the comparison. Briefly comments on similarities in tone between Herbert's "Even-song" and Agrippa d'Aubigne's "Prière du Soir."

✍§ 291. Cropper, Margaret. "George Herbert." In *Flame Touches Flame*, pp. 1–28. London, New York, Toronto: Longmans, Green and Co.

Presents Herbert as an Anglican saint. An idealized biographical sketch that uses the poems as autobiographical records of Herbert's religious experience and sensibility. Calls *The Country Parson* "one of the foundation books of the life of the parish priest in our communion, and when it was published after Herbert's death it became one of the formative books of the next period" (p. 14).

✍§ 292. Gibbs, J. "An Unknown Poem of George Herbert." *TLS*, 30 December, p. 857.

Reproduces a heretofore unknown Latin poem ("Perigrinis Almam

Matrem invisentibus") written in Herbert's script and found in a copy of the 1620 edition of the works of James I. The first two lines of the poem (with minor revisions) are found on page 459 of F. E. Hutchinson's edition (entry 223).

◄§ 293. GREEN, JULIEN. *Journal: 1943–1945.* Paris: Librairie Plon. 234p.
Comments briefly on Herbert in two journal entries: (1) 25 May 1943, reflects on his reactions to rereading Herbert's poetry; calls it "la poésie en sourdine" (p. 38); (2) 16 October 1945, comments on "The Collar": "Je retrouve dans un poème de George Herbert tout l'essentiel de ma conversion, et même plusieurs détails très précis" (p. 241). States that Gide and he looked for the poem in the Oxford anthology and were unable to locate it.

◄§ 294. GROS, LÉON-GABRIEL. "Métaphysiques anglais, du raisonnement en poésie." *Cahiers du Sud* 293:3–30.
Critical preface to a group of translations into French of several seventeenth-century poems, including Herbert's "Vertue." Evaluates metaphysical poetry in terms of Eliot's criticism. Praises Herbert as "le meilleur des poètes religieux de l'Eglise Anglicane" and calls him "le plus fidèle des disciples de Donne" (p. 18). "Ses vers sont aussi durs que ceux de son maître, il abuse des images, mais c'est dans un langage simple et direct qu'il exprime les pensées les plus bizarres" (p. 18).

◄§ 295. HERBERT, GEORGE. *George Herbert's Country Parson: Selected Passages,* edited by G. M. Forbes. London: Faith Press; New York: Morehouse-Gorham Co. xiii, 56p.
Introduction (pp. vii–xii) is a general appreciative essay that stresses that *The Country Parson* is "an idealized seventeenth century portrait" (p. viii) that may have, nonetheless, a lesson for modern men who "have drifted away from the country to the more artificial 'civilization' of our towns" (p. xii). Herbert's "The Author to the Reader" (p. xiii); selected passages (pp. 1–54); index (pp. 55–56). No notes and no commentary.

◄§ 296. McADOO, H. R. *The Structure of Caroline Moral Theology.* London, New York, Toronto: Longmans, Green and Co. xii, 179p.
Attempts "to assemble and to analyse Caroline writing on moral theology with a view to producing a picture of the science as a whole during the period" (p. ix) and "to show that Anglicanism had a well-defined plan of approach to moral theology, clear-cut principles and a positive concept of the science as it should be" (p. x). Several references to Herbert, especially to the country parson's use of moral theology in *A Priest to the Temple* and Herbert's devotion to the liturgy and to the practice of catechizing. Chapter 6, "The Spiritual Life in the English Church,"

(pp. 138–72) presents an overall view of Anglican piety during the period. Bibliography.

◄§ 297. MURDOCK, KENNETH B. *Literature and Theology in Colonial New England.* Cambridge, Mass.: Harvard University Press. xi, 235p.

References to Herbert throughout. Points out that, unlike most other Anglican writers of the seventeenth century, Herbert was read by the Puritans in America "because he concentrated his work on what was for the Puritan the core of religious life—the direct relation of the individual to God" (p. 149). He appealed also because his imagery, compared with Donne's, was restrained and because "there are few of his lines that even a Puritan could consider dangerous in their appeal to man's vagrant passions" (p. 154). Contrasts Herbert's attitude toward wit, music, art, etc. with those of the Puritans: for Herbert "a poem or a piece of music, a witty sermon or an embroidered Communion cloth, might serve as a proper offering" (p. 24).

◄§ 298. ROBERTS, J. RUSSELL. "Emerson's Debt to the Seventeenth Century." *AL* 21:298–310.

Surveys the influence of the seventeenth century on Emerson. Points out that Herbert was Emerson's favorite metaphysical poet and suggests that reading Herbert influenced his own poetry. Notes that William Ellery Channing on one occasion mistook one of Emerson's poems for one by Herbert.

◄§ 299. TATE, ALLEN. "Johnson on the Metaphysicals." *KR* 11:112–30.

Reprinted in *The Forlorn Demon: Didactic and Critical Essays* (Chicago: Henry Regnery Co., 1953), pp. 112–30; *Collected Essays* (Denver: Alan Swallow, 1959), pp. 488–506.

Reconsiders Dr. Johnson's estimate of the metaphysical poets. In particular, develops a contrast in the use of figurative language, with Dr. Johnson and his critical assumptions on one side and the metaphysical poets on the other. No direct mention of Herbert.

1950

◄§ 300. ARMS, GEORGE, and KUNTZ, JOSEPH M. *Poetry Explication: A Checklist of Interpretations since 1925 of British and American Poems Past and Present.* New York: Swallow Press and William Morrow & Co. 187p.

Rev. ed. by Joseph Kuntz (Denver: Swallow Press, 1962).

Lists seventeen critical essays on Herbert's poems. The revised edition of 1962 lists thirty-one explications of Herbert's poems.

BENJAMIN, EDWIN B. "Herbert's 'Vertue.' " *Expl* 9:item 12.
ents on the structure of "Vertue," on the contrast built up be-
: first three stanzas of the poem and the last.

~§ 302. BULLETT, G. W. "Some Seventeenth-Century Poets." In *The English Mystics*, pp. 94–112. London: Michael Joseph.
Maintains that, although the poems of *The Temple* are expressions of sincerity and saintliness, they are not mystical. Says that Herbert's poems are "very unequal in merit, pious conceits and trivialities mingling or alternating with things of a freshness and beauty that silence criticism" (p. 102). Brief biographical sketch.

~§ 303. BUSH, DOUGLAS. "The New Science and the Seventeenth-Century Poets." In *Science and English Poetry: A Historical Sketch, 1590–1950*, pp. 27–50. New York: Oxford University Press.
Reprinted, Oxford University Paperback, 1967.
Brief comment on Herbert to show that he, like most writers of his time, was convinced of the "priority of religious and moral insight over knowledge of the external world" (p. 38). Although Herbert praised Bacon, he shows little interest in science per se.

~§ 304. DAICHES, DAVID, and CHARVAT, WILLIAM, eds. "The Seventeenth Century." In *Poems in English, 1530–1940*, pp. 53–121. Edited with critical and historical notes and essays. New York: Ronald Press Co.
General introduction to seventeenth-century poetry. Comments on Herbert's principal themes and major characteristics. Suggests that Herbert's metaphysical qualities "consist largely in the way he pushes his imagery to its logical conclusion, however far-fetched the 'conceit' that might result, and in his ability to take images from everyday life and play with them intellectually until they became impressive symbols of spiritual reality" (p. 55). Compares Herbert briefly to Crashaw, Donne, and Vaughan. Anthologizes four of Herbert's poems (pp. 73–76) with notes (pp. 660–61).

~§ 305. EMPSON, WILLIAM. "George Herbert and Miss Tuve." *KR* 12:735–38.
A reply to Rosemond Tuve's disagreement (entry 310) with the author's interpretation of "The Sacrifice" in *Seven Types of Ambiguity*. While agreeing with some of Tuve's objections, Empson concludes that he "cannot feel that the mass of erudition she brings down like a steam hammer really cracks any nuts" (p. 735). Agrees with Tuve that a critic should not create an entirely new poem by his reinterpretation of it and that he "should entirely concentrate on how the poem was meant to take

effect by its author and did take effect on its first readers" (p. 738). "But," he adds, "this formula includes the way in which it took effect on them without their knowing it, and that opens an Aladdin's Cave of a positively limestone extent and complexity" (p. 738).

⟨§ 306. KEAST, WILLIAM R. "Johnson's Criticism of the Metaphysical Poets." *ELH* 17:59–70.
Reprinted in *Essential Articles for the Study of John Donne's Poetry*, edited by John R. Roberts (Hamden, Conn.: Archon Books, 1975), pp. 11–19.
Reevaluates Johnson's criticism of the metaphysical poets in an attempt to determine "how far our disappointment with Johnson's treatment of the metaphysical poets reflects genuine deficiencies in Johnson and how far it reflects merely our own present conviction that Donne is a greater poet than, say Gray or even Milton" (pp. 59–60), and to determine how much of our disagreement with Johnson simply reflects "our preferences for a critical theory that specializes in detailed accounts of metaphorical structure to one that emphasizes the general condition of literary pleasure" (p. 60). Argues that given Johnson's assumptions and premises about the nature and function of poetry his censure of metaphysical poetry is understandable and just. Points out that Johnson developed no comprehensive literary theory but applied his taste and judgment to individual writers. Suggests that Johnson's comments on the metaphysicals can be more readily put into a proper perspective if one reads his *Life of Cowley* "in relation to the *Rambler*, the *Preface to Shakespeare*, and the other *Lives*" (p. 61). No specific mention of Herbert.

⟨§ 307. MAHOOD, M. M. *Poetry and Humanism.* New Haven: Yale University Press. 335p.
Reprinted, Port Washington, N.Y.: Kennikat Press, 1967; New York: W. W. Norton, 1970.
Herbert is mentioned frequently in this study of Christian humanism and the arts. In "Two Anglican Poets" (pp. 22–53) the author compares and contrasts Herbert with Christina Rossetti. Shows Herbert's influence and comments on her imitation of him, especially in "Sweet Death." Comments on Herbert's "theocentric assurance of faith," the bravado and audacity in his poetry, his ability to invent parable and to convey a sense of play, and his uses of the emblem and Petrarchan traditions. Discusses Herbert's "acceptance of the human condition as one of tension" (p. 31) and illustrates the point by discussing "The Temper (I)," "The Flower," and "The Pulley." Mentions the importance of certain philosophical notions in Herbert's verse, such as The Great Chain of Being, the idea of correspondences, and cosmic harmony. Throughout compares Herbert with Vaughan, Donne, and Milton.

ß. Nicolson, Marjorie Hope. *The Breaking of the Circle: Studies ı the Effect of the "New Science" Upon Seventeenth Century Poetry*. Evanston: Northwestern University Press. xxii, 193p. Rev. ed., New York: Columbia University Press, 1960.

Many references to Herbert in this study of the impact of the New Science on the literary imagination of the seventeenth century. Points out that, with the encroachment of a mechanistic view of the world, the cosmological metaphors (especially the circle) that grew out of an earlier world view ceased to have the force of actuality and became more similes. Uses Herbert's verse primarily to illustrate the world view commonly held before the introduction of the New Science. Suggests that Herbert, perhaps more than any other religious poet of the period, "taught the happiness of limitation and restraint" (p. 156) and that thus his works "might be called that word reiterated in so many of them—'Content' " (p. 156). Unlike many of his time, Herbert "put aside the restlessness of the too-inquiring mind" and "discovered the truly 'vast' things with which man need concern himself" (p. 157). Points out, for example, that Herbert, although he knew both the old and new astronomy, was not particularly stirred by it. For him, "The world and the universe might be threatened by scientists and philosophers, the circles broken, but man was all symmetry" (p. 159). Argues that Herbert "found shelter from the incomprehensible universe in faith" (p. 160).

◄§ 309. Symes, Gordon. "The Paradoxes of Poetry." *English* (London) 8:69–73.

Discusses "The Collar" as an example of the complex uses of Christian paradox. Suggests that the basic paradox of the poem is "the all-embracing fatherhood of God which extends as well to the rebellious as to the devout" (p. 72). A further paradox proceeds from this one: "There can be no freedom except in submission to God" (p. 72). Contrasts the poem with Francis Thompson's "The Hound of Heaven": "Thompson's effects are not those of paradox at all. The paradox stands outside the poem, to be accepted by the reader as a condition of his enjoying the poem. It does not grow *out* of the poem, as Herbert's does" (p. 73).

◄§ 310. Tuve, Rosemond. "On Herbert's 'Sacrifice.' " *KR* 12:51–75.

Challenges William Empson's treatment of "The Sacrifice" in *Seven Types of Ambiguity* and warns against the excesses and limitations of the "New Critics." Shows that Herbert's poem is not "original" (in Empson's sense of the word), "for its basic invention or structural situation, the sequence of ironies upon which it is built, the occurrence, setting and application of the refrain which binds it together, the very collocation of antitheses which make up the poem, are none of them

Herbert's" (p. 52). Points out that the poem "belongs with two inter-linked groups, both well-known, of medieval lyrics; both groups belong as does his poem to a larger group, the Complaints of Christ to his People, and all apparently have their spring in the liturgical office of Holy Week, most obviously (for one group) in the *Improperia* or Reproaches of Good Friday" (p. 52). Comments on various typological, legendary, and liturgical elements that inform the poem to show that when one reads it in the light of the tradition in which it was written "it takes on a richness, a depth, complexity and moving power" (p. 57) that cannot be had otherwise. For a more extended treatment, see Tuve, *A Reading of George Herbert*, entry 344. For a reply, see William Empson, entry 305.

⤳§ 311. WALLERSTEIN, RUTH. *Studies in Seventeenth-Century Poetic.*
  Madison: University of Wisconsin Press. x, 421p.
 Several references to Herbert but no extended treatment. Comments briefly on Herbert's use of the emblem tradition and compares him with Marvell: "*On a Drop of Dew* and *The Coronet* remind us of the work of George Herbert, whose poems like *The Collar* they closely re-semble in their religious motif, in their treatment of image, and in metrical structure" (p. 162). Suggests that Herbert helps in understand-ing the religious feeling of Marvell's *Appleton House* (pp. 303–5) and points out that Herbert's "Constancie" was "surely one germ of Words-worth's *Character of a Happy Warrior*" (p. 261).

⤳§ 312. WEDGWOOD, C. V. *Seventeenth-Century English Literature.*
  Home University Library of Modern Knowledge, 218. London:
  Geoffrey Cumberlege and Oxford University Press. 186p.
 Reprinted, 1961, 1970.
 States that Herbert's poetry "has a serenity which is already beyond passion. For that reason he can never stir the emotions as Crashaw or Donne can stir them; but he can convey the still wonder of unperturbed devotion more truly than any other poet" (p. 83).

⤳§ 313. WIMSATT, W. K., JR. "Verbal Style: Logical and Counterlogi-
  cal." *PMLA* 65:5–20.
 Reprinted in *The Verbal Icon: Studies in the Meaning of Poetry* (Lexington: University of Kentucky Press, 1954), pp. 201–17.
 A study of verbal style in order "to correlate certain areas which have been noticed separately by earlier criticism: certain prose figures or merits defined in classical rhetoric, certain logical faults of prose, espe-cially as defined by H. W. Fowler in his *Modern English Usage*, and certain poetic figures defined both by classical rhetoric and by recent semantic criticism" (p. 5). Discusses the pun as a "fully developed coun-

terlogical figure" (p. 11) and comments specifically on Herbert's use of the pun *son-sun* in "The Sonne" and the pun on *rest* in "The Pulley."

◄§ 314. ZITNER, SHELDON P. "Herbert's 'Jordan' Poems." *Expl* 9:item 11.

Comments on the symbolic possibilities of Herbert's title for his two Jordan poems. Finds in a book of emblems, *Emblemata et Epigrammata Miscellanea Selecta ex Stromatis Peripateticis*, gathered by Fayi and published in 1610 at Geneva, some Latin verses that contrast the purity of the Jordan with the vile landscape through which it flows. Sees a possible parallel between this symbol and Herbert's contrast between moral and secular poetry in the two poems.

1951

◄§ 315. BATESON, F. W. "Contributions to a Dictionary of Critical Terms. II. Dissociation of Sensibility." *EIC* 1:302–12.

Reprinted in *Essays in Critical Dissent* (Totowa, N.J.: Rowman and Littlefield, 1972), pp. 142–52; *Essential Articles for the Study of John Donne's Poetry*, edited by John R. Roberts (Hamden, Conn.: Archon Books, 1975), pp. 58–65.

Traces the development of T. S. Eliot's notion of "dissociation of sensibility" to the critical writings of Rémy de Gourmont, particularly his *Problème du Style* (1902), which provided Eliot "with a *framework* to which his own critical ideas and intuitions—even then incomparably profounder and more original than Gourmont's—were able to attach themselves" (p. 308). "What he has done . . . has been to transfer to the nation Gourmont's analysis of the mental processes of the individual. The unified sensibility that Gourmont found in Laforgue, Mr. Eliot finds in the England of the early seventeenth century" (p. 307). Points out certain inconsistencies in Eliot's uses of the term "dissociation of sensibility" and traces the evolution of Eliot's thinking. Concludes, "Its use today as a loose, honorific synonym for 'taste' and 'personality' can only be deprecated" (p. 312). For a reply by Eric Thompson, see entry 343; for Bateson's reply to Thompson, see entry 329.

◄§ 316. BETHELL, S. L. *The Cultural Revolution of the Seventeenth Century*. London: Dennis Dobson. 161p.

Reprinted, 1963.

Divided into two parts: (1) a discussion of the concept of dissociation of sensibility, especially as it relates to certain theological questions, and (2) a study of Vaughan. Mentions Herbert throughout. Comments briefly on such matters as Herbert's possible assistance in translating Bacon's *Advancement* into Latin, his uses of the conceit, his influence on Vaughan, his hymns, and his Welsh background. Compares Herbert with Crashaw, Donne, and Vaughan.

◄§ 317. BICKHAM, JACK M. "Herbert's 'The Collar.' " *Expl* 10:item 17.
In part a reply to Dan Norton, entry 259. Points out the triple verbal
pun in the title of the poem—collar, choler, caller. Suggests that Herbert
is choleric about the collar "only until he hears the voice of the *caller*,
God"; thus, "the *caller* is more important in end effect than is the symbolic 'collar' or the mood of 'choler.' "

◄§ 318. BLACKBURN, WILLIAM. "Lady Magdalen Herbert and Her Son
George." *SAQ* 50:378–88.
Presents a biographical sketch of Herbert and his mother and outlines their relationship. Suggests that, as a result of his mother's constant supervision, Herbert's personal life and his poetry reflect a feeling of
dependence. Maintains that a constant theme in Herbert's poetry is "the
dependence of the soul on God, though some of his most poignant poems,
such for example as 'The Collar,' show him in rebellion against God's
discipline—just as indeed the child is often in rebellion against the discipline of the parent. The figure is eloquent of Herbert's concept of religion: religion is a state of being tied to God—even as a child is tied to
its mother's apron string" (p. 388).

◄§ 319. BROWER, REUBEN ARTHUR. *The Fields of Light: An Experiment
in Creative Reading.* New York: Oxford University Press. xii, 218p.
Reprinted as a Galaxy Book, 1962.
Reprinted in part in *Perspectives on Poetry*, edited by James L. Calderwood and Harold E. Toliver (New York: Oxford University Press, 1968),
pp. 98–108.
Attempts "to demonstrate some methods of reading analysis and to
use them in discovering designs of imaginative organization in particular
poems, plays, and novels" (p. xi). In discussing tonal patterns, the author comments on Herbert's "Love (III)" (pp. 27–31), discussing primarily its "trio of tones—the reserved decently colloquial manner of the
narrator and within the story the intimate deprecatory voice of the guest
and the exquisite politeness and assurance of the host" (p. 29). Shows
that in the poem "the gentle resolution of a deep conflict is expressed
through a contrast between tones and the implied inner action of the
drama" (p. 31). In discussing basic methods for interpreting metaphor,
the author comments on "The Windows" (pp. 44–48) and presents a
detailed diagram of the poem's metaphorical design. In a section on
sound, the author uses the third stanza of "The Windows" to illustrate
his point (pp. 59–61).

◄§ 320. EMPSON, WILLIAM. *The Structure of Complex Words.* London:
Chatto & Windus. 451p.
Contains an explication of stanza 3 of "Jordan (I)" (p. 188). Shows

how the stanza "gets its play from pastoral sentiment and patronage" (p. 188).

◈§ 321. HERBERT, GEORGE. Four Poems of Herbert. Translated by Joseph H. Summers. *Quarterly Review of Literature* 6:211–12.

Translation of four of Herbert's Latin poems into English: (1) "In Angelos" from *Lucus* ("The Angels"), (2) "Horti, deliciae *Dominae*" from *Memoriae Matris Sacrum* ("The Gardens: to the Memory of Magdalen Herbert"), (3) "Homo, Statua" from *Lucus* ("Man, the Statue"), and (4) "Patria" from *Lucus* ("Homeland").

◈§ 322. PRAZ, MARIO. "The Critical Importance of the Revived Interest in Seventeenth-Century Metaphysical Poetry." In *English Studies Today*, edited by C. L. Wrenn and G. Bullough, pp. 158–66. London: Oxford University Press.

Reprinted in *Essential Articles for the Study of John Donne's Poetry*, edited by John R. Roberts (Hamden, Conn.: Archon Books, 1975), pp. 3–10.

Maintains that the revival of interest in the metaphysical poets, especially Donne, in the twentieth century "has not only resulted in a change of perspective in literary criticism, but has also furthered the reaction against the critical standards and poetic theory of romanticism: Donne, we may say without fear of exaggeration, has had in the last thirty years a catalytic function" (p. 166). Argues that the revaluation of the metaphysical poets "has been more than a literary fashion, has resulted not only in the adoption of certain images, in the cult of certain conceits and imaginative processes: it has rather amounted to the awareness of a similar disposition of spirit, of the same complexity in facing life, of the same ironical reaction" (p. 163). Outlines T. S. Eliot's key role in this process. No specific mention of Herbert.

◈§ 323. SILVER, LOUIS H. "The First Edition of Walton's *Life of Herbert*." HLB 5:371–72.

Presents a collation of the complete first edition of Walton's *Life of Herbert* (1670) as it left the printer. Accounts for the two title pages involved.

◈§ 324. SMITH, HAROLD WENDALL. " 'The Dissociation of Sensibility.' " *Scrutiny* 18:175–88.

Reexamines Eliot's theory and suggests that the split between thought and feeling can be traced to its social and religious roots. Argues that Eliot's evaluation of Donne and the metaphysicals was in effect an effort to canonize his own tastes and reflects the tensions of his own sensibility. By the time of the metaphysicals, "The two realms of abstract and sensible had already been divided; it was in the distance which separated them that the 'metaphysician' worked between them, and Eliot's very term 'unification' implies both elements must have been clearly distinguishable and in need of being utterly fused into one" (p. 178). No specific disscussion of Herbert.

◄§ 325. SUMMERS, JOSEPH H. "Herbert's Form." *PMLA* 66:1055–72.
Reprinted in *George Herbert: His Religion and Art* (entry 369), pp. 73–94.
Discusses Herbert's attitude toward form and order in religion and art. Suggests that Herbert saw the ritual of the Church as a means of achieving a state of grace: "If every aspect of it was understood, it could teach the way of salvation and the beautiful pattern of God's creation. Proper worship resulted in an ethical and spiritual ordering of the worshipper's life" (p. 1057). From this notion follows Herbert's concept (perhaps derived in part from St. Augustine) that a work of art should reflect the divine pattern of creation and that "an unethical life or poem by definition represented that lack of order called 'ugly' or 'evil'—not a positive quality, but an absence of the good and beautiful" (p. 1058). Discusses Herbert's hieroglyphic view of the world and experience and comments on his uses of typology and emblems in his poetry. Maintains that for Herbert poetry was an act of worship and/or of edification, not direct autobiographical revelation or mere self-expression. Suggests that the title, *The Temple*, is a symbol "for all the types of order in the universe, both God's and man's" (p. 1065). *The Temple* is "the symbolic record, written by a poet, of a 'typical' Christian life within the Church" (p. 1066). Discusses in particular "The Collar" as "one of Herbert's most deliberate ventures in 'hicroglyphic form' " (p. 1069); the poem, a formalized picture of chaos, reflects in its form the disordered life of self-will. Thus, for Herbert, the composition of poems "was the act of the craftsman who shapes the imperfect materials of his own suffering as well as joy into a pattern symbolic of the divine order" (p. 1072).

◄§ 326. VAN DOREN, MARK. *Introduction to Poetry: Commentaries on Thirty Poems*. New York: William Sloane Associates. xxviii, 568p.
Reprinted, 1962, 1966; New York: Hill and Wang, 1968.
Explication of "The Flower" (pp. 69–73). Discusses theme, stanzaic intricacies, uses of sound and metaphor, and tone.

1952

◄§ 327. BAKER, HERSCHEL. *The Wars of Truth: Studies in the Decay of Christian Humanism in the Earlier Seventeenth Century*. Cambridge, Mass.: Harvard University Press. xi, 390p.
Examines "the traditional and the emerging concepts of 'truth'—theological, scientific, political, and other—whose collision generated such

heat and even light in the age of Milton" (p. vii). The author adds, "Yet in attempting to seek out the origin of this transformation in the early Renaissance and to sketch the progress through the earlier seventeenth century I have sought to indicate the intellectual and emotional pressures which shaped men's conception of 'truth' and of their capacity to attain it, and to suggest some of the consequences for literature" (p. vii). Several references to Herbert that clearly place him within the intellectual framework of his time. Comments on Herbert's conception of Providence and on his love for tradition and for the Anglican establishment. Shows that both Donne and Herbert stayed rather closely within the ecclesiastical tradition.

◄§ 328. BARUCH, FRANKLIN R. "Donne and Herbert." *TLS*, 30 May, p. 361.

Points out that in *The Church-Porch* (stanza 14) Herbert appropriates line 30 from Donne's "To Mr Tilman after he had taken orders." For a reply, see J. B. Leishman, entry 338.

◄§ 329. BATESON, F. W. "The Critical Forum: 'Dissociation of Sensibility.' " *EIC* 2:213–14.

Reply to Eric Thompson (entry 343), who challenges Bateson's attack on the notion of "dissociation of sensibility" (entry 315). Insists, "However much we dress it up, the Dissociation of Sensibility cannot be made respectable. It's a lovely mouthful, full of sound and fury, but unfortunately it doesn't signify anything" (p. 214).

◄§ 330. BOTTRALL, MARGARET. "George Herbert and 'The Country Parson.' " *Listener* 47:558–59.

General appreciative comments about *The Country Parson*. Places the work within a seventeenth-century context and suggests that, although the book is not autobiographical and is instead Herbert's conception of the life of the ideal parson (somewhat like a seventeenth-century character essay), Herbert indirectly reveals much about himself in it: "Only a man who loved pastoral work could have written of it so understandingly" (p. 559). Sees *The Country Parson* as an important document of social history and also as an important commentary on Herbert's poetry.

◄§ 331. BUSH, DOUGLAS. *English Poetry: The Main Currents from Chaucer to the Present*. London: Methuen; New York: Oxford University Press. ix, 222p.

General critical commentary on Herbert's poetry. Says, "The poetry of Herbert is a record of religious experience more central and comprehensive, and more humble, than Donne's" (p. 60). Comments on Herbert's use of the emblematic technique: "Whatever their themes and manner and length, Herbert's best poems are organized wholes. Usually his battles are fought under our eyes, and the issue may be in doubt, yet every image, line, and phrase contributes to the developing pattern; there is no fumbling or rambling" (p. 62).

⊷§ 332. CAZAMIAN, LOUIS. *The Development of English Humor.* 2 parts. Durham: Duke University Press. viii, 421p.

Studies the development of English humor from the Old English period through the Renaissance. Maintains that Herbert, as well as such religious poets as Crashaw, Vaughan, Lord Herbert, and Traherne, are humorless poets: "The devout seriousness of their purpose precludes the possibility of a half-conscious element of intentional grotesqueness in their manner" (p. 365, n. 1). Suggests that "their conceits do not lend themselves to any suspicion of double meaning" (p. 388).

⊷§ 333. D[AVENPORT], A[RNOLD]. "Five Notes on George Herbert." N&Q 197:420–22.

Corrections or supplements to F. E. Hutchinson's commentary on five difficult passages in *The Works of George Herbert* (entry 223): (1) *The Church-Porch* (stanza 33). Points out that the word *cracked* in the seventeenth century had the special meaning of *bankrupt.* Thus, Herbert is saying: "If you play for higher stakes than you can afford you will go bankrupt; your wife and children will be impoverished; your servants will be turned off; and at length your ancestral name will survive only in the armorial window of the family chapel in the parish church, of interest to antiquarians, but no longer important as a name of a prominent family" (p. 421). (2) "Superliminare." Argues that the two quatrains should be regarded as two parts of one poem and that Herbert's quatrains correspond to the two parts of the Sybil's speech in the *Aeneid* (6.258 ff.). (3) "The Sacrifice" (lines 121–23). Suggests that Herbert is referring to Exodus 17. Herbert has Christ saying: "I am accused of calling myself king of the Jews, but the people rejected me and say that Caesar is their sole King: it was Caesar, forsooth! who cleft the rock in Horeb, when, as now, the people denied my Lordship and my presence. I cleft the rock for them then, and I pour out my blood for them now, but neither then nor now have I touched their hearts" (p. 421). (4) "The Quidditie" (line 12): "I am with thee, and *most take all.*" The phrase is a gambling phrase. Herbert is saying "that worldly people value this or that for the pleasure, honour, profit, etc. it provides, and scorn poetry as deficient in these ways; but he himself when writing his religious poetry is 'with God' and in that communion finds that he far surpasses the worldly in his possession of the very things they value, in pleasure, honour, profit, etc. In any competition with them he 'scoops the pool' " (p. 422). Sees three possible interpretations of the title of the poem. (5) "The Jews" (lines 5–6): "Who by not keeping once, became a debter;/ And now by keeping lose the letter." Herbert is saying: "The Jews, who, in the person of

Adam, by not keeping the one commandment, became sinners . . . and had to be reinstated and controlled by Mosaic Law . . . , and now, by keeping to the Mosaic Law, losing Christ who lets us lose both from the sin of Adam and from subservience to the letter of the old law" (p. 422).

◄§ 334. DEUTSCH, BABETTE. "Wars and Rumors of Wars." In *Poetry in Our Time*, pp. 348–77. New York: Henry Holt and Co.

Comments briefly on Herbert's influence on Louis MacNeice, especially the echoes from Herbert's "Sighs and Grones" in "Prayer Before Birth" (pp. 364–67).

◄§ 335. ELDREDGE, FRANCES. "Herbert's 'Jordan.'" *Expl* 11:item 3.

Suggests that Herbert's title "Jordan" refers primarily to the sacrament of baptism: "The Christian sacrament of baptism, with its significance of spiritual cleansing, regeneration, and consecration to the Christian vision, was the essential connotation . . . in the concept 'Jordan.'" In the two poems Herbert is "seeking regeneration and consecrating his talents to the highest service he knew."

◄§ 336. GARDNER, HELEN. "Appendix G: Donne's Latin Poem to Herbert and Herbert's Reply." In *John Donne: The Divine Poems*, edited with introduction and commentary by Helen Gardner, pp. 138–47. Oxford: Clarendon Press.

Discusses the date of Donne's Latin poem to Herbert (probably January 1615), its title and setting in both the 1650 edition of Donne's poems and in Walton's *Life* (1658), and the nature of Herbert's Latin and English verses printed with it. Argues that Herbert's verses do not form one poem but are separate verses written at different times.

◄§ 337. HOWELL, A. C. "Christopher Harvey's *The Synagogue* (1640)." *SP* 49:229–47.

Points out that the title page of the first edition of Harvey's *The Synagogue* closely resembles that of *The Temple*, which it obviously imitates; it was also frequently bound with *The Temple*. Philemon Stephens, "the enterprising seller of theological and devotional books, saw the possibility of bringing together these two volumes of verse as a good money-making proposition. And so his shop, the Gilded Lion, became the headquarters for Herbert's and Harvey's poems, inseparable for 200 years after 1650" (p. 232). Shows that "not until the appearance of a volume edited by R. Edwards . . . in 1806 did Herbert's *The Temple* appear in an edition separate from *The Synagogue*" (p. 233). Comments on how *The Synagogue* was both an imitation of *The Temple* and was also intended to supplement it.

⋘§ 338. LEISHMAN, J. B. "Donne and Herbert." *TLS*, 13 June, p. 391.
Reply to Franklin Baruch, entry 328. Points out that not only did F. E.
Hutchinson in his edition of Herbert (entry 223) note that line 30 of
Donne's "To Mr Tilman after he had taken orders" appear in stanza 14
of Herbert's *The Church-Porch*, but also that it appears, slightly revised,
in *The Country Parson*.

⋘§ 339. MAZZEO, JOSEPH ANTHONY. "A Critique of Some Modern Theo-
     ries of Metaphysical Poetry." *MP* 50:88–96.
Reprinted in *Seventeenth Century English Poetry: Modern Essays in
Criticism*, edited by William Keast (entry 480), pp. 63–74, rev. ed. (en-
try 707), pp. 77–88; *Discussions of John Donne*, edited by Frank Kermode
(Boston: D. C. Heath & Co., 1962), pp. 118–25; *John Donne's Poetry:
Authoritative Texts, Criticism*, edited by A. L. Clements (New York:
W. W. Norton & Co., 1966), pp. 134–43.
Comments on several modern theories about the nature of metaphysical poetry, such as the idea that metaphysical poetry is a decadent, exaggerated use of the Petrarchan and troubadour tradition; is best accounted
for by the influence of Ramist logic; is closely allied to the baroque; or is
closely related to the emblem tradition. Approaching the problem from
the perspective of sixteenth- and seventeenth-century theorists, especially
Giordano Bruno, Baltasar Gracián, and Emmanuele Tesauro, the author
finds all modern theories wanting and at times inconsistent. Argues,
"The principle of universal analogy as a poetic, or the poetic of correspondences, offers . . . a theory of metaphysical poetry which is simpler, in
great harmony with the evidence, and freer from internal contradictions
than the major modern theories that have yet been formulated" (p. 89).
Points out that, according to the contemporary critics, "the conceit itself
is the expression of a correspondence which actually obtains between
objects and that, since the universe is a network of universal correspondences or analogies which unite all the apparently heterogeneous elements of experience, the most heterogeneous metaphors are justifiable.
Thus, the theorists of the conceit justify the predilection of the 'school
of wit' for recondite and apparently strained analogies by maintaining
that even the more violent couplings of dissimilars were simply expressions of the underlying unity of all things" (pp. 88–89). No specific references to Herbert.

⋘§ 340. RAIZISS, SONA. *The Metaphysical Passion: Seven Modern Amer-
     ican Poets and the Seventeenth-Century Tradition*. Philadelphia:
     University of Pennsylvania Press. xv, 327p.
Reprinted, Westport, Conn.: Greenwood Press, 1970.
Discusses the influence of, and the similarities between, the metaphysi-
cal poets of the seventeenth century and the work of certain modern

poets, especially T. S. Eliot, John Crowe Ransom, Allen Tate, Robert Penn Warren, Hart Crane, Elinor Wylie, and Archibald MacLeish. Argues, "If, from many of Donne's poems, we remove a seventeenth-century construction here and there and revert an inversion, we discover the experience and language of contemporary writing" (p. xiii). Part 1 (pp. 3–56) examines the temper of metaphysical poetry, its subject matter, methods, moods, and wit. Part 2 (pp. 59–164) discusses the sources of the metaphysical impulse, those tensions and conflicts that are parallel between the seventeenth and the twentieth centuries. Part 3 (pp. 167–241) discusses seven modern poets in the light of the preceding comments. Refers throughout to Herbert, primarily by way of illustration and comments briefly on some of his major themes and images, his uses of ambiguity and wit, etc. Sees the psychology of Herbert's poetry, as compared with Donne's, as "an apparently simpler and more direct kind" (p. 100). Briefly compares Herbert with Donne, Hopkins, Wylie, Eliot, Ransom, Anna Branch, Emily Dickinson, Emerson, MacLeish, and Samuel Greenberg.

◄§ 341. Ross, MALCOLM MACKENZIE. "Analogy and Metaphor: A Note on the Decline of the Metaphysical Style." *SCN* 10:13.

Summary of the argument that is more fully presented in *Poetry and Dogma: The Transformation of Eucharistic Symbols in Seventeenth Century English Poetry* (entry 368). Sees a direct relationship between the decline of metaphysical style and the ascendancy of certain radical revisions of dogma, especially the dogma of the Eucharist. Suggests, "In the Eucharistic poetry of the Catholic Anglicans the world of flesh is clearly cut off from the world of spirit." Points out that in Herbert's "The H. Communion" "all sense of the analogical *participation* of the natural order in the divine disappears" and that thus "in Herbert there is to be had the spectacle of analogical language dissolving into metaphor" (p. 13).

◄§ 342. SUMMERS, JOSEPH H. "Herbert's 'Trinitie Sunday.'" *Expl* 10: item 23.

Considers the poem, a prayer for Trinity Sunday, as one of Herbert's "most artful formal hieroglyphs." Points out the functional uses of the number *three* in the poem: "The poem is not merely a witty exercise in divine numerology: the ingenuity clarifies the central meaning." Close reading of each line of the poem.

◄§ 343. THOMPSON, ERIC. "The Critical Forum: 'Dissociation of Sensibility.'" *EIC* 2:207–13.

Challenges F. W. Bateson, entry 315. Suggests that Eliot's study of F. H. Bradley is central to understanding his concept of "dissociation of sensibility." For a reply by Bateson, see entry 329.

◄§ 344. TUVE, ROSEMOND. A *Reading of George Herbert.* Cl.
University of Chicago Press; London: Faber and Faber; Toronto:
W. J. Gage & Co. 215p.
Reprinted, 1965.
Prefatory notes (pp. 9–10) explain that, in references to modern positions on Herbert, these "sets of ideas cannot be equated with 'The New
Criticism', although most all of the 'New Critics' take some or all of the
positions discussed" (p. 9). Attempts "to show that criticism can be
richer and truer if it will remain willing to bring all methods to bear,
including those which scholarship can provide" (p. 10). Table of plates
(pp. 13–16). Part 1: " 'The Sacrifice' and Modern Criticism" (pp. 19–
99), portions of which were published previously (entry 310). Challenges
the critical presuppositions and attempts to repair the ignorance of many
modern critics. Suggests that the poem should "speak so far as possible in
its own voice" (p. 22), that "a poem is most beautiful and most meaningful to us when it is read in terms of the tradition which gave it birth"
(p. 22). Although the primary purpose is to read Herbert, a critical theory
emerges. Not only presents a detailed reading of "The Sacrifice" but
specifically points out the inadequacies of William Empson's reading of,
and his critical position on, the poem in *Seven Types of Ambiguity* (entry 108). Shows that although "The Sacrifice" is a great and original
poem, its "basic invention or structural situation, the sequences of ironies
upon which it is built, the occurrence, setting, and application of the refrain which bind it together, the very collocation of the antitheses which
make it up, are none of them Herbert's" (p. 24). Comments on the poetical, typological, iconographical, and liturgical conventions of the poem
in order to show that "much that is 'outside' a poem to us was well inside
it to our forefathers, and still is to some readers" (p. 27). Uses the poem
as a vehicle for criticizing the excesses of modern critics who fail to
combine scholarship with their criticism. Shows that Herbert's originality
must be seen in relation to the tradition and that thereby one is able
"to perceive with greater pleasure those leaps and those masterful ordering actions of the single human mind by which new relationships are
made and new unities created" (p. 79). Part 2 (pp. 103–203) contains
several subsections. In the introduction to part 2, the author announces
her intention to explain and illustrate a number of traditional symbols
in Herbert's verse and thereby to demonstrate "what characterizes writing
in the symbolic mode" (p. 103). Points out that, as a Christian poet,
Herbert "sees the world, both outside and inside himself; he sees it as a
web of significances not as a collection of phenomena which we may
either endow with significance or leave unendowed. He writes not of
events and facts, but of meanings" (pp. 103–4). (1) "Images as Language" (pp. 112–37) discusses the problem of figures and language by
considering a group of Herbert's poems that "use the set of conceits
clustered around the ancient symbol of Christ as the miraculous grape-

bunch which figured forth the inheritance of the Chosen People, crossing over Jordan to the Promised Land" (p. 112). Comments also on the
tradition of this Old Testament figure in the graphic arts. Comments on
such poems as "The Bunch of Grapes," "The Agonie," "Sion," "The
Bag," and "Good Friday" to show their typological and iconographical
antecedents. Proposes to show "that symbols are a language which enables poems to be permanently valid, and that if we will learn the language, which is in some cases an archaic and difficult one, we shall not
mistake the poet's tone of voice but accurately take his meanings even
across intervening centuries" (p. 134). (2) "Wit" (pp. 137–58) argues
that many of the details that to modern readers of Herbert seem most
novel and witty are "either outright conventions in traditional allegorical
materials, or take their spring from such inherited symbols" (p. 138).
Comments on such images as the gilded *tabernaculum* or box, the image
of man as God's music, the crucified Christ as a lyre, the devotional uses
of red and white, etc., in order to show that if "we approach them inno-
cent of their long use, traditional overtones, and serious fitness deriving
from long-familiar connexions, we not only outright lose shades of meaning but we destroy the delicacy and decorous justness of the tone" (p.
158). (3) "Explanation" (pp. 158–82) explains the iconographical conventions used in "Sunday," "Peace," "Church-rents and schisms," "Justice (II)," and "Whitsunday," which contain some apparently bizarre
figures according to certain modern readers but which were clear and
uneccentric to readers in Herbert's time. Discusses other poems that
would have demanded a great deal from Herbert's contemporaries, such
as the reference to "Joseph's coat" in "Church-musick." (4) "Jordan"
(pp. 182–203) discusses the two Jordan poems and maintains that "a better understanding of these two poems will illuminate some seven or eight
others whose interrelations are revealing, and the process will serve to
uncover basic elements in Herbert's poetic theory, which in turn are in-
extricable from his conceptions of the significance of human life" (p.
182). Three notes: (1) a note on the accessibility of materials used, to
the sixteenth- and seventeenth-century English reader (pp. 204–11); (2)
a note on conventions of quoting used in this book (pp. 211–13); and (3)
a note for students interested in certain types of texts (pp. 214–15).
Concludes by pointing out that the book, by design, does not have an
index because the author did not want it to be used as a "dictionary of
symbols or as a repertory of specific sources."

⋙ 345. WILEY, MARGARET L. "Postscript: The Despair of God." In
    *The Subtle Knot: Creative Skepticism in Seventeenth-Century
    England*, pp. 277–81. London: George Allen & Unwin.
    Comments briefly on Herbert's "The Sacrifice" as a poem that attempts
to reveal God's frustration in his attempts to break through man's rejec-

tion of his love and truth. Presents a hypothetical soliloquy by God, who examines his own despair at reaching man.

1953

᠅§ 346. BETHELL, S. L. "Gracián, Tesauro, and the Nature of Metaphysical Wit." *Northern Miscellany of Literary Criticism* 1:19–40.

Reprinted in *Discussions of John Donne*, edited by Frank Kermode (Boston: D. C. Heath & Co., 1962), pp. 136–49; *The Metaphysical Poets: A Selection of Critical Essays*, edited by Gerald Hammond (entry 783), pp. 129–56.

Agrees with Rosemond Tuve's position in *Elizabethan and Metaphysical Imagery: Renaissance Poetic and Twentieth-Century Critics* (entry 279) but attempts "to supplement and somewhat rectify her account of metaphysical poetry by means similar to her own, that is by going to contemporary theorists" (p. 20). Since early seventeenth-century England produced almost no theorists on the nature of wit, the author presents an account of metaphysical wit and of the nature of the conceit based primarily on a reading of Baltasar Gracián's *Agudeza y Arte de Ingenio* (1642) and Emmanuele Tesauro's *Il Cannocchiale Aristotelico* (1654). Suggests that both Gracián and Tesauro "are engaged with the wider functions of literary criticism, so what they have to say applies almost as much to English as to Spanish or Italian poetry" (p. 22). Maintains, "There is, of course, no suggestion that they are 'sources' of anything or 'influences' on anybody. But, coming as they do after Europe had been soaked for a half a century in metaphysical wit, we might expect them to articulate the methods by which poets and other writers had been perhaps only half-consciously working" (p. 22). No specific references to Herbert.

᠅§ 347. BORGERHOFF, E. B. O. " 'Mannerism' and 'Baroque': A Simple Plea." *CL* 5:323–31.

Explores the difficulty of using the terms *baroque* and *mannerism* in literary discussions, especially about French literature, yet maintains that, in spite of the controversial nature of the terms, both have a literary usefulness. No specific mention of Herbert, but Donne is cited as a mannerist poet.

᠅§ 348. BOULTON, MARJORIE. *The Anatomy of Poetry*. With an introduction by L. A. G. Strong. London: Routledge & Kegan Paul. xiii, 189p.

Brief comments on several individual poems of Herbert by way of illustrating the nature and function of poetry: "Redemption" (pp. 107–8), "Discipline" (pp. 109–10), "Love (III)" (pp. 130–31). Notes Herbert's uses of pattern poems (p. 12).

⊷§ 349. Burke, Kenneth. "On Covery, Re- and Dis-." *Accent* 13:218–26.

An assessment of Rosemond Tuve's position in *A Reading of George Herbert* (entry 344) that, in order to understand and appreciate Herbert, the reader must study and understand the cultural, linguistic, and religious traditions that the poems reflect, especially the liturgical and iconographical contexts. Contrasts this emphasis on "re-covery" of the past with the tendency of many modern critics to engage in "dis-covery," to find "new things about the workings of Herbert's mind by applying modern terms quite alien to his thinking" (p. 218). Argues that Tuve's conception of art is perhaps too narrow and that if one accepts her position too rigidly there are still left many "quandries that concern both 'psychological' and 'sociological' motives" (p. 226) but considers "these quandries as problems of 'knowledge' that works of art do not resolve for us, though they give us invaluable material for use in our search, a search over and above the delight that we can have if we read and ponder texts with the help of such able investigators as Miss Tuve" (p. 226).

⊷§ 350. Duncan, Joseph E. "The Revival of Metaphysical Poetry, 1872–1912." *PMLA* 68:658–71.

Reprinted in *Discussions of John Donne*, edited by Frank Kermode (Boston: D. C. Heath & Co., 1962), pp. 126–35. In revised form appears as chapter 4 of *The Revival of Metaphysical Poetry: The History of a Style, 1800 to the Present* (entry 429), pp. 113–29.

Suggests that Herbert J. C. Grierson's edition of Donne (1912) "marked the end of the first stage of the metaphysical revival" (p. 658) and that T. S. Eliot's essays "were not so much a new note as a sensitive formulation of ideas that had become familiar by 1912" (p. 658). Traces the ever-growing acceptance of metaphysical poetry from 1872 (Grosart's edition of Donne) to 1912. Although the essay is primarily concerned with the nineteenth-century fascination with Donne the man and surveys the background of Eliot's criticism of the metaphysicals, Herbert is mentioned in several places and the essay serves to illustrate the changing attitude toward all the metaphysical poets.

⊷§ 351. Knieger, Bernard. "Herbert's 'Redemption.'" *Expl* 11:item 24.

Paraphrases "Redemption" and suggests that in order to understand the sonnet fully one must understand "the significance of the act narrated in the last line." Suggests that the meaning of the poem is further complicated by Herbert's "dual use of chronological sequence." "It is as if in a moment of spiritual depression Herbert visualizes, in contemporary terms, the overwhelming sacrifice which permits his spiritual well-being, and which makes his own suffering seem petty indeed." Comments in some detail on the phrase *dearly bought*.

◆§ 352. LEACH, ELSIE A. "John Wesley's Use of George Herbert." *HLQ* 16:183–202.

Comments on the forty-nine adaptations of Herbert's poems made by John Wesley for inclusion in the various editions of his hymnal. Proposes "to suggest some reasons why Wesley's fondness for Herbert in spite of neo-classical hostility to the metaphysical poets and, in addition, to analyze in more detail than did Hutchinson [entry 168] the nature of the changes Wesley made in the *Temple* poems" (p. 184). Suggests that Wesley was particularly attracted to those poems of Herbert that celebrate the struggle of the inner life of the religious man and to those that emphasize eschatological or soteriological themes, especially those embued with a spirit of Arminianism: "Both the personal revelation and the Arminian themes would particularly appeal to Wesley, for they suited the evangelical fervor and the theology of Methodism" (p. 192). Shows how Wesley regularized the meter and the line and stanza lengths of Herbert's poems, how he simplified the thought and imagery, and how he often changed the tone and diction in order to reconcile eighteenth-century critical theory and taste with the emotional fervor of enthusiasm.

◆§ 353. MALLOCH, A. F. "The Unified Sensibility and Metaphysical Poetry." *CE* 15:95–101.

Attempts to limit more precisely the terms *unified sensibility* ("an epitome of all that is most cryptic and pretentious in modern criticism" [p. 95]) and *metaphysical poetry* and to indicate the relationship between the two. Concludes, "The relation of the unified sensibility to metaphysical poetry is the relation of poetic process to poetic technique. Certain techniques can validly be said to distinguish Donne, Herbert, Crashaw, and Marvell as a school (and there are significant differences within that school). The unification of sensibility, on the other hand, is a judgment on a poet's mode of creation, whatever the nature of his techniques" (pp. 100–101).

◆§ 354. MAZZEO, JOSEPH ANTHONY. "Metaphysical Poetry and the Poetic of Correspondence." *JHI* 14:221–34.

Discusses the revival of interest in the nature and function of metaphor among certain European critics and rhetoricians in the seventeenth century, especially Baltasar Gracián, Emmanuele Tesauro, Cardinal Sforza-Pallavicino, Pierfrancesco Minozzi, and Matteo Pellegrini, and concludes that these theorists "envisaged a poet's universe as a complex system of universal analogical relationships which the poet expressed and revealed" (p. 234). Suggests that such a universe "contained relationships which no longer exist for us; they have been eliminated from our perception by Baconianism and Cartesianism. What may seem to us strange and far-fetched similitudes were often truths, even commonplaces, in their world of insight" (p. 234). No specific references to Herbert.

≈§ 355. Mourgues, Odette de. *Metaphysical Baroque & Précieux Poetry*. Oxford: Clarendon Press. vii, 184p.

Compares French poets whom the author considers "metaphysical"— a term that she distinguishes from "baroque" and "précieux"—and certain late sixteenth- and early seventeenth-century English poets, including Herbert. Argues, "There exists in French poetry, not a metaphysical school, but a metaphysical 'line' beginning as early as 1544 with Scève's *Délie*, dodging the Pléiade, running in an underground way through scientific poetry, coming to the surface again at the end of the sixteenth century and giving its last scattered manifestations in some minor poets of the mid-seventeenth century" (p. 10). Shows how Herbert is metaphysical, not baroque. Briefly compares Herbert with Jean de La Ceppède.

≈§ 356. Noakes, Aubrey. "The Mother of George Herbert." *ContempR* 183:39–45.

Appreciative biographical sketch of Magdalen Herbert. Comments also on the life of George Herbert and Sir John Danvers. Includes a detailed description of Danvers's house.

≈§ 357. Perkins, David. "Johnson on Wit and Metaphysical Poetry." *ELH* 20:200–17.

Reevaluates Dr. Johnson's attitude toward metaphysical poetry, especially his *"favorable* approach to qualities—such as 'wit' and 'novelty' in the uses of imagery and language—that are now commonly associated with the 'metaphysical' style" (p. 201). Points out the value that Johnson places on "intellectual activity in the language of poetry" (p. 202) and on wit. Redefines Johnson's concept of wit. Points out that Johnson quotes Herbert seventy-eight times in the *Dictionary*. Although Johnson's admiration for the metaphysical poets was not complete nor without certain reservations, it was "strong enough, however, to make him the first critic to analyze and define them—in a sense, even to resurrect and justify them critically" (p. 217).

≈§ 358. Ross, Malcolm M. "A Note on the Metaphysicals." *HudR* 6: 106–13.

Discusses the decline of Christian poetic sensibility in the seventeenth century. Argues that the change can best be seen in "those Christian symbols which at one and the same time are rooted in dogma and which convey—or seek to convey—the immediate sense of existence" (p. 107). Comments on the breakdown of the Christian symbol from analogy to mere metaphor as a result of the reform of Christian dogma. Suggests that in Anglican poetry, such as Herbert's, "hovering precariously as it must between Catholic and Protestant symbol, that one is able to see most clearly a far-reaching crisis in the Christian aesthetic" (p. 107). Comments on Herbert's eucharistic theology as reflected in his poetry and shows that in these poems one can observe "analogical language dissolving into simple metaphor" (p. 111). Concludes that in Herbert, "metaphor succeeds analogy with the immediacy of a first echo—and with the poignant loveliness of something very near yet very far because irretrievable" (p. 112).

◆§ 359. THORNTON, ROBERT D. "Polyphiloprogenitive: The Sapient Stulers." *Anglican Theological Review* 35:28–36.
Comments on Herbert's views on preachers and preaching, especially on his concept of the Word. Argues that "The Windows" may be the primary impulse for T. S. Eliot's "Sunday Morning Service" and maintains that "no poem written in the more than three hundred years since 'The Windows' seems so close to Herbert's" (p. 30). Compares the two poems and compares Herbert's and Eliot's views on the Word: "Both emphasize the thought that no man can presume to be a Christian and certainly not presume to be a priest of God until he had learned of pride and humility. Furthermore, he cannot learn of these until he has gone back to the study of the Word" (p. 33).

1954

◆§ 360. AKRIGG, G. P. V. "George Herbert's 'Caller.'" *N&Q*, n.s. 1:17.
Suggests that since the major action of "The Collar" is the calling that occurs in the last few lines of the poem perhaps Herbert originally entitled it "The Caller" and a copyist made a mistake in transcription.

◆§ 361. BOTTRALL, MARGARET. *George Herbert*. London: John Murry. 153p.
Reprinted, Folcroft, Pa.: Folcroft Library Editions, 1971.
Chapter 6, "Herbert's Craftsmanship," reprinted in *Seventeenth Century English Poetry: Modern Essays in Criticism*, edited by William Keast (entry 480), pp. 238–51.
Chapter 1, "The Layman" (pp. 1–24). Calls Herbert a great poet but not a major one: "His greatness lies in the way he handles great concepts" (p. 1). Suggests that in poetical theory Herbert is closer to Sidney than to Donne: "Herbert's wit was fired not by the example of Donne but by the paradoxical nature of Christianity itself" (p. 2). Comments on the influences of Anglicanism, music, and classical studies on Herbert. Chapter 2, "The Priest" (pp. 25–48). Outlines Herbert's life as a priest and comments on his marriage to Jane Danvers and his friendship with Nicholas Ferrar. Chapter 3, "Literary Remains" (pp. 49–66). Bibliographical survey of Herbert's writings, both poetry and prose, Latin and

English. An overview of his literary production. Discusses the themes and structure of *The Temple*. Chapter 4, "The Country Parson" (pp. 67–82). Critical discussion of Herbert's posthumously published pastoral treatise, calls it "a practical treatise, in which Herbert explores the methods by which a contemporary parson could strengthen the hold of the established church upon the hearts and minds of the people of rural England" (p. 68). Sketches the historical and religious context of the work; for instance, points out that Herbert stresses the need for public worship because the reformed liturgy had not yet become fully familiar to the rural folk. Surveys major themes in *The Country Parson* and relates them to Herbert's poetry: "Coming to *The Country Parson* with Herbert's poetry already in mind, we recognize occasional similarities of phrasing as well as constant similarities of temper" (p. 79). Chapter 5, "Herbert's Themes" (pp. 83–98). Comments on Herbert's particularly Christian uses of analogy and metaphor ("his constant tendency to co-ordinate and harmonize" [p. 84]) and his fundamentally orthodox view of the world as "a divinely organized harmony" (p. 85). Suggests that "his most frequent and dearest theme is the redemptive love of Christ" (p. 88). Comments on the traditional sources of Herbert's imagery, especially the Bible and typology. Compares Herbert with Hopkins. Chapter 6, "Herbert's Craftsmanship" (pp. 99–116). Discusses Herbert's originality, experimentation, and economy in meter, forms, structures, "his architectonic skill" (p. 99). Presents the tension in Herbert between elaboration and ingenuity and his conscious striving for simplicity and directness. Comments on the musicality of much of Herbert's verse and his colloquial rhythms. Discusses the complex, conceptual, yet unobtrusive nature of Herbert's imagery, especially pointing out the influence of the Bible and emblem books. Chapter 7, "Literary Affinities" (pp. 117–33). Comments on the influence of Donne and suggests that "his indebtedness has been exaggerated" (p. 117). Compares Herbert also with Lord Herbert of Cherbury, Jonson, Wyatt, and especially Sidney. Chapter 8, "The Christian Poet" (pp. 134–47). Discusses the particular temper of Herbert's Christian vision, his general disinterest in the purely speculative issues of theology, and his joy and self-confident devotional spirit. Compares the religious sensibility of Herbert with that of Crashaw, Vaughan, and Christopher Harvey. Outlines briefly Herbert's reputation and concludes, "Today Herbert's reputation is higher than it has been since the end of the seventeenth century" (p. 146). Selected bibliography.

⋙ 362. CRUTTWELL, PATRICK. *The Shakespearean Moment and Its Place in the Poetry of the 17th Century*. London: Chatto & Windus. 262p.

Argues that at the end of the sixteenth century Shakespeare and the metaphysical poets were participating with the same qualities in the richest moment in English poetry: "The mature Shakespearean or meta-physical style—which, it must be repeated, is the same style used for dif-ferent purposes and in different *milieux*—emerged in the last years of the sixteenth century and remained the most fruitful style for the first few decades of the next." Discusses the conditions of life that allowed the building of bridges between all subjects and things and elaborates on what caused the end of the metaphysical style: Puritanism, the Common-wealth Interregnum, and the resulting differences in thinking about the human condition. Several references to Herbert but no extended dis-cussion. Briefly contrasts Herbert and Donne and also contrasts Herbert and other representatives of the "Shakespearean moment" with the Puri-tans and points out that when the former express "an ascetic revulsion from and rejection of the sensuous, their asceticism seems to express it-self, paradoxically, in thoroughly sensuous terms, so that the physical world has returned, as it were, by a backdoor" (p. 140). Sees Herbert's use of domestic imagery and colloquial language as a reflection of the "Shakespearean moment." Briefly contrasts Herbert and Lord Herbert of Cherbury. The conclusion divides the age into two great types of mind and places Herbert on the side represented by the following characteris-tics: Anglo-Catholicism, traditional medieval theology, native popular art, sensuousness allowed to permeate all things, courtly splendor, at-tempts to preserve what remained of the medieval Continental unity, monarchist sympathies and a hierarchical view of society, pessimism and skepticism about the possibility of human improvement, and a dramatic and tragic sense (pp. 252–53).

◄§ 363. EMSLIE, MACDONALD. "Herbert's 'Jordan I.' " *Expl* 12:item 35.
   Line-by-line explication of "Jordan (I)." Comments on such phrases as "false hair" (line 1), "winding stair" (line 3), "painted chair" (line 5), "Catching the sense at two removes" (line 10), etc. Sees the poem as an attack on those who make the writing of religious verse "over-elaborate or who convey religious themes through pastoral allegory." Comments on possible Platonic elements in the poem.

◄§ 364. LAWRENCE, RALPH. "The English Hymn." *E&S* n.s. 7:105–22.
   Discusses the development of the English hymn. States that the hymn, as we know it, did not fully emerge until 1623 with Wither's *Hymnes and Songs of the Church* and that it was not until 1707 that "the first authentic hymnal appeared: Dr. Isaac Watt's *Hymns and Spiritual Songs in Three Books*" (p. 106). Suggests the main differences between a re-ligious poem and a hymn and says that Herbert's "The Elixir," when sung, loses much of its particular charm. Maintains that the seventeenth century, while producing some hymns of rare distinction, "was primarily an age of Psalters, these being translations made from the Genevan

Psalters in metrical form" (p. 106). Suggests that there are some affinities between John Keble and Herbert but that *The Christian Year* "is far inferior to *The Temple*" (p. 115).

◆§ 365. MARTZ, LOUIS L. *The Poetry of Meditation: A Study in English Religious Literature of the Seventeenth Century.* Yale Studies in English, vol. 125. New Haven: Yale University Press. London: Oxford University Press. xiv, 375p.
  Rev. ed., 1962.
  Pages 135–44 reprinted in *The Modern Critical Spectrum*, edited by Gerald Jay Goldberg and Nancy Marner Goldberg (Englewood Cliffs, N.J.: Prentice-Hall, 1962), pp. 244–50.
  Pages 211–48 (with revisions from the 2d ed.) reprinted in *Seventeenth Century English Poetry: Modern Essays in Criticism*, edited by William Keast (entry 480), pp. 144–74, rev. ed. (entry 707), pp. 118–51.
  Pages 220–23 and 228–48 reprinted in *John Donne: A Collection of Critical Essays*, edited by Helen Gardner (Englewood Cliffs, N.J.: Prentice-Hall, 1962), pp. 152–70.
  The primary purpose of this study is "to modify the view of literary history which sees a 'Donne tradition' in English religious poetry. It suggests instead a 'meditative tradition' which found its first notable example not in Donne but in Robert Southwell" (p. 3). Argues that the metaphysical poets, though obviously widely different, are "drawn together by resemblances that result, basically, from the common practice of certain methods of religious meditation" (p. 2). Herbert is mentioned throughout. Two complete chapters are devoted to him: (1) chapter 7, "George Herbert: in the Presence of a Friend," discusses the influence of, and Herbert's affinities to, St. François de Sales, Sir Philip Sidney (especially his translations of the psalms), the *Imitation of Christ*, and Girolamo Savonarola; (2) chapter 8, "George Herbert: The Unity of *The Temple*," argues that *The Temple* has a structure built primarily upon the art of mental communion. Other important issues discussed in relation to Herbert: (1) the uses of meditative structure in Herbert's poems, (2) "The Sacrifice" as a meditation on the liturgy of Holy Week, (3) devotion to the Virgin Mary, (4) the influence of the method of self-examination, especially the *Spiritual Combat* of Lorenzo Scupoli, (4) the art of sacred parody, the literature of tears, and various meditations on death. In addition to those already mentioned, Herbert is compared and contrasted with Donne, Southwell, Vaughan, and Crashaw.

◆§ 366. MAYCOCK, ALAN. *Chronicles of Little Gidding.* London: Society for Promoting Christian Knowledge. 120p.
  Presents "an account, first of the events covered by the twenty years between Nicolas's death in 1637 and the death of John Ferrar in 1657,

and then of various episodes and happenings connected with Little Gidding which take us on almost to the middle of the eighteenth century" (p. 1). Several references to Herbert. Points out that John Ferrar's accounts for 1649 show that he sent to various settlers in Virginia no less than 197 books, including copies of Herbert's poems. In a letter to his son, John Ferrar commented on the friendship between Nicholas Ferrar and Herbert, "your uncle's most dear friend (of whom it was said by them that knew them both there was one soul in two bodies)" (p. 89). Suggests that it was perhaps the publication of *The Country Parson* in 1652, with an introduction by Barnabas Oley, that determined John Ferrar to write his own short life of Nicholas Ferrar in 1653 or 1654.

◄§ 367. MOLONEY, MICHAEL F. "A Suggested Gloss for Herbert's 'Box Where Sweets. . . .' " *N&Q*, n.s. 1:50.
Suggests that "A box where sweets compacted lie" in "Vertue" may not be a box of perfumes (as F. E. Hutchinson suggests) but rather a music box.

◄§ 368. ROSS, MALCOLM MACKENZIE. *Poetry and Dogma: The Transformation of Eucharistic Symbols in Seventeenth Century English Poetry.* New Brunswick: Rutgers University Press. xii, 256p.
Studies "some of the consequences for religious poetry in England of the Protestant revision of Eucharistic dogma" and maintains, "The dogmatic symbolism of the traditional Eucharistic rite had nourished the analogical mode of poetic symbol, indeed had effected imaginatively a poetic knowledge of the participation (each with the other) of the natural, the historical, and the divine orders" (p. vii). Reprints "George Herbert and the Humanistic Tradition," entry 277 (pp. 135–57). Herbert is frequently mentioned throughout this study of the influence of the revolution in Christian dogma on the poetic act. Sees in Herbert the breakdown of the analogical symbol. Argues that there is a "certain tension which obtains in his work between a Catholic sensibility and an urgent, if uneasy Protestant dogmatism" (p. 176). Suggests that Herbert is linked to the Catholic tradition "not so much by his use of traditional typology and iconography as by his intense and immediate feeling for the Person of Christ" (p. 176). Points out a number of Catholic and even Counter-Reformation elements in Herbert's art but sees his Protestant views on the Eucharist as "the spectacle of analogical symbol dissolving into simple metaphor" (p. 181). Argues that Herbert's rhetoric is "a displaced rhetoric, a Catholic rhetoric Protestantized but always looking backward. It is the end-point of a moving cycle, of a steady process of deterioration in the analogical symbol from Shakespeare onwards, a cycle in poetry reflecting a decline in dogma and in habits of mind and heart that were rooted in dogma" (p. 219).

◄§ 369. SUMMERS, JOSEPH H. *George Herbert: His Religion and Art.* Cambridge, Mass.: Harvard University Press; London: Chatto & Windus. 246p.
Reprinted, 1968.

Chapter 4, "The Conception of Form," first appeared as "Herbert's Form" (entry 325). Reprinted in *The Metaphysical Poets: Key Essays on Metaphysical Poetry and the Major Metaphysical Poets,* edited by Frank Kermode (entry 647), pp. 230–51; and *The Metaphysical Poets: A Selection of Critical Essays,* edited by Gerald Hammond (entry 783), pp. 157–81.

Chapter 6, "The Poem as Hieroglyph," reprinted in *Seventeenth Century English Poetry: Modern Essays in Criticism,* edited by William Keast (entry 480), pp. 215–37; rev. ed. (entry 707), pp. 225–47.

Full-scale study of Herbert's religion as it is reflected in his poetry and an interpretation of the poetry in the light of his religious convictions and sensibilities. Explores the symbolism and traditions of the Church that inform Herbert's art. "The major assumption of this book is that George Herbert . . . is one of the best lyric poets who has written in the English language" (p. 7). The book is divided into three major sections: the first three chapters consider Herbert's poetic reputation, his life, and his religious thought and sensibility; chapters 4 and 5 discuss Herbert's theories of form and language, "both basic to his poetic and religious practice" (p. 7); and the final section applies these concepts to the poems. Chapter 1, "Time and *The Temple*" (pp. 11–27), surveys Herbert's reputation and influence as a poet both in his own time and later. In his own day, "except for John Cleveland, he was the most popular of the so-called 'metaphysical poets', sacred or profane" (p. 11). Emphasizes that art and religion are inextricably woven together in *The Temple.* Chapter 2, "The Life" (pp. 28–48), rejects the notion that Herbert was a simple, naive saint and mystic and presents him as a devout, sophisticated, complex man of his times. Questions a strict autobiographical reading of the poems. Chapter 3, "Religion" (pp. 49–69), surveys the diversity of religious opinion in England in the early seventeenth century and presents Herbert's religious thought and sensibilities as reflected in his poems, translations, and prose works. Chapter 4, "The Conception of Form" (pp. 73–94), argues that Herbert's use of form in the poetry reflects his religious convictions, his "analogical habit of mind and the belief that order, measure, proportion, and harmony are both divine and beautiful" (p. 76). Discusses the significant arrangement of the poems in *The Temple* and rejects George Herbert Palmer's reordering: "The composition of the poems, imitative as they were of that ordering which he had experienced and which he hoped to experience again, was the act of a craftsman who shapes the imperfect materials of his own suffering as well as joy into a pattern symbolic of divine order" (p. 94). Chapter 5, "The Proper Language" (pp. 95–119), surveys Herbert's views on the nature and function of language, especially "the implication that the beauty of language, like the soul's, can live only if it is 'lost' to the proper object" (p. 119). Comments on Herbert's love of language, which was always kept in check by rational control, and points out his "insistence on propriety and the equal insistence that language is finally unimportant when compared with the spirit" (p. 119). Chapter 6, "The Poem as Hieroglyph" (pp. 123–46), discusses Herbert's "art which conceals art" (p. 135). "The hieroglyph represents to Herbert a fusion of the spiritual and material, of the rational and sensuous, in the essential terms of formal relationships" (p. 145). Suggests that the pattern poems are the most developed of hieroglyphs. Chapter 7, "Verse and Speech" (pp. 147–55), discusses Herbert's metrical inventiveness and his uses of counterpoint, rhythm, sound, and diction. "In Herbert's poems subject and image do not determine speech; they are transformed by it" (p. 152). Chapter 8, "Music" (pp. 156–70), comments on Herbert's lifelong interest in music and his uses of musical effects and metaphors. Suggests that music best explains the sound patterns, tone, and form in many of the poems. "About a fourth of the poems in *The Temple* concern music directly" (p. 157). Chapter 9, "Allegory and Sonnet: A Traditional Mode and a Traditional Form" (pp. 171–84), discusses Herbert's experimentation with the sonnet ("he sought to transform and to revitalize the conventional so as to make it freshly available to serious poetry" [p. 171]) and his complex uses of allegory, especially in its then-popular Christian form. Chapter 10, "Conclusions" (pp. 185–90), presents a summary of several major points about Herbert's art. Suggests, for example, "We can fully realize Herbert's poetic achievement—or almost any one poem in *The Temple*— only within the light of ideas, beliefs, and conventions of early seventeenth-century England" (p. 185), and, "For Herbert, Christianity provided the means of giving order and universal significance to his personal experience" (p. 186). Appendix A, "Mr Herbert's Temple & Church Militant Explained and Improved" (pp. 191–94) discusses George Ryley's annotations and explanation of the poems in *The Temple* (1714/ 1715), which, though primarily theological, "often provide the key to many of the passages and poems which are difficult for the modern reader of Herbert" (p. 191). Appendix B, "Bacon and Herbert" (pp. 195–97), briefly discusses the relationship between the two men, stressing the areas of their agreement on matters of religion and morality. Notes (pp. 198–237). Index (pp. 239–47).

◅§ 370. WILLY, MARGARET. "The Poetry of Donne: Its Interest and Influence Today." *E&S*, n.s. 7:78–104.

Discusses certain likenesses between the metaphysical poets, particularly Donne, and certain modern poets. Maintains that the kinship between the seventeenth and the twentieth centuries "penetrates far deeper than that relatively superficial kind: rooted as it is in broadly similar social conditions, which, in the literature of both ages, evoked certain responses that correspond strikingly in spirit and technique" (pp. 79–80). Although Donne is the main poet mentioned, Herbert is also considered. Comments briefly on the affinities between Herbert and Hopkins.

ও§ 371. YOUNG, SIMON. "George Herbert." *TLS*, 15 January, p. 41.
Requests information on Herbert for a projected biography.

1955

ও§ 372. BLUNDEN, EDMUND. "Some Seventeenth-Century Latin Poems by English Writers." *UTQ* 25:10–22.
Translates into English two Latin poems by Herbert: "On Sacred Music" ("De Musicâ Sacrâ") and "To Pallas Athene" ("Innupta Pallas, nata Diespitre"). General comments on Herbert's Latin verse. Suggests that in these poems, "which amount to about a fourth part of Herbert's whole extant works, a view of Herbert is found which is not quite that of the poems in English" (p. 12). Comments in particular on *Parentalia*. Translations also of Donne, Crashaw, and Milton.

ও§ 373. BUSH, DOUGLAS. "Seventeenth-Century Poets and the Twentieth Century." *Annual Bulletin of the Modern Humanities Research Association*, no. 27, pp. 16–28.
Comments on the revival of interest in the metaphysical poets, especially Donne, from the nineteenth century through the twentieth century and gives reasons for the extraordinary attention given the metaphysical poets by both scholars and practicing poets, especially during the 1920s and 1930s, and for the decline of interest since that period, especially among practicing poets. Considers also the effects of the metaphysical revival on the fate of Milton in the twentieth century and concludes that Milton, "far from having been dislodged from his throne, appears to sit more securely than ever on a throne that has partly new and even more solid foundations" (p. 26). Suggests, "Amateur criticism restored Donne and banished Milton, scholarly criticism kept Donne and restored Milton" (pp. 26–27). No specific comment on Herbert.

ও§ 374. COLERIDGE, SAMUEL TAYLOR. *Coleridge on the Seventeenth Century*. Edited by Roberta Florence Brinkley with an introductory essay by Louis I. Bredvold. Durham, N.C.: Duke University Press. xxxviii, 704p.
Reprinted, New York: Greenwood Press, 1968. Selections reprinted in *The Metaphysical Poets: A Selection of Critical Essays*, edited by Gerald Hammond (entry 783), pp. 59–60.
Collection of Coleridge's comments on the seventeenth century ar-

ranged under seven headings: (1) the seventeenth century in general, (2) the philosophers, (3) the divines, (4) science, (5) literary prose, (6) poetry, and (7) the drama. Several references to Herbert, whom Coleridge calls "the every way excellent George Herbert" (p. 275). Especially note the collection of Coleridge's specific comments on Herbert (pp. 533–40). In a letter to W. Collins, Coleridge remarks: "I find more substantial comfort now in pious George Herbert's 'Temple' . . . than in all the poetry since the poems of Milton" (p. 533).

◆§ 375. DAVENPORT, A. "George Herbert and Ovid." N&Q 200:98.

Points out that the sequence of thought in Herbert's "Vertue" occurs in Ovid's *Ars Amatoria*, book 2, lines 111 ff. "It is worth pointing out since it enables us to watch Herbert's imagination in the art of developing and enriching the Ovidian outline."

◆§ 376. DUNCAN-JONES, ELSIE. "Benlowes's Borrowings from George Herbert." RES, n.s. 6:179–80.

Points out two possible borrowings from Herbert in Edward Benlowe's *Theophilia*: (1) canto 2, line 91 echoes lines from "Bitter-sweet" and (2) canto 9, line 17 appropriates a line from the first verse of *The Church-Porch*.

◆§ 377. ESCH, ARNO. *Englische Religiöse Lyrik des 17. Jahrhunderts: Studien zu Donne, Herbert, Crashaw, Vaughan*. Buchreihe der Anglia Zeitscrift für englische Philologie, 5. Tübingen: Max Niemeyer. xi, 225p.

Studies the problems of religious poetry of the period by analyzing and comparing the works of individual poets. Chapter 3 (pp. 11–27) deals specifically with Herbert's poetry, especially with various poetic structures. Classifies Herbert's poems into five main types: (1) chain poems (those in which a stanza could be added or subtracted or possibly stanzas could be interchanged without damaging the poem); (2) definition poems (such as "Prayer (I)"); (3) poems based on verbal or visual patterns (such as "Easter-wings" and "Paradise"); (4) poems clearly symmetrical in structure, often built on antithesis, with two main parts (such as "Death"); (5) poems containing a tripartite structure. Argues that in the last category are found Herbert's best poems and maintains that this structure suggests the influence of Quintilian's rhetoric, especially as it was used by the early Fathers of the Church in their sermons. Analyzes a number of poems in this last category, including "The Bunch of Grapes," "Peace," "Divinitie," "Redemption," "Love (III)," "Miserie," "Mortification," "Discipline," "Jesu," "Life," "Aaron," "The Collar," and "The Quip."

◄§ 378. GROOM, BERNARD. 'The Spenserian Tradition and Its Rivals to
1660." In *The Diction of Poetry from Spenser to Bridges*, pp. 43–
73. Toronto: University of Toronto Press; London: Geoffrey Cumberlege, Oxford University Press.

Comments briefly on Herbert's "classical neatness and conciseness
of style" (p. 62) and on "the controlled fervour and the precision of his
unaspiring style" (p. 63). Suggests that Herbert's chief effects "come
from some simple phrase tellingly reserved, unerringly placed" (p. 63).
Suggests also that Herbert's diction is plain, so that "those who do not
enter into the spirit of his poetry find it sometimes 'quaint' " (p. 63).
Briefly compares Herbert and Vaughan.

◄§ 379. ROSENTHAL, M. L., and SMITH, A. J. M., *Exploring Poetry*. New
York: Macmillan Co. xli, 758p.

Contains a brief discussion of "Vertue" (pp. 415–17), commenting
especially on Herbert's figures of speech and on what the authors call
the "process of elimination." Comments also on "The Pulley" (pp.
544–45), especially on its concentrated intellectual manner and dramatic elements. Several briefer references and questions on other poems.

◄§ 380. SELLS, ARTHUR LYTTON. "Southwell." In *The Italian Influence
in English Poetry: From Chaucer to Southwell*, pp. 306–35. Bloom-
ington: Indiana University Press.

Brief comments on the possible influence of Southwell and the spirit
of the Counter-Reformation on Herbert's poetry: "It was through the
intermediary of Southwell, whose works were widely read and admired
in England, that the better literary theories of the Counter-Reformation
entered into the fabric of Anglican poetry as well as of Catholic" (p.
311). Suggests several close parallels between Herbert's poetry and that of
Southwell.

◄§ 381. SYPHER, WYLIE. *Four Stages of Renaissance Style: Transforma-
tions in Art and Literature, 1400–1700*. Anchor A44. Garden
City, N.Y.: Doubleday & Co. 312p.

Studies the development of various Renaissance styles from 1400 to
1700, stressing relationships between literature and the fine arts. The
metaphysical poets are discussed as examples of the mannerist style. In
art history, mannerism "represents a 'formal dissolution of a style'—the
style of renaissance art founded upon the concepts of proportion and
harmony and unity" (p. 102). In literature, this style exemplifies Eliot's
notion of "dissociation of sensibility" and Herbert J. C. Grierson's
idea that Donne and the metaphysical poets "are 'more aware of disintegration than of comprehensive harmony' " (p. 103). Several refer-

ences to Herbert. Comments on his tension between "calm, assured piety and his agitated awareness of things in the world" (p. 169), discusses his use of metaphor and image, and briefly compares him with Crashaw.

∾§ 382. Watson, George. "Hobbes and the Metaphysical Conceit." *JHI* 16:558–62.
Maintains that the metaphysical conceit was killed by a change in literary theory and illustrates this change by referring to the critical writings of Hobbes. Suggests that, in time, the conceit lost its intellectual force and was dismissed as mere sound. No specific mention of Herbert. For a reply, see T. M. Gang, entry 389.

∾§ 383. Wickes, George. "George Herbert's Views on Poetry." *RLV* 21:344–52.
Collects various scattered statements concerning Herbert's view of poetry as reflected in his poems: "No less than one quarter of his poems reflect his preoccupation with his role as poet" (p. 345). Also finds similar comments in *A Priest to the Temple*. Considers two main aspects of Herbert's poetic theory: his concern with content and his conscious efforts in technique. Points out some of the more explicit statements and themes that reflect Herbert's view on the uses of poetry in the religious life and also comments on the less explicit views on poetic techniques and tastes. Comments on Herbert's uses of wit and on the highly pictorial quality of his verse. Suggests that the essential principle of his poetry is "to inform and inflame or—to use the characteristic seventeenth century expression of Nicholas Ferrar—to «enrich the World with pleasure and piety»" (p. 352).

1956

∾§ 384. Cox, R. G. "A Survey of Literature from Donne to Marvell." In *From Donne to Marvell*, edited by Boris Ford, pp. 43–85. The Pelican Guide to English Literature, vol. 3. London and Baltimore: Penguin Books.
Reprinted several times (with minor revisions).
Very broad survey of poetry and prose from Donne to Marvell. Discusses Herbert in a subsection entitled "The Metaphysical Manner and Religious Poetry" (pp. 54–59). Compares Herbert with Donne, Crashaw, Quarles, Vaughan, and Marvell. Comments briefly on those elements usually associated with Herbert's verse: courtly urbanity of language, allegorical vividness, musical verse forms, neatness, homely wit, intensity, effects of surprise, control of tone, dramatic sense, purity of diction, proverbial and colloquial uses of language, etc. Says that Her-

bert's best work "embodies the religious temper of the seventeenth century at its finest and most humane" (p. 57).

◄§ 385. DENONAIN, JEAN-JACQUES. *Thèmes et formes de la poésie "métaphysique": Étude d'un aspect de la littérature anglaise au dixseptième siècle.* Publications de la faculté des lettres d'Alger, 18. Paris: Presses universitaires de France. 548p.

Attempts to define as precisely as possible the nature of metaphysical poetry. After an introduction (pp. 5–18) in which the author states his purpose and challenges several of the better-known definitions, the book is divided into five major parts: (1) a tentative definition of metaphysical poetry (pp. 21–95); (2) an analysis of major themes in metaphysical poetry (pp. 99–326); (3) a discussion of the psychological processes by which the themes of the poetry are developed and expanded (pp. 329–64); (4) a study of poetic forms utilized by the metaphysical poets (pp. 367–449); and (5) a conclusion that seeks to discern the unifying characteristics of metaphysical poetry (pp. 453–80). Three sections of the book deal specifically with Herbert: (1) the religious themes of George Herbert: meditations on religious occasions and theological themes, pain of sin, ingratitude toward God and rebellion, contrition and submission to the will of God, prayer, actions of grace, worship, mystical effusions, blind confidence in the intercession of Christ, proselytism (pp. 185–220); (2) images, metaphor, and conceit in Herbert (pp. 389–93); and (3) poetic technique in Herbert (pp. 426–36). Among the several appendixes, two deal specifically with Herbert: (1) the chronology of George Herbert (pp. 485–86) and (2) the structure of prosody in Herbert (pp. 505–10). Some negative attitudes expressed: "A la médiocrité de l'inspiration, Herbert ajoute un mauvais goût impardonnable dans ses conceits, même si l'on tient compte de la psychologie et des habitudes du temps" (p. 393). Selected bibliography.

◄§ 386. ENRIGHT, D. J. "George Herbert and the Devotional Poets." In *From Donne to Marvell*, edited by Boris Ford, pp. 142–59. The Pelican Guide to English Literature, vol. 3. London and Baltimore: Penquin Books.

Calls Herbert "one of the strongest poetic personalities in English" (p. 142). Comments on Herbert's quiet tone; his uses of homely imagery and rhetoric; his combining of courtly and popular elements; and his sense of drama, immediacy, and intimacy. Outlines the major themes of Herbert's poetry; "foremost among them are the Incarnation, the Passion and the Redemption" (p. 145). Suggests that the most serious criticism that can be leveled against Herbert is "the rather clumsy way in which the scales are occasionally weighted against earthly pleasures as opposed to heavenly bliss" (p. 146). Compares and contrasts Herbert with Vaughan and Crashaw.

 ◄§ 387. FORD, BORIS, ed. *From Donne to Marvell*. The Pelican Guide
to English Literature, vol. 3. London and Baltimore: Penquin
Books. 277p.

Reprinted several times (with minor revisions).

Herbert is mentioned throughout this collection of original essays on
various seventeenth-century topics. Essays in which Herbert is given
special consideration have been entered separately in this bibliography
(see entries 384, 386). Selective bibliography of Herbert and Herbert
criticism (pp. 261–62).

◄§ 388. FRANKENBERG, LLOYD. *Invitation to Poetry: A Round of Poems
from John Skelton to Dylan Thomas Arranged with Comments*.
Garden City, N.Y.: Doubleday & Co. 414p.

Very brief critical comments on "A true Hymne" (pp. 62–63) and on
"Vertue" (pp. 163–64).

◄§ 389. GANG, T. M. "Hobbes and the Metaphysical Conceit: A Reply."
JIII 17:418–21.

In part a reply to George Watson, entry 382. Challenges Watson's
interpretation of Hobbes's critical theory. Second part of the essay is devoted to a discussion of the metaphysical conceit. Suggests that Herbert
and Donne "even when they do not use the terminology of metaphysics,
play with concepts in a manner which they have learnt from the meta-
physicians" (p. 419). Maintains that it was possible for metaphysical
poets "to use the language and assumptions of metaphysics because they
believed these to have a validity. But to play on ideas which have become
meaningless is pointless. And this, surely, is what happened in the fifties
and sixties of the seventeenth century: both the verbiage and the general
method had become, or were fast becoming, meaningless" (p. 419). Suggests that what makes a conceit "metaphysical" is "not the wildness of
the comparison, but the fact that the comparison is between a concrete
thing and an abstraction, and that the double meanings are produced by
taking the concrete part of the comparison 'seriously,' that is, writing literally about the vehicle of the metaphor" (p. 421). Points out that in
Herbert's poetry "the non-literal language that is treated literally is often
the language of the Bible, the Prayer-book, and common proverbial expressions" (p. 421).

◄§ 390. HERBERT, GEORGE. *The Country Parson and Selected Poems by
George Herbert*, edited by Hugh Martin. A Treasury of Christian
Books Series. London: SCM Press. 125p.

Contains a biographical introduction with brief critical comment on
The Country Parson and the poems (pp. 7–10). Calls Herbert "the father
of the religious lyric" (p. 8). Reprints *The Country Parson* (pp. 11–96)
and selected poems (pp. 97–125) without notes or commentary.

◄§ 391. HILBERRY, CONRAD. "Two Cruxes in George Herbert's 'Redemption.'" N&Q 201:514.

Comments on the phrase *small-rented lease* in "Redemption" (line 4) and sees a possible biographical reference in the first quatrain: "Herbert, in taking orders and committing himself later to parochial life, was certainly cancelling an old lease in which he had not thrived and accepting a new 'small-rented' one in its place." Gives several possible interpretations of the use of the word *land* (line 7): (1) land=dust, man; (2) land=Christ; (3) land=Eden and, typologically, Calvary.

◄§ 392. KORETZ, GENE M. "The Rhyme Scheme in Herbert's 'Man.'" N&Q 201:144–46.

Discusses the intricate design and formal order in "Man." Points out that of all the poems in *The Temple*, "Man" "is the only one in which the rhyme scheme is consistently varied in stanzas of equal lengths" (p. 145). Shows how the formal symmetry of the poem is related to the poem's subject: "Since man occupied the central position in the chain of being, serving as mediator between the material and spiritual realms, and since the natural world was created for his sustenance and pleasure, the poem provides a comprehensive treatment of the whole of creation with relation to man. Implicit in the world-picture which Herbert presents are the concepts of unity enveloping diversity, order governing abundance and variety—and it is these concepts which the poet has sought to embody in the poem's structure" (p. 145).

◄§ 393. KORNINGER, SIEGFRIED. *Die Naturaufassung in der englischen Dichtung des 17. Jahrhunderts.* Weiner Beiträge zur englischen Philologie, 64. Vienna and Stuttgart: Wilhelm Braumüller. 260p.

Discusses changing attitudes toward nature in the seventeenth century. Uses poetry as the source material for studying two major groups of questions: (1) how does man face his environment, what does he understand of it, and how does he depict it? and (2) to what extent is man's attitude toward nature expressed in his poetic works, and what inspirations and artistic impulses does the poetry derive from the investigation of nature? Finds in Herbert's poetry an interest in nature and natural phenomena, which he shares with most of his contemporaries. Many illustrations drawn from Herbert's poetry.

◄§ 394. MANNING, STEPHEN. "Herbert's 'The Pearl', 38." *Expl* 14:item 25.

Explicates Herbert's symbolic uses of the silk twist in line 38 of "The Pearl" and concludes that symbolically the silk twist "is faith, by which God both conducts and teaches man how to climb to Him." Supports such a reading by referring to the commentaries of Rabanus Maurus, Rupertus of Deutz, and the English translator of Beza.

⊷§ 395. RAO, A. V. "The Religious and Meditative Poetry of England."
Prabuddha Bharata; or Awakened India (Calcutta), pp. 139–42.

Briefly comments on some of the major devotional and mystical poets
of England from the thirteenth century to T. S. Eliot. Assures Indian
readers that "a rich vein of religious, devotional, and meditative poetry
runs through the literature of England, though at first sight it would
seem incredible, because the English people have been looked on as fight-
ers, colonizers, empire-builders, sturdy John Bulls, a 'nation of shop-
keepers', and what not—anything but mystics and devotional poets" (p.
139). Briefly mentions Herbert and suggests that he is simpler than
Donne, "though not altogether free of 'wit' " (p. 141).

⊷§ 396. SMITH, A. J. "An Examination of Some Claims for Ramism."
RES, n.s. 7:348–59.

Reprinted in *Essential Articles for the Study of John Donne's Poetry*,
edited by John R. Roberts (Hamden, Conn.: Archon Books, 1975), pp.
178–88.

Challenges primarily Rosemond Tuve's claim in *Elizabethan and
Metaphysical Imagery: Renaissance Poetic and Twentieth-Century Critics* (entry 279) that Ramism "provides a satisfactory explanation not only
of certain major elements in so-called 'Metaphysical' poetry, but even of
the very thought processes of the greatest 'Metaphysical' poet, Donne"
(p. 348). Discusses the nature of Ramism, in particular its relation to
verse. Concludes that "too much has been made of the attempt at reform
in teaching method called Ramism, in itself and as an influence" (p. 359)
and that "for the true explanation of 'Metaphysical' qualities and techniques one need seek no farther than the great sixteenth-century tradition
of which Ramism was but a backwater—that of *wit* as it was developed
in conventional rhetoric" (p. 359). No specific mention of Herbert. For
a reply, see George Watson, entry 420.

⊷§ 397. TILLYARD, E. M. W. *The Metaphysicals and Milton.* London:
Chatto & Windus. vii, 87p.

Examines the supposed opposition between the metaphysicals and
Milton. Maintains that Milton was "a great figure looking back to the
Middle Ages and forward to the spirit and achievements of eighteenth-
century puritanism. But his larger surprises and ironies are in harmony
with the requirements of his age and of course are largely inspired by
them. He was very much of a person, yet he did not thrust his personality
overmuch into his poetry and he chose to inhabit the general centre rather
than to construct a private bower, or perform dazzling acrobatics, near
the circumference. He is more like Jonson and Marvell than he is like
Donne and Crashaw. Donne, on the other hand, was a great innovator
but with a narrower, more personal talent. He made people heed him, he
stirred them up, he contributed to the age's vitality. But he remains the

exception, and his admirers will do him no good in the long run if they pretend he was anything else" (p. 74). Rejects the notion of a "school of Donne." Claims that Herbert is closer to Milton "in many motions of his mind" (p. 2) than he is to Donne. Says that Donne's "direct influence on Herbert was undoubted but it extended to a smaller proportion of his poems than is often thought" (p. 58).

◄§ 398. WELLEK, RENÉ. "The Criticism of T. S. Eliot." SR 64:398–443.
Reviews Eliot's basic comments on the metaphysical poets (pp. 437–40) and points out that, although his criticism has proved to be an important impetus to the so-called metaphysical revival, his ideas are, for the most part, neither original nor consistent and that he is the first critic to link the metaphysical poets so definitely with the French symbolists. Briefly comments on Eliot's evaluation of Herbert: "He rates Herbert more high [than Donne] as a great master of language, as a sincere devotional poet, as an anatomist of feeling, as a trained theologian, and as a man who, in his short life, went much further along the road to humility than Donne" (p. 439). Points out Eliot's insistence that *The Temple* be considered "as a continuous religious meditation with a planned, intellectual framework" (p. 439). Suggests that Eliot considers Vaughan inferior to Herbert.

1957

◄§ 399. COLLMER, ROBERT G. "Herbert's 'Businesse', 15–30." *Expl* 16: item 11.
Comments on five different possible meanings for, or kinds of, death in lines 20–30 of "Businesse": "(I) redemptive, or Christ's; (II) spiritual, that is, separation of the human being from God in this life; (III) eternal, that is, separation of the human in the future life; (IV) transformatory, or separation of the soul from the world and sin, which is achieved by applying the merits of Christ's crucifixion and resurrection to the soul; (V) natural, separation of the soul from the body."

◄§ 400. GARDNER, HELEN, ed. *The Metaphysical Poets*. Selected and edited by Helen Gardner. Baltimore: Penquin Books. 328p.
Reprinted, 1959, 1961, 1963, 1964.
Rev. ed., 1966.
2d ed., London: Oxford University Press, 1967; rpt., 1967.
Pages xix–xxiv reprinted in *Seventeenth Century English Poetry: Modern Essays in Criticism*, edited by William Keast (entry 480), pp. 50–62; rev. ed. (entry 707), pp. 32–44.
An anthology of metaphysical poetry in which Herbert is represented by twenty-four poems. Brief biographical note and selected bibliog-

raphy. The introduction outlines and comments on the major characteristics of metaphysical poetry, especially its concentration, its uses of the conceit, its argumentative and persuasive tone and structure, its various dramatic elements, its strong sense of the real and actual, its individuality, etc. Comments briefly on "Mortification," stressing Herbert's individuality in treating "the old theme of the stages of human life and the traditional lessons of the *Ars Moriendi*" (p. 27).

৺§ 401. GREGORY, HORACE, and ZATURENSKA, MARYA, eds. *The Mentor Book of Religious Verse*. A Mentor Book. New York: New American Library of World Literature. xxviii, 238p.

Anthology of religious verse arranged according to the liturgical calendar. The introduction (pp. xv–xxviii) comments on the rediscovery and appreciation of religious poetry in the twentieth century. Comments briefly on how very much Herbert was appreciated by Coleridge, Emerson, and Emily Dickinson. Includes seven poems by Herbert.

৺§ 402. KERMODE, FRANK. " 'Dissociation of Sensibility': Modern Symbolist Readings of Literary History." In *Romantic Image*, pp. 138–61. London: Routledge and Kegan Paul.

The relevant parts of this chapter that deal with the metaphysical poets and the seventeenth century are explored in much expanded form in "Dissociation of Sensibility," entry 403.

৺§ 403. ———. "Dissociation of Sensibility." KR 19:169–94.

Reprinted in *Essential Articles for the Study of John Donne's Poetry*, edited by John R. Roberts (Hamden, Conn.: Archon Books, 1975), pp. 66–82.

Challenges Eliot's theory of "dissociation of sensibility" and points out that the tension between reason and theological truth was not solely confined to, nor begun in, seventeenth-century England. As far as poetry is concerned, especially metaphysical poetry, the theory is simply an "attempt on the part of Symbolists to find an historical justification for their poetics" (p. 194). Discusses how the term and concept are closely related to the twentieth-century revival of metaphysical poetry. No specific references to Herbert. In a much-revised form, the same ground is covered in " 'Dissociation of Sensibility': Modern Symbolist Readings of Literary History" (entry 402).

৺§ 404. LEVANG, DWIGHT. "George Herbert's 'The Church Militant' and the Chances of History." PQ 36:265–68.

Points out that Samuel Ward of Ipswich, a Puritan preacher, was imprisoned in 1635 for making a statement in a sermon that is strikingly close to lines 235–36 of *The Church Militant* ("Religion stands on tip-toe in our land,/ Readie to passe to the *American* strand.")

405. MILES, JOSEPHINE. *Eras & Modes in English Poetry.* Berkeley and Los Angeles: University of California Press. xi, 233p. Rev. ed., 1964.

Questions the theory of dividing English poetry arbitrarily into historical periods and defines three recurrent modes in poetry based upon the various kinds of sentence structure and word usage favored by English poets: the clausal or predicative, the phrasal or sublime, and the balanced or classical. Considers the clausal or active predicative mode as the most English and traces it to Chaucer. In this mode one finds such a variety of poets as Chaucer, Skelton, Wyatt, Sidney, Donne, Jonson, Herrick, Herbert, Cowley, Coleridge, Byron, Browning, Hardy, Cummings, Frost, and Auden. The clausal mode lends itself to passionate argumentation, natural discourse in verse, abrupt movement, clausal connectives, and a preponderance of verbs over adjectives. In appendix A (pp. 215–30) the author shows, by means of a statistical table, that Herbert belongs to the clausal mode. Chapter 2, "The Language of the Donne Tradition" (pp. 20–32) is a revision of an article by the same title in *KR* 13 (1951): 37–49. Although Herbert is not directly mentioned in this chapter, many of the general observations could be applied to his poetry.

406. MOLONEY, MICHAEL F. "A Note on Herbert's 'Season'd Timber.' " *N&Q*, n.s. 4:434–35.

Comments on stanza 4 of "Vertue" to illustrate the complexity of Herbert's "imagistic texture." Suggests that the "primary likeness which Herbert wishes to stress between the virtuous soul and seasoned timber is . . . that just as the latter resists the structural strains placed upon it without warping or bowing, so the former resists with complete integrity the burden of temptation" (p. 435). Shows how a "simple simile . . . veils a subtle metonymy" (p. 435).

407. SCOTT, A. F. *The Poet's Craft: A Course in the Critical Appreciation of Poetry.* Cambridge: University Press. xi, 219p.

Divided into five sections: (1) reproductions of a number of manuscript poems, many of them original drafts, often showing the poets' corrections; (2) first published versions of several poems with more widely accepted revisions; (3) raw materials used by several poets (North, Golding, etc.); (4) several translations of Greek and Latin poems into English by different hands; and (5) a number of unsigned poems grouped together for comparison and contrast. Reproduces Herbert's

"Perfection" ("The Elixir") from the Williams MS (pp. 4–5) and includes "Love (III)" in the fifth section.

⌐§ 408. TAYLOR, IVAN EARLE. "Cavalier Sophistication in the Poetry of
George Herbert." *Anglican Theological Review* 39:229–43.

Challenges the notion that Herbert is a "plastic saint" and argues that in his poetry he "gives evidence of being basically a cavalier; that is to say, a courtly seventeenth century aristocrat concerned to a remarkable degree with interests generally associated with the cavaliers: wine, game, women, sophisticated conversation, dress, and the like" (p. 230). Classifies and discusses under four major headings the images, allusions, and metaphors in Herbert's poetry "that reveal him as a true cavalier and sophisticate": (1) stewardship and the ways the lord of a manor relates to his tenants concerning such matters as the proper uses of grants and leases; considerations of court life, great places, and proper upbringing of a gentleman; (2) rich clothing, silks, weaving knots, etc.; (3) wine, drinking, cating, etc.; (4) wit, courtesy, love dalliance, the art of language. Argues, "There are, moreover, many references, here and there throughout the poems, to such sophisticated activities as gambling, falconry, gardening, to jewels and perfumes, and, of course, to music" (pp. 230–31).

1958

⌐§ 409. ADAMS, ROBERT M. "Metaphysical Poets, Ancient and Modern." In *Strains of Discord: Studies in Literary Openness*, pp. 105–45. Ithaca, N.Y.: Cornell University Press.

Suggests that the most distinguishing feature of metaphysical poetry is wit, a "wit based upon a difficult metaphor, intellectual or abstract in its nexus, rather than naturalistic, involving more often an esoteric analogy than a superficial, single-level physical resemblance, and giving always the sense of a difficulty overcome" (p. 107). Comments on the dramatic element in Herbert's poetry: Herbert, Donne, and Marvell are poets "who play with a contrast between spheres of existence: the microcosm and the macrocosm or the stadium of heavenly simplicity and that of worldly complexity or the sphere of contemplation and the sphere of action" (p. 111). Thus, their style is metaphysical "precisely as it juxtaposes points of view which are in some ways compatible, in others not— as it carries out a juxtaposition which involves a strain" (p. 111). In a subsection of the essay entitled "Auden and Herbert," the author compares the simplicity of style, the seemingly artless quality, and the quiet and graceful tone of Herbert's poetry with the strenuous, difficult, allusive, and restless quality of the metaphysical verse of Auden and Empson. Comments on Herbert's deliberate and inventive devices for achieving simplicity, especially his uses of shaped verse and stanzaic patterns. Calls "Love (III)" an exquisite example of "a metaphysical poem so close to metaphysical reality that it needs no impurities of style, no dramatization or assertion of self; yet its very comportment, its quiet and easy grace, are dramatically eloquent" (p. 124).

∞§ 410. ADLER, JACOB H. "Form and Meaning in Herbert's 'Discipline.'" N&Q, n.s. 5:240–43.

Shows through a stanza-by-stanza analysis of "Discipline" that "in spite of an apparent (and in a sense genuine) simplicity and austerity, the effect of the poem is both complex and powerful" (p. 243). Points out how various elements in the poem contribute to the total effect: "The short lines with end-pause; the particularly short third lines; the direct word-order and easy-seeming rime; the rod and the vivid imagery of love as a man of war which are together expressive of the central idea of the poem; the first and last stanzas, which need to be similar and need to be different: all contribute to the tension between two conflicting emotions toward God which the poem builds up and resolves" (p. 243).

∞§ 411. BUSH, DOUGLAS. "Tradition and Experience." In *Literature and Belief*, edited by M. H. Abrams, pp. 31–52. English Institute Essays, 1957. New York: Columbia University Press.

Reprinted in *Engaged and Disengaged* (Cambridge, Mass.: Harvard University Press, 1966), pp. 143–63.

Discusses non-Christian responses to, and experience of, poetry that is firmly rooted in Christian belief. Makes several references to Herbert by way of illustration. Argues, "The great poetry of religious meditation, the poetry that really comes home to modern readers who do not share the beliefs it embodies, is that which extends beyond the particular creed and personality of its author, which grows out of and embraces general human experience" (pp. 40–41). Suggests that such an appeal is what the modern reader finds in Herbert: Herbert's "greater poems are greater because they deal with worldly allurements, rebellious self-will, the desire for discipline and humility and for the renewal of spiritual energy, with conflicts and aspirations and defeats and victories that belong to all human life" (p. 39). Contrasts Herbert's modern appeal with that of Donne and Crashaw.

∞§ 412. EVANS, G. BLAKEMORE. "George Herbert's 'Jordan.'" N&Q, n.s. 5:215.

Supports the interpretation of the title of Herbert's two Jordan poems put forward by A. B. Grosart: "(a) That he was crossing into the Promised Land; (b) That thereupon Jordan was to be his Helicon—the Lord, not the Nine Muses, the source of his inspiration" (p. 215). Supports this position by references to Christopher Harvey's *The Synagogue* (2d ed., 1647) and to some anonymous lines appearing in a memorial poem included in Herbert's *The Temple* (10th ed., 1674): "In both passages, with specific reference to Herbert's poetry, we find a sacred height . . . compared to Parnassus, and Christ's blood . . . to an implied Helicon" (p. 215).

◄§ 413. HAGSTRUM, JEAN H. "The 'Baroque' Century." In *The Sister Arts: The Tradition of Literary Pictorialism and English Poetry from Dryden to Gray*, pp. 93–128. Chicago: University of Chicago Press.

Comments on the emblematic quality of Herbert's poetry and calls him "the most emblematic of poets" (p. 100). Points out that the titles of many of Herbert's poems "are graphic in an emblematic way and seem almost to take the place of engraved design" (p. 98); that "The Posie," in fact, "even uses the technical language of the device or impresa" (p. 98); and that "the graphically conceived icon in Herbert's verse often provides its organizing form" (p. 100). Suggests that *The Temple* "resembles a book of *imagini*, like Cesare Ripa's *Iconologia*" (p. 99): "Herbert's collection of poems represents the same kind of subject, limited of course to the church, its symbols and its seasons, its feasts and its fasts" (p. 99). Recognizes that the symbolic and metaphysical meanings of objects, rather than the objects themselves, are the concern of Herbert's poetry, but still maintains that because of Herbert's emblematic method he "belongs to the iconic and pictorialist tradition" (p. 100).

◄§ 414. HILBERRY, CONRAD. "Herbert's 'Dooms-day.'" *Expl* 16:item 24.

Outlines the basic argument of "Dooms day," which is a "striking illustration of George Herbert's very sure control of tone: the first four stanzas are a bizarre, partly comic plea for an early Doomsday; then the last stanza shifts the tone slightly and unfolds a new center of seriously religious meaning."

◄§ 415. JOSELYN, SISTER M. "Herbert and Hopkins: Two Lyrics." *Renascence* 10:192–95.

Compares and contrasts Herbert's "Affliction (I)" and G. M. Hopkins's "Carrion Comfort" and suggests that the subject of both poems is similar: "A trial of faith more or less intense . . . favorably resolved at the end though at the cost of severe personal sacrifice" (p. 192). Yet points out that "in tenor and decorum, every nuance and strategy of feeling, the two poems could hardly differ more" (p. 192). Presents a close reading of Herbert's poem.

◄§ 416. MITTON, C. LESLIE. "George Herbert's 'The Country Parson.'" *Expository Times* 69:113–15.

Appreciative essay on *The Country Parson* by a clergyman. Stresses that even today Herbert's book "is particularly applicable to the minister, but words of homely wisdom abound, many of which are also of significance for every one who seeks to live the Christian life" (p. 114).

◄§ 417. NOVARR, DAVID. *The Making of Walton's Lives.* Cornell Studies in English, edited by M. H. Abrams, Francis E. Mineka, and William M. Sale, Jr., 41. Ithaca, N.Y.: Cornell University Press. xvi, 527p.
Discusses Walton's biographical methodology and makes important comments on the various subjects of the *Lives.* Herbert is mentioned throughout, especially in the sections devoted to Donne. Chapter 10, "The 'Almost Incredible Story' of George Herbert," is devoted to the *Life of Herbert* (1670) and its subsequent revisions. Comments on Walton's long interest in Herbert before the writing of the *Life.* Outlines Walton's intention, point of view, and sources in writing the biography. Concludes that Walton "had put a halo about Herbert's head, had made a case that the halo glorified even noble and learned heads, and had shown the clergy precisely how they, too, could obtain halos. His revisions serve only to show that he was himself pleased by his accomplishment" (p. 361). Shows that Walton did not "go to great trouble to get detailed biographical information" (p. 488) and that thus the *Life* is "full of inaccuracies and gaps" (p. 488). Shows how Walton used Herbert's poetry and prose to create a portrait of Herbert as "a prototype of the good parson" (p. 488). Appendix B, "Walton and the Poems about Donne's Seal" (pp. 503–6), comments on Herbert's reply. Appendix D, "The Publication of the *Life of Herbert*" (pp. 510–12), presents bibliographical information. Appendix F, "Walton on Herbert's Resignation of His Fellowship" (pp. 516–20), discusses Walton's reason for dropping his reference to Herbert's resignation of his fellowship.

◄§ 418. RICKEY, MARY ELLEN. "Rhymecraft in Edward and George Herbert." *JEGP* 57:502–11.
Proposes "to examine the range of rhyme designs used by both men and to determine what light, if any, can be cast on the relationship of their rhymecraft" (p. 502). Presents a tabulation of the "rhyme formulas and number of nonrepeated stanza forms" employed by each (pp. 503–4). Shows that "George Herbert uses 48 rhyme plans in 169 stanzas while Edward Herbert uses 44 rhyme plans in 62 stanzas" (p. 504). Points out that such innovators as Campion, Donne, Southwell, and Raleigh cannot match the Herberts in range of pattern. Enumerates some of the so-called oddities of Herbert's verse found in the earlier work of Edward Herbert—for instance, the hieroglyphic (shaped poem), the convention of the echo, the use of a shift in stanza form within a poem, and the use of rare or unknown stanza forms. Shows that Edward's experimentation with rhyme and his ingenuity are more extensive than George's

and concludes that the younger brother appropriated some formal qualities from the older brother: "It is especially curious that several of the
highly wrought lyrics of holy Mr. Herbert should have been suggested to
him by the more flippant verse of Lord Herbert of Cherbury" (p. 511).

◆§ 419. WARNKE, FRANK J. "Jan Luyken: A Dutch Metaphysical
Poet." *CL* 10:45–54.
Argues that metaphysical poetry "constitutes a style, unlike the continental baroque, and that this style is not limited to English poetry" (p.
46). Suggests, "No body of continental verse demonstrates more tellingly the presence of this analogous something than does the religious
poetry of the seventeenth-century Dutchman Jan Luyken (1649–1712)"
(p. 46). Compares and contrasts Luyken with Herbert and suggests that
the Dutch poet is more closely related to Vaughan or Traherne than he
is to Herbert or Donne: he belongs "to that last phase of metaphysical
poetry, in which the traditional view of the world expresses itself through
a meditative attention to observed nature, an attention which in many
ways anticipates that of those romantics who a century and a half later
were also to look for the Creator in the creation" (pp. 53–54).

◆§ 420. WATSON, GEORGE. "Ramus, Miss Tuve, and the New Petro-
machia." *MP* 55:259–62.
Challenges in part A. J. Smith's attack (entry 396) on Rosemond
Tuve's claims for Ramism in her study, *Elizabethan and Metaphysical
Imagery: Renaissance Poetic and Twentieth-Century Critics* (entry 279).
Agrees with Smith that Tuve's argument is "too ambitious and will not
stand" (p. 260) but concludes that Ramism, "as far as the English were
concerned, was a quick handbook for logic with Cambridge and Puritan
associations. It is still not clear that there is any need to seek a connection between Ramism and English poetry; but, if one must be sought at
all, the neo-Ramists might surely have found a happier hunting-ground
than the poems of men as un-Puritanical and unsimple as the English
metaphysicals" (p. 262). No specific mention of Herbert.

◆§ 421. WILSON, EDWARD M. "Spanish and English Poetry of the Seventeenth Century." *Journal of Ecclesiastical History* 9:38–53.
Tries "to show that there was unity as well as diversity in two contemporary religious literatures and to hint at the sources of that unity"
(p. 38). Suggests that "in each country there was a common way to
express religious truths in vivid everyday terms" and that this "was partly
due to the fact that both countries had a medieval heritage in common,
but still more to the fact that a devotional literature spread from Spain
through Roman Catholic Europe into England in spite of fundamental
differences of religious belief and practice" (p. 53). Discusses the art of
sacred parody and the uses of divine analogy (or continued metaphor)

in English and Spanish devotional poetry. Points out Herbert's parody of Sidney and calls "Redemption" the best example of the continued metaphor in English. Compares Herbert briefly with Alonso de Ledesma, Lope de Vega, and Valdivielso. Comments on possible Spanish influence on Herbert and discusses also the influence of the art of discursive meditation on the various poets of the period.

1959

⁍§ 422. Anon. [Smith, A. J.] "Anglicanism and the Poets." *TLS*, 20 March, pp. 153–54.

Comments on the great diversity of Anglican poets and suggests that many of them, though not always agreeing on points of doctrine, often seem to share "an understanding of the peculiarly indefinable Anglican temperament" (p. 153). Suggests that the local nature of the Anglican Church accounts for a great deal of this diversity: "The ability of Anglican poets . . . to take upon them the prevailing attitudes of their age can occasionally make clear distinctions difficult, and the absence of an inflexible orthodox line has led many critics into what in one sense are almost bizarre comparisons between, for example, Wordsworth and Vaughan, for intellectually these poets differ greatly" (p. 153). Several references to Herbert by way of illustrating the Anglican temperament of the seventeenth century.

⁍§ 423. Attal, Jean-Pierre. "Qu'est-ce que la poésie 'métaphysique'?" *Critique* (Paris) 15:682–707.

Review of six critical studies: (1) Denonain's *Thèmes et formes de la poésie «métaphysique»* (entry 385); (2) Odette de Mourgues's *Metaphysical Baroque and Précieux Poetry* (entry 355); (3) Alan Boase's *Sponde* (Geneva: Pierre Cailler, 1949); (4) Boase's "Poètes Anglais et Français de l'Époque Baroque" (entry 290); (5) Joan Bennett's *Four Metaphysical Poets* (entry 147); (6) T. S. Eliot's "The Metaphysical Poets" (entry 56). Maintains that metaphysical poetry is indeed metaphysical in that it deals with first principles and first causes, that it is above all concerned with truth rather than beauty, and that it scorns the heritage of the classics and traditional poetic phraseology: "Ils se sont tournés verse quotidien et le familier pour atteindre la «réel»" (p. 706). Compares Herbert and Donne: "Alors que Donne soumet l'apparence au sacré (ce qui explique en partie sa liberté d'images qui n'ont qu'un but: signifier ce sacré), Herbert et Vaughan la soumettent plutôt au divin; l'apparence est pour eux «l'inépuisable livret d'une inépuisable musique»" (p. 702).

⁍§ 424. Boyd, George W. "What Is 'Metaphysical' Poetry?" *MissQ* 12:13–21.

Traces the meaning of the term *metaphysical poetry* from Dryden to the present, "taking account of its sometimes gradual, sometimes drastic shifting and giving especial attention to the wide-ranging discussion of the subject in the criticism of the past decade" (p. 13). Maintains that the "classic definition and delineation of metaphysical poetry laid down by Messrs. Grierson, Eliot, and Williamson . . . has not been superseded in modern criticism, indeed, that it has hardly been basically modified" (p. 21). Sees the work of Joseph Mazzeo and Louis Martz as possible new directions. No specific mention of Herbert.

✎§ 425. CHUTE, MARCHETTE. *Two Gentle Men: The Lives of George Herbert and Robert Herrick.* New York: E. P. Dutton & Co. 319p. Reprinted, London: Secker & Warburg, 1960.

Part 1 (pp. 11–152) presents a biographical account of Herbert for the common reader with brief critical comments on Herbert's poetry, which is seen primarily as autobiographical. Appendix: "Walton's Biography of Herbert" (pp. 277–82) comments on Walton's intention and methodology in the *Lives.* Challenges in particular Walton's contention that Herbert entered politics because of worldly ambition, a "case of manipulation, one that adds a great deal to the effectiveness of the story of a saint who forsook the world but one which has no support outside of Walton's pages" (p. 279). Also questions Walton's account of the reasons Herbert became a deacon. Bibliography (pp. 283–97).

✎§ 426. ———. "A Biographer and Two Dear Friends She Never Met." *NYHTB,* 27 December, pp. 1, 11.

Explains why she enjoyed writing *Two Gentle Men: The Lives of George Herbert and Robert Herrick* (entry 425): "I already knew, before I began the book, that I loved them both as poets but after I made their acquaintance I found I loved them as people too" (p. 1). Presents a brief biographical sketch of Herbert and Herrick.

✎§ 427. COLIE, ROSALIE L. "Constantijn Huygens and the Metaphysical Mode." *GR* 34:59–73.

Examines the religious verse of Huygens, the Dutch translator of Donne's poems, to determine the validity of Huygens's claim of being a metaphysical poet. Points out a number of parallels between Huygens and the metaphysical poets and concludes that his "religious poetic, his mode of metaphoric usage, his choice of meter, all show the poet's persuasive belief in God's original wit and in his own lesser wit, set to sing his praises of God's creativity, working simultaneously in the physical and spiritual worlds of which metaphysical poetry is made" (p. 73). Notes that Huygens possessed a copy of Herbert's poetry and finds many parallels between the religious verse of Huygens and that of Herbert, especially echoes of "The Flower," "The Collar," "The Sacrifice," "Christmas," "The H. Scriptures (II)," and "Jordan (II)." Says that

Huygens, like Herbert, "managed to maintain in his poems an intellectual tension rising from his awareness of the necessarily paradoxical bases
of his religious life and to force upon his readers a sharp and articulate
religious understanding" (p. 67).

◄§ 428. DREW, ELIZABETH. *Poetry: A Modern Guide to Its Understanding and Enjoyment*. New York: W. W. Norton & Co. 287p.
Brief explication of "Love (III)" (pp. 245–47). Calls the poem "a
little symbolic drama of personal experience, where the Christian ethic
shines out in all its simple beauty" (p. 245). Brief mention of "Vertue"
(p. 107) and "The Flower" (p. 142).

◄§ 429. DUNCAN, JOSEPH E. *The Revival of Metaphysical Poetry: The
History of a Style, 1800 to the Present*. Minneapolis: University of
Minnesota Press. 227p.
General, broad review of the critical reputation of the metaphysical
poets from their own time to the present. Emphasizes "the line of successive interpretations rather than individual evaluations, and treats
poetic style as a vital force guiding creative efforts in a later period" (p.
5). Attempts "to show in what ways the metaphysical style, as it was interpreted and varied through successive periods, was both like and unlike the metaphysical style of the seventeenth century" (p. 4). Divided
into ten chapters: (1) "The Early Conceptions of Metaphysical Poetry"
(pp. 6–28); (2) "Seeds of Revival" (pp. 29–49); (3) "John Donne and
Robert Browning" (pp. 50–68); (4) "The Beginnings of the Revival in
America" (pp. 69–88); (5) "The Catholic Revival and the Metaphysicals" (pp. 89–112); (6)"The Metaphysical Revival: 1872–1912" (pp.
113–29); (7) "Yeats, Donne and the Metaphysicals" (pp. 130–42); (8)
"Eliot and the Twentieth-Century Revival" (pp. 143–64); (9) "Metaphysicals and Critics since 1912" (pp. 165–81); and (10) "Metaphysical
Florescence" (pp. 182–202). Chapter 3 first appeared as "The Intellectual Kinship of John Donne and Robert Browning" in *SP* 50 (1953):81–
100, here slightly revised; chapter 6 first appeared as "The Revival of
Metaphysical Poetry, 1872–1912" (entry 350), here slightly revised. Many
references throughout to Herbert. Comments on Herbert's influence on
many later poets and surveys the appreciative evaluation of him by many
notables, including Coleridge, Margaret Fuller, Emerson, Lowell, and
especially John Keble, G. M. Hopkins, Francis Thompson, and Yeats.

◄§ 430. EMERSON, RALPH WALDO. "Ben Jonson, Herrick, Herbert, Wotton." In *Early Lectures of Ralph Waldo Emerson*, vol. 1 (1833–
1886), edited by Stephen E. Whicher and Robert E. Spiller, pp.
337–55. Cambridge, Mass.: Harvard University Press.

Emerson's lecture to the Society for the Diffusion of Useful Knowledge at the Masonic Temple in Boston on 31 December, 1835. The editors suggest that Emerson's choice of writers for this lecture may have been in part motivated by his concern at the time about the function of language as symbol. As early as 1831 Emerson in the *Journal* had commented on Herbert's use of language. In the lecture, Emerson says that Herbert "is a striking example of the power of exalted thought to melt and bend language to its fits of expression" (p. 350) and maintains that Herbert excels "in exciting that feeling we call the moral sublime" (p. 352). Praises Herbert's diction and quotes from "Vertue," "Confession," "The Elixir," "Providence," and "Affliction (I)."

◀§ 431. GAMBERINI, SPARTACO. *Poeti Metafisici e Cavalieri in Inghilterra*. Biblioteca dell' «Archivium Romanicum»: Serie 1: Storia-Letteratura-Paleografia, vol. 60. Florence: Leo S. Olschki. 269p.

Discriminates between such critical terms as *wit, conceit, metaphysical poetry, euphuism, baroque,* and *mannerism.* Compares and contrasts Donne, Jonson, and Chapman as leaders of different poetic schools. Presents a general survey of Herbert's work for an Italian audience (pp. 83–92). Comments primarily on the thematic concerns of Herbert's poetry and on his religious sensibilities. Calls *The Temple* "il diario intimo che con scrupolosa esattezza annota ogni moto dell'anima" (p. 86) and suggests, "Forse per questo scrupolo di verità, nell' ansia di osservare e definire ogni stato d'animo, nel non permettere mai il minimo abbandono, la poesia del Herbert non è lirica, intendendo questo genere come canto, abbandono alato all'émpito del sentimento. Manca la lirica, c'è la preghiera, l'analisi, l'introspezione, l'argomentazione, ma non il canto" (p. 86). Compares Herbert with Lyly, Benlowes, Lord Herbert, and especially Vaughan.

◀§ 432. HART, A. TINDALL. "Saints and Sinners." In *The Country Clergy in Elizabethan & Stuart Times, 1558–1660*, pp. 137–64. London: Phoenix House.

Brief biographical account of Herbert as a Laudian clergyman. Outlines some of his main tenets concerning the living of a Christian life, especially as these apply to a country parson.

◀§ 433. RATHMELL, J. C. A. "Hopkins, Ruskin and the Sidney Psalter." *London Magazine* 6:51–66.

Primarily discusses the influence of the *Sidney Psalter* on G. M. Hopkins, especially on his "terrible sonnets." Suggests that Herbert also owes a great deal to the *Psalter* and briefly comments on Herbert's influence on Hopkins. Sees the modern metaphysical revival beginning, not in 1912 with the publication of Herbert J. C. Grierson's edition of Donne, but in the 1860s with Ruskin's and Hopkins's great admiration for Herbert.

❧ 434. RICHMOND, H. M. "The Intangible Mistress." *MP* 56:217–23.

Discusses various treatments of the theme of the unknown or unknowable mistress, a stock theme of Renaissance poetry, as a way of distinguishing what is genuinely metaphysical in so-called metaphysical poetry. Only incidentally comments on Herbert. Points out that "prettily conceited verse dealing with quaint situations is particularly a Caroline specialty" and that "to this vein many of the poems of George Herbert, for example, could be more readily assimilated than to that of Donne's verse, to the stringent scholasticism of which they offer no parallel" (p. 222). Suggests also that Herbert, although he writes religious poems exclusively, gives one a "more secular sense of delight than is produced by the intense scrutiny to which Donne subjects even pagan themes" (p. 222).

❧ 435. TUVE, ROSEMOND. "George Herbert and *Caritas*." *JWCI* 22: 303–31.

Reprinted in *Essays by Rosemond Tuve*, edited by Thomas P. Roche, Jr. (Princeton: Princeton University Press, 1970), pp. 167–206.

Discusses the nature of Christian love in Herbert's poems and shows the intellectual fineness of his theology of love. Suggests that the primary conflict in Herbert is not between his secular ambitions and his religious calling but rather between his will and the demands of God's love. His fundamental torment is that he does not fully respond to God's love. Points out that Herbert writes "much more of God's love for man than of what man's love to God should be" (p. 308). States that Herbert "celebrates in poem after poem God's love for man, Agape, and the single revelation of it in Christ's Incarnation and Passion" (p. 314). Comments on various distinctions that must be made between secular poetry and Herbert's religious love poetry. For example, unlike the secular love poet, Herbert "never mentions, or implies, or fears, that his love is unrequited" (p. 310); likewise, he is "so entirely convinced and aware of the boundless love received from the one he loves that this is a *datum* in the most unhappy, the most tormented of the poems" (p. 311).

❧ 436. UNTERMEYER, LOUIS. "After the Renaissance." In *Lives of the Poets: The Story of One Thousand Years of English and American Poetry*, pp. 137–69. New York: Simon & Shuster.

Brief biographical sketch of Herbert. Comments on some of the more salient features of his poetry: its playfulness, piety, double meanings, metaphorical ingenuity, wit, and technical experimentation. Calls the poetry "a union of play and passion which allows Herbert to embody his most profound reflections in anagrams and acrostics, shaped stanzas, and picture poems" (p. 139). Comments on the "fusion of solemnity and virtuosity" (p. 140). "Quiet, alternately courtly and colloquial, this is a poetry which begins in wonder and ends in certainty" (p. 142).

1960

⋙ 437. ALLEN, DON CAMERON. "George Herbert: 'The Rose.'" In *Image and Meaning: Metaphoric Traditions in Renaissance Poetry*, pp. 67–79. Baltimore: Johns Hopkins Press.
Rev. and enlarged ed., 1968.
Discusses the classical and Christian symbolic uses of the rose that inform Herbert's poem "The Rose." Shows that Herbert "brings in the Christian meanings of the flower and permits the pagan rose to be contrasted with the spiritual one" (p. 68). In antiquity the rose had a double metaphoric tradition: it stood not only for transient worldliness but also represented drunken revelry and riot. Thus to some early Christians the rose was a sign of the deceits of the world. Later the rose was transformed into a symbol of love and virginity and a sign of those who scorned the world, especially the martyrs. The rose was particularly associated with the Virgin Mary and ultimately with Christ, who, from the twelfth century on was often called the mystic rose. Shows that in Herbert's poem "the rose of fleeting worldly pleasure is also the Christian and his God, a God who is love, but who is also judge and sentencer. So there are two flowers, an earthly one and a heavenly one; and on this doctrine of the rose, the poem of Herbert rests" (pp. 78–79).

⋙ 438. CROSSETT, JOHN. "Did Johnson Mean 'Paraphysical'?" *Boston University Studies in English* 4:121–24.
Says that if one studies Dr. Johnson's dictionary as well as his general critical vocabulary, a vocabulary often taken from Longinus, it is possible to trace the origin and the precise meaning of the term *metaphysical* as Johnson used it in *The Lives of the Poets*. Concludes that Johnson merely "substituted 'metaphysical' for the non-existent 'paraphysical,' willingly or otherwise accepting the confusion in the exact meanings of *meta* and *para*; and that he wished 'metaphysical' to express the notion of deviating from nature by being excessive and contrary to nature" (p. 124). Suggests that Johnson's main criticism of the metaphysical poets was "that they did violate nature; the word that he chose to categorize them was intended to convey this notion" (p. 124).

⋙ 439. ELLRODT, ROBERT. *L'Inspiration personnelle et l'esprit du temps chez les poètes métaphysiques anglais*. Paris: José Corti. 2 parts in 3 vols.
Part 1 (vols. 1 & 2): 2d ed. (with new bibliography), 1973.
General introduction (pp. 14–77) reviews various definitions of metaphysical poetry using certain historical, stylistic, and psychological grounds

and dismisses each as inadequate. Presents a tentative definition of metaphysical poetry and concludes that, since the metaphysical conceit comes from "la perplexité de l'esprit en présence des contradictions inhérentes à l'existence," Herbert as well as Donne and Marvell "sont les vrais 'poètes métaphysiques', car leur poésie reproduit la démarche même et l'inquiétude du métaphysicien" (p. 30). Part 1, "Les Structures fondamentales de l'inspiration personnelle," is divided into two volumes. Volume 1, "John Donne et les poètes de la tradition chrétienne" is further subdivided into two books: "John Donne" (pp. 80–264) and "Les Poètes de la tradition chrétienne" (pp. 265–452). In the second book, one chapter is specifically devoted to Herbert (pp. 267–373). This chapter has four major sections: (1) "Le temps et l'espace," (2) "Mode de conscience et de sensibilité," (3) "Mode de pensée et formes d'expression," and (4) "Donne et Herbert, poètes métaphysiques." Throughout the chapter the author contrasts and compares Herbert to Donne. States, "L'habitude de penser sur deux plans à la fois, la perception simultanée de vérités parallèles et contraires, indissociables et distinctes, telle est la «forme» d'esprit qui apparente Donne et Herbert" (p. 341). Comments specifically on Donne's and Herbert's perceptions of time and space; discusses the autobiographical elements in the poetry of each; contrasts and compares Donne's and Herbert's uses of hyperbole, litotes, paradox, and irony; comments in detail on Herbert's attitude toward the Eucharist and compares it with the Calvinistic position; and evaluates the applicability of the term *metaphysical* to Herbert. In the last section of this chapter Herbert is contrasted with Crashaw (pp. 375–452). Volume 2 of part 1 is divided into two books: "Poètes de transition" (pp. 9–170) and "Poètes mystiques" (pp. 171–399). Throughout Herbert is compared to Lord Herbert of Cherbury, Cowley, Marvell, Vaughan, and Traherne. Three tables summarize the various major characteristics of the metaphysical poets (pp. 411–12, 416, 422). In part 2 (pp. 9–400) the author discusses the social, psychological, and literary origins of metaphysical poetry at the turn of the sixteenth century.

440. HERBERT, GEORGE. *Selected Poems of George Herbert, with a few representative poems by his contemporaries,* edited by Douglas Brown. London: Hutchinson Educational. 159p.

Prefatory note (pp. 5–6); contents (pp. 7–9); short biographical portrait (pp. 11–15); early records: selections from Walton's *Life* and Nicholas Ferrar's preface to *The Temple* (pp. 16–21); a note on the social and literary setting (pp. 22–25); selections from Herbert's poetry as well as a few poems by Sidney, Southwell, Vaughan, Carew, Donne, Marvell, and Henry King, arranged into four major groups: hymns and anthems, his quick-piercing mind, the many spiritual conflicts, and poetry of meditation (pp. 27–100); critical commentary and notes on each section and on individual poems (pp. 101–50); short bibliography (p. 151), and glossary (pp. 153–60).

◄§ 441. HUGHES, RICHARD E. "Conceptual Form and Varieties of Religious Experience in the Poetry of George Herbert." *Greyfriar: Siena Studies in Literature* 3:3–12.

Discusses the idea of form as concept and argues that Herbert's works "*de facto* are more a question of concept than precept" (p. 6) and that "there is a tense ambivalence in Herbert's poetry which can be seen once we extend behind the disciplinary elements of his forms to the concepts which his forms embody" (p. 6). States, "A single, consecrated subject-matter; an edifying and persuasive intention; poetry as recapitulation: behind all of these lies one concept. This concept might be generally termed the rhetorical viewpoint" (p. 6). Suggests that Herbert's rhetorically oriented conceptualism consists of three main ingredients: (1) a belief in probability; (2) "the belief that probability gives grounds for action, and that reasonable men will act on probability, once it is presented" (p. 7); and (3) "the belief that isolated phenomena, experiences, perceptions find their real value when they can be absorbed into or subordinated to the abstract realm of probability" (p. 7). Argues that the "temptation in criticizing Herbert is to overstress the orderliness of his poetry, and to overlook the rich complexity of the concept which lies behind that orderliness" (p. 9). Discusses the techniques of Herbert's rhetoric, especially commenting on his uses of figures and tropes. Comments in some detail on "Redemption," "The Collar," "Christmas," "Easter," and "The Pilgrimage" as poems that involve the search for God, in which Herbert "combines two varieties of religious experience, and moves from a detached, intellectualized expression into an expression of simultaneous realities" (p. 11).

◄§ 442. KNIEGER, BERNARD. "The Religious Verse of George Herbert." *CLAJ* 4:138–47.

Suggests that Herbert's poems do not "merely dramatize the philosophy of an Anglican priest" but rather "illuminate the situation of all men" (p. 138). Discusses some of the major themes of Herbert's spiritual struggle. Points out in particular the extensive use of business imagery in Herbert's poems of conflict. Comments on this imagery in "Jordan (II)," "Affliction (I)," "The Pearl," and "Redemption" as a way of generally introducing Herbert's poetry as a whole. Concludes, "Because 'selling' and 'buying' are to him very strong symbols for states of impotency and value respectively, because he conceives the relation between God and man as almost expressible in legal terms, and because he is so intimate and confident in his intercourse with God that he can employ even the language of business when talking to Him and about Him, for all these

reasons George Herbert employs business imagery with telling effect"
(p. 147).

◆§ 443. LEACH, ELSIE. "More Seventeenth-Century Admirers of Her-
    bert." N&Q, n.s. 7:62–63.
Notes certain seventeenth-century admirers and imitators of Herbert
not mentioned in F. E. Hutchinson's edition (entry 223), including
Thomas Washbourne in *Divine Poems* (1654), John Rawlet in *Poetick
Miscellanie* (1687), Samuel Speed in *Prison-Pietie: Or, Meditations
Divine and Moral* (1677), Richard Baxter in *Poetical Fragments* (1681),
Daniel Baker in *Poems upon Several Occasions* (1697), W. S. in *The
Poems of Ben. Jonson Junior, Being a Miscelanie of Seriousnes, Wit,
Mirth, and Mysterie* (1672), and John Hall in *Jacobs Ladder: or, the
Devout Souls Ascention to Heaven, in Prayers, Thanksgivings, and Praises*
(2d ed., 1676).

◆§ 444. ————. "Lydgate's 'The Dolerous Pyte of Crystes Passioun'
    and Herbert's 'The Sacrifice.' " N&Q, n.s. 7:421.
Points out parallels between Herbert's "The Sacrifice" and Lydgate's
"The Dolerous Pyte of Crystes Passioun" (Early English Text Society,
extra series 107[1911]:250–52), especially the complaint. Suggests that
this is the only medieval poem that renders into English the specific complaint used by Herbert.

◆§ 445. MARTZ, LOUIS L. Foreword to *The Poems of Edward Taylor*,
    edited by Donald E. Stanford. New Haven: Yale University Press.
    lxii, 543p.
Reprinted in *The Poem of the Mind: Essays on Poetry, English and
American* (entry 578), pp. 54–81.
In his foreword Martz compares and contrasts Herbert and Taylor,
pointing out the pervading influence of Herbert, especially on *Preparatory
Meditations*. Relates both Herbert and Taylor to the larger meditative
tradition but also points out specific echoes and borrowings from Herbert. Concludes that Taylor "appears to have had a mind saturated with
Herbert's poetry, and the result is that a thousand tantalizing echoes of
Herbert remain for the most part untraceable because the meditative
voice of Herbert has been merged with Taylor's own peculiar voice" (p.
xiv). Rejects the notion that Taylor is "a quaint primitive who somehow,
despite the Indians, managed to stammer out his rude verses well enough
to win the title of 'our best Colonial poet' " (p. xviii). Stanford's notes
to Taylor's individual poems point out several specific borrowings from
Herbert.

◆§ 446. MILES, JOSEPHINE. *Renaissance, Eighteenth-Century, and Mod-
    ern Language in English Poetry: A Tabular View*. Berkeley and
    Los Angeles: University of California Press. iii, 73p.

Presents information gathered from two hundred poets, from Chaucer to the present, "in such a way as to suggest the basic patterns of relation between poet and poet in the use of language, and at the same time to provide the most straightforward chronological arrangement of materials for those who may have other questions to ask, about single poets, single eras, single types, or single terms" (p. 1). Tabulates Herbert's use of language, pointing out, for instance, the number of nouns, adjectives, and verbs in the first one thousand lines of *The Temple* (through "Mattens" in F. E. Hutchinson's edition [entry 223]). Lists the most frequently used adjectives, nouns, and verbs in Herbert's verse.

◄§ 447. MONTGOMERY, ROBERT L., JR. "The Province of Allegory in George Herbert's Verse." *TSLL* 1:457–72.
Discusses the allegorical elements in Herbert's symbolic method. Points out that basically his symbols are analogies. Distinguishes between the meditative and allegorical modes and attempts to define the allegorical elements of Herbert's method and to indicate which of his poems can be properly labeled allegorical. Suggests that "the fable is the core of Herbert's allegorical method" (p. 463) and points out three criteria for distinguishing his allegorical lyrics: "A fable (or fiction structure) in control of the poem, the symbolic character of the fable, and fantasy or conceit" (p. 465). Concludes, "Allegory as a kind of larger symbol and vital form, is, in Herbert's hands, his most versatile tool" (p. 472).

◄§ 448. PETTET, E. C. *Of Paradise and Light: A Study of Vaughan's Silex Scintillans*. Cambridge: University Press. x, 216p.
Throughout this study, Herbert's influence on Vaughan is discussed and specific borrowings, echoes, and parallels are documented. Chapter 3, "Herbert's Poetry" (pp. 51–70), traces the extent and specific nature of Herbert's influence on *Silex Scintillans*. Points out not only the general inspiration that Vaughan got from Herbert but also comments on features of his style as well as on direct borrowings of specific images, titles, metrical forms, and even lines and half-lines from *The Temple*. Particularly sees Herbert's influence in Vaughan's use of homely images and metaphors. Argues, however, that "in theme, attitude, and spirit . . . the poems of *Silex Scintillans* owe little to Herbert" (p. 52). Concludes this survey by remarking: "All considered, there is little doubt that Herbert's poetry exercised an immense influence on the composition of *Silex Scintillans*. On the other hand, in spite of this great indebtedness to *The Temple*, Vaughan's work, particularly the flower of it, remains richly individual and, in all that essentially matters, entirely distinctive from Herbert's. Certainly the two writers can be regarded as true poetic twins; but, like Coleridge and Wordsworth, they are twins of the dissimilar type" (p. 70).

📌 449. STAMBLER, ELIZABETH. "The Unity of Herbert's 'Temple.'"
    Cross Currents 10:251–66.

Challenges in part the attempts of Louis Martz (*The Poetry of Meditation: A Study in English Religious Literature of the Seventeenth Century*, entry 365) and Joseph Summers (*George Herbert: His Religion and
Art*, entry 369) to account for the unity of *The Temple*. Offers a partial
explanation for the unity of the volume by discussing the "ways in which
The Temple as a whole resembles a volume of courtly love poetry—the
Vita Nuova, Petrarch's *Rime*, *Astrophel and Stella*—as individual poems
of *The Temple* resemble lyrics of the courtly love tradition" (p. 252).
Finds "resemblances in several important details and in two fairly large
general themes, the theme of loss and the theme of discipline which
brings the protagonist at last to a condition of purified desire" (p. 252).
Discusses such unifying details as the dramatic persona; the unceasing
shifts of states of feeling that record a wide range of emotion; Herbert's
references to *The Temple* as a whole and to his desire that single poems
be placed within the context of the whole; the unifying effect of the title
of the volume; the flow of time and the ordered chronology of the poems;
the chain of images in the first fourteen poems, in which the protagonist
is transformed from an inanimate object to an animate one; the recurring
images, especially sun-stone, measure, and eyes. Agrees that Herbert's "reordering and revitalizing of the form of the courtly love volume is an entirely characteristic display of his talent, on the same principle as his
utilization of Christian typologies or tracts of meditation" (p. 252).

1961

📌 450. ALVAREZ, A. *The School of Donne*. London: Chatto & Windus.
    202p.

Attempts "to show how Donne affected the language and form of
poetry in a way that is still peculiarly meaningful to us, and is rapidly
becoming yet more meaningful" and tries "to define a kind of intelligence which, though it was first expressed at the end of the sixteenth
century, is still vital and urgent" (p. 12). Argues for the notion of a
"School of Donne," united not so much by various poetical methods
and techniques as by the intellectual attitude and tone that formed it:
the desire to portray dramatically in poetry the complexities of thought
and feeling. Chapter 3, "The Poetry of Religious Experience" (pp. 67–
90), deals specifically with Herbert (pp. 67–83) and Vaughan (pp. 83–
90). Calls Herbert the "only poet to use Donne's discoveries for wholly
original ends" (p. 67). Points out Herbert's debt to Donne ("but his
debt is nowhere as specific as that of the other Metaphysicals [p. 68]),
especially his peculiar intensity and his use of common, conversational
language in religious verse. Attempts to point out, however, definite ways

in which Herbert clearly differs from Donne, for example, in his uses of the Bible, in his wit, and in his complex simplicity. Sees Herbert's simplicity, however, as "not the measure by which he fell short of Donne, but of the distance he went beyond him" (p. 70) and argues that Herbert's wit and ingenuity are best seen in his inventive verse forms. Concludes that Herbert's "contribution to religious poetry is large and his own. But the ground in which it could flower had been cleared by Donne" (p. 83). Comments specifically on "Jordan (I)," "The Forerunners," "Home," "The Pearl," and "Love (III)." Compares Herbert also with Crashaw, Vaughan, Marvell, Cowley, Hopkins, and Southwell.

◄§ 451. BANZER, JUDITH. " 'Compound Vision': Emily Dickinson and
      the Metaphysical Poets." *AL* 32:417–33.
   Argues that Dickinson, like Herbert and the other metaphysical poets, "practiced the metaphysical awareness of the unity of experience" (p. 417) and maintains, "The discipline that wrought many of her poems was the metaphysical one of a 'Compound Vision' by which the eternal is argued from the transient, the foreign explained by the familiar, and fact illuminated by mystery" (p. 417). Comments on Dickinson's familiarity with the metaphysical poets ("her pencil-markings of several poems argue close attention to their vision and technique" [p. 418]) and shows that her poems themselves are "the crucial argument for her knowledge of Donne or Herbert" (p. 418). Points out many similarities between Herbert and Dickinson, especially their uses of material conceits to illustrate transcendent realities, their uses of "homely images of safe enclosure" (p. 421), and their reflective practices, "which put Herbert forever in the divine presence" and result in "Emily's habit of strolling with Eternity" (p. 423). Sees both poets in the meditative mode and suggests specific echoes of Herbert in Dickinson's poetry.

◄§ 452. BLUM, IRVING D. "The Paradox of Money Imagery in English
      Renaissance Poetry." *SRen* 8:144–54.
   Argues against the somewhat standard opinion that money imagery is used in Renaissance poetry only to depict "the crass, prosaic details of existence" (p. 144) and gives a number of examples to show that, in fact, oftentimes money imagery, "like the sonnet, . . . is used to cast light upon all facets of life—the beautiful and the ugly, the generous and the miserly, the good and the evil" (p. 145). Suggests that such images "remain well within the Petrarchian and Spenserian conventions and, indeed, well within the poetic tradition of the entire English Renaissance" (pp. 144–45). Comments on such usage in Spenser, Gascoigne, Wyatt, Sidney, Daniel, Shakespeare, Chapman, Donne, and Herbert. Points out that, like many others, Herbert did not "scorn to borrow the qualities of money to define fanciful things in metaphor, while expressing

disdain for wealth in literal references" (p. 153). Shows Herbert's rejection of money in "Avarice" but notes his metaphorical uses of it in *The
Church-Porch* (lines 1–2, 109–10, 429–30) and in "The Pearl."

❧ 453. COLLMER, ROBERT G. "The Meditation on Death and Its Ap-
     pearance in Metaphysical Poetry." *Neophil* 45:323–33.
  Discusses the *meditatio mortis* tradition and comments on some of its
appearances in the poetry of Herbert, Donne, Vaughan, and Crashaw.
Points out a number of ways in which Herbert's attitude toward death
is reflected in his poetry, especially in "Repentance," "Church-monuments," and "Mortification." Suggests that Herbert, unlike Donne and
Vaughan, does not present descriptions of the more gruesome aspects of
death.

❧ 454. DALGLISH, JACK. *Eight Metaphysical Poets.* Edited with an
     introduction and notes by Jack Dalglish. New York: Macmillan
     Co. viii, 184p.
  General introduction to the nature and style of metaphysical poetry
(pp. 1–10). Considers the intellectual and introspective nature of much
metaphysical poetry, its fusion of thought and feeling, its uses of imagery
and conceits, its verse movement and dramatic qualities, etc. Anthologizes selections from Donne, Herbert, Carew, Crashaw, Vaughan, King,
Marvell, and Cowley (pp. 11–126). Herbert is represented by sixteen
poems with commentary and notes on individual poems. Presents in the
notes for Herbert (pp. 137–47) a biographical sketch and a brief essay
on some of the general characteristics of Herbert's poetry, such as his
themes, conversational tone, uses of complex metrical forms, technical
skill and inventiveness, and uses of imagery and the conceit.

❧ 455. GASKELL, RONALD. "Herbert's 'Vanitie.' " *CritQ* 3:313–15.
  Briefly compares Herbert and Jonson and concludes that Herbert's
is "a discipline more deeply moral, more completely a discipline of sensibility" (p. 313). Presents a close reading of "Vanitie," commenting on
Herbert's sensitive use of language and technical subtleties. Briefly compares Herbert to Keats. For three replies, see John Blackie, E. P. Smith,
and Ronald Gaskell, entry 473.

❧ 456. HART, JEFFREY. "Herbert's *The Collar* Re-Read." *Boston Uni-
     versity Studies in English* 5:65–73.
  Reprinted in *Seventeenth Century English Poetry: Modern Essays
in Criticism*, edited by William Keast (rev. ed., entry 707), pp. 248–56.
  Suggests that to see "The Collar" only in terms of "the struggle between discipline and pleasure, between the duties of a clergyman and the
satisfactions to be derived from the natural life, or . . . the struggle between God's will and the speaker's rebellious Heart" (p. 66) is to miss

the full complexity and import of the poem. Reading the poem "in the context of Herbert's other poems, and with reference to the tradition which informs his imagery with meaning" (p. 66), the author sees the poem as representing "in psychological terms the events of the Christian moral drama—the Fall, the Atonement, and the Redemption" (p. 66). Describes the moral events of the poem: "Just as the moral disorder entailed by the rebellious Adam and Eve was overcome by Christ's sacrifice, so the moral disorder of the speaker's rebellion is to be finally overcome by the sacrament of the Eucharist" (p. 66). Suggests, "The brilliance of the poem lies in the fact that it expresses rebellion and atonement in the same vocabulary, and by so doing epitomizes its central idea: that rebellion necessarily entails, because of God's justice and mercy, atonement" (p. 66). Presents a detailed reading of the poem and comments on its structure and form; its uses of images, puns, symbols, and double entendre; and its dramatic development.

◄§ 157. HERBERT, GEORGE. *The Poems of George Herbert*. With an introduction by Helen Gardner. The World's Classics, no. 109. 2d ed., London, New York, Toronto: Oxford University Press. xxi, 285p.

Reprinted, 1964, 1967, 1969, 1972, 1974. (The text of this edition is based on F. E. Hutchinson's text [entry 223]. An earlier edition in this series was edited by Arthur Waugh in 1907 and was based on Grosart's text.)

Contents (pp. v–xiii); introduction by Helen Gardner (pp. xv–xx); bibliographical note (p. xxi); text of *The Temple* (pp. 1–189); English poems in the Williams MS not included in *The Temple* (pp. 191–96); poems from Walton's *Lives* (pp. 197–98); doubtful poems (pp. 199–214); *Musae Responsoriae* (pp. 215–36); *Passio Discerpta* (pp. 237–42); *Lucus* (pp. 243–56); *Memoriae Matris Sacrum* (pp. 257–68); *Alia Poemata Latina* (pp. 269–77); appendix: *Pro Supplici Evangelicorum Ministrorum in Anglia* (pp. 279–85). In the introduction Helen Gardner comments on the general characteristics of Herbert's poetry, such as its grace of style, wit, intellectual vivacity, sincerity, precision and design, and the range of verse forms. Praises Herbert's "spiritual subtlety and delicacy" (p. xix) and says that "few devotional poets so exercise the mind" (p. xx). Comments briefly on the arrangement of the poems in *The Temple*, rejects the notion that the poems are simply a narrative account of the poet's spiritual progress, and concludes that, excluding some poems in the opening and the conclusion of the volume, "the connexions from poem to poem are not systematic: they are subtle relations of theme and mood and thought, groups of poems forming variations on the ground theme of the book, the love of God for man" (p. xviii). Suggests, "The source of the struggles in *The Temple* does not lie in a conflict between the world and a call to serve God at his altar; but in the difficulty of learning to say truly in any calling 'Thy will be done' " (p. xvii). Comments also briefly on Herbert's reputation.

❧§ 458. HOLLANDER, JOHN. *The Untuning of the Sky: Ideas of Music in English Poetry, 1500–1700.* Princeton: Princeton University Press. xii, 467p.

Reprinted, 1970.

Discusses certain beliefs about the nature and function of music during the Renaissance and about how English poetry of the sixteenth and seventeenth centuries expressed and employed these beliefs. Describes "the successive stages in the de-mythologizing of poetry's view of music" (p. 19) and suggests, "From the canonical Medieval Christian view that all human music bears a definite relation to the eternal, abstract (and inaudible) 'music' of universal order, to the completely de-Christianized, use of such notions in late seventeenth-century poetry as decorative metaphor and mere turns of wit, a gradual process of disconnection between abstract musical mythology and concrete practical considerations of actual vocal and instrumental music occurs" (p. 19). One section of chapter 5, " 'The Sacred Organs Praise,' " entitled "Herbert's Musical Temper" (pp. 288–94) discusses the wide range of musical images, puns, conceits, and terminology as well as the more generalized musical effects in Herbert's poetry. Suggests that the musical conceit "is seldom unconnected with some other, more central and governing one in each poem. It is as if the image of music were always running along beneath the surface of all of Herbert's poems, breaking out here and there like the eruption of some underground stream, but exercising always an informing, nourishing function" (p. 294). Argues that Herbert's "almost constant use of 'sing' for 'pray' represents a personal as well as a conventional figure; it is the actual image of the poet-divine playing and singing in secluded retirement that lurks behind so many of the musical conceits in his poetry" (p. 288). Comments specifically on "The Thanksgiving," "The Temper (I)," "Repentance," "Deniall," "The Quip," "Ephes. iv.30. *Grieve not the Holy Spirit*," "Dooms-day," "Easter," and "Easter-wings."

❧§ 459. HOWARTH, R. G. "Notes on Vaughan." *N&Q*, n.s. 8:184–85.

Rejects A. H. Bullen's suggestion in *More Lyrics from the Song-books of the Elizabethan Age* (1888) that the poem beginning "Yet if his majesty our sovereign lord" is by Vaughan. Suggests that it resembles Herbert but is inferior and more likely the work of one of Herbert's many imitators. Also says that the poem "Cry, bold but blessed thief," which Norman Ault includes in his *Poets' Life of Christ* (entry 64) and his *Seventeenth-Century Lyrics* (London, New York: Longmans, Green and Co., 1928) may be by Herbert, but again thinks that it is doubtful.

⊷§ 460. Hughes, R. E. "George Herbert's Rhetorical World." *Criticism* 3:86–94.

Argues that "a commitment to rhetoric, instead of limiting a writer to a learned facility, actually involves him in a complex frame of reference, that rhetoric, properly defined, might better be called a *weltanschauung* than a *discipline*; and that to view rhetoric in this light is a considerable help in understanding and appreciating much of the poetry of George Herbert" (p. 86). First discusses rhetoric generically and theoretically and then applies his conclusions specifically and analytically to some of Herbert's poems, particularly "Prayer (I)," "The Agonie," "Redemption," "Christmas," "Easter," and "The Pilgrimage." Primarily concerned with showing that in Herbert's poetry "rhetoric is not simply technique, not simply discipline, but is a way of looking at experience and ideas" (p. 88). Comments on Herbert's use of allegory as a way of subordinating "the specious world of appearances to the real world of abstractions" (p. 88). Suggests that all Herbert's themes are related to the probability of the communion between the human spirit and God and that all his poetry insists "on this probability; and if he could not *prove* that probability, as a logician might, he could *demonstrate* it, as a rhetorician would: through trope, which presented both the attributes and the uniqueness of God" (p. 88).

⊷§ 461. Jennings, Elizabeth. "The Lyric Intervention: Herbert and Vaughan." In *Every Changing Shape*, pp. 72–82. London: Dufour Editions; Philadelphia: Dufour Editions, 1962.

Sees Herbert primarily as a mystical poet, a visionary. Comments through examples drawn from various of Herbert's poems on the nature of his religious experience: "He explored and depicted all the stages of approach to God, from the articulate, discursive prayer of the beginner to the wordless prayer of the man far advanced in the spiritual life" (p. 74). Points out various major features of Herbert's verse: its simplicity, directness, wide range of images, use of paradox, colloquial diction, and especially its dramatic elements. Sees the dominating theme of all Herbert's poetry as one of "flight from and return to God" (p. 73). Briefly compares and contrasts Herbert and Vaughan.

⊷§ 462. Leishman, J. B. *Themes and Variations in Shakespeare's Sonnets.* London: Hutchinson & Co. 254p.

Comments on the "religiousness" of Shakespeare's sonnets and sees an affinity between them and Herbert's poetry, especially in their uses of the theme of "compensation": "I can find nothing in other love-poetry really comparable with his [Shakespeare's] many variations on the theme of what I have called 'compensation', and I think the only things in other poetry of which they really 'remind' me are some of those poems

where George Herbert expresses, or, as it were, revivifies his conviction
that his 'pearl of great price' is a more than sufficient compensation for
all that either he himself or the world may have supposed him to have
resigned or forgone" (p. 216). Suggests that some of Donne's more
serious love poems may have served as stylistic models for Herbert's religious love poems. Briefly comments on George Herbert Palmer's attempt to reorder Herbert's *The Temple* (entry 1) to make it fit a notion
of spiritual biography and quotes Aldous Huxley's comment about Herbert's poetry reflecting "inner weather" (see entry 138).

ও§ 463. LIEVSAY, JOHN LEON. *Stefano Guazzo and the English Renais-
    sance, 1575–1675.* Chapel Hill: University of North Carolina Press.
    xii, 344p.

Discusses Guazzo's contribution to English proverb lore and presents
a list of more than fifty of the so-called outlandish (foreign) proverbs
in G. H.'s *Witts Recreation. Selected from the finest Fancies of Moderne Muses. With a Thousand Outlandish Proverbs* (1640), often
attributed to Herbert, that can be found in either Guazzo's *Civil conver-
satione* or his *Dialoghi piacevole.* Suggests that the writer of *Witts Recreation* adapted them either directly from Guazzo or perhaps indirectly
from Florio's *Second Frutes.* Points out that proverbs from *Witts Recreation* also appear in *Comes Facundus in Via: The Fellow-Traveler*
(1658) and in N. R.'s *Proverbs English, French, Dutch, Italian, and
Spanish. All Englished and Alphabethically Digested* (1659). Calls the
latter "a shameless steal from the *Outlandish Proverbs*" (p. 321).

ও§ 464. PAGNINI, MARCELLO, ed. *Lirici Carolini e Repubblicani.* Collana
    di Letterature Moderne, 15. Naples: Edizione Scientifiche Italiane.
    xii, 420p.

Anthology of seventeenth-century English poetry for the Italian reader.
Contains a general introduction to the lyrical poetry of the period as well
as critical comment on each of the poets included (pp. 3–40). Textual
note (pp. 41–42) and a selected bibliography of critical works on the
period and on individual poets (pp. 43–51). Herbert is represented by
twenty poems and a brief biographical sketch and bibliographical note
(pp. 129–60).

ও§ 465. SANDERS, WILBUR. "Herbert and the Scholars." *Melbourne
    Critical Review* 4:102–11.

Explores the question "of how far Herbert's poetry depended upon his
predecessors, upon contemporary religious thought, and upon traditional
and liturgical symbolism" (p. 102) by examining the work of four recent
critics: Louis Martz (*The Poetry of Meditation: A Study in English
Religious Literature of the Seventeenth Century,* entry 365), Rosemary

Freeman (*English Emblem Books*, entry 284), Rosemond Tuve (*A Reading of George Herbert*, entry 344), and Malcolm MacKenzie Ross (*Poetry and Dogma: The Transformation of Eucharistic Symbols in Seventeenth Century English Poetry*, entry 368). Argues that Martz, Tuve, and Freeman overstate their cases in claiming that Herbert's cultural environment made his poetry possible and maintains that "poetry cannot be discussed at all except in terms of its meaning to us now" (p. 108). Agrees with Ross that Herbert was "caught in a process of social decay which reinforces his natural impulse away from a comprehensive humanism into a defensive and personal mysticism" (p. 110) and maintains that actually Herbert "estranged himself from the intellectual currents of his time and committed himself to a deliberate reaction" (p. 111).

≈§ 466. Souris, André, comp. and arr. *Poèmes de Donne, Herbert et Crashaw mis en musique par leurs contemporains G. Coperario, A. Ferrabosco, J. Wilson, W. Corkine, J. Hilton.* Transcriptions et réalisation par André Souris après des recherches effectuées sur les sources par John Cutts. Introduction par Jean Jacquot. Paris: Editions du centre national de la recherche scientifique. xix, 26p.

Comments briefly in the introduction on Herbert's interest in music and the importance of music in his poetry (pp. x–xi). Presents John Wilson's musical setting for "Content" (Bodleian Library Ms. Mus. b. 1, ff. 50ᵛ 51).

≈§ 467. Tuve, Rosemond. "Sacred 'Parody' of Love Poetry, and Herbert." *SRen* 8:249–90.

Reprinted in *Essays by Rosemond Tuve*, edited by Thomas P. Roche, Jr. (Princeton: Princeton University Press, 1970), pp. 207–51.

Discusses some conceptions of Herbert and his predecessors concerning the relationship between sacred and profane love poetry. Comments in detail on Herbert's "A Parodie," a sacred parody of William Herbert, third earl of Pembroke's poem "Soules joy, now I am gone" (sometimes attributed to Donne). Discusses various Renaissance meanings of the word *parody* and concludes, "Not any of these descriptions accurately describe the relation Herbert's poem bears to its original" (p. 251). Argues that there "is a parallelism between the two poems extending throughout their length, but it is not conceptual, and . . . had little to do . . . with 'turning' another poet's sense and thus obliquely commenting thereon, or with the intention of substituting good love for bad by displacing naughty verses" (p. 254). Suggests rather that the word *parody* in Herbert's title is a musical term and implies that Herbert set his words to the same musical setting that Pembroke had used for his verse. Points out numerous contemporary and earlier examples of this practice of using secular music for sacred verse and vice versa without the intention of converting the one to the other. The author indicates that she has been unable to find the exact piece of music presumably used by both Herbert and Pembroke but sets down how she searched for it and the problems involved. Makes a very close comparison between the two poems and shows that Herbert's poem, in spite of some obvious parallelism, is on an entirely different subject than Pembroke's: these comparisons "demonstrate usefully the nature of a parodic relation which imitates *form*, and is unarguably divorced from the interest in evoking conceptual ambiguities which we attribute to practically all literary interaction of the sacred and the profane" (p. 285). Presents a hypothetical setting with music for both poems in order to illustrate the effects of musical parody.

✍§ 468. WARNKE, FRANK J. *European Metaphysical Poetry.* The Elizabethan Club Series, 2. New Haven and London: Yale University Press. xi, 317p.

Anthology of French, German, Dutch, Spanish, and Italian metaphysical poetry. The introduction (pp. 1–86) distinguishes between baroque and metaphysical style. The latter is considered as one of several related styles that can be seen within the generic category of the baroque. Suggests that the European metaphysical poets show "the extent to which not only the Baroque style but also its Metaphysical variation ought to be regarded as international phenomena, further manifestations of the real unity of our culture" (p. 4). States, "Metaphysical poetry is associated in the minds of its readers with the work of one man, John Donne. Yet, since every poet has his individual voice as well as his adherence to a collective style, one cannot simply make a touchstone of Donne's style in determining what poetry is Metaphysical; certain of his crucial themes, techniques, and emphases will occur in all Metaphysical poetry, but others will not. Metaphysical poetry has, when tried on the ear, a 'metaphysical' sound; that is to say, it sounds significantly like the poetry of John Donne. But each Metaphysical poet has also the unique sound of the individual poet" (p. 5). Discusses some of the characteristic elements of Donne's style but throughout compares and contrasts Herbert with Donne, Crashaw, Vaughan, and Marvell. Argues that all the metaphysical poets "display differing aims and differing sensibilities; they are united by a set of shared stylistic traits—ingenious metaphor, consistent intellectuality, radically all-inclusive diction, and colloquial tone—and, ultimately, by a shared habit of vision—the tendency to view their experience in the light of total reality, with a consequent concern for metaphysical problems and contradictions" (p. 21). Comments on specific features of Herbert's poetry: its ingenuity and intellectuality; its uses of paradox and homely images; its didacticism and simplicity; its uses of allegory, conceit, and concrete diction; its functional structure; etc.

Compares Herbert to a number of European poets, such as Friedrich von Spee, Herman Dullaert, Jean de La Ceppède, Jean-Baptiste Chassignet, Paul Fleming, Jacobus Revius, Constantijn Huygens, Martin Opitz, Lope de Vega, Jean de Sponde, and Jan Luyken.

⇥§ 469.WILLIAMSON, GEORGE. "Caroline Wit." In *The Proper Wit of Poetry*, pp. 43–62. Chicago: University of Chicago Press.

Traces the changing concept of wit from the Jacobean era through the Caroline and Interregnum periods to the Augustan Age and attempts to indicate what particular fashions prevailed, how each generation understood the nature and function of wit in a slightly different way, and how finally there was a gradual separation of the facetious and the serious, of nature and fancy. Comments briefly on Herbert's commitment to simplicity and on his more ingenious uses of wit and accounts for this by suggesting that Herbert believed that the poet must use the "bait of pleasure" to win his readers.

1962

⇥§ 470. ALLEN, WARD SYKES. "A Note upon George Herbert's 'The Pearl. Matth. 13.45.'" *N&Q*, n.s. 9:212–13.

Points out that the allusion in "The Pearl" to the head and pipes that feed the press (lines 1–2) may have been suggested by an interpretation of Zech. 4.12 in the preface to the Authorized Version of the Bible. "Translators to the Reader" says: "If you ask what they had before them, truly it was the *Hebrew* text of the Old Testament, the *Greek* of the New. These are the two golden pipes, or rather conduits, wherethrough the olive brances empty themselves into the gold." Points out several other images in the preface that suggest images in Herbert's poem.

⇥§ 471. AUSTIN, ALLEN C. "T. S. Eliot's Theory of Dissociation." *CE* 23:309–12.

Argues that Eliot's theory of dissociation of sensibility has been variously misunderstood by modern critics, especially F. W. Bateson, Basil Willey, Frank Kermode, and W. K. Wimsatt, Jr. Maintains that Eliot primarily laments the split that occurred in the seventeenth century between wit and emotion, ideas and images, and language and sensibility. Suggests that Eliot "is lamenting the loss of intellectual poetry, the amalgamation of intellectual and emotional experience" (p. 311). No specific references to Herbert.

⇥§ 472. BEAURLINE, L. A. "Dudley North's Criticism of Metaphysical Poetry." *HLQ* 25:299–313.

Comments on a now-forgotten essay on the various fashions of seven-h-century poetry by Dudley North (1581–1666) published in his collected writings, entitled *A Forest of Varieties* (1645). Reproduces the text of this essay, one of the few contemporary statements about early seventeenth-century poetry. Argues that North's essay "is in direct contradiction to Miss Tuve's theory that fashionable Jacobean poetry was basically the same in theory and practice as Elizabethan poetry" (p. 299) and points out that North objects strongly that "the new poetry violates propriety in amatory verse" (p. 299). No specific references to Herbert.

◄§ 473. BLACKIE, JOHN; Smith, E. P ; and Gaskell, Ronald. "Herbert's 'Vanitie.' " *CritQ* 4:80–81.

Two replies and an answer by the author to Ronald Gaskell's essay, "Herbert's 'Vanitie,' " entry 455. Blackie objects to Gaskell's suggestion that Herbert misused the word *mellowing* in the fourth stanza of the poem. Shows that it meant "soft, loamy, rich" as applied to soil and that "this is precisely the ultimate effect that frost has on soil" (p. 80). Smith objects more generally to Gaskell's reading of the poem, specifically dislikes Gaskell's emphasis "on the parallels between the openings of the first three stanzas . . . when one ignores . . . those between the second halves of each of these stanzas" (p. 80), and believes that an understanding of the sexual overtones in the poem is crucial to an understanding of its complex theme. Gaskell, in his answer, agrees with Blackie's point and agrees with Smith that the sexual overtones are present in the third stanza.

◄§ 474. BOWERS, FREDSON. "Herbert's Sequential Imagery: 'The Temper.' " *MP* 59:202–13.

Argues that the order of the poems in *The Temple* "is not random but is planned according to developing sequences that work out major themes" and that "within these sequential poems Herbert develops clusters of images that are appropriate not only for the poem in which they appear but also—in some sense—exist coincidentally with the individual poems and apply independently to the great central theme of the section and then of *The Temple*" (p. 202). Comments on the "narrative continuity" of one such sequence but suggests, "More continuity is discoverable in the poems of this sequence than is found merely in the progression of formal ideas or in links at end and beginning" (p. 203). Especially significant is "the development of certain strains of images that independently form a commentary on the announced theme for any poem" (p. 203). Illustrates this Herbertian device by comments on "The Temper (I)," especially on "some of the accumulated meanings of the title . . . as they are worked out either in the poem itself or as ascertainably present from the evidence of the preceding sequential imagery" (p. 203).

◄§ 475. BRADNER, LEICESTER. "New Poems by George Herbert: The Cambridge Latin Gratulatory Anthology of 1613." *RN* 15:208–11.

Announces the discovery of two heretofore unknown Latin poems by Herbert: one on the visit of Frederick, the Elector Palatine, and Prince Charles to Cambridge University in 1613; the other an epithalamium for Frederick and Princess Elizabeth, daughter of James I, who were married on 14 February 1613. The poems were found in a two-part volume, originally in Frederick's library but now at the Vatican (MS Palat. lat. 1736). There were approximately sixty contributors to the volume, including, in addition to Herbert, Giles Fletcher and William Gager. Reproduces the two Latin poems by Herbert and comments briefly on each.

◄§ 476. DUCKLES, VINCENT. "John Jenkins's Settings of Lyrics by George Herbert." *Musical Quarterly* 48:461–75.

Comments briefly on Herbert's interest in music and his extensive use of musical imagery in his poetry. Points out that there is a "surprising lack of Herbert lyrics set to music by his contemporaries" (p. 462). Comments primarily on a set of partbooks found in the library of Christ Church College, Oxford (MSS 736–38) that contains six lyrics from *The Temple* with musical settings by John Jenkins and states that "these are the earliest known examples of Herbert's lyrics with music" (p. 462). The six settings include (1) "The shephards sing, but shall I silent be" (strophe 2 of "Christmas"); (2) "Awake, sad heart, whom sorrow ever drowns" (from "The Dawning"); (3) "O take thy lute and tune it" (last three stanzas of "Ephes.iv.30. *Grieve not the Holy Spirit*"; (4) "And art Thou grievéd, sweet and sacred Dove" (first three stanzas of "Ephes.iv.30. *Grieve not the Holy Spirit*"); (5) "Then with our trinity of light" (last four stanzas of "The Starre"); and (6) "Bright spark, shot from a brighter place" (first four stanzas of "The Starre"). Analyzes the musical settings and argues, "Our appreciation of George Herbert is not complete until we have experienced his poetry within the framework provided by John Jenkins's music" (p. 475). Illustrations.

◄§ 477. ELIOT, T. S. *George Herbert*. Writers and Their Works, no. 152. London: Longmans, Green and Co. 36p.

Reprinted in American ed. (Lincoln: University of Nebraska Press, 1964). American ed. includes, in addition to Eliot's study, Frank Kermode's *John Donne* (1957) and Margaret Willy's *Three Metaphysical Poets: Richard Crashaw, Henry Vaughan, Thomas Traherne* (1961).

Divided into three sections. 1: A biographical sketch of Herbert. Asserts, "To think of Herbert as a poet of a placid and comfortable piety is to misunderstand utterly the man and his poems" (p. 14). 2: Calls *The Temple* "a coherent sequence of poems setting down the fluctuations of emotion between despair and bliss, between agitation and serenity, and the discipline of suffering which leads to peace of spirit" (p. 23) and insists, "We cannot judge Herbert, or savour fully his genius and his art, by a selection to be found in an anthology; we must study *The Temple* as a whole" (p. 15). Calls Herbert a major poet in his own right who should not be unfavorably compared with Donne. Compares Donne's "Batter my heart" and Herbert's "Prayer (I)" in order to show their differences: "Both men were highly intellectual, both men had keen sensibility: but in Donne thought seems in control of feeling, and in Herbert feeling seems in control of thought" (p. 17). In Donne there is "much more of the *orator*; whereas Herbert . . . has a much more intimate tone of speech" (p. 18). Donne's poetry is witty; Herbert's, "magical" (p. 18). Yet Herbert is "closer in spirit to Donne than is any other of 'the school of Donne' " (p 20). Comments on the exclusively religious subject matter of Herbert's poetry and insists that his poems are valuable, even to the nonbeliever, precisely because of their content: "The poems form a record of spiritual struggle which should touch the feeling, and enlarge the understanding of those readers also who hold no religious belief and find themselves unmoved by religious emotion" (p. 19). 3: Returns to a comparison of Herbert and Donne, pointing out a number of lines that remind the reader of their relationship, yet pointing out that Herbert's originality and resourcefulness of invention in metrical forms have "no parallel in English poetry" (p. 31). Selective bibliography (pp. 35–36).

⊷§ 478. FITTS, DUDLEY, ed. *Herbert*. Selected, with an introduction and notes by Dudley Fitts. The Laurel Poetry Series. New York: Dell Publishing Co. 191p.

Reprinted, 1966.

Introduction (pp. 9–22); bibliography (pp. 22–23); chronology (pp. 24–25); note on the text (p. 26); a selection from the English poems based primarily on F. E. Hutchinson's text (entry 223) with minor alterations (pp. 27–185); notes on individual poems (pp. 186–91). Suggests in the introduction that Herbert is more admired today than read, primarily because the modern reader is often embarrassed or bored "by the expression of so direct and personal a faith as Herbert's was" (p. 10), especially since his poetry lacks the rhetorical splendor, sensationalism, and mystical rhapsody of more popular metaphysical poets. Argues that *The Temple* has something to say to the modern reader because it presents "an important human argument: a man's attempt to discover himself, to define and to refine away what is selfish and vacillating and cowardly in his nature, to fix a goal for his life's course, and to submit himself to the demands imposed by that goal" even if Herbert's way of doing these things "is stated in terms of a specific religious system" (p. 13). Comments on Herbert's complex simplicity, especially as it is reflected in such poems as "Love unknown" and "Love (III)" as well as in his stanzaic inventiveness and artistry.

◄§ 479. GRIEDER, THEODORE. "Philip Pain's 'Daily Meditations' and the Poetry of George Herbert." *N&Q*, n.s. 9:213–15.

Points out possible borrowings from Herbert's poetry in the *Daily Meditations* (1668) of Philip Pain, a somewhat obscure American Puritan poet. Pain uses the form of several of Herbert's poems, certain meters and rhythms, as well as specific images and figures. For a reply, see Norman Farmer, entry 523.

◄§ 480. KEAST, WILLIAM R., ed. *Seventeenth Century English Poetry: Modern Essays in Criticism.* A Galaxy Book, 89. New York: Oxford University Press. 434p.

Rev. ed., 1971 (see entry 707).

Collection of previously published items. Contains five general essays on metaphysical poetry: (1) H. J. C. Grierson, "Metaphysical Poetry." From *Metaphysical Lyrics & Poems of the Seventeenth Century* (entry 58), pp. xiii–xxxviii. (2) T. S. Eliot, "The Metaphysical Poets" (entry 56). (3) F. R. Leavis, "The Line of Wit." From *Revaluation: Tradition & Development in English Poetry* (London: Chatto & Windus, 1936, 1949; New York: W. W. Norton Co., 1947), pp. 10–36. (4) Helen Gardner, "The Metaphysical Poets." From *The Metaphysical Poets* (entry 400), pp. xix–xxxiv. (5) Joseph Anthony Mazzeo, "A Critique of Some Modern Theories of Metaphysical Poetry" (entry 339). There are two previously published essays specifically on Herbert: (1) Joseph H. Summers, "The Poem as Hieroglyph." From *George Herbert: His Religion and Art* (entry 369), pp. 123–46. (2) Margaret Bottrall, "Herbert's Craftsmanship." From *George Herbert* (entry 361), pp. 99–116.

◄§ 481. LEACH, ELSIE. "Yeats's 'A Friend's Illness' and Herbert's 'Vertue.'" *N&Q*, n.s. 9:215.

Suggests that Yeats's "A Friend's Illness," written for Lady Gregory, contains several possible echoes from "Vertue."

◄§ 482. LOTT, BERNARD. "M. E. *Drinken* and *Drink* in George Herbert." *IJES* 3:132–34.

Challenges Rosemond Tuve's interpretation (*A Reading of George Herbert*, entry 344) of a line in a medieval religious lyric ("And thou wyth eysyl drinkest to me"). Tuve claims that the line resembles Herbert's colloquial style for exalted subjects and interprets the line by saying, "The vinegar as a kind of toast which 'thou drinkest to me' is typical of what happens in this tradition, and long before Herbert used it" (p. 133). Lott argues that such an interpretation is "unscriptural and makes no good sense" but that "*drink* used causatively to mean 'to hand or present a person beverage for his use; to give drink to' is well attested, and gives the correct meaning here" (p. 133).

◄§ 483. PRAZ, MARIO. "Il Barocco in Inghilterra." In *Manerismo, Barocco, Rococò: Concetti e Termini*, pp. 129–46. Problemi Attuali di Scienza e di Cultura, no. 52. Rome: Accademia Nazionale dei Lincei.
Translated into English in *MP* 61 (1964): 169–79.
Maintains that the baroque was essentially alien to English sensibility and taste. Suggests that Milton, Crashaw, Beaumont and Fletcher, and Dryden were to differing degrees influenced by baroque models. Sees Donne as a mannerist, not a baroque poet. No specific comment on Herbert. Discusses the revival of interest in metaphysical poetry in the twentieth century.

◄§ 484. RAUTER, HERBERT. "Eine Anleihe Sternes bei George Herbert." *Anglia* 80:290–94.
Maintains that Sterne was familiar with Herbert's work and that in at least two places in *Tristram Shandy* he is influenced by Herbert: (1) Walter Shandy's comments on jest and wit in chapter 5 reflects strophe 40 of *The Church-Porch*, and (2) the character of Yorkic is influenced by Herbert's *The Country Parson*, as is especially reflected in Yorkic's comments on the catechism.

◄§ 485. REES, T. R. "T. S. Eliot, Rémy de Gourmont, and Dissociation of Sensibility." In *Studies in Comparative Literature*, edited by Waldo F. McNeir, pp. 186–98. Louisiana State University Studies: Humanities Series, no. 11. Baton Rouge: Louisiana State University Press.
Reviews the modern critical controversy over Eliot's concept of "dissociation of sensibility," especially F. W. Bateson's attack (see entries 315, 329), and attempts to explain and defend Eliot's use of the term in the light of its Continental sources, especially the work of Rémy de Gourmont. No specific references to Herbert.

◄§ 486. SANDERS, WILBUR. " 'Childhood Is Health': The Divine Poetry of George Herbert." *Melbourne Critical Review* 5:3–15.
Challenges critics, like L. C. Knights and Rosemond Tuve, who maintain that Herbert "is not only a good, competent poet, but a great one" (p. 3). Argues that many of Herbert's poems are "drastically flawed," "sound stuffy and churchy, deal too largely in abstractions, and abound in examples of what one could call a sort of verbal imprecision" (p. 3). Suggests that much of Herbert's poetry is "poetical exhibitionism disguised thinly as piety" (p. 4); regards his simplicity as "simulated sim-

plicity, the uncritical adoption of a simple 'manner'" (p. 4) and "an effort of self-abasement which ends in a new and pernicious form of self-aggrandizement, a type of poetic exhibitionism before an indulgent and pious audience" (p. 5); maintains that Herbert's "preoccupation with subjective experience . . . frequently lands him in sentimentality" (p. 6); and concludes that Herbert "displays more negative submission than positive assent" to the notion of a divinely appointed order in the universe and that "his doubts and his beliefs are never brought into any comprehensive concord" (p. 13). Presents critical evaluations of "The Collar," "Affliction (I)," "Love (III)," "The Pearl," and "The Forerunners."

❧ 487. SLOANE, WILLIAM. "George Herbert's Reputation, 1650–1710: Good Reading for the Young." *N&Q*, n.s. 9:213.

Points out six pieces of evidence that show that children of different religious preferences and social classes were urged to read Herbert's poetry during the period 1650–1700: (1) an undated letter from Peter Sterry, chaplain to Cromwell, to his son; (2) Henry Delaune in *Patrikon doron. Or a legacy to his sons* (1651; rev. and enlarged, 1657); (3) Charles Hoole in 1660; (4) Thomas White in *A little book for little children* (1674); (5) Dr. Thomas Willis in *The key to knowledg, opening the principles of religion; and the path of life, directing the practice of true pietie; design'd for the conduct of children and servants, in the right way to heaven and happiness* (1682); and (6) Joseph Downing in *The Young Christian's Library* (1710). Concludes that the "sophisticated eighteenth-century reader was presumably content to relegate Herbert to the nursery and the servants' quarters" (p. 213).

❧ 488. STARKMAN, MIRIAM K. "Noble Numbers and the Poetry of Devotion." In *Reason and Imagination: Studies in the History of Ideas, 1600–1800*, edited by J. A. Mazzeo, pp. 1–27. New York: Columbia University Press; London: Routledge & Kegan Paul.

Primarily a critical examination and defense of Herrick's *Noble Numbers*. However, throughout Herrick is compared to Herbert as a devotional poet. Dislikes the term *religious metaphysical* and argues that a more critically appropriate term would be *poetry of devotion*, which is more "hospitable to the symbolic, the meditational, and the emblematic" elements of the religious poetry of the period; which allows "for the various figurative modes that were actually employed, for genres from the couplet to the epic"; which allows room "for the didactic couplet as well as the affective prayer"; and which "is susceptible of being used with historical as well as intrinsic signification" (p. 23). Mentions Herbert's use of gnomic verse in *The Church-porch* and suggests that it may have come from Southwell or perhaps even from the so-called wisdom poetry of collections such as *Tottel's Miscellany*.

৯১ 489. STEPHENSON, WILLIAM E., ed. *Select Hymns Taken Out of Mr. Herbert's Temple (1697)*. With an introduction by William E. Stephenson. Augustan Reprint Society, no. 98. Los Angeles: William Andrews Clark Memorial Library, University of California. vii, 45p.

Facsimile edition of *Select Hymns*, first published by Thomas Parkhurst, the well-known Presbyterian bookseller, in 1697, and currently in Dr. Williams' Library, London. The adapter is unknown but his intention is clearly to turn some thirty-two of Herbert's poems into hymns "suitable for congregational singing by the nonconformist worshippers known as Dissenters" (p. i). The introduction points out that the collection "shows clearly which elements of Herbert's poetry a later age valued" (p. i). Outlines the state of congregational singing in the 1690s among the Dissenters. Maintains that the adapter chose the poems to be included on the basis of their themes rather than their stanzaic patterns.

৯১ 490. STORY, G. M. "Herbert's *Inventa Bellica*: A New Manuscript." *MP* 59:270–72.

Announces the discovery of a manuscript in Chetham's Library, Manchester (Mun. A.3.48), that contains a text of Herbert's "Inventa Bellica." Describes the manuscript and argues that it "offers a text which throws further light on the claims of *Inventa Bellica* to preference over Herbert's unrevised *Triumphus Mortis* and should help to restore the polished version to its proper place in the poet's canon" (p. 270). Presents a transcription of "Inventa Bellica" from the Chetham manuscript (pp. 271–72).

৯১ 491. SWARDSON, H. R. "George Herbert's Language of Devotion." In *Poetry and the Fountain of Light: Observations on the Conflict between Christian and Classical Traditions in Seventeenth-Century Poetry*, pp. 64–82. Columbia: University of Missouri Press; London: G. Allen & Unwin.

Although Herbert, like Donne, banished classical mythology from his poetry and stands in "a kind of negative relation to poetry in the classical literary tradition" (p. 64), the author argues, "In the broad sense of 'classical' Herbert's poetry does reflect intensely one aspect of the tension between the Christian tradition and the classical tradition: the opposition between spiritual sincerity and skill in poetry, or, more crudely, between simple truth and contrived art" (p. 81). Points out that, although Herbert is often praised for his simplicity and straightforwardness, in practice he does not often follow his own advice to say simply, "My God, My King." In fact, "his plain intention is always curled with metaphors, even in the very poems that reject this strategy" (p. 73). Argues that only occasionally is Herbert able to relax this sense of tension and conflict; more often he shows a general distrust of sensuous and ornate images as

well as of the more ingenious forms of wit and rhetoric. Comments on
"Jordan (I) and (II)" "The Forerunners," "Sunday," "The Pearl," "The
Collar," "Deniall," and "The Flower."

◄§ 492. WALKER, JOHN DAVID. "The Architectonics of George Herbert's *The Temple.*" *ELH* 29:289–305.
Attempts to show that not only the physical structure of the Hebraic
temple but also the complex symbolism associated with it were significant
influences on the structure of *The Temple*. Comments on the tripartite
division of *The Temple* (*The Church-Porch, The Church, The Church
Militant*) and sees in this division (1) a spatial architectural analogy
with the Hebraic temple (porch, holy place, holy of holies), (2) a possible cosmological and symbolic interpretation based on this architectural
division and derived from various Church Fathers and early Christian
writers (the lower, middle, and upper regions of the cosmos, in other
words, the earth, heaven, and heaven of heavens), and (3) a tripartite
temporal structure of Christian progression (youth, maturity, old age and
death, or, more profoundly, "from primal obedience to Christ, to maturity in affliction, to the ultimate destiny of union with God" [p. 291]).

◄§ 493. WILLIAMSON, KARINA. "Herbert's Reputation in the Eighteenth
Century." *PQ* 41:769–75.
Assesses Herbert's popularity during the eighteenth century in order to
show that there were admirers "who, against all the weight of literary
fashion, continued to honor and perpetuate his name" (p. 770). Lists
editions of Herbert's poetry and collections in which his poems appeared
during the period and presents favorable comments by a number of admirers, most of whom were churchmen and/or hymn collectors whose
"respect for his writing sprang less from literary judgments than from
religious sympathy" (p. 772). Points out that Herbert "was read (or sung
or paraphrased), it seems, not for the virtues of his style but rather in
spite of them, for the truth of his rendering of Christian attitudes and
beliefs" (p. 772). Supports this position by commenting on the many
adaptations, changes, and mutilations made in the poems to suit various
eighteenth-century tastes, especially those made by Wesley.

◄§ 494. WOLFE, JANE E. "George Herbert's 'Assurance.'" *CLAJ* 5:213–
22.
Views "Assurance" as "a most vital and significant chapter" in Herbert's spiritual development, one that "may not be omitted from a spiritual biography which one would desire to intuit from a reading of his
poems" (p. 222). Argues that in the poem Herbert "expressed most
firmly and with unmistakable finality" his "full assurance of his salvation" and "his unqualified acceptance by God" (p. 213). Presents a detailed, stanza-by-stanza analysis of the dramatic argument of the poem

and comments on several important elements, especially its skillful uses of tone and its many biblical echoes in both imagery and diction.

1963

◄§ 495. ADAMS, HAZARD. "Metaphysical Poetry: Argument into Drama." In *The Context of Poetry*, pp. 75–99. Boston: Little, Brown & Co.

Discusses some of the general characteristics of metaphysical poetry (diction, rhythms, conceits, wit) and stresses the dramatic elements. Comments briefly on Herbert as a religious poet who "developed drama out of traditional theological paradoxes" (p. 93). Suggests that Herbert's complexity is, for the most part, "that of traditional religious analogies and emblems, of allegory, which often explains its own meaning" (p. 94).

◄§ 496. COHEN, J. M. *The Baroque Lyric.* London: Hutchinson University Library. 207p.

Comments on Herbert's uses of typology, the sources of his imagery (such as, traditional architecture, the liturgy, medieval poetry, iconography), the uses of music and auditory imagery, and the architectural complexity of *The Temple.* Places Herbert's poetry "on the borderline between the religious and the mystical" (p. 177): "For while it speaks of deep personal experience, it invariably does so in the context of church doctrine" (p. 177). Likewise, suggests that Herbert's poetry "expresses a supreme paradox: it is personal and impersonal at the same time, because when he writes as a poet, it is with that part of himself which is immortal man" (p. 174). Compares and contrasts Herbert with Donne, Crashaw, Vaughan, Lope de Vega, Jean de La Ceppède, Argensola, Malherbe, and Bach.

◄§ 497. COLIE, R. L. "*Logos* in *The Temple*: George Herbert and the Shape of Content." *JWCI* 26:327–42.
Reprinted as chapter 6 in *Paradoxia Epidemica: The Renaissance Tradition of Paradox* (entry 565), pp. 190–215.

Maintains, "It is in the speculum of the great mystical, self-explanatory notion of the divine *logos* . . . that Herbert's poetry may be most helpfully reflected" and, "The difficulties involved in the doctrine of the *logos,* once understood in relation to Herbert's verse, may clarify some of the content and method of that verse and serve as a model, an emblem, for the difficulties inherent in both his subject-matter and his method" (p. 328). Examines in some detail with many examples drawn from numerous poems "the uses of the Word, intradeical and extradeical, in Herbert's verse," and tests the hypothesis "that from his manipulation of the paradoxes inherent in the *logos*-doctrine we can read the problems in his verse and his versing" (p. 329).

◄§ 498. CUBETA, PAUL M. "Ben Jonson's Religious Lyrics." *JEGP* 62: 96–110.

Finds a number of resemblances between Jonson's religious lyrics and Herbert's, especially certain tonal qualities. Suggests that Jonson's "A Hymne to God the Father" reminds one of Herbert's "Discipline" and that the diction and sentence structure of "To Heaven" "points ahead a few years to Herbert's easy, relaxed rhythms" (p. 109).

◄§ 499. DANIELS, EDGAR F. "George Herbert's 'Balm and Bay'—Synonyms?" *SCN* 20:63 (item 205).

Comments on Herbert's use of the phrase *balm and bay* in "Sunday" (line 5). Rejects previous interpretations of *bay* and argues that the word "is intended as an alliterative synonym of *balm*, in the old rhetorical tradition of 'might and main' and 'vim and vigor' " (p. 63). Suggests that the whole phrase simply means "the easement of care." Supports this interpretation by reference to George Ryley's commentary in *Mr Herbert's Temple & Church Militant Explained & Improved* as well as by reference to Herbert's use of a similar rhetorical device in *A Priest to the Temple*.

◄§ 500. EMPSON, WILLIAM. "Herbert's Quaintness." *New Statesman*, n.s. 65:18.

Primarily a review of T. S. Eliot's *George Herbert* (entry 477). In particular, Empson responds to Eliot's dismissal of his comments on "The Sacrifice," which first appeared in *Seven Types of Ambiguity* (entry 108) and which were severely challenged by Rosemond Tuve in *A Reading of George Herbert* (entry 344). Reasserts his original argument, insists that the various ambiguities of the poem spoil it, and maintains that it demonstrates Herbert's own embarrassment about the paradoxes of Christianity. Explains his original position in more detail, while at the same time readily admitting that it was probably a mistake "to drag in Freud" and that several of the more outrageous puns that he pointed out originally are clearly impossible.

◄§ 501. FREEMAN, ROSEMARY. "Parody as a Literary Form: George Herbert and Wilfred Owen." *EIC* 13:307–22.

Discusses the kind of parody that is neither satirical nor comic but "is based upon known literary examples, in which the aim is creating a meaning that is positive and constructive, not absurd" (p. 307). Comments on Herbert's "A Parodie" as an example of a poem that uses the formulas of love poetry but redirects them to the service of religion. Shows that this "transference of profane to sacred use is a constantly recurring feature in Herbert's work; much of it reflects the form and feeling of love poetry, now directed to a personal God" (p. 309). Comments on "Jordan (I)" and "Jordan (II)" as "examples of literary criticism from Herbert in which judgment is passed on the subjects of contemporary verse" (p. 310) and that serve as an apologia for Herbert's approach. Points out that in "Dulnesse" Herbert "remains very close to the idiom of secular love lyrics so that it enables the poem to work on two planes at once" (p. 313). Mentions other poems in which "the achievements of amatory verse are imitated yet made merely contributory" (p. 315), such as "The Glance," "The Answer," "Clasping of hands," and "Mans medley." Comments, in the second part of the essay, on Wilfred Owens's war poetry, which, like Herbert's, combines the "evocative style of contemporary love poetry with a more serious subject" (p. 315).

◄§ 502. FRYXELL, LUCY DICKINSON. "George Herbert: Anti-Metaphysical Poet?" *Discourse* (Concordia College) 6:293–99.

Comments on the tension in Herbert between simplicity and conscious artistry and argues that he "was pulled in two directions in his attitude toward the language appropriate for religious poetry" (p. 295). Herbert sees poetry as a means of leading men to God and thus recognizes the merits of simplicity and plainness, but he also sees poetry as prayer and thus recognizes that "the finest language that the human mind can invent is the best choice for reflecting God's infinite beauty" (p. 298). Thus, although Herbert distrusts the wit and ingenuity that modern critics focus on in his poetry, he is, nonetheless, much concerned about art and art forms. "To him the poet is the artist working for God, and in the orientation toward God anything that calls attention and admiration to the workmanship is inappropriate; but his integrity as an artist requires that he use the best materials available to him, and that he employ those materials with the greatest skill of which he is capable" (p. 298). Suggests that Herbert, if he were alive today, would disapprove of the inordinate attention given to his artistry, wit, and ingenuity by modern critics: "He would feel that his search for the best way of expressing 'Thou art still my God' has become perhaps a stumbling block to the fulfillment of one purpose of his poems" (p. 298).

◄§ 503. HASTINGS, ROBERT. " 'Easter Wings' as a Model of Herbert's Method." *Thoth* 4:15–23.

Presents a detailed explication of "Easter-wings" in order "to show that in its form, especially in its structure, diction, and imagery, the poem may be made to serve as a model of Herbert's emblematic mode of expression" (p. 15). States that the main theme of the poem is "one of alienation from God through sin, and redemption from sin through faith in the risen Christ, evidenced in the form of the paradox, that sin and its effects are made, for the believer, the very instruments of God's purposes, through the atonement of Christ's passion and the power of His spirit" (p. 16). Comments in detail on various formal characteristics of the poem that reenforce its theme—the visual patterns, structure,

rhyme scheme, line lengths, metrics, images, metaphors, and diction—
and shows that its typological or emblematic characteristics are typical of
Herbert's poetry in general.

✥§ 504. HERBERT, GEORGE. *George Herbert.* Selected by David Herbert.
    Pocket Poets. London: Vista Books. 48p.
Selection of forty-one poems from *The Temple* with no notes and no
commentary. Brief, one-page introduction to Herbert's life and poetry by
David Herbert.

✥§ 505. JOSELYN, SISTER M. "Herbert and Muir: Pilgrims of Their Age."
    Renascence 15:127–32.
Compares and contrasts Herbert and Edwin Muir. Suggests that they
resemble each other in their "tendency toward paradox, prevailing sweetness of tone, use of narrative situations to reveal moral or spiritual truths,
self-conscious dialogue with the Deity, frequent use of the quatrain, simple diction and so on" but that their great difference "lies in the degree
of certainty with which each is able to close off the dialogue with conscience—or God" (p. 127). Discusses a number of Muir's poems that in
varying degrees resemble or differ from Herbert's and sees each poet as
reflecting the particular religious sensibility and tensions of his age.

✥§ 506. KRANZ, GISBERT. "George Herbert: Ein Dichter des Anglikan-
    ertums." *Hochland* 55:235–46.
General introduction to Herbert for the German reader. Brief history
of Herbert's influence on poets of his own time as well as on later poets.
Biographical sketch. Maintains, "In Herberts Dichtung ist das Christ-
liche nicht ohne Verständnis des Künstlerischen, das Küntlerische nichte
ohne Verständnis des Christlichen zu erfassen" (p. 237). Presents a brief
analysis of the major structure and symbols of *The Temple* and compares the musical quality of Herbert's poetry with that of Donne.

✥§ 507. KUNA, F. M. "T. S. Eliot's Dissociation of Sensibility and the
    Critics of Metaphysical Poetry." *EIC* 13:241–52.
Shows that dissociation of sensibility is simply "a poetic theory, and
nothing more, which cannot be applied to any poetry written before the
eighteenth century without distorting all historical truth, and which
must not be separated from its original context" (p. 243). Argues that
Eliot's concept can be applied only to modern poetry and that it is primarily the result of Eliot's theorizing about the nature of his own early
poetry. No specific reference to Herbert.

✥§ 508. LEACH, ELSIE. "Some Commercial Terms in Seventeenth-
    Century Poetry." *N&Q*, n.s. 10:414.
Points out that Herbert's use of the business term *market-money* in

The Church-Porch (line 375) antedates the first recorded instance in the *OED* (1891).

❧ 509. MARTZ, LOUIS L., ed. *The Meditative Poem: An Anthology of Seventeenth-Century Verse.* With an introduction and notes. Anchor Seventeenth-Century Series, AC6. Garden City, N.Y.: Doubleday & Co. xxxii, 566p.

Reprinted in hardback (Stuart Editions), New York: New York University Press, 1963.

Rev. ed., *The Anchor Anthology of Seventeenth Century Verse*, vol. 1. Garden City, N.Y.: Doubleday & Co., 1969; reprinted as *English Seventeenth Century Verse*, vol. 1 (1973).

Introduction to *The Meditative Poem* is partially reprinted in *The Poem of the Mind: Essays on Poetry, English and American* (entry 578), pp. 33–53.

The introduction (pp. xvii–xxxii) distinguishes between metaphysical and meditative poetry and outlines the essential features of the meditative mode, suggesting that "the central meditative action consists of an interior drama, in which a man projects a self upon a mental stage, and there comes to understand that self in the light of a divine presence" (p. xxxi). Includes sixty-eight poems by Herbert (pp. 141–229) with commentary and notes (pp. 534–38).

❧ 510. PÉREZ GÁLLEGO, CÁNDIDO. "La Iglesia anglicana como estructura y símbolo en George Herbert." *RL* 23:117–21.

Argues that the symbol of the Christian Church confers unity on *The Temple*. Discusses the double significance of the Church both as a physical and spiritual symbol: "Un símbolo: la Iglesia. Pero un símbolo de doble significacion, puesto que además de tener entidad en el poema va alvergando todos los momentos de arrepentimiento que en ella ocurren. Después, una Iglesia real, con una arquitectura visible y concreta. *The Temple* es un gran edificio religioso, de nobles armonías, donde los esfuerzos del autor consisten en conjugar la materialidad del símbolo— un templo—con el camino que conduce al estado de la gracia" (p. 121).

❧ 511. RICKEY, MARY ELLEN. "Herbert's Technical Development." *JEGP* 62:745–60.

Reprinted in a much revised form as chapter 4 of *Utmost Art: Complexity in the Verse of George Herbert* (entry 584), pp. 103–47.

Studies Herbert's poetry "to show that a number of formal differences between his early and later work exist, and that these differences are sufficiently alike in kind to enable one to see a concerted direction in which his writing was moving at the time of his death" (p. 745). Examines "the differences between the sixty-nine 'earlier' poems [in the

Williams MS] and the additional 'later' poems which appeared in *The Temple* in 1633" (p. 745). Maintains that, although all Herbert's poems exhibit more similarities than differences, the following significant changes occur: (1) an increasing use of figurative titles, due to Herbert's realization that a title "could function much like an additional, and highly desirable, unit of imagery" (p. 747); (2) the use of more than one stanza form in a single poem; (3) a decreasing production of sonnets, probably accounted for by Herbert's interest in more original stanza forms; (4) the use of different kinds of hieroglyphs, "moving away from absolute physical imitation of the topic of his verse, to what might be called a 'semi-hieroglyphic', in which some less conspicuous formal quality reinforces the matter of the poem" (p. 749); (5) an increasing number of so-called contrapuntal poems: of the poems in the Williams manuscript only 47 percent are contrapuntal whereas 64 percent of the new poems in *The Temple* fit this category; (6) an increasing use of longer and more elaborate stanza forms; (7) an increasingly careful use of feminine endings, which Herbert came to regard "as expressing weakness and disorder" (p. 751) and to use for conscious effects; (8) an increasing use of stanza linking; and (9) an increasingly careful use of variation for dramatic purposes, with a rather detailed comment on the complexity of variations in "The Collar." Concludes that the differences between the "early" and "later" poems show Herbert's "increasingly fine and delicate control of the adjustment of form to substance as well as a more subtle approach to this adjustment" (p. 760).

◆§ 512. SPARROW, JOHN. "Hymns and Poetry." *TLS*, 11 January, p. 32.
Points out that several poems by Herbert, Donne, Crashaw, and other religious poets of the period are adapted for congregational singing and included in the *Collection of Hymns* (London, 1754), edited by John Gambold for the "Brethren's Church" of the Moravians. Also points out that two of Herbert's poems are printed with musical settings in Playford's *Harmonia Sacra* (book 1).

◆§ 513. SWANSTON, HAMISH. "The Second 'Temple.'" *DUJ* 25:14–22.
Reexamines the affinity between Herbert and Crashaw, commenting on certain technical features that both exhibit (such as use of language, means of manipulating the metaphor, recurring verbal patterns) and pointing out similar constructive elements (especially their uses of the conceit). Notes the similarity of their general attitudes toward sensible and suprasensible objects. Does not suggest that Herbert "is a fully developed baroque poet, but merely that he could have given encouragement to Crashaw" (p. 17). States that a number of critics in both the seventeenth and eighteenth centuries recognized the many affinities between the two poets.

◆§ 514. WATSON, GEORGE. "The Fabric of Herbert's *Temple*." *JWCI* 26:354–58.

Comments on Herbert's "audacity" in his use of God-mistress analogies, original metrical and stanzaic patterns, puns, figure poems, and other stylistic devices and suggests that this "intense and ostentatious use of technique encourages the reader to seek deliberation elsewhere in *The Temple*, even where it has not hitherto been sought—in the title and order of the poems" (p. 355). Maintains that the temple that Herbert has in mind is not a parish church or specific building but rather that he is using the term metaphorically to describe himself as a priest: "The temple, for Herbert, signified his final commitment to the priestly life and his submission to divine love" (p. 357). Concludes that Herbert "lacked the temperament to build a whole collection of poems united by a single 'emblem' or visual image" (p. 357) but that there are "some grounds for thinking that the opening of *The Temple*, at least, was designed to exemplify the titular metaphor" (p. 356).

1964

◆§ 515. ATTAL, JEAN-PIERRE. "L'image 'métaphysique.'" *MdF* 351: 270–95.

Defines the metaphysical image as giving spiritual significance to things, joining disparate phenomena, creating surprising effects, causing the reader to reason, and opposing the abstract and the concrete. Suggests that the poet who creates metaphysical images is more a beholder than a participant in life. Maintains that the metaphysical image has flourished from the sixteenth century onward because of the secularization of life. Comments on Scève, Bunyan, Poc, and Raymond Roussel and suggests that Donne more than Herbert composed metaphysical images.

◆§ 516. BERRY, LLOYD E., comp. *A Bibliography of Studies in Metaphysical Poetry, 1939–1960*. Madison: University of Wisconsin Press. xi, 99p.

A continuation of Theodore Spencer's and Mark Van Doren's *Studies in Metaphysical Poetry: Two Essays and a Bibliography* (entry 202). Lists 1,147 critical studies on metaphysical poetry from 1939 to 1960. "Entries were compiled after a search of more than 1000 journals, about 480 of which are not listed in the PMLA bibliography" (jacket). No annotations. There are 102 items specifically on Herbert.

◆§ 517. BLANCHARD, MARGARET M. "The Leap into Darkness: Donne, Herbert, and God." *Renascence* 17:38–50.

Contrasts the religious sensibilities of Herbert and Donne as they are reflected in the poetry. Studies the tone and the visual and auditory images in the work of each poet and concludes that Herbert's relationship to God tends to be a very personal and intimate one, whereas Donne's tends to be more objective. In Herbert's poetry God speaks and is more often directly addressed than in Donne's poetry: "Herbert's religious poetry, enriched by the presence and voice of God, does then speak of a more significant spiritual relationship than does Donne's more objective poetry; this is not to say that Donne's struggle with a silent God is less gripping to us on a human level" (p. 50).

⋘§ 518. BROADBENT, J. B. *Poetic Love*. London: Chatto & Windus. vii, 310p.

Presents a history of love poetry from the twelfth century to the Enlightenment primarily in terms of the problem of duality of the body and soul. Argues that the metaphysical poets separate the spheres of sacred and human love, even though they use human love as a metaphor of divine love. Comments on Herbert as a religious love poet and calls him a "Christian in the deepest Pauline and Augustinian sense" (p. 107). Praises Herbert's poems as being "remarkable for their variety of little genres, and of levels of religious experience" (p. 108). Points out in particular that Herbert's poetry, unlike Donne's, is musical and defines the quality of its music. Maintains that both Herbert and Donne in their poetry are less concerned with presenting the transcendent God than with dramatizing "a struggle between God and themselves" (p. 95). Points out a central paradox of Herbert's poems: "For all their intricate artistry, they do not present themselves (as Milton's obtrusively do) as art, but present rather the divinity which they affirm" (p. 112). Compares and contrasts Herbert with Donne, Hopkins, and Eliot.

⋘§ 519. DANIELS, EDGAR F. "Herbert's 'The Quip', 23." *Expl* 23:item 7.

Comments on the first half of line 23 of "The Quip" ("Speak not at large"). Disagrees with those who interpret "at large" as meaning "in a general way" and argues that the phrase more appropriately means "at length, in full, fully." "It is the main point of the poem that God's reply is to be a 'quip,' a short stinging statement, and so He is urged not to speak at length in a point-by-point refutation but to answer everything in a single sentence."

⋘§ 520. ———. "Herbert's 'The Quip,' Line 23: 'Say, I Am Thine.' " *ELN* 2:10–12.

Points out that line 23 of "The Quip" is ambiguous and can be read either "say that I (man) am Thine (God's)," as George Herbert Palmer suggests, or "say, 'I (God) am thine (man's).' " Argues that the thematic unity of the poem "is possible only if the half-line is read as a direct quotation: God's quip is the climactic statement of the poem, minimizing the rewards of the world (beauty, money, glory, and intellectual association) by placing God himself in the balance against them" (p. 12).

◄§ 521. ELLRODT, ROBERT. "Scientific Curiosity and Metaphysical Poetry." MP 61:180–97.

Accounts for the prevailing scientific curiosity in metaphysical poetry and for the differences in the use of science among the various poets. Points out that Herbert "deplored that man's attention should stray through the Creation instead of turning to the Creator" (p. 195) but that he did not hold science in contempt. Unlike Donne, Herbert "seems ingenuously persuaded that man's intelligence can penetrate any mystery in Nature" (p. 195), and thus he "only disowns the search of the scientist because it does not lead man to God" (p. 195). Like Bacon, Herbert separated science from religion, but for an entirely different reason: Bacon "wished to free philosophy from theological fetters" while Herbert "would rather free the Christian from intellectual subtleties" (p. 195). Yet Herbert is not hostile to natural philosophy nor does he view learning as useless; he recognizes "the *human* value of science" (p. 195). Argues that Herbert's "underlying rationality kept him from wholly surrendering to emotion, ecstasy, or wonder" (pp. 195–96), and thus he is "like Donne and unlike Crashaw in stressing paradox rather than mystery or miracle" (p. 196). Points out specific examples of Herbert's admittedly sparing use of scientific images.

◄§ 522. ENGLAND, MARTHA WINBURN. "The First Wesley Hymn Book." BNYPL 68:225–38.

Reprinted in *Hymns Unbidden: Donne, Herbert, Blake, Emily Dickinson, and the Hymnographers* (New York: Public Library, 1966), pp. 31–42.

Comments on the adaptations of poems from *The Temple* in John Wesley's *A Collection of Psalms and Hymns* (published in Charleston, S.C., in 1737). Discusses Wesley's great admiration of Herbert as evidenced in his various collections of hymns, his publication of Walton's *Life of Herbert* in 1753, and his publication of selections from Herbert's poems in 1773.

◄§ 523. FARMER, NORMAN. "The Literary Borrowings of Philip Pain." N&Q, n.s. 11:465–67.

In part a reply to Theodore Grieder, entry 479. Argues that Philip Pain, a minor American Puritan poet, "probably knew his Quarles better than his Herbert" (p. 467). Discusses the relative popularity of the two seventeenth-century English poets and concludes that we can "ill-afford to reject the possibility that Pain had as great a working familiarity with

Quarles as with Herbert" (p. 466). Shows that many of the so-called borrowings, both general and specific, attributed to Herbert can also be found in Quarles.

◀§ 524. FISCH, HAROLD. "Hebraic Poetry." In *Jerusalem and Albion: The Hebraic Factor in Seventeenth-Century Literature*, pp. 56–62. New York: Schocken Books.

Discusses the biblical lineage of Herbert's poetry. Points out that Herbert's meditative poetry "has its roots deep in the Psalter, and its simplicity is that of the Psalmist" (p. 57). Maintains that psalms are typically "a song for two voices addressing one another in the intimate drama of the covenant-relation" (p. 59) and sees this dialectical strain as typical of much of Herbert's poetry: "His characteristic poetry reveals a certain tension owing to the juxtaposition cither in sequences or in balance of the various opposing forces of the religious life" (p. 61). Suggests that Herbert may be more appropriately called a "dialogic" poet rather than a metaphysical poet. Describes Herbert's poetry as that particular kind of meditative poetry that is "strenuous, earnest, and controlled; it brings together the various powers of the soul into a unity—the contemplative and active, the rational and the emotional" (p. 60). Comments briefly on Herbert's rendering of Psalm 23 and several other poems, including "An Offering," "Complaining," and "The Collar."

◀§ 525. HOWARTH, R. G. "The Chronology of George Herbert's Poems." In *A Pot of Gillyflowers: Studies and Notes*, pp. 82–83. Cape Town, South Africa.

Evaluates George Herbert Palmer's attempt to date and to arrange Herbert's poems in chronological order (entry 1) and F. E. Hutchinson's objections to such an ordering (entry 223). Suggests that when one considers "Jordan (II)," in which Herbert renounces his earlier excesses in poetry, "it will be found that Palmer's order is fairly well borne out; though he may, as Hutchinson declares he does, inadvisedly separate some related pieces" (p. 83).

◀§ 526. HUGHES, RICHARD E. "George Herbert and the Incarnation." *Cithara* 4:22–32.

Maintains that the central issue in Herbert's poetry is the Incarnation and argues that Herbert "did not merely write *about* the Incarnation: he saw poetry itself as a miniature version of the Incarnation, and each divine poem as a microcosm of the Incarnation" (p. 24). Thus, the "doctrine provided Herbert, not only with subject, but with form, technique and meaning" (p. 24). Comments on Herbert's sacramental sense, his delight in order, his uses of music, and his understanding of the tradition of the Logos as part of his incarnational view. Presents a detailed reading of "Love (III)" in order to demonstrate "how Herbert fashions his poetry so that the entire poetic process becomes incarnative" (p. 29).

◄§ 527. KENNER, HUGH, ed. *Seventeenth Century Poetry: The Schools of Donne and Jonson.* New York: Holt, Rinehart and Winston. xxxiii, 508p.

Contents (pp. iii–viii); editor's note (pp. ix–x); introduction (pp. xi–xxxii); selected bibliography (p. xxxiii); chronological chart (p. xxxiv); selections from the poetry of Donne, Jonson, Lord Herbert, Henry Wotton, Aurelian Townshend, Richard Corbett, Henry King, Herbert, Crashaw, Vaughan, Traherne, Herrick, Carew, Suckling, William Habington, Lovelace, Waller, Denham, Cleveland, Cowley, and Marvell (pp. 1–499); index (pp. 500–508). Brief headnote on Herbert and a selection of twenty-eight poems with short explanatory notes (pp. 199–225).

◄§ 528. MELCHIORI, GIORGIO. *Poeti metafisci inglesi del Seicento.* Scala Reale. Antologie Letterarie, no. 4. Milan: Casa Editrice Dr. Francesco Vallardi. 673p.

Anthology of seventeenth-century English poetry for the Italian reader. The introduction (pp. 1–45) is divided into seven subsections: (1) Eufuismo, (2) Wit eufuistico e wit metafisico, (3) Universo medievale e «nuova filosofia», (4) Il linguaggio del Manierismo, (5) L'evoluzione barocca, (6) Dalla meditazione alle visione, and (7) La poesia metafisica oggi. Selective general bibliography (pp. 53–58). Contains a brief introduction to Herbert's life and poetry (pp. 267–69). Calls Herbert a mannerist and suggests, "In lui davvero si trova quella precaria e sottilmente bilanciata fusione del colloquiale e del cosmico, di pensiero e sentimento, che è la caratteristica più genuina della grande poesia «metafisica» del primo Seicento; fusione già apparirà imperfetta nella fase barocca di questa poesia, in poeti come Crashaw e Cowley" (p. 268). Very selective Herbert bibliography (p. 269). Translates into Italian verse thirty-five of Herbert's poems. Notes to the poems (pp. 646–49).

◄§ 529. SPARROW, JOHN. "George Herbert and John Donne among the Moravians." *BNYPL* 68:625–53.

Reprinted in *Hymns Unbidden: Donne, Herbert, Blake, Emily Dickinson and the Hymnographers* (New York: Public Library, 1966), pp. 1–28.

Comments on John Wesley's lifelong admiration for Herbert's poetry, evidenced by his including several poems (somewhat abridged) from *The Temple* in his *Collection of Moral and Sacred Poems* (1744) and also by his publishing in 1773, when he was seventy years old, a collection of twenty-three poems (again abridged) entitled *Select Parts of Mr. Herbert's Sacred Poems.* In addition, Wesley demonstrated his admiration for Herbert's poems by adapting six of them for congregational singing in 1737 and another six in 1738. In 1739, John and Charles Wesley published their *Hymns and Sacred Poems* and "of the 138 pieces in this book, no fewer than forty-two were adaptations from Herbert (including ten of the twelve that he had already published); all were designated as being 'From Herbert,' and in almost every case they retained their original titles" (p. 626). Comments also on adaptations of Herbert that appear in the Moravian hymnbook entitled *A Collection of Hymnes* (1754). Thirty poems by Herbert (including four from Harvey's *Synagogue*) were included, only ten of which had been previously adapted by Wesley. Compares Wesley's adaptations with those of the Moravian collection.

ᴥᔤ 530. WARNER, OLIVER. "George Herbert." In *English Literature: A Portrait Gallery*, pp. 28–29. London: Chatto & Windus.

Brief biographical sketch and an engraved portrait of Herbert based on a drawing by Robert White. The portrait first appeared in Walton's *Life* (1670). States that it is "the only representation of Herbert to have survived" (p. 28).

ᴥᔤ 531. WARNKE, FRANK J. "Sacred Play: Baroque Poetic Style." *JAAC* 22:455–64.

Discusses how intellectual play, dramatic projection, and mythic embodiment coexist in the work of certain English and Continental baroque poets, including Herbert. Suggests an approach to baroque poetry, "a way which may conceivably help us understand how a poem may be both serious and not serious, and how its style may partake simultaneously of the frivolous, the dramatic, and the profound" (p. 455). Comments briefly on Herbert's uses of intellectual play: anagrams, acrostics, pattern poems, and various technical effects achieved by the very form of the poem (as, for example, in "Deniall" or "Trinitie Sunday"). Suggests that in *The Temple*, Herbert "plays at the game of salvation—all in the most serious possible manner" (p. 463). His art is "an experience of the spirit which, being different from life, affords a ground from which to perceive and celebrate life" (p. 463). Briefly compares Herbert's poetry to Bach's *Musikalisches Opfer*, in which, "a joyful mirthful virtuosity is at the service of devout religious sensibility, and serves it best by being joyous and mirthful" (p. 463).

1965

ᴥᔤ 532. ALLCHIN, F. R. "George Herbert's 'Rope of Sands.'" *TLS*, 6 May, p. 356.

Queries Geoffrey Tillotson (entry 561) and James Kinsley (entry 546) about a possible link between Herbert and "his senior contemporary in North India, Tulsī Dās, who wrote of a vain task as 'twining a rope of dust specks with which to bind a lordly elephant'" (p. 356).

◆§ 533. BEATY, JEROME, and MATCHETT, WILLIAM H. *Poetry: From Statement to Meaning*. New York: Oxford University Press. 353p.

General introduction to the study of poetry. Brief comments on the originality and experimental quality of Herbert's stanzaic forms. Mentions "The Altar" (p. 105), "Easter-wings" (p. 323), and "The Flower" (pp. 323–24).

◆§ 534. BEMENT, PETER. "George Herbert's 'Rope of Sands.'" *TLS*, 29 April 1965, p. 331.

Reply to Geoffrey Tillotson, entry 561. Points out that on at least three occasions Chapman used phrases very similar to Herbert's *rope of sands*. Suggests that Chapman's source is likely Erasmus's *Adagia*, as is pointed out by Frank L. Schoell in *Études sur l'humanisme continental en Angleterre à la fin de la renaissance* (Paris: Champion, 1926), pp. 50–51.

◆§ 535. COLEMAN, MARION MOORE. "George Herbert's 'Rope of Sands.'" *TLS*, 29 April, p. 331.

Reply to Geoffrey Tillotson, entry 561. Points out the use of the phrase *rope of sands* in Adam Mickiewicz's poem "Pani Twardowska." The Twardowski legend is a combination of the Faust and Tyll Eulenspiegel legends.

◆§ 536. COLLMER, ROBERT G. "The Function of Death in Certain Metaphysical Poems." *McNR* 16:25–32.

Reprinted in *BSE*, see entry 566.

Discusses the treatment of death in the poetry of Herbert, Donne, Vaughan, and Crashaw. Suggests that Herbert, in contrast to Donne, emphasizes in his poetry "unitive death, not divisive death" (p. 28); he views death simply "as part of God's system" (p. 29). Thus Herbert "did not view death as a frightful experience; he said virtually nothing about the physical ravages of death" (p. 28). Maintains that Herbert is "closer to Crashaw than to any other metaphysical poet in his belief that death is primarily positive" (p. 29).

◆§ 537. DANIELS, EDGAR F. "Herbert's 'The Quip,' Line 15: A 'De-Explication.'" *AN&Q* 3:115–16.

Argues that line 15 of "The Quip" ("He scarce allow'd me half an eie") has been overread by both George Herbert Palmer and F. E. Hutchinson and that if it is allowed "to have its simple say without these exegeses, it makes excellent sense and verse" (p. 116). Glory personified, like the other personified appeals in the poem, shows his general contempt for the poet in his own quite characteristic way: "Conceived as a pompous person walking past the poet, he does not condescend to give him a glance" (p. 116).

⇜§ 538. DERRY, WARREN. "George Herbert's 'Rope of Sands.'" TLS, 29 April, p. 331.
Reply to Geoffrey Tillotson, entry 561. Points out the proverbial nature of the phrase *rope of sands* for expressing the notion of vain labor. Finds use of it in the works of Lucius Junius Columella.

⇜§ 539. ELIOT, T. S. "To Criticize the Critic." In *To Criticize the Critic and Other Writings*, pp. 11–26. New York: Farrar, Straus & Giroux.
Eliot comments on his role in the modern revival of interest in metaphysical poetry: "I think that if I wrote well about the metaphysical poets, it was because they were poets who had inspired me. And if I can be said to have had an influence whatever in promoting a wider interest in them, it was simply because no previous poet who had praised these poets had been so deeply influenced by them as I had been" (p. 22). He adds: "As the taste for my own poetry spread, so did the taste for the poets to whom I owed the greatest debt and about whom I had written. Their poetry, and mine, were congenial to that age. I sometimes wonder whether that age is not coming to an end" (p. 22). Points out that for pure delight and pleasure he turns now more and more to the poems of Herbert, rather than to those of Donne: "This does not necessarily involve a judgment of relative greatness: it is merely that what has best responded to my need in middle and later age is different from the nourishment I needed in my youth" (p. 23).

⇜§ 540. ENDICOTT, ANNABEL M. "The Structure of George Herbert's *Temple*: A Reconsideration." UTQ 34:226–37.
The purpose of this essay is "to deny emphatically the structural analogy between Herbert's *Temple* and the Hebrew one" as suggested by John David Walker (entry 492), "to provide some additional knowledge about the use of this symbol in the Renaissance, and to show that Herbert would almost certainly have been aware of its complexities and its disadvantages" (p. 226). Comments on the traditional typology of the temple as found in the works of Joseph Hall, Donne, and Guillaume du Bartas to show not only that the image was a common one in the Renaissance but also to point out that "the tradition itself was by no means simple, and allowed much scope for individuality" (p. 233). Discusses "just how much of the *Hebraic* nature of the Temple could be implied by Herbert's use of the name" (p. 232). Concludes that if one demands an overall pattern for *The Temple*, then a "three-fold structure of didactic, lyrical, and satirical poems" (p. 236) would be more appropriate

than any attempt to impose the structure of the Hebraic temple onto this diverse collection of poems.

᪲§ 541. GREENWOOD, E. B. "George Herbert's Sonnet 'Prayer': A Stylistic Study." *EIC* 15:27–45.

Detailed stylistic analysis of "Prayer (I)" in which the critic attempts "to marry the old rhetoric . . . with the new linguistics founded by Saussure and the stylistics of Alonso" (pp. 27–28). Sees Herbert's sonnet as "a kind of *mimesis* of inner speech" (p. 29) and argues that its very structure exemplifies the central point of the poem, namely that "we can only understand 'something' of it [prayer], not everything" (p. 42). Comments on the structure, rhetorical features (such as the use of asyndeton —the omission of conjunctives), the highly concentrated metaphors, and various rhythmic and phonetic characteristics. Especially explains in detail some of the more important metaphors in the poem. Contains an appendix on apposition as a mode of expression. See also Helen Vendler, review of *Essays on Style and Language: Linguistic and Critical Approaches to Literary Styles*, edited by Roger Fowler, *EIC* 16 (1966): 457–63; and Greenwood, entry 595.

᪲§ 542. HERBERT, GEORGE. *The Latin Poetry of George Herbert: A Bilingual Edition*. Translated by Mark McCloskey and Paul R. Murphy. Athens, Ohio: Ohio University Press. vii, 181p.

Introduction (pp. v–vii); contents (pp. viii–ix); Herbert's Latin and Greek poems (F. E. Hutchinson's text [entry 223]) with English translations of facing pages (pp. 1–175); notes (pp. 177–81). In the introduction the translators point out that Herbert's Latin poetry "is not only in the tradition of the Anglo-Latin poetry of his time, but it also reveals significant and little-known sides of his character and style" (p. v). Brief comments on the Anglo-Latin tradition.

᪲§ 543. HUNTER, JIM. *The Metaphysical Poets*. Literature in Perspective. London: Evans Brothers. 160p.

Introduction to metaphysical poetry intended for the "ordinary man who reads for pleasure" (p. 5). Contains nine brief chapters: (1) Background; (2) Characteristics of Metaphysical Poetry; (3) Verse; (4) Diction; (5) Imagery; (6) John Donne; (7) George Herbert; (8) Vaughan, Marvell, Crashaw, and Others; and (9) Critical Estimate Over the Years. Selected bibliography. The chapter on Herbert (pp. 108–24) presents a biographical account and a general survey of his poetry. Comments primarily on the ingenuity and wit of Herbert's poems: "They are technically some of the most complex in English" (p. 111). Contains brief critical comment on several individual poems, especially "The Collar" ("for all its serious intention it must have given Herbert some amusement to create" [p. 114]), "Church-monuments" ("his finest hieroglyph" [p. 115]), "The Pearl," "Frailtie," and "The Forerunners." Stresses Herbert's variety and asks that one's evaluation of Donne not be used to misjudge Herbert, "who is one of the best English poets in most things, and the best of all in some things" (p. 122).

◄§ 544. INGLIS, FRED, ed. *English Poetry, 1550–1660.* London: Methuen & Co. xix, 242p.
Anthology that contains twenty-one of Herbert's poems (pp. 145–64), brief notes (p. 220), and a short biographical sketch (p. 226). The introduction to the poetry of the period (pp. 1–36) mentions Herbert throughout.

◄§ 545. JENNINGS, ELIZABETH. "The Seventeenth Century." In *Christianity and Poetry*, pp. 48–63. Faith and Fact Books, 122. London: Burns & Oates.
General survey of religious poetry in England during the seventeenth century. Calls Herbert "the most satisfying minor poet of the whole seventeenth century" (p. 53). Suggests that "Love (III)" is "one of the most exquisitely simple poems in English about Holy Communion" (p 54).

◄§ 546. KINSLEY, JAMES. "George Herbert's 'Rope of Sands.'" *TLS*, 29 April, p. 331.
Reply to Geoffrey Tillotson, entry 561. Points out that *rope of sands* is proverbial for "something having no coherence or binding power."
Suggests that the word *anneal'd* in line 3 of "Love joy" may be a pun fabulous application of a commonplace." See also F. R. Allchin, entry 532.

◄§ 547. KIRKWOOD, JAMES J., and WILLIAMS, GEORGE WALTON. "Anneal'd as Baptism in Herbert's 'Love-Joy.'" *AN&Q* 4:3–4.
Suggests that the word *anneal'd* in line 3 of "Love-joy" may be a pun on *aneled* (anointed) and thus may have reference to the holy oil of chrism used from earliest Christian times in the administering of the sacrament of Baptism. Points out various typological connections in the poem.

◄§ 548. LEITER, LOUIS H. "George Herbert's Anagram." *CE* 26:543–44.
Presents a detailed explication of "Anagram of the Virgin Marie." Argues that, although at first the poem appears "to be only a trick, only a joke or oddity," it captures in fact "the essence of a particular kind of

poetic sensibility" (p. 543) and "performs a sacrament of prophecy and praise" (p. 544). For a reply, see Robert E. Reiter, entry 583.

⋘§ 549. LUCAS, F. L. "George Herbert's 'Rope of Sands.' " TLS, 29 April, p. 331.

Reply to Geoffrey Tillotson, entry 561. Points out a Cornish legend of the wicked Tregeagle who was condemned to make ropes of sand. Also points out that The Oxford Dictionary of English Proverbs contains ten examples (including Erasmus and Hudibras) and that the phrase was proverbial in the seventeenth century for performing futile tasks. Challenges Tillotson's suggestion that Ruskin had Herbert in mind when he used the phrase.

⋘§ 550. MacCAFFREY, ISABEL G. "The Meditative Paradigm." ELH 32:388–407.

Evaluates Louis Martz's The Paradise Within: Studies in Vaughan, Traherne, and Milton (New Haven: Yale University Press, 1964) in which Martz discusses the effects of the Augustinian meditative tradition on the three poets. Disagrees with the notion that the meditative poem forms a specific genre but maintains that what Martz describes is "a literary paradigm, convention, or fiction in which a particular kind of thematic concern expresses itself habitually in—implies or demands—particular structural characteristics" (p. 390). Comments on two distinct meditative traditions, "one concerned with eucharistic and liturgical emblems, the other with a fictive 'landscape of the soul' " (p. 394). Compares Herbert briefly with Vaughan in the light of these traditions.

⋘§ 551. MacNEICE, LOUIS. Varieties of Parables. Cambridge: University Press. vii, 156p.

Several references to Herbert throughout, especially to his overt parable poems (such as "Redemption"), his uses of the plain style and of traditional symbols, and his skillful uses of allegory and paradox. Says that Herbert "is not only less strained or straining than the other so-called Metaphysical poets, but a good deal less 'poetical' than certain prose writers of the period such as Jeremy Taylor and Sir Thomas Browne" (p. 47). Suggests that Herbert anticipates Bunyan and has certain clear links with Spenser.

⋘§ 552. MOHANTY, HARENDRA PRASAD. "George Herbert's 'The Collar.' " IJES 6:114–16.

Argues that the poem "presents a metaphysical ambivalence, the opposition between renunciation and enjoyment, submission to collar and revolt from commitment" (p. 114). Sees a double conflict at the heart of the poem, "one positive, the other negative, one the attraction of the senses, the other the illusory nature of the divine" (p. 115). Praises various elements in the poem: its complexity, dramatic tension, wide-ranging imagery, colloquial speech rhythms, etc. "Only the mood is turbulent but everything else is controlled, bound in the tight organization of balances, rhythmic stresses, half-rhymes, internal rhymes, alliterations, and onomatopoeia" (p. 116).

◄§ 553. OSTRIKER, ALICIA. "Song and Speech in the Metrics of George Herbert." *PMLA* 80:62–68.
Tries to account for the various paradoxes in Herbert's poetry "by isolating in metrical terms, the apparently irreconcilable modes of 'song' and 'speech' which have been observed in Herbert by several critics, notably Joseph H. Summers; by discovering what conventions they derive from and how Herbert used and changed what he learned from others; and by showing how the prosodic causes serve as instruments of an overall poetic vision in *The Temple*" (p. 62). Comments on the pervasive influence of the Elizabethan song on Herbert and argues that its most significant influence "lies in the structuring of his stanza-patterns, in which one finds the most important metrical qualities cultivated by the lyricists: complexity and variety, strictness of form, and concurrence of sound with sense" (p. 62). Discusses also the speech elements in Herbert's verse by examining his uses of blank verse, especially "how he used, or abstained from using, the tricks of accentual variety, caesural irregularity, and over-flow, common to blank verse" (p. 66). Maintains that "the 'song' elements in Herbert's prosody are supplied by the structure of his stanza-patterns; while the 'speech' elements are given by internal rhythmic variation" (p. 68) and concludes that "the poet's treatment of stanza and rhythm helps produce not only his mingled voices of singing and speaking, but affects every aspect of his poetic expression" (p. 68).

◄§ 554. PACEY, DESMOND. "Easter Homage to George Herbert." *The Atlantic Advocate* 55:40–44.
Appreciative sketch of Herbert's life and personality. Describes a visit to Salisbury and Bemerton. Five photographs.

◄§ 555. PEEL, DONALD F. "Syncretistic Elements in Seventeenth Century Metaphysical Poetry." *Northwest Missouri State College Studies* 29, no. 2:3–20.
Considers the effects of the "new philosophy" in the development of metaphysical poetry: "The poetry was born in the disintegration of medieval scholasticism as a universal mode of thought. But whereas the scientists hailed that destruction as a victory, the poets saw the moral vacuum so created was not being adequately filled by the 'new philosophy'" (p. 3). Herbert is mentioned in several places, primarily by way of illustration. Concludes that the metaphysical poets, unlike the positivistic scientists, "were more constructive than destructive, more inter-

ested in holding up an affirmative ideal than in exposing the false" (p. 20). Aware of the tensions and problems created by the new science, the metaphysical poets actively addressed themselves to solving the moral dilemma created by the destruction of the old system.

◄§ 556. PURCELL, HENRY. "With Sick and Famish'd Eyes" [Words by George Herbert]. In *The Works of Henry Purcell*, vol. 30, *Sacred Music*, part 4, *Songs and Vocal Ensemble Music*, edited by Anthony Lewis and Nigel Fortune. London: Novello and Co., pp. 94–97.
Presents Purcell's musical adaptation of certain stanzas of Herbert's "Longing."

◄§ 557. SCHEURLE, WILLIAM H. "A Reading of George Herbert's 'Content.'" *LangQ* 4, nos. 1–2: 37–39.
Detailed analysis of "Content" in order to examine the spirit of Herbert's religious humility and "to show that the language, figures, and images used by Herbert belonged to a general storehouse of terms and beliefs utilized by other divines of the period" (p. 37).

◄§ 558. STEESE, PETER. "Herbert and Crashaw: Two Paraphrases of the Twenty-Third Psalm." *Journal of Bible and Religion* 33:137–41.
Compares Herbert's and Crashaw's paraphrases of Psalm 23 and contrasts their achievements in this genre with the mediocre rendition of Sternhold and Hopkins. Shows that Herbert "closely follows the simple dignity of the Scriptures, yet he uses words and phrases which bring various interpretations to the mind of the reader and at the same time creates a sense of poetic unity" (p. 139). Says that both Herbert's and Crashaw's paraphrases "represent a level of achievement seldom equalled in the history of the genre" (p. 141).

◄§ 559. STRAVINSKY, IGOR. "Memories of T. S. Eliot." *Esquire*, August, pp. 92–93.
Stravinsky reports that Eliot said to him that the best parts of his essay on Herbert were the quotations and that he regretted "he had not had a 'sense of his audience' while writing it—though he certainly knew his audiences were the English 'lit' departments of several hundred thousand American universities" (p. 92). Also reports that Eliot announced, "Herbert is a great poet . . . and one of a very few I can read again and again" (p. 92).

◄§ 560. THORPE, JAMES. "Herbert's 'Love (III).'" *Expl* 24:item 16.
Suggests that "Love (III)" is not only related to the service of Holy Communion but "is in fact a dramatization of the central portion of

that service, from the Exhortation following the offertory through the Administration of the Elements." Presents, through detailed allusions to the Book of Common Prayer, an allegorical interpretation of the poem in which the Eucharist is figured as a feast. Argues that the poem allows for a four-fold interpretation as found in medieval scriptural exegesis: (1) literal (simply the invitation to dinner), (2) allegorical (the eucharistic feast), (3) tropological (a dialogue between the soul and love), and (4) anagogical (the reception of the soul into heaven).

⊷§ 561. TILLOTSON, GEOFFREY. "George Herbert's 'Rope of Sands.'" *TLS*, 22 April, p. 320.

Comments on the phrase *rope of sands* in line 22 of "The Collar." Points out that in his *Royal Academy Notes* Ruskin uses the phrase. Ruskin's editors, E. Cook and A. Weddeburn, apparently unaware of the Herbert allusion, refer the reader to Scott's notes on his *Lay of the Last Minstrel*, which contain a reference to a certain Michael Scott, a thirteenth-century scholar and magician, who tells of keeping a demon busy by engaging him "in the hopeless and endless task of making ropes out of sea-sand" (p. 320). Tillotson states that he has been unable to discover how Herbert may have come onto the legend. For replies, see F. R. Allchin, entry 532; Peter Bement, entry 534; Marion Moore Coleman, entry 535; Warren Derry, entry 538; James Kinsley, entry 546; and F. L. Lucas, entry 549.

⊷§ 562. WAGNER, LINDA WELSHIMER. "Donne's Secular and Religious Poetry." *LHR*, no. 7, pp. 13–22.

Compares Herbert's "The Flower," Vaughan's "The Flower," and Donne's "The Blossom" and "Holy Sonnet II," "poems related through subject matter rather than through category" (p. 13), in order to show various likenesses and differences. Suggests that Herbert's poems "combine elements of metaphysical religious poetry and the personally urgent lyric creating a unified expression of devout, almost passionate, belief" (p. 16). Maintains that the chief parallel among the three poets is their pervasive conversational tone and that the chief differences "stem from the poets' concepts of nature as well as their religious beliefs" (p. 20). Concludes that a study of the four poems highlights Donne's influence on Herbert and Vaughan: "In their choice of images, point of view, poetic craft, and positive expression of feelings, these later poets couple techniques of both Donne's secular and religious poems" (pp. 21–22). Agrees with Helen Gardner's statement that Herbert's poems "can be regarded as a species of love poetry" (p. 22).

⊷§ 563. WHITING, PAUL. "Two Notes on George Herbert." *N&Q*, n.s. 12:130–31.

(1) Comments on stanza 51 of "The Sacrifice." Argues that Herbert

is not merely restating a conventional concept when he describes Christ, the new apple, nailed to the "dry tree" of the cross; actually, through this image the "sin-tree" (the tree of knowledge of good and evil) becomes transformed into the "life-tree" (the tree of life also found in the Garden): "The Eden-fruit brought death, but the new apple, which is Christ, brings life" (p. 130). Thus Herbert has "extended the meaning-area of an apparently traditional concept, and only a reading that bears in mind the familiar Scriptural background involved will really be adequate" (p. 130). (2) Comments on lines 9–12 of "Easter." Suggests that in the image of Christ stretched out on the cross, which is likened to the fine tuning of a musical instrument, "we see that the sinews are stretched not only in order to temper them correctly, but specifically to reach a key high enough for the adequate celebration of 'this most high day' " (p. 131). Points out that church music in Herbert's day was in a high key.

564. WOODHOUSE, A. S. P. "The Seventeenth Century: Donne and His Successors." In *The Poet and His Faith: Religion and Poetry in England from Spenser to Eliot and Auden*, pp. 42–89. Chicago and London: University of Chicago Press.

Comments on the general conditions of English religion and poetry in the seventeenth century that made the period such an important one for religious verse. Contrasts the lives and the religious sensibilities of Herbert and Donne. Sees Herbert's struggle as primarily one against the attractions of the world while Donne's was with "the world, the flesh, and the devil of doubt and cynicism" (p. 67). Maintains that in temper and attitude Herbert resembles John Keble. Briefly discusses the influence of Herbert on Crashaw and Vaughan.

1966

565. COLIE, ROSALIE L. *Paradoxia Epidemica: The Renaissance Tradition of Paradox*. Princeton: Princeton University Press. xx, 553p.

Chapter 6, "*Logos* in *The Temple*" (pp. 190–215), first appeared in *JWCI*, see entry 497. Throughout this study Herbert is mentioned. Comments on the use of "rhopographical" images (images of "insignificant objects, odds and ends") and "rhypological" images (images of low and sordid things) in Herbert's poetry. Points out that Dionysius the Areopagite recommends such images as "appropriate to attempt comprehension of the divine essence" (p. 25) and that their use was practiced by certain Hellenistic painters. Argues that this tradition explains "the curious habit of devotional poets' using 'low things' in immediate juxtaposition to the highest, such as Herbert's likeness of Christ to a bag, or of God to a coconut, and Donne's of the flea's triple life to the Trinity" (p. 25).

✑§ 566. COLLMER, ROBERT G. "The Function of Death i
Metaphysical Poems." *BSE* 6:147–56.
First appeared in *McNR*, see entry 536.

✑§ 567. CURTIS, JARED R. "William Wordsworth and English Poetry
of the Sixteenth and Seventeenth Centuries." *CLJ* 1:28–39.
Comments briefly on Wordsworth's acquaintance with Herbert's poetry and prose. Notes that Wordsworth owned a copy of *Herbert's Remains* (1652) and that he refers to *The Country Parson* in "Sacred
Religion." Questions whether or not Wordsworth knew *The Temple*
but thinks it is possible that Wordsworth's concept of his own great work
as a cathedral may have been derived from Herbert. Points out also that
Emerson saw certain resemblances between Herbert's "Constancie" and
Wordsworth's "Character of a Happy Warrior" but suggests that the
similiarities are extremely slight.

✑§ 568. DANIELLS, ROY. "The Mannerist Element in English Literature." *UTQ* 36:1–11.
Briefly discusses certain manneristic elements in Herbert's poetry,
especially the note of striving for the moment of divine illumination.
Herbert's poetry is often a record of an experience "which is more
than conventionally devotional and less than mystical" (p. 8); what he
achieves is "the sudden vision of a transcendental world, of a highly personal kind and of great delicacy" (p. 8). But he is " 'ever in warres' and
must rise to each instant of serenity by a fresh effort of dedication" (p. 8).
Comments also on Shakespeare, Bacon, Donne, Vaughan, Traherne, and
Marvell.

✑§ 569. ENDICOTT, ANNABEL M. " 'The Soul in Paraphrase': George
Herbert's 'Library.' " *RN* 19:14–16.
Suggests that the paradox of "The Parson's Library" in *A Priest to the
Temple* may come from one of Donne's sermons on the penitential psalms
(tentatively assigned by Donne's editors to the winter of 1624–1625).
Speculates on "whether Donne's linking of David and Solomon, poet and
preacher, sheds any new light on the relationship between *A Priest to the
Temple* and *The Temple*" (p. 15), and suggests that "*The Temple*, by
combining the functions of David and Solomon, becomes an act of public worship, rather than of private devotion; the full appropriateness of its
title becomes clearer; and the reader is spared the frequently embarrassing
sensation that he may be eavesdropping on the intimate conversation between a man and his God" (p. 16).

✑§ 570. FITTS, DUDLEY. "The Collar." In *Master Poems of the English
Language*, edited by Oscar Williams, pp. 147–51. New York: Trident Press.

Calls "The Collar" "a miniature drama of revolt against moral authority, a brief violence stilled by a single word almost before it has got well under way" (p. 149). Rejects autobiographical readings of the poem: "The predicament is general: every one of us has known the collar and has longed to slip it. If we were passionate enough, and metrists sufficiently accomplished, we might write the first thirty-two lines of 'The Collar'; so far, it is a superbly adolescent outburst. It is in the last four lines however—indeed, in the last five words—that we watch the transformation into superb poetry" (pp. 150–51). Comments on the technical finesse of the poem and praises Herbert's control.

⋙ 571. HANLEY, SISTER SARA WILLIAM, C.S.J. "George Herbert's 'Ana $\left(\begin{smallmatrix}\text{Mary}\\\text{Army}\end{smallmatrix}\right)$ gram.' " ELN 4:16–19.

Points out that in the 1633 edition of The Temple the two-line anagram was moved (perhaps by Herbert himself) from its original position between "Church-musick" and "Church-lock and key" and placed between "Avarice" and "To all Angels and Saints." Argues that the poem in its present context takes on additional meaning and that, in fact, in the three poems "we have a tightly knit group, united not in a gradually developing sequence but as a strikingly contrasted pair of poems linked by a third poem placed deliberately between them" (p. 19). Discusses the imagery, wit, conceit, and general cleverness of the anagram.

⋙ 572. ———. "Herbert's 'Frailtie.' " Expl 25:item 18.

Sees echoes of the Spiritual Exercises of St. Ignatius Loyola in the tripartite structure of "Frailtie" (the three stanzas corresponding to the exercise of the memory, understanding, and will) and in the reference in lines 9–10 to "both Regiments;/ The worlds, and thine" (similar to Ignatius's meditation on the Two Standards).

⋙ 573. KNEPPRATH, H. E. "George Herbert: University Orator and Country Parson." Southern Speech Journal 32:105–12.

Comments on Herbert's activities and achievements as a student, teacher, and practitioner of the art of public speaking. Argues that Herbert's views on the purpose and means of rhetoric changed when he became a country parson: "He found that what constitutes gravity, elevation, transparency, and conciseness in a speech depends not so much on the niceties of invention, arrangement, and language as taught by sixteenth- and seventeenth-century logic and rhetoric as it does upon an understanding of the nature and beliefs of an audience" (p. 112). Examines the few comments on rhetoric found in The Country Parson.

⋙ 574. KNIEGER, BERNARD. "The Purchase-Sale: Patterns of Business Imagery in the Poetry of George Herbert." SEL 6:111–24.

Points out with many examples drawn from the poems that Herbert frequently uses commercial imagery "to express the very heart of his devotional experience" (p. 111). Such business terms as *debtor, creditor, debt, purchase, sold, commerce, expense, wages, price, profit,* and *business* "play a crucial role in Herbert's strategy of communication" (p. 112). Points out, as an example, that Herbert's "use of *selling* is representative of his employment of business-commercial terminology," for though "he characteristically uses this concept in a seemingly-pejorative sense (in the context of betrayal), this same term simultaneously incorporates within itself the magnitude of God's love for mankind as exemplified by his voluntarily subjecting himself to the utmost degradation for man's sake: from this point of view, paradoxically, the term could not have a more positive content" (pp. 116–17). Suggests that Herbert may have been influenced by his observance of the immense expansion of English commerce during his own day, by the Puritan work ethic, and by the use of such imagery in the Bible. Argues that in part his usage is shaped by his "conception of the blood-sacrifice of Christ: that is, Herbert conceived of the crucifixion as a purchase-sale in which Christ, going about God's business, purchased (for man) mankind's salvation at the cost of His own degradation and agony" (p. 111). Also argues that Herbert "conceives of commerce and of business employment as useful or potentially useful activities, indeed a sign of God's providence" (p. 124).

٭§ 575. ———. "Teaching George Herbert in Israel—and in America? *CLAJ* 10:143–48.

Concerned with making Herbert's poetry acceptable and meaningful for modern students, whether Israeli or American, who do not share Herbert's religious beliefs nor his commitment to otherworldliness. Suggests that the teacher of Herbert must emphasize close critical readings of the poems and must point out their universality: "We must relate the psychological conflicts and the specific religious concerns of Herbert to our own psychological conflicts and our search for centers of value while simultaneously demonstrating the artistic achievement of one of the masters of English verse" (p. 148). Illustrates this approach by presenting a series of questions for the study of "Vertue." Comments on "Vanitie" and "The Pearl" as being central to an understanding of Herbert's universality.

٭§ 576. LA GUARDIA, ERIC. "Figural Imitation in English Renaissance Poetry." In *Actes du IVe Congrès de l'Association Internationale de Littérature Comparée,* edited by François Jost, pp. 844–54. The Hague and Paris: Mouton and Co.

Compares and contrasts medieval and Renaissance figuralism. Comments on the special character of Renaissance figuralism, maintaining that the Renaissance poet participated in two worlds, the ideal and the mundane, or to use Sidney's terms, the golden and the brazen. Illustrates his arguments by commenting on the treatment of nature, love, and art in a number of Renaissance poems. Briefly comments on Herbert's "Jordan (II)," suggesting that "love" becomes a figura in the poem.

᷅§ 577. McGILL, WILLIAM J., JR. "George Herbert's View of the Eucharist." *LHR*, no. 8, pp. 16–24.
Comments on Herbert's theology and his religious sensibility, particularly on his eucharistic theology. Argues that an examination of Herbert's eucharistic theology, as found in his poems and in *The Country Parson*, "shows that while he rejects out of hand certain doctrines [such as transubstantiation and impanation], he does not propose any substitute dogmatic formulation" (p. 24). Herbert clearly believes in the Real Presence but "he declines to speculate further, thus reflecting one of the principal characteristics of the Church to which he belonged, his primary concern for God's grace and man's salvation, and his preoccupation with the tasks of devotion" (p. 24). Maintains, however, that Herbert's piety was "intensely liturgical, even sacramental, in its expression" and that "it was in the eucharist that it had its fullest manifestation" (p. 24).

᷅§ 578. MARTZ, LOUIS L. *The Poem of the Mind: Essays on Poetry, English and American*. New York: Oxford University Press. xiii, 231p. Reprinted in paperback, 1969.
Collection of previously published essays and one essentially new essay that discuss poetry "of the interior life, where the mind, actually aware of an outer world of drifting, unstable forms, finds within itself the power to create coherence and significance" (p. ix), "selected and arranged with the aim of suggesting an underlying continuity when read in the present sequence" (p. ix). Three essays discuss Herbert: (1) Chapter 3, "Meditative Action and 'The Metaphysick Style'" (pp. 33–53) in a shorter version first appeared in the introduction to *The Meditative Poem: An Anthology of Seventeenth-Century Verse* (entry 509) and includes also material from an essay on Donne in *Master Poems of the English Language*, edited by Oscar Williams (New York: Trident Press, 1966). Discusses the nature of meditative action in seventeenth-century English poetry and attempts to distinguish between meditative action and metaphysical style. Suggests that Herbert is linked to Donne not so much by style as by their both sharing the meditative mode. (2) Chapter 4, "Edward Taylor: Preparatory Meditations" (pp. 54–81) originally appeared in the foreword to Donald E. Stanford's edition of *The Poems of Edward Taylor* (entry 445). Comments on the influence of Herbert on Taylor and shows how the two poets differ in their uses of metrics, diction, imagery, etc. (3) Chapter 5, "Whitman and Dickinson: Two Aspects of the Self" (pp. 82–104), essentially a new essay, contains passages from a review-article on Thomas Johnson's edition of Emily Dickinson's

poems (1955) in *UTQ* 26 (1957):556–65. Brief comparison of Herbert and Dickinson.

◄§ 579. MILES, JOSEPHINE, and SELVIN, HANAN C. "A Factor Analysis of the Vocabulary of Poetry in the Seventeenth Century." In *The Computer and Literary Style: Introductory Essays and Studies,* edited by Jacob Leed, pp. 116–27. Kent Studies in English, no. 2. Kent, Ohio: Kent State University Press.

Reprinted in *The Metaphysical Poets,* edited by Gerald Hammond (entry 783), pp. 182–96.

Presents a "factor analysis of the sixty nouns, adjectives, and verbs used at least ten times in a consecutive thousand lines by each of at least thirty poets in the seventeenth century" to see if such an analysis will reveal "a number of factors useful for characterizing certain groups of poets and poetic habits of style" (p. 116). Herbert's *The Church* is included in this study. Shows, for example, that Donne's word usage has much in common with that of such poets as Carew and Shirley and "least with Herbert, Wither, and Milton" (p. 121). Argues that certain emphases become more obvious through such a study than they do in literary histories, such as "the primacy of the Donne tradition; the ethical allegiance of Herbert to Jonson; the early innovative forces of Sandys and Quarles toward the Biblical aesthetic; and the isolation of Vaughan from his religious confrères, in contrast to the surprising general continuity in Prior and Pomfret" (p. 125).

◄§ 580. MOLLENKOTT, VIRGINIA RAMSEY. "George Herbert's Life of Love of God." *Christianity Today* 10, no. 24:11–13.

Laments the fact that Herbert is not read nor greatly appreciated by modern evangelicals. Points out that in the seventeenth and eighteenth centuries he was greatly respected by Nonconformists. Outlines some of the main features of Herbert's religious sensibility as reflected in his poetry. Maintains that "the most important insight that Herbert's poetry offers the twentieth-century evangelical is his concept of organic Christian living" (p. 12) and suggests, "It was precisely Herbert's Christocentricity that made him most completely himself as a creative individual" (p. 13).

◄§ 581. ————. "The Many and the One in George Herbert's 'Providence.'" *CLAJ* 10:34–41.

Argues, "Providence" is Herbert's "equivalent to Spenser's 'Cantos of Mutabilitie' or to Hopkins' 'Pied Beauty' and its central motif is that of the One in the Many and the Many in the One" (p. 34). Believes that Herbert found his theme of the "oneness of Providence behind the multiplicity of phenomena" (p. 35) in the Apocrypha, specifically in the Wisdom of Solomon 8:1. Presents a detailed reading of the poem.

◄§ 582. PENNEL, CHARLES A., and WILLIAMS, WILLIAM P. "The Unity
of *The Temple*." *XUS* 5:37–45.

Comments on the unity of the central portion of *The Temple*, "that
portion which follows the purification on the porch and the sacramental
celebration of the first fourteen poems in 'The Church' and which pre-
cedes the group of poems on 'last things' with which 'The Church' closes"
(p. 37). Suggests that Herbert "patterned the poems which lead from the
sacrament to death and judgment as a pilgrimage" and that "the progress
of the pilgrim soul, under the care of Christ's church, is the *leit-motif* of
the central portion of *The Temple*" (p. 38). Traces out this design and
suggests that "The Pilgrimage," although not a "key" to *The Temple*,
offers "itself as a useful trope for illuminating 'The Church' " (p. 39).

◄§ 583. REITER, ROBERT E. "George Herbert's 'Anagram': A Reply to
Professor Leiter." *CE* 28:59–60.

In part a reply to Louis H. Leiter, entry 548. Comments on the phrase
pitch His tent in "Anagram of the Virgin Marie." Points out that in the
Greek version of John 1:14 (usually translated as "and the word was
made flesh and dwelt among us") the verb *eskenosen* literally means
pitched a tent. Argues, "the wit of the poem, the appropriateness of the
anagram, and the meaning of the poem are directly dependent upon the
literal meaning of the Greek text" (p. 60).

◄§ 584. RICKEY, MARY ELLEN. *Utmost Art: Complexity in the Verse of
George Herbert*. Lexington: University of Kentucky Press. xv, 200p.

Part of chapter 4 originally appeared as "Herbert's Technical Development" (entry 511).

Proposes "to examine the nearly paradoxical co-existence of complexity
and seeming simplicity in Herbert's English poetry, to point out tropological materials hitherto overlooked, and, by exploring the development
of his art and his own statements about the nature of divine poetry, to
show his endeavor to concentrate a great store of motifs in small and un-
pretentious verses" (pp. xiv–xv). Chapter 1, "The Classical Materials"
(pp. 1–58), argues that Herbert used many classical allusions, images, and
motifs and that he used these "as tellingly as he did his familiarity with
the English Church, the natural world, or the teachings of the Fathers"
(p. 2). Unlike his Elizabethan predecessors and unlike many of his
contemporaries, Herbert thoroughly weaves these materials so skillfully
into the very texture of his verse that the modern reader may miss them
altogether. Cites numerous examples of Herbert's use of classical materials and maintains that his main purpose for using them is "the
consistent demonstration of the degree to which the happiness of the
Christian surpasses that of the pre-Christian, or natural, man and of the
contrast between God's total concern for His creatures and the meretri-

cious activities of the deities of the ancients" (p. 57). Thus, Herbert once again "demonstrates the propriety of subordinating the natural to the divine" (p. 58). Chapter 2, "Sacred Quibbles" (pp. 59–91), attempts to show that Herbert's serious puns and witty quibbles "constitute a weightier component of his verse than is generally conceded" (p. 60). Points out many examples to show that, unlike Donne, who "moves freely from one trope to another," Herbert frequently sustains in one poem two or more metaphorical systems simultaneously, thus allowing him "to sound his imagerial notes in polyphonic fashion" (p. 60). Presents a partial catalogue of Herbert's uses of serious puns "which briefly introduce new metaphorical dimensions by overlapping two or more figures" (p. 72) and argues that for Herbert "the neatness of the pun made possible the balance and harmony of some of his best poems" (p. 91). Chapter 3, "Quiddities: The Titles" (pp. 92–102), comments on Herbert's highly original uses of titles for the poems of *The Temple*. Cites a number of examples to show both the often-missed metaphorical complexity of many of his titles and the spareness of many others, which "set off the richness of the arguments within the poems" (p. 102). Chapter 4, "Time's Pruning Knife: The Development" (pp. 103–14), reviews several aspects of Herbert's development as a poet by comparing the first and second halves of *The Temple*, by comparing the poems in the Williams MS with those written later, and by commenting on the revisions in the Williams MS. Discusses Herbert's increasingly mature handling of imagery and invention and argues, "The nature of Herbert's revisions, his increasingly fine discipline of his imagery, and his progressive shifting from literal to metaphorical titles—suggest a gradual change in his conception of the devotional lyric" (p. 120). Illustrates that when "one examines the early and late sections of *The Temple*, he does indeed find that the two groups contain different *kinds* of poems" (p. 120). Comments also on Herbert's mastery of versification and his highly original stanzaic inventions to show that, like the changes in his handling of imagery, his prosodic mutations also "evince his steady pursuit of precision and concentration of idea" (p. 134). Chapter 5, "The Clothing of the Sonne: Complexity in Apparent Simplicity" (pp. 148–79), discusses Herbert's theory of poetry and comments on his complex simplicity. Argues that it is "a kind of simplicity on our part, as well as myopia, if, noting that Herbert is genuinely holy, we insist on reading his verse as jejune. For its primary impact to be one of lowly-hearted praise is precisely what he intended; and a refusal to recognize that a well-equipped adult mind has been painstakingly disciplined to make this humility possible springs from our obstinacy, not Herbert's deficiency" (p. 178). Appendix: "Herbert and William Alabaster" (pp. 180–84) comments on various resemblances between the two poets, points out specific parallels, and suggests that Herbert may have known Alabaster's English poetry in manuscript. Notes (pp. 185–95); index (pp. 196–200).

◄§ 585. STEWART, STANLEY. *The Enclosed Garden: The Tradition and the Image in Seventeenth-Century Poetry.* Madison, Milwaukee, London: University of Wisconsin Press. xiv, 226p.

Considers the figure of the enclosed garden as it appeared in the poetry of the late sixteenth and seventeenth centuries. Shows that the proper context for an understanding of such poems as Herbert's "Paradise" and Marvell's "The Garden" is this tradition. Shows the extensive use of the tradition, based on the allegorization of the Song of Songs, in Herbert's poetry. Discusses also Herbert's particular uses of time in his poetry. Mentions Herbert throughout with specific comments on individual poems, including "Paradise," "The Thanksgiving," "Longing," "The Flower," "The Crosse," "Even-song," "Life," "Time," "Sunday," "Employment," and "In Solarium."

◄§ 586. ———. "Time and *The Temple.*" SEL 6:97–110.

Discusses the structural integrity of *The Temple,* especially the function of *The Church Militant* in the design of the whole. Maintains that the placement of *The Church Militant* "is a hieroglyphic of a temporal relation" and argues, "The absence of intensity in 'Church Militant,' like that in 'Church Porch,' cannot be detached from the function of the poem within the larger structure" (p. 105). Unlike the voice in *The Church,* which reflects the anxieties and struggles of man with time (and thus change), the speaker in *The Church Militant* "sees the world with the vision of one in a state outside of life, a state which was achieved by the proper redemption of time" (p. 105). Argues then that *The Church Militant* is "an apocalyptic poem" and that "its tone is detached and austere because its speaker sees the past, the present, and the future with equal clarity" (p. 105). *The Church Militant,* unlike *The Church,* which portrays the struggles of man in time, is concerned "with the movement of the Church throughout all time" (p. 105).

1967

◄§ 587. BARNES, T. R. "The Seventeenth Century." In *English Verse: Voice and Movement from Wyatt to Yeats,* pp. 58–116. Cambridge: University Press.

Comments briefly on some of the major elements of Herbert's verse, especially the conceits, concentration, colloquial tone, dramatic elements, rhythms, music, rejection of the pastoral, complexity, etc. Presents a close reading of "The Windows" and "Jordan (I)."

◄§ 588. BLOCK, HASKELL M. "The Alleged Parallel of Metaphysical and Symbolist Poetry." CLS 4:145–59.

Reprinted in *Comparative Literature: Matter and Method,* edited by

Alfred Owen Aldridge (Urbana: University of Illinois Press, 1969), pp. 90–105.

Denies that there is a basic parallel between metaphysical and symbolist poetry. Tries to account for the alleged likenesses by reviewing the criticism of T. S. Eliot, Cleanth Brooks, and others. Discusses also those critics who deny the likeness and suggests properties of both kinds of poetry that prove them basically unlike. No specific reference to Herbert.

᪣§ 589. BROWN, WILLIAM J. "Herbert's 'The Collar' and Shakespeare's 1 *Henry IV.*" *AN&Q* 6:51–53.

Comments on the pun *collar-choler* in Herbert's poem. Argues that at the beginning of the poem "the *cause* of his unhappiness is felt to be the 'collar,' whereas in truth it is his 'choler'. When, in the final stanza, the anger of his rebellion is seen in perspective as a childish tantrum, the implication is that true happiness lies in submission to the will of God— in acceptance of the 'collar' " (p. 51). Comments on Shakespeare's pun on *collar-choler* in 1 *Henry IV* and notes various correspondences between Herbert's poem and the play: the pun "with the idea of religious restraint and sobriety as responsible for blasting the joys of youth is unusual and reinforced by strong verb similarities: blow, sigh, and abroad" (p. 52). Poses the question of whether or not Herbert may have had Shakespeare's play in mind while composing his poem.

᪣§ 590. CHAMPION, LARRY S. "Body Versus Soul in George Herbert's 'The Collar.' " *Style* 1:131–37.

Argues that "The Collar" is not simply a continuous statement of rebellion but is rather "a carefully articulated dialogue between the body and the soul" (p. 131). Divides the poem into four sections: (1) lines 1–16 (the body rebels); (2) lines 17–26 (the soul replies); (3) lines 27–32 (the body replies to the soul's reply); and (4) lines 33–36 (God's command for humility is set forth through the soul, and the body, "its audacity obliterated by the simple command, presents itself in childlike obedience" [p. 133]). Shows how the narrative, the metrical structure, and the imagery combine to support such a reading and argues that the ending of the poem is neither a surprise nor an abrupt conclusion.

᪣§ 591. CHARLES, AMY M. "George Herbert: Priest, Poet, Musician." *Journal of the Viola da Gamba Society of America* 4:27–36.

Discusses the subtlety, complexity, and pervasiveness of music in Herbert's poetry and comments on the central role that it played in his life: "In a very real sense, music *was* Herbert's sustenance on earth and its upward movement his most treasured avenue to God" (p. 36). Points out that, although there are numerous musical allusions in Herbert's poetry, his "open use of musical language and imagery is less than would be expected, if one looks only for the terms in a musical glossary" (p. 27). For example, Herbert mentions the viol only once (in *The Country Parson*) yet figures of tuning and strings "provide some of Herbert's most effective musical figures" (p. 28). Cautions against finding musical allusions where none were intended (such as references to "measure," "score," "springs," etc.) Points out that, although many of Herbert's poems were set to music by later musicians, few of his hymns and anthems are in general use today as hymns, primarily because of their stanzaic complexities and subtleties. Comments on Herbert's skillful uses of sound in his poetry and suggests, "It is doubtful that he would have used them so widely had his sense of the sound of words not been developed and refined by his music" (p. 35).

592. FERRY, ANNE DAVIDSON, ed. *Religious Prose of Seventeenth-Century England*. Borzoi Anthology of 17th-Century English Literature, vol. 5. New York: Alfred A. Knopf. 258p.

Contains a general critical introduction to the nature and varieties of religious prose during the period (p. 3–29). Reproduces chapter 7 of Herbert's *A Priest to the Temple* (pp. 241–43).

593. FOSTER, D. W. "George Herbert." *Theology* (London) 70: 68–76.

An appreciative essay that comments on Herbert's modern relevancy: "He gives us depth, complication, and immediacy of experience" (p. 73). Argues that Herbert's sanctity, though real, is "far removed from *sancta simplicitas*" (p. 69) and attempts to demythologize accounts of Herbert's life. Comments on the complex religious sensibility and poetic excellence of Herbert's verse and suggests that the modern reader can respond to Herbert in the same way that he can respond to "the life and work of Gandhi, Dolci, or Pope John without necessarily sharing their tenets" (p. 70). Discusses briefly the comprehensive biblical symbolism that informs Herbert's poetry and exemplifies this richness by commenting on "Affliction (I)." Contrasts Herbert and Keble.

594. FRENCH, ROBERTS W. "Herbert's 'Vertue.'" *Expl* 26:item 4.

Discusses the meaning of the word *coal* in the last stanza of "Vertue" and argues that it should be taken in the sense of "glowing coal" or "red-hot coal" rather than "cinder" or "ashes" in order to sustain the main simile of the stanza. For a reply, see Dan S. Collins, entry 639.

595. GREENWOOD, E. B. "Putting the 'Romance' Back into Stylistics: A Reply to Helen Vendler." *EIC* 17:256–57.

Reply to Helen Vendler's review of *Essays on Style and Language:*

Linguistic and Critical Approaches to Literary Styles, edited by Roger Fowler, in *EIC* 16 (1966):457–63. Defends his reading of Herbert's "Prayer (I)" (see entry 541).

◄§ 596. HERBERT, GEORGE. *A Choice of George Herbert's Verse*. Selected with an introduction by R. S. Thomas. London: Faber and Faber. 95p.

Presents a biographical sketch of Herbert and relates him to the historical period. Sees Herbert as a reflection of the best in seventeenth-century Anglican sensibility. Suggests that Herbert's relevance to the modern world "is bound up with the relevance of Christianity, and with the possibility of a fruitful relationship between Christianity and poetry" (p. 15) and that he "commands a way of life for the individual that is still viable" (p. 17). Maintains that Herbert's poetry "is proof of the eternal beauty of holiness" (p. 17). Selections from *The Temple* and from Walton's *Life*.

◄§ 597. ———. *George Herbert: Selected Poetry*, edited by Joseph H. Summers. Signet Classic Poetry Series, edited by John Hollander. New York and Toronto: American Library; London: New English Library. xxxviii, 288p.

Contents (pp. v–viii). Introduction by Joseph H. Summers (pp. ix–xxvii). A general note on the text by John Hollander (p. xxix). A note on this edition (pp. xxxi–xxxiii). Chronology (pp. xxxv–xxxvi). Selected bibliography (pp. xxxvii–xxxviii). *The Temple* (pp. 41–265). Poems from the Williams MS excluded from *The Temple* (pp. 267–75). Poems from Walton's *Lives* (pp. 277–78). Translations of Herbert's Latin poems (pp. 279–80). Doubtful poems (pp. 281–84). Index of first lines (pp. 285–88). In the introduction, Summers calls Herbert "the author of the best extended collection of religious lyrics in English, a man whose art is as unquestionable as is his spiritual authenticity" (p. ix). Comments on ways for the inexperienced reader to approach the poems of Herbert. Comments primarily on *The Church-Porch* because it is most likely to present problems to the reader. Bases his text of the poems primarily on F. E. Hutchinson's edition (entry 223). Contains explanatory notes.

◄§ 598. MILES, JOSEPHINE. *Style and Proportion: The Language of Prose and Poetry*. Boston: Little, Brown and Co. ix, 212p.

Discusses how "words and structures of language in literature differ from era to era, from place to place, from kind to kind" in order "to gain a more general view of literary styles of language" (p. v). Analyzes sixty poetical texts and sixty prose texts, including Herbert's *The Church* (through "Mattens").

�’§ 599. MOLLENKOTT, VIRGINIA R. "Christian Humanism Through the
Centuries." In *Adamant and Stone Chips: A Christian Humanist
Approach to Knowledge*, pp. 31–52. Waco, Tex.: Word Books.

Says that Herbert's "The Elixir" "admirably summarizes the Christian
humanist approach to life, to the environment and the duties of this
world" (p. 50). Points out three detriments to Christian living: activism,
secularism, and fragmentation. Suggests that Richard Sibbes perhaps alludes to Herbert's central metaphor in his *A Learned Commentary*
(1656).

�’§ 600. NOMACHI, SUSUMU. "George Herbert: Man's Innate Trust in
the Eternal." *The Annual Collection of Critical Studies* (Gasku-
shuin University, Tokyo) 14:1–51.

Comments on Donne's influence on Herbert and contrasts their spiritual sensibilities and inner conflicts: "While Donne's was a furious battle in which external elements participated, Herbert's was a conflict of
introspection; his was the sort of question to be dealt with in his own
breast, hidden from vulgar eyes" (p. 3). Discusses Herbert's interest in
concrete things, his refinement of taste, and his love of neatness and sees
these qualities as reflecting a feminine element in Herbert's nature.
Points out a number of manifestations of Herbert's feminine character
in the language of his poems and in his verse forms and rhyme schemes.
Comments on Herbert's dualism both in his response to the world outside himself and to the various competing antitheses in his own mind.
Contrasts Herbert's view of beauty and order with the views of Donne
and Vaughan and suggests that Herbert's sense of orderliness and his
attention to minute detail, seen as feminine qualities, may have been
influenced by his mother. Analyzes in detail "Prayer (I)" as an example
of Herbert's feminine mind and method and comments on *The Church-
Porch* and "Discipline" as examples of Herbert's intuitive manner. Concludes by discussing the development of Herbert's thought, especially
his idea of God and death, and maintains, "The minute care, feminine
in its essential character, for the matters of daily life, never for a moment
deserted Herbert's mind" (p. 51).

�’§ 601. PETERSON, DOUGLAS L. *The English Lyric from Wyatt to
Donne: A History of the Plain and Eloquent Styles*. Princeton:
Princeton University Press. vi, 391p.

Traces the development of the lyric during the sixteenth century,
stressing the medieval origins of the plain and eloquent styles and accounting for the changes and relative importance of both. Sees Herbert as a master of the plain style and suggests that he—along with
Vaughan, Traherne, Crashaw, and other devotional poets of the seventeenth century—continues "a tradition of anticourtly and otherworldly
verse originating in the simple didactic poetry of the Middle Ages and

becoming in the seventeenth century the dominant and most vigorous mode of English lyric" (pp. 356–57). Points out that Herbert, like Donne, was strongly opposed to "studied eloquence as well as courtly love poetry" and that he "avoids those schemes which in the sonnets contribute to the mellifluousness of the sugared style" (p. 240). Several references to Herbert and to individual poems of Herbert throughout.

⋖§ 602. POGGI, VALENTINA. *George Herbert*. Testi e saggi di letterature moderne, 10. Bologna: Casa Editrice Prof. Riccardo Pàtron. 263p.

Divided into three major chapters: (1) "Il poeta di Dio" (pp. 13–130); (2) "Finito e infinito in *The Temple*" (pp. 131–201), and (3) "Il 'Final Twist' " (pp. 203–52). Chapter 1 is subdivided into three sections. (1) "Il sacro ministero della poesia" presents a brief biographical sketch of Herbert, discusses the major themes of his poetry, and comments on the relationship between poetic language and the expression of religious sentiments in his poems. (2) "Il volto di Dio" surveys Herbert's presentation of God in the poems and suggests that he views God primarily as a friend rather than as a lover or a father. (3) "La condizione umana" comments on man's relationship to God in Herbert's poetry and suggests that the image of dust is a major key to understanding *The Temple*. Presents a detailed reading of "Easter-wings." Chapter 2 is subdivided into two sections. (1) "Il senso dello spazio e l'angoscia del vuoto" considers the theme of temptation in *The Temple* and concludes that Herbert views temptation as a condition of man's free will. Points out that Herbert associates open spaces and freedom of movement with danger and temptation. (2) "La mesura del posto e la casa interiore" suggests that Herbert associates joy and peace with confined spaces. Chapter 3 describes this poetic closure in Herbert's poems, especially his use of surprise endings and reversals. Presents a close reading of "Affliction (I)," "Redemption," "Prayer (I)," "Frailtie," "Constancie," "The Collar," "The Pulley," "The Flower," and "Sinne (I)." Selected bibliography (pp. 253–57).

⋖§ 603. REILLY, R. J. "God, Man, and Literature." *Thought* 42:561–83.

Suggests, "Since the writer's felt apprehension of his relationship to God shapes his literary imagination, it might well be used as a principle of classification of literature" (p. 561). Outlines five basic categories: (1) "the 'rapt' writers, those who have a sense, or awareness, of their intimate union with God" (p. 568); (2) "the 'excited' writers, those who also apprehend that the relationship between God and man is an intimate one, but whose apprehension is more intellectual than that of the writers in Group I" (p. 568); (3) "the 'normal' writers or 'humanistic' writers, those who accept the close relationship posited for them by their religions or philosophies but for whom the relationship is not existentially central"

(p. 568); (4) "the writers in whose work there is less than normal recognition of the relationship, whether or not their religion or philosophy posits such a relationship" (p. 568); and (5) "the 'fervid deniers' of the relationship" (p. 568). Places Herbert in the second category.

◄§ 604. ROSCELLI, WILLIAM JOHN. "The Metaphysical Milton (1625–1631)." *TSLL* 8:463–84.

Comments on the possible influence of the metaphysical poets on Milton and concludes, "(1) in at least six English poems which he composed between 1625 and 1631 and which have survived, Milton does employ images which can properly be considered metaphysical; (2) the use of metaphysical images, in general, is restricted to poems whose ostensible subject is death; (3) some of these metaphysical images find parallels in the poems of George Herbert, but the echoes are not so strong as to suggest direct influence; (4) the internal evidence provided by the English poems substantially confirms Raleigh's judgment that Milton was 'untouched' by Donne" (p. 484). Suggests that the differences between Milton and Herbert are not so great as those between Milton and Donne. Sees specific resemblances between stanza 5 of "On the Death of a fair Infant" and Herbert's "Death," between the proem of "On the Morning of Christ's Nativity" and Herbert's "Christmas," and between lines 79–82 of "On the Morning of Christ's Nativity" and Herbert's "Whitsunday," lines 13–16.

◄§ 605. RUTHVEN, GREY. *For George Herbert.* Cambridge, Mass.: Pym-Randall Press.

An original five-stanza poem on Herbert.

◄§ 606. STARKMAN, MIRIAM K., ed. *Seventeenth-Century English Poetry*, vol. 1. Borzoi Anthology of 17th-Century English Literature, vol. 1. New York: Alfred A. Knopf. xiii, 294, viiip.

Contains a general critical introduction to metaphysical poetry (pp. 3–24). Calls Herbert "the source and well-spring of devotional poetry for the seventeenth century" (p. 8). Outlines the major themes of *The Temple* and comments on the various influences that shaped Herbert's art—the liturgy, iconography, emblem books, music, etc. Contrasts Herbert briefly with Donne and Vaughan. Presents a brief biographical sketch of Herbert (p. 111) and reproduces fifty-five poems from *The Temple* (pp. 112–60), with brief explanatory notes. Selective bibliography (p. 292).

◄§ 607. TAYLER, EDWARD W., ed. *Literary Criticism of Seventeenth-Century England.* Borzoi Anthology of 17th-Century English Literature, vol. 4. New York: Alfred A. Knopf. xii, 427, vp.

Contains a general critical introduction to the literary criticism of the seventeenth century (pp. 3–32). Presents a brief introduction to Herbert (pp. 259–60) and reproduces "My God, where is that ancient heat towards thee," "Love (II)," "Jordan (I) and (II)," and "A Wreath" (pp. 260–62), all poems that deal with the important question of the relationship of poetry and religion.

≈§ 608. WEISS, WOLFGANG. "Note on Herbert's 'The Collar.'" *N&Q,* n.s. 14:93.
Suggests that both the image of the collar in the title and the images *rope of sands* and *good cable* in the poem "express the idea of thraldom in the relationship of god and man" and are derived from the old etymology of the word *religio* (*ligare,* to bind).

≈§ 609. WHITLOCK, BAIRD W. "From the Counter-Renaissance to the Baroque." *BuR* 15:46–60.
Discusses certain differences between sixteenth-century and seventeenth-century art forms, between the Counter-Renaissance (ca. 1520–1620) and the baroque (ca. 1620–1720). Suggests that Donne and Herbert "represent the shift that took place between the two periods" (p. 48). Points out, for example, that "both created a new poetic form in nearly every poem they wrote, but Donne's metrical and rhyme innovations very seldom add to the unification or meaning of the whole poem, whereas Herbert's variations almost without exception do" (p. 48). Considers Herbert as a baroque poet and sees *The Temple* as offering "good evidence of the manner in which the Baroque poet sought to organize his previously separate works into a more unified sequence than the mere chronological or even haphazard collections of the previous century" (p. 57). Mentions briefly the formal methods of unification found in "Man," "The Collar," "Church-floore," and *The Church-Porch.*

≈§ 610. WILLIAMSON, GEORGE. *Six Metaphysical Poets: A Reader's Guide.* New York: Farrar, Straus and Giroux. 274p.
Presents a general introduction to Herbert's poetry and gives a brief biographical sketch (pp. 94–118). Contains prose summaries of the arguments of sixteen major poems. Comments primarily on Herbert's wit and ingenuity and suggests, "He seems to have found his mode of wit or rhetoric in the Bible, or its familiar illustration" (p. 102). Suggests that Christ's parables "also supply the key to Herbert's poetry in method, imagery, and diction" (p. 102). Maintains that Herbert "is more like Donne than appears on the surface" (p. 118). Brief bibliography (pp. 263–65).

≈§ 611. WINTERS, YVOR. "Aspects of the Short Poem in the English Renaissance." In *Forms of Discovery,* pp. 1–120. Chicago: Alan Swallow.

Critical discussion of "Church-monuments" (pp. 83–88). Calls the poem "the last word in the sophistication of the plain style" and one of "the most impressive short poems in the English Renaissance" (p. 84). Praises its "quiet profundity" and its "impeccable organization" (p. 87). Comments in some detail on the various relationships between the syntax of the poem and its lines and between the syntax and the stanzaic form and considers such matters as enjambment, punctuation, sentence lengths, rhythm, diction, metaphor, and tone. Points out that the poem has no exclusively Christian references: "The poem deals with the vanity of life and the necessity of preparing for death" (p. 86). Suggests that in many respects the poem is uncharacteristic of Herbert's poetry, much of which is marred by "cloying and almost infantile pietism" that "leads him into abject clichés" (p. 88).

◄§ 612. ZIEGELMAIER, GREGORY. "Liturgical Symbol and Reality in the Poetry of George Herbert." ABR 18:344–53.
Points out pervasive liturgical elements in Herbert's poetry, many of which are hidden from the modern reader unfamiliar with both the liturgy itself and the habit of mind it produces and reflects. Suggests that Herbert turns to the liturgy "sometimes for its power to concentrate dogma, but more often for its emotional effects" (p. 345). Maintains that Herbert's "originality is more devotional than strictly liturgical" (p. 349). Concludes that Herbert "intuitively finds the objects proper to his sense and turns them into praise: the rhythms and colors of the emblems, sculpture, vestments, the music of song and organ, of smell, of the upward wreathing of incense; the use of body in gestures and movements in the handling of material things used in worship; the use of the lips in the mystery of words. His words have their spirit, their evocative power; gestures their vitality, meaning. And for those students for whom sacrifice and altar are realities, the liturgical element in George Herbert preserves its reality too" (p. 353).

1968

◄§ 613. BUCHLOH, PAUL GERHARD. "George Herbert: The Pulley." In *Die englische Lyrik: Von der Renaissance bis zur Gegenwart*, edited by Karl Heinz Göller, 1:159–65. Düsseldorf: August Bagel.
Detailed explication of "The Pulley." Points out that the basic conceit of the poem is built upon an altered version of the Greek myth of the box of Pandora. Stresses that God is presented in the poem in very human terms. German prose translation of the poem.

◄§ 614. BUCKLEY, VINCENT. *Poetry and the Sacred*. New York: Barnes and Noble. 244p.
Discusses "the variety of modes and directions which the religious im-

pulse in literature may take" (p. 3). Calls Herbert and Hopkins "the two most centrally religious poets in the language" (p. 1). Comments briefly on the dramatic elements of Herbert's poetry and calls it "the drama of contrived imaginative situations" (p. 31); in other words, Herbert's drama is basically rhetorical. "I do not suggest that Herbert did not feel the dramas he proposes in his poetry; but I do think that the dramatic forms in which he proposes them are at a large remove from his initial feeling of them" (p. 31). Laments the fact that Herbert's dramatic poems have become widely regarded as a prototype for Christian poetry. Contrasts Herbert with a number of religious poets, especially Greville, Donne, Henry King, Wordsworth, Hopkins, Dylan Thomas, and Theodore Roethke.

◄§ 615. CALDWELL, HARRY B.; SAMAHA, EDWARD E., JR.; and FRICKE, DONNA G., comps. "George Herbert: A Recent Bibliography, 1960–1967." *SCN* 26:54–56.

Lists 138 items on Herbert published between 1960 and 1967. No annotations. Divided into five sections: (1) editions and anthologies, (2) milieu and general studies, (3) theme and structure, (4) analyses of individual poems, and (5) miscellaneous. See also Humphrey Tonkin, "A Bibliography of George Herbert 1960–1967: Addenda," entry 660.

◄§ 616. CARNES, VALERIE. "The Unity of George Herbert's *The Temple*: A Reconsideration." *ELH* 35:505–26.

Suggests that the tripartite division of *The Temple* derives its thematic unity from an extended metaphor or analogy between religion and art, between man's religious activities and his aesthetic activities. In *The Church-Porch* the persona is seen as the preacher expressing the revealed Word of God, in *The Church* the persona is viewed as the poet who expresses through his art the Word, and in *The Church Militant* the speaker is seen as the redeemed soul that unites the secular word and the sacred Word. Stylistically there is a parallel movement from didactic image, to symbol, to myth. Man's recreation of this cycle in his attempts to communicate with God prefigures man's ultimate reconciliation of his soul to God.

◄§ 617. DAVIES, H. NEVILLE. "Sweet Music in Herbert's 'Easter.'" *N&Q*, n.s. 15:95–96.

Comments on the appropriateness of lines 11–12 of "Easter" ("His stretched sinews taught all strings, what key/ Is best to celebrate this most high day") and points out the commonly accepted notion in the seventeenth century that a high musical key was associated with sweetness and love. Argues that the music that "may be played on a fully stretched string was known primarily not for its suitability for devotional use *per se*, but for its *sweetness*" (p. 95). Finds an analogue in Lyly's

Euphues. Notes also the familiar reference to Christ as *Jesu dulcissime* and points out that "the sweet music produced by Christ when stretched on the Cross is a particular idea which would have been well known to Herbert and his contemporaries" (p. 95). Concludes that Herbert's "sweet music is, therefore, the fittest with which to celebrate the triumph of love over sin and death, for through its sweetness the hearer could ecstatically experience the love of God" (p. 96).

◄§ 618. Gorlier, Claudio. "La Poesia di George Herbert." In *La Poesia metafisica inglese*, pp. 81–105. Biblioteca di studi inglesi e americani, 1. Milan: La Goliardica.

Biographical sketch of Herbert and a critical evaluation of the poetry, stressing in particular its dramatic elements. Comments on the major themes of Herbert's poetry and sees the major tension in the poems as being between God and man. Reproduces Giorgio Melchiori's prose translations of "The Altar," "Jordan(II)," "Discipline," "Love (III)," "Death," "Artillerie," "The Pearl," and "Redemption" and presents brief explications and comments on each.

◄§ 619. Hanley, Sara William, C.S.J. "Temples in *The Temple*: George Herbert's Study of the Church." *SEL* 8:121–35.

Argues that the title, *The Temple*, is a major metaphor that gives unity to the whole volume as well as to certain clusters of individual poems within the work: "*The Temple* is, literally, a book about temples, and the plot of the book concerns man's gradual efforts to 'enter' the temple of his own soul, the temple of his Christian Church, and the eternal temple of the people of God, finding at the center of each temple the God who created it and inhabits it" (p. 122). Comments in detail on a group of tightly knit poems beginning with "Mattens" and ending with "Trinitie Sunday" and suggests that this cluster of poems presents a discussion "of the nature of the Church, the source of grace" (p. 123). Sees "Mattens," "Sinne," and "Even-song" as studies and examples of the Church's prayer; the five so-called furniture poems that follow "focus attention on the symbol of the Church as heart, as building, as body of the faithful, and as the New Jerusalem" (p. 121); and the final poem in the sequence, "Trinitie Sunday," celebrates this major feast of the Church "with a litany-like prayer" (p. 121). Thus, the "furniture poems" are not inferior, as has been suggested, but rather form an essential part of *The Temple*.

◄§ 620. Harbinson, M. J. "A Crux in Herbert's 'The Sacrifice.'" *N&Q*, n.s. 15:96–98.

Interprets lines 121–24 of "The Sacrifice" ("Why, Caesar is their onely King, not I:/ He clave the stonie rock, when they were drie;/ But surely not their hearts, as I well trie:/ Was ever grief, &c.). Suggests that certain passages in Josephus's *Antiquities of the Jews* provide a key to this puzzling stanza. Notes that in a passage preceding the only reference to Christ in Josephus, the historian describes the force that Pilate (acting as Caesar's delegate) used to put down a riot begun by the Jews when he attempted to build conduits to bring water into Jerusalem. Argues, "An illuminating parallel then appears between Pilate as Caesar's procurator dealing with the mob rioting over taxes spent on the aqueduct, and Pilate as Caesar's procurator dealing with the mob calling for Christ's death" (p. 98). Also notes that Pilate's method of dealing with the mob in both cases "has obvious relevance to the nature of imperial power. Peace must be bought at the lowest price—contrast the price Christ is willing to pay" (p. 98). Suggests that Herbert was most likely familiar with these passages from Josephus.

•◄§ 621. HERBERT, GEORGE. *The Temple* (1633). Scolar Press Facsimile. Menston, Eng. Scolar Press. 11, 195p.
Facsimile of the 1633 edition (original size) of *The Temple* (British Museum: Shelf-mark C 58.a.26). Brief bibliographical introduction. *Short-Title Catalogue* 13183.

◄§ 622. HONIG, EDWIN, and WILLIAMS, OSCAR, eds. *The Major Metaphysical Poets of the Seventeenth Century: John Donne, George Herbert, Richard Crashaw, and Andrew Marvell.* New York: Washington Square Press. 902p.
This anthology contains a detailed critical introduction to metaphysical poetry (pp. 1–33) by Edwin Honig. The Herbert section (pp. 321–501) contains a brief biographical sketch, *The Temple*, English poems not included in *The Temple*, and poems from Walton's *Lives*. Selective bibliography prepared by Milton Miller and Beverly Goldberg (pp. 867–77).

◄§ 623. HOWARD, THOMAS T. "Herbert and Crashaw: Notes on Meditative Focus." *GorR* 11:79–98.
Maintains that, although both Herbert and Crashaw were products of a similar religious tradition and shared a devotion to the liturgy, the sacraments, and spiritual meditation, there is a fundamental difference between the two poets, primarily one of focus: "Whereas Herbert's vision of religion and the world was a truly sacramental one, albeit tempered with an Anglican reticence about becoming too baroque, Crashaw felt at home in the excruciating physical forms of Counter-Reformation meditation, an idea which is borne out in his shift to Rome as well as his poetic focus" (p. 84). Suggests that Herbert's "devotional and meditative posture takes the form of scrutiny, analysis, self-calumny, dialogue with God, reflection on the implications of grace, and so forth, with the full consciousness of liturgical and traditional forms and the significance of

ecclesiastical ornament, the figural, and sacramental understanding of the creation as 'God-bearing images' "; whereas Crashaw "is disposed to adoration, and baroque elaboration of objects of veneration as though by the artistic expansion of the object the soul will be that much the more impressed and aware of its overwhelming debt of gratitude" (p. 84). Comments on a number of Herbert's poems in order to illustrate the particular nature of his religious convictions and sensibilities and then contrasts these with Crashaw's.

◄§ 624. LEVITT, PAUL M., and JOHNSTON, KENNETH G. "Herbert's 'The Collar' and the Story of Job." *PLL* 4:329–30.
Points out a number of striking similarities in both the dramatic situation and the imagery of "The Collar" and the Book of Job. For example, both the speaker of the poem and Job are rebels "against the austerities inherent in a life of denial and obedience" (p. 329); both weep and sigh in their trials, neither fully rejects God though both question God's providence, and "the faith of both men is confirmed when they hear the voice of God" (p. 330). Even the reversal of Herbert's last line recalls Job's exclamation, "Thou shalt call, and I will answer thee." Points out also several possible parallel images.

◄§ 625. METTEDEN, A. K. "On Reading Old Poets." *Nigeria Magazine* (Lagos) 98:251–57.
Presents a selection of "old masters" for the pleasure of his reading audience, including "The Pulley" and lines from "Man." Presents a brief biographical note on Herbert, whom he calls "one of the first and greatest Metaphysical poets" (p. 257).

◄§ 626. MURRIN, MICHAEL. "Poetry as Literary Criticism." *MP* 65: 202–7.
Comments on "Jordan (II)" as literary criticism and suggests that the poem is written "in a metaphysical style and that it represents a negative judgment on that style, presented as if it were on stage in a dramatic action, where a problem is set up and answered in eighteen lines" (p. 202). Also comments on "Jordan (I)," an allegorical poem that attacks allegory. Concludes that Herbert "deliberately wrote an allegorical poem when he was attacking allegory, just as he wrote metaphysically when attacking metaphysical poetry" (p. 203). Warns that the modern critic, therefore, "must consider the whole poem, both form and content, as a complex critical statement" (p. 206); otherwise, he misrepresents the poet's position.

◄§ 627. RYAN, THOMAS A. "The Poetry of John Danforth." *PAAS* 78: 129–93.
Briefly points out that John Danforth (1660–1730), a minor Puritan

poet, alludes to Herbert's "Anagram of the Virgin Marie" in his elegy on Mrs. Mary Gerrish. Suggests that such an allusion shows that the Puritans "had no qualms about reading or even quoting such Anglican poets of the time as Herbert or Quarles" (p. 133).

⋙ 628. SMITH, BARBARA HERRNSTEIN. *Poetic Closure: A Study of How Poems End*. Chicago and London: University of Chicago Press. xvi, 289p.

Discusses the relationship of thematic structure to poetic closure in "Vertue" (pp. 67–70): "What gives this poem so much of its power is the fact that so many elements in its formal and thematic structure conspire to bring about closure at the conclusion of the *third* stanza. The fourth stanza, however, is hardly anticlimatic: on the contrary, it has the effect, entirely appropriate to its theme, of a revelation—that which is known beyond what can be demonstrated logically" (p. 69). Discusses briefly three major principles of thematic structure in "Mortification": "Two of them are sequential, one being a series, the other a logical development. The third principle, a recurrent conceit, is in effect paratactic" (p. 113). Shows how the conclusion of the poem "derives its expressive power and stability from the complex relation of these three principles and from other nonstructural elements as well" (p. 113). Comments also on the sequential structure and the allegorical elements of "Redemption" and calls its conclusion "extraordinarily moving": "As the reader is drawn into the allegorical world of tenants and property transactions, he follows the events as in a fictional narration—even though their religious significance is always apparent. The conclusion is experienced with a double shock of surprise and recognition" (pp. 125–26).

⋙ 629. STEIN, ARNOLD. *George Herbert's Lyrics*. Baltimore: Johns Hopkins Press. xliv, 221p.

Condensed version of chapter 1 published in *The Poetic Tradition: Essays on Greek, Latin, and English Poetry*, edited by Don Cameron Allen and Henry T. Rowell (entry 630), pp. 99–122.

A shorter version of chapter 1 reprinted in *Seventeenth Century English Poetry: Modern Essays in Criticism*, edited by William Keast (rev. ed., entry 707), pp. 257–78.

Chapter 2 published as "George Herbert's Prosody," entry 631.

The purpose of this study is to demonstrate "why Herbert is one of the great masters of lyric poetry" (p. vii) and to show that his lyrics "are the expression of a complex and subtle mind, uniquely aware of itself and its fertile deceptions yet trusting the depths of feeling, and trusting his own power to invent and order imaginative explorations of personal experience" (p. viii). Divided into five sections: (1) an introduction (pp. xiii–xliv) that outlines briefly the history of the plain style from its classical origins through the early Christian era to the seventeenth century and that locates the metaphysicals in this tradition. Argues that the plain style, although based on the natural rhythms of speech, has always depended on careful artistry and discipline and is not necessarily free from obscurity. Chapter 1, "The Art of Plainness" (pp. 1–44), discusses Herbert's attitude toward poetry and argues that his art of plainness "is an art, not a summary feature" (p. 44). Shows that one of Herbert's major themes is poetry itself. Analyzes the tension between Herbert's desire for simplicity and sincerity and his need to use rhetoric, metaphor, and language in order to create poems. Demonstrates that his art of plainness "does not bear a single stamp, and his arguments with God are conducted with great freedom and inventiveness" (p. 26). Suggests that the major devices of Herbert's plainness are "not traditional figures but psychological gestures and movements" (p. 27). Illustrates the range of Herbert's art of plainness by closely examining "The Temper (I)," "The Pearl," and "Death," and argues that the power of the plain style "lies in the passion excluded, in the resistance mastered, and in the deliberate grace of saying difficult things with ease" (p. 43). Chapter 2, "The Movement of Words" (pp. 45–84), discusses "the basis of Herbert's metrical rhetoric, the expressive movement of words by which he brings into focus and controls the particular discriminations of his meanings" (p. 45). Primarily comments on stress, juncture, and phrasing and shows that Herbert's metrical style "is characterized by the frequency of its colloquial phrasing and by the inventive ease with which he adjusts colloquial and metric phrasing to each other" (p. 53). Shows how stress, juncture, and phrasing "work together to create an order of separate and overlapping forms" and how "the balance between apparently independent, informal elements and apparently controlled formal elements is capable of endless variation" (p. 58). Discusses and illustrates certain primary patterns: advancing intensity of stress, loosening and contracting of rhythmical movements, and augmenting or diminishing of established patterns. Suggests that Herbert's "techniques for ordering the movement of language are significant in themselves" and that "they resemble metaphor in both establishing and discovering meanings" (p. 84). Chapter 3, "Complaint, Praise, and Love" (pp. 85–135), discusses complaint, praise, and love "in part as the subjects of [Herbert's] poetry, in part as thematic ideas which move and develop in their own characteristic ways but which are significantly related to each other" (p. 85). Points out that one of the primary causes for complaint in Herbert's poetry is the grief that man feels when he confronts his failure to love God fully. Argues that Herbert's "lyric gifts are not fully engaged by lament pure and simple" (p. 96), since "the expression of pain and longing is always qualified by something else—by his disciplined detachment, by his imaginative ability to perceive and relate what he finds real within and without himself" (p. 97). Shows that in Herbert's poetry "every complaint is also, more or less, a declaration of praise and love" (p. 97). Examines various difficulties that the religious poet encounters in his attempt to praise God and especially comments on Herbert's "master metaphor of praise, music, an art that for him not only expresses but represents both meaning and feeling" (p. 110). Suggests that Herbert approaches his central theme of love in three ways: (1) a movement away from love, an effort to escape; (2) a movement toward love, aiming to force love; and (3) contemplation of love. Chapter 4, "Questions of Style and Form" (pp. 137–210), points out that Herbert does not often repeat the situations and plots of his most significant poems and suggests that he consistently keeps a delicate balance between "the elements of individuality and freedom" and "the commitment to significant form and specific beliefs" (p. 139). Compares the earlier and revised versions of "The Elixir" and "Easter" so that "we can gain some insight into what did and did not satisfy Herbert in terms of a whole poem" (p. 139). Analyzes a number of individual poems in terms of closed form (poems that turn back and close in on themselves, such as "A Wreath," "Sinnes round," "H. Baptisme (II)," and "Aaron") and in terms of open form (poems that have an expanding movement outward, such as "Easter-wings," "Trinitie Sunday," and "The Odour"). Offers detailed explications of "Mortification," "Life," "Vertue," "Love (III)," and "The Flower." Concludes by commenting briefly on Herbert's attitude toward the imagination and by suggesting that Herbert "is a splendid master of that basic illusion upon which his poetry depends, that the language and forms of art are only another, if better, way to talk naturally" (p. 208).

◄§ 630. ———. "George Herbert: The Art of Plainness." In *The Poetic Tradition: Essays on Greek, Latin, and English Poetry*, edited by Don Cameron Allen and Henry T. Rowell, pp. 99–122. Percy Graeme Turnbull Memorial Lectures on Poetry. Baltimore: Johns Hopkins Press.

Reprinted (in part and expanded) in *George Herbert's Lyrics* (entry 629), pp. 1–44.

Comments on the great complexity of Herbert's plain style and his mastery of the rhetoric of sincerity (the "art by which he may tell the truth to himself and God" [p. 107]). Argues that Herbert "does not give us a single, consistent attitude toward expression, that his art of plainness does not bear a single stamp, and that his arguments with God are conducted with great freedom and inventiveness" (p. 106); thus, when "we take a single example as our model to copy, we become aware of statements on the other side and of stylistic demonstrations that force us to widen our definitions" (pp. 106–7). Points out that Herbert achieves his rhetoric of sincerity not primarily by traditional figures but by "psychological gestures and movements" (p. 107). Illustrates Herbert's art of plainness by commenting in detail on three poems: "The Temper

(I)," "The Pearl," and "Death." Argues that the power of the plain style "lies in the passion excluded, in the resistance mastered, and in the deliberate grace of saying difficult things with ease" (p. 121). Evaluates Coleridge's comments on Herbert and suggests that two important points emerge: "First, it is clear that Herbert is a master who draws a leading thought through authentic obstacles which both test and refine the ultimate expression of that thought. Secondly, the rhetorical proof of character lies in the poet's convincing demonstration that *he* becomes what he says, that the flow and shape of his words lead to a unity of eloquence and wisdom, and that he is at the expressive center of what he concludes" (p. 122).

ఆౕ 631. ———. "George Herbert's Prosody." *Lang&S* 1:1–38.

Reprinted in revised form in *George Herbert's Lyrics* (entry 629), pp. 45–84; and in *Perspectives in Poetry*, edited by James L. Calderwood and Harold E. Toliver (New York: Oxford University Press, 1968), pp. 169–77.

Studies "the basis of Herbert's metrical rhetoric, the expressive movement of words by which he brings into focus and controls the particular discriminations of his meanings" (p. 1). Argues that Herbert's techniques "for ordering the movement of language are significant in themselves" (p. 38). Shows how Herbert sets up a tension between colloquial and metrical phrasing and how each phrase is fully sensitive to those that follow or precede it: "Stress, juncture, and phrasing work together, then, and create an order of separate and overlapping forms which may express the fullest possible variety or may give concentrated prominence to a limited range of effects" (p. 9). Comments on the loosening and contracting of rhythmical movement in Herbert's poetry, pointing out "the ways in which the rhythmic flow of emphasis resembles the power of metaphor to control and establish meaning while discovering new and unexpected meanings" (p. 34). Scans numerous lines from individual poems to illustrate his points and presents an extended discussion of "Employment (I)" and "The Crosse."

ఆౕ 632. UNRAU, JOHN. "Three Notes on George Herbert." *N&Q*, n.s. 15: 94–95.

(1) Comments on the use of *thankfull glasse* in "The H. Scriptures (I)," lines 8–9. Suggests that Herbert is referring to a mirror, perhaps a wish-fulfilling mirror as described by Girolamo Cardano (Cardanus) in *De Rerum Varietate Libri XVII* (1557). If this is Herbert's intent, then *thankfull* should be interpreted as *pleasing* or *agreeable*. (2) Suggests that Herbert's allusion to *ebony box* in "Even-song," lines 21–23, may refer to the well-known medicinal properties of ebony and that the lines may thus be interpreted to read: "Just as poisonous liquids are rendered harmless by enclosure in a box of ebony, so the frustrations and tensions

of the day, described by Herbert in the preceding stanza, are neutralized by night and sleep" (p. 94). Finds a similar use of ebony in Arthur Golding's translation of *The excellent and pleasant worke of Iulius Solinus* (1587). (3) Comments on lines 37–45 of "Love unknown." Points out that Pliny, Solinus, and several Elizabethan and seventeenth-century writers comment on the idea that only blood is "capable of softening the otherwise indestructible diamond" (p. 94). Notes the use of the idea in Thomas Johnson's *Cornucopiae, or diuers secrets* (1595) and in Donald Lupton's *Emblems of rarieties* (1636).

◄§ 633. WALCUTT, CHARLES CHILD, and WHITESELL, J. EDWIN, eds. "Herbert." In *The Explicator Cyclopedia*, 2:147–57. Chicago: Quadrangle Books.

Reprints the following *Explicator* articles on poems by Herbert: (1) "Businesse" (Robert G. Collmer, entry 399); (2) "The Collar" (Dan S. Norton, entries 250, 259; T. O. Mabbott, entry 248; Jack M. Bickham, entry 317); (3) "Dooms-day" (Conrad Hilberry, entry 414); (4) "Jordan" (Sheldon P. Zitner, entry 314; Frances Eldredge, entry 335; Macdonald Emslie, entry 363); (5) "The Pearl" (Stephen Manning, entry 394); (6) "The Pulley" (D. S. Mead, entry 256); (7) "Redemption" (Bernard Knieger, entry 351); (8) "Trinitie Sunday" (Joseph H. Summers, entry 342); (9) "Vertue" (Herbert Marshall McLuhan, entry 234; Edwin B. Benjamin, entry 301).

◄§ 634. WHITLOCK, BAIRD W. "The Baroque Characteristics of the Poetry of George Herbert." *Cithara* 7:30–40.

Argues that Herbert, not Crashaw, is "the most typical English baroque poet" (p. 30) and maintains, "To study the characteristics of the Baroque without seeing George Herbert as a central figure in the movement is to miss most that is central to the concept" (p. 39). Cites some twelve generally accepted major characteristics of baroque art and illustrates each with specific examples drawn from Herbert's poems. Comments on such baroque elements as the insistence on achieving unity "*by* form rather than *in* form" (p. 30), the sacramental sense of art being an "outward sign of an inward grace," the rejection of classical forms, the movement from closed to open form and from clarity to obscurity or relative clarity, the indirect method of progression or "serpentine approach to beauty" (p. 37), the preference for small size, the quest for illusion, and the belief in the unity of all the arts.

1969

◄§ 635. ANON. "Weekend Competition #2053." *New Statesman* n.s. 78:95.

Reports that a pub is to be opened at Bemerton to encourage church-going. Invites competitors "to compose verses by Herbert on this new development, or by other literary figures on places associated with them which may be similarly refurbished: e.g. Tennyson on the conversion of Farringford into a hotel, Wordsworth on the Labour Exchange that now occupies the Cockermouth birthplace, etc." Reproduces four poems submitted to the competition.

⊷§ 636. ASALS, HEATHER. "George Herbert and Hugh of St. Victor's 'Soliloquium de Arrha Animae.'" N&Q, n.s. 16:368–70.
Suggests that Herbert is drawing on a well-established tradition when he employs money imagery in *The Temple* and specifically points out that "the function of the governing money image in Herbert's 'Dialogue' quite exactly parallels the function of the money image in Hugh's *Soliloquium*" (p. 369). Also suggests that Herbert may have found in the *Soliloquium* a model for the numerous internal dialogues in *The Temple*.

⊷§ 637. ———. "The Voice of George Herbert's 'The Church.'" ELH 36:511–28.
Shows that the psalms and the pre-1633 Christian commentaries on the psalms (especially those of St. Augustine) exercised a much more profound influence on *The Church* than has been usually recognized. Points out many verbal echoes from the psalms but argues that this kind of influence is minimal in comparison to more significant considerations. Argues that the voice in the psalms was often identified by the Christian commentators as that of Christ's Body or of the Church and that this identification enables Herbert to create a plural identity for the speaker of *The Church*: "By echoing the voice of the Psalmist, Herbert expands the dimensions of the 'I' of his poetry" (p. 513). Thus the multiple speakers in the poems (Christ, David, the Christian, everyman, etc.) are really all various voices of one voice, the Church, and likewise all the various voices "are the voice of one man—all the 'I's are one 'I'" (p. 516). Shows how this concept explains the many shifts in point of view found between the poems and even within the same poem. Comments also on how the concepts of affliction and suffering in *The Church* are shaped by the views expressed by the Christian commentators on the psalms: "As the voice of the Church is one with the voice of Christ, so also are the complaints of the Church one with the complaints of Christ" (p. 519). Explains how "the development of 'The Church' dramatizes the gradual acknowledgment by the speakers in 'The Church' of the fact that the real speaker in all the poems is the voice of 'The Church'" (p. 519). Also compares Herbert's uses of verb tense with Hebrew usage, pointing out that, in Hebrew, tense is not related to time but to the kind of action described, completed or not completed. Thus, for example, the use of the past tense in "Love (III)" "is meant to be seen as a figure of speech declaring the fact that the reconciliation of 'The Church' with God in

God's time is as sure as done" (p. 525), and likewise Herbert's various pleas in the poems that God remember him "are not ultimately requests but figures expressing the condition of 'The Church' in this world" (p. 527).

⊷§ 638. BAGG, ROBERT. "The Electromagnet and the Shred of Platinum." *Arion* 8:407–29.

Argues that Reuben Arthur Brower's *The Fields of Light: An Experiment in Creative Reading* (entry 319) exemplifies the serious limitations of Eliot's impersonal theory and insists that "personality is the organizing vitality of art" and that Eliot's theory "is a menace whenever it stops us from realizing that the greatness of a poem like 'Love' is in its power to convince us, by its inexhaustible nuance of experience beyond the power of the artist to will, that its voice is not an ad hoc construction, but a mode of being" (p. 429). Presents a brief Freudian reading of "Love (III)," maintaining that the primary appeal of the poem "is the almost geisha-like care and thoughtfulness of Love; shyness and unworthiness before Christ is felt as unworthiness in an encounter full of sexual ambience" (p. 428). Christ is seen metaphorically as a woman appearing in a dream to soothe the sexual anxiety of the poet, all of which is a metaphor for Christ's power.

⊷§ 639. COLLINS, DAN S. "Herbert's 'Vertue.'" *Expl* 27:item 50.

Reply to Roberts W. French, entry 594. Suggests that in stanza 4 of "Vertue" Herbert has in mind "live coal," which permits him "to distinguish the dead cinder into which the world of flesh turns at death from the live coal which yet glows in the center ('chiefly') of the mass." Suggests also that the best gloss of the image is stanza 2 of "Employment (II)."

⊷§ 640. CRUM, MARGARET, ed. *First-Line Index of English Poetry 1500–1800 in Manuscripts of the Bodleian Library Oxford*. 2 vols. New York: Index Committee of the Modern Language Association; Oxford: Clarendon Press. x, 1–630; 631–1257p.

First-line index of English poetry (1500–1800) in manuscripts of the Bodleian up to 1961. Five indexes: (1) Bodleian manuscripts listed by shelf marks; (2) index of authors; (3) index of names mentioned; (4) index of authors of works translated, paraphrased, or imitated; and (5) index of references to composers of settings and tunes named or quoted. Contains thirty-three main entries for Herbert.

⊷§ 641. DENIS, YVES. "Poèmes métaphysiques." *NRF* 17:235–46.

General introduction to the nature of metaphysical poetry. Contains a brief biographical sketch of Herbert and translations of "Redemption" and "Love (III)" into French (pp. 241–43).

⊷§ 642. DOLAN, PAUL J. "Herbert's Dialogue with God." *Anglican Theological Review* 51:125–32.

Through an examination of the various stances and attitudes of the speaker and listener in "Dialogue," "The Temper (I)," "Discipline," "Christmas," "The Thanksgiving," and "The Collar," the author shows that one of the distinctive characteristics of Herbert's poetry is his skillful uses of the dialogue mode and suggests that those poems "concerned with God's bargain with man or the contractual conditions of salvation" (p. 125) are particularly important "because these reveal most distinctly the nature of Herbert's concept of man's relationship to God Whom he petitions and the God to Whom he repents" (p. 126).

⊷§ 643. ERICSON, EDWARD E., JR. "A Structural Approach to Imagery." *Style* 3:227–47.

Discusses imagery by analyzing "the external structure and arrangement of images" (p. 227) in order to "tell us something about the methods which a particular poet employed in constructing his poems—or at least the imagistic pattern within his poems" (p. 228). Comments on the structural types of Herbert's imagery as a way of illustrating the general approach and classifies his images into several categories: simple, extended, running, images within images, images within images within images, and images within images within images within images. Examines the structural pattern of images in "Prayer (I)," "Grief," "Vanitie," "Mortification," "The Rose," "The World," "The Pilgrimage," "Redemption," "Artillerie," "Assurance," "Church-rents and schismes," and "The Bag." Suggests that most of the poems can be divided into two major patterns: (1) those that "are unified from beginning to end through the use of imagery" and (2) those that use "separate blocks of images connected end to end" (p. 229). Most of Herbert's poems fall into the second category but argues that the best poems fall into the first.

⊷§ 644. FOGELMAN, ROGER. "Revision and Improvement in George Herbert's *The Temple*." *Nassau Review* (Nassau Community College) 1:65–85.

Comments on the nature of Herbert's revision of several of the poems in *The Temple*. Argues that "a comparison of certain poems in the Williams MS and the Bodleian MS shows that Herbert's revisions were inspired, on occasion, by the wording and imagery of other of his poems" (p. 78) and that the revisions "show the development of significant attitudes in Herbert's religious thought" (p. 79), especially "an emphasis upon the positive aspects of the human condition, and a deepening awareness of the general or universal nature of man's relation to his fellow-man and to God" (p. 79). Comments in particular on the revision of "Easter," "Whitsunday," "Praise (I)," and certain lines in *The Church-Porch*, "Faith," and "The Sacrifice."

◄§ 645. FORSYTH, R. A. "Herbert, Clough, and Their Church-Windows." *VP* 7:17–30.

Suggests that Herbert's "The Windows" is a possible source for the
unusual window imagery found in Arthur Hugh Clough's "Epi-strauss-
ium," Clough's statement on what constitutes essential Christianity.
Argues that Clough's poem does not simply echo Herbert's in material
or style and is not simply a parody of a Victorian reworking of a seventeenth-century poem; rather maintains that Clough uses the imagery of
Herbert's poem to underline his own religious beliefs. In "The Windows"
Herbert says that it is only by becoming Christ-like that man can become
the true Christian; Clough in his poem ironically finds that his rejection
of the historical Jesus does not destroy his religious beliefs but rather
allows him to discover more readily and more clearly essential Christianity. Contains a close reading of "The Windows."

◄§ 646. HUNTLEY, FRANK L. "Dr. Johnson and Metaphysical Wit; or,
Discordia concors Yoked and Balanced." *Papers of the Midwest
Modern Language Association* 1:103–12.

Attempts to view the metaphysical poets from Dr. Johnson's perspective, primarily by explaining Johnson's use of the phrase *discordia concors*. Distinguishes between "two modes of imitating world harmony,"
the classical and the Christian, and "describes and illustrates the difference in feeling and shape that one mode produces in Denham and
Pope; and the other, in Donne and Herbert" (p. 104). "One pattern
imitates the natural balance between the elements of fission and fusion;
the other more daringly combines a lower into a higher value to achieve a
third. The balanced pattern is Pythagorean and Empedoclean and consists of two's and four's; the yoked pattern is Platonic and Christian, and
often appears in three's and five's" (p. 104). Uses the first three stanzas
of Herbert's "Easter" and the first four lines of "The H. Scriptures (II)"
to illustrate the Christian mode, "an upward struggle from a lower entity to its opposing higher entity in order to achieve a third which is
brand new" (p. 110). Suggests that Dr. Johnson is not ridiculing the
metaphysicals but views the Augustans and the metaphysicals from a
"classical" viewpoint.

◄§ 647. KERMODE, FRANK, ed. *The Metaphysical Poets: Key Essays on
Metaphysical Poetry and the Major Metaphysical Poets*. Edited
with introduction and commentary by Frank Kermode. Fawcett
Premier Literature and Ideas Series, edited by Irving Howe. New
York: Fawcett Publications. 351p.

General introduction to metaphysical poetry by Frank Kermode (pp.
11–32) with a brief introduction to Herbert (pp. 25–26): "Herbert employed traditional pious themes, from the liturgy and from the resources
of Biblical typology, with such originality that he created new forms and

almost a new tone in English poetry" (p. 25). A collection of twenty-six previously published essays and/or selections from book-length studies arranged under five major headings: (1) The English Background, (2) Baroque, (3) Metaphysical Poetic, (4) The Major Metaphysical Poets, and (5) Epilogue. Although several of the items in this collection make reference to Herbert and are important in understanding the nature of metaphysical poetry in general, only two items are specifically on Herbert: (1) A selection from Walton's *Life of Mr. George Herbert* (pp. 225–29) and (2) Joseph H. Summers's "Herbert's Conception of Form" (pp. 230–51) from *George Herbert: His Religion and Art* (entry 369), pp. 73–94, 219–21.

৽§ 648. LEVITT, PAUL M., and JOHNSTON, KENNETH G. "Herbert's 'The Collar': A Nautical Metaphor." *SP* 66:217–24.

Comments on the "boat-of-the-mind" metaphor, "which enriches, clarifies, and organizes 'The Collar' " (p. 217). Argues that recognition of the pervasive nautical imagery of the poem in no way destroys the standard Christian interpretation of the poem but rather shows that Herbert's speaker is proposing "to embark on a worldly voyage" (p. 217). Comments on a possible nautical meaning of the title: "a band (or garland) of rope which helps to support the main mast, to restrain the motion of the mast, and thus to ensure a safe voyage" (p. 218). Thus, the title suggests that it would be "as disastrous for the speaker to renounce his Christian life of discipline, denial, and restraint ('to slip the collar' as the phrase went) as it would be for the sailor to cut the collar supporting the mast" (p. 219). Comments on various possible nautical meanings of "the board" (line 1), "abroad" (line 2), "lines" (line 4), "rode" (line 4), "Loose as the winde, as large as store" (line 5), "suit" (line 6), "bayes" (line 14), "garlands" (line 15), "hands" (line 18), "cage" (line 21), "rope of sands" (line 22), "Good cable" (line 24), "Away" (line 27), "deaths head" (line 29). Suggests that Herbert's speaker maintains "that the religious man must weather a spiritual storm, as it were, before he can arrive at a spiritual calm" (p. 224). Thus, when the speaker achieves peace of mind, he "no longer desires to set sail in search of worldly pleasures" (p. 224). For a reply, see D. F. Rauber, "Critics and Collars," entry 713.

৽§ 649. LLOYD, J. D. K. "Where Was George Herbert Born?" *Archaeologia Cambrensis* 118:139–43.

Indicates that there is no positive evidence to support the claim that Herbert was born at Montgomery Castle. Suggests that he was most likely born at Eyton-on-Severn in Shropshire, the home of his maternal grandmother, Lady Margaret Newport. Surmises that Herbert was probably baptized either in the chapel there or in the church in Wroxeter.

✒§ 650. McGuire, Philip C. "Herbert's Jordan II and the Plain Style."
   MichA 1, no. 3–4: 69–74.
Suggests that Herbert's rejection of figures of diction and of stylistic
embellishments in "Jordan (II)" was influenced by statements about the
proper style for private prayer found in various Renaissance devotional
manuals and handbooks on prayer as well as by the tradition of classical
plain style. Presents a close reading of "Jordan (II)."

✒§ 651. Martz, Louis L. *The Wit of Love: Donne, Carew, Crashaw,
   Marvell.* University of Notre Dame Ward-Phillips Lectures in English Language and Literature, vol. 3. Notre Dame, Ind., and London: University of Notre Dame Press. xv, 216p.
Series of four lectures (revised and expanded) that were first delivered
at the University of Notre Dame in March 1968. Only brief references to
Herbert. Suggests that Herbert is neither a mannerist nor a baroque poet
but that in his poetry he "achieves the perfect harmony of a High Renaissance symbol" (p. 136). Compares briefly the careers of Herbert and
Carew (pp. 151–52) and the devotional poetry of Herbert and Crashaw
(pp. 136–37) and of Herbert and Marvell (pp. 154–56).

✒§ 652. Merrill, Thomas F. " 'The Sacrifice' and the Structure of Religious Language." *Lang&S* 2:275–87.
Discusses the structure of religious language and maintains that it "is
the same as everyday language but *put to a special use*," that use being
"communication to and about God" (p. 276). Discusses "The Sacrifice"
as an excellent model for analyzing the language of devotional poetry
and argues that from a structural analysis of the poem it would seem that
the real subject of it "is a crucial piece of Christian dogma—the Hyposta-
tic Union" (p. 287). Disagrees with the conclusions of William Empson
and Rosemond Tuve about the poem.

✒§ 653. Miner, Earl. *The Metaphysical Mode from Donne to Cowley.*
   Princeton: Princeton University Press. xix, 291p.
Pages 118–58 reprinted in *Seventeenth Century English Poetry: Modern Essays in Criticism*, edited by William Keast (rev. ed., entry 707),
pp. 45–76.
Pages 99–117 reprinted in *The Metaphysical Poets: A Selection of
Critical Essays*, edited by Gerald Hammond (entry 783), pp. 197–214.
The purpose of this study is "to discriminate poetic features that are
particularly important to the Metaphysical style and differences possible
within the style: in other words, what is lasting and what changes, what
is general to the style and what is peculiar to individual writers" (p. xi).
Argues (1) that metaphysical poetry is "private in mode, that it treats
time and place in ways describable in terms of the 'dramatic,' the 'nar-

rative,' the transcendent, the 'meditative,' and the 'argumentative'—and
that these terms provide in their sequence something of a history of the
development of Metaphysical poetry" (p. xi); (2) that "the wit of Metaphysical poetry can be characterized as definition that is, as those logical
or rhetorical processes bringing together or separating (whether in metaphor or idea) matters of similar or opposed classes; and as that dialectic,
or those processes, that extend such matters by their relation in logical and
rhetorical procedures" (pp. xi–xii); and (3) that "the thematic range of
Metaphysical poetry can best be represented in terms of satiric denial
and lyric affirmation" (p. xii). Chapter 1, "The Private Mode" (pp. 3–
47), argues that the private mode is "the chief 'radical' of Metaphysical
poetry, that feature differentiating it from the social and public modes of
other poetry written in modern English before the late eighteenth century and the Romantic poets" (p. x). Chapter 2, "Forms of Perception:
Time and Place" (pp. 48–117), explores various "forms, modes and structures of Metaphysical poems in terms of their version of time and space"
(p. x). Chapter 3, "Wit: Definition and Dialectic" (pp. 118–58), defines the "major feature of Metaphysical wit in terms reflecting the poets'
use of an older logic and rhetoric" (p. xi). Chapter 4, "Themes: Satire
and Song" (pp. 159–213), comments on "the thematic range of Metaphysical poetry in terms of complementary elements" (p. xi), in terms
of song and satire, "the former a tendency to affirmation, the latter a
tendency to denial, both being capable of expression in lyricism or in
satire, or in mixtures" (p. xi). Chapter 5, "Three Poems" (pp. 214–71),
examines in detail Donne's "The Perfume," Herbert's "The Flower," and
Marvell's "The Nymph complaining for the death of her Faun." Herbert
is mentioned throughout and compared and contrasted with Donne,
Vaughan, Crashaw, Marvell, Traherne, Cowley, and Quarles. Deals with
Herbert's dramatic qualities, his uses of the meditative tradition and the
emblem tradition, and his particular kind of wit. Comments more or less
extensively on "Artillerie," "Bitter-sweet," *The Church-Porch*, "The Collar," "Grace," "Jordan (I)," "Life," "Love (III)," "The Pearl," "Prayer
(I)," "The Pulley," "The Quip," "The Sacrifice," "The Temper (I),"
and "Vertue," and presents a detailed reading of "The Flower" (pp. 231–
46). Relates "The Flower" to the tradition of the poetry of meditation,
the emblem tradition, and the tradition of the soul's vicissitudes.

⇜§ 654. MULDER, JOHN R. *The Temple of the Mind: Education and
    Literary Tastes in Seventeenth-Century England.* Pegasus Back-
    grounds in English Literature. New York: Pegasus. viii, 165p.
  Mentions Herbert frequently in this background study of significant
aspects of seventeenth-century education and sensibility. Argues that, although education does not account for the literature of the period, an
understanding of the curriculum helps the modern reader "to recover the
way in which Browne or Herbert was read by his contemporaries; and

such knowledge is likely to bring us closer to the author's intention" (p. xvii). Chapter 1 discusses the training offered students in language, logic, and rhetoric. Chapter 2 studies the emphasis of the curriculum on logical and dialectical argumentation. Chapter 3 comments on seventeenth-century fondness for word play. Chapter 4 discusses the central role that religion played in the formation of the seventeenth-century reader and writer. Chapter 5 discusses Nowell's *Catechism* as an example and synopsis of religious ideas generally shared by the writers of the period. Chapter 6 outlines the basic principles of biblical typology and the prevalence of typological thinking in the age. Comments on the rhetorical method of argument in Herbert's "Employment (II)" (pp. 65–66) and his uses of logic and debate in such poems as "Deniall," "The Quidditie," "The Reprisall," "The Thanksgiving," "H. Baptisme (I) and (II)," "The Temper (I) and (II)," "Love (I)," "Church-monuments," and "Church-musick," especially stressing Herbert's arranging of poems in pairs in order to form complex inner relationships. Discusses Herbert's use of titles that have complex and multilevel meanings, especially "The Agonie," "Divinitie," "Unkindnesse," "The Temper (I)," "Mans medley," "The Storm," "The Size," "Redemption," "Businesse," and "Dialogue" (pp. 73–79). Comments on "Man" as reflecting a typical seventeenth-century attitude toward man in the hierarchy of creation (pp. 103–4). Presents examples drawn from *The Temple* to illustrate generally accepted religious notions of the time and argues that an understanding of the nuances of mood and meaning in many of Herbert's poems requires knowledge of generally accepted religious views such as those contained in Nowell's *Catechism* (pp. 115–20). Gives a close reading of "The H. Scriptures (II)" as an example of Herbert's uses of biblical typology (pp. 130–31) and comments on the wide-ranging influence of typological thinking on the structure and design of *The Temple* (pp. 138–41). Suggests that the poems preceding "Coloss. iii.3" "lay the foundations of the doctrines of redemption and the mysteries of faith" and that those following the poem emphasize "the difficulties the Christian encounters in building on these foundations" (p. 142). Contrasts briefly Herbert's and Milton's approaches to typology, arguing that Herbert's interpretation "is reminiscent of the Epistle to the Hebrews, in which Old Testament types prefigure the antitypes of the New, and both in turn anticipate the full revelation of heaven" (p. 146), while Milton recalls the approach of St. Paul.

⊸§ 655. MURRIN, MICHAEL. *The Veil of Allegory: Some Notes Toward a Theory of Allegorical Rhetoric in the English Renaissance.* Chicago and London: University of Chicago Press. x, 224p.
   Briefly discusses Herbert as an allegorist: "He cast his *Temple* in allegorical form and used the traditional metaphors and symbols of the Christian-biblical tradition" (p. 195). Points out that Herbert's style is

"simple, his wit restrained, and his allegory depends upon popular symbols, unfamiliar to us but well-known in the seventeenth-century" (p. 195). Suggests that Herbert, "more than anyone perhaps, put into effect the old principle: *ars est celare artem*" and that, as far as the more elaborate forms of allegory are concerned, Herbert "is a sign of the end" (p. 196). Concludes that the allegory that survived the change "was of the simplified, clear type which Herbert used but—after Bunyan—without the profundity of his Christian symbols" (p. 197).

᪵§ 656. RUTHVEN, K. K. *The Conceit.* The Critical Idiom, edited by John D. Jump, vol. 4. London: Methuen & Co. 70p.
Discusses the word *conceit*, the theoretical basis of conceits, some common types of conceits, and the decline of the conceit. Mentions Herbert throughout and briefly comments on his uses of typology, as evidenced in "The Agonie."

᪵§ 657. SHAWCROSS, JOHN R., and EMMA, RONALD DAVID, eds. *Seventeenth-Century English Poetry.* Lippincott College English Series. Philadelphia and New York: J. B. Lippincott Co. xvii, 636p.
Contains a general introduction to seventeenth-century poetry (pp. 1–11) and a general bibliography (pp. 13–15). Presents a brief introduction to Herbert's life and works, with a selective bibliography (pp. 196–98), and reproduces forty-four poems from *The Temple*, with explanatory notes (pp. 198–239).

᪵§ 658. SHELTON, A. J. "George Herbert's 'Employment (II).'" *Critical Survey* 4:92–95.
Presents a close reading of "Employment (II)" and suggests that it is "fluctuation of mood that provides the major interest as one examines the poem in detail" (p. 95). Argues that the poem develops "in terms of a series of cryptic statements rather than a logical and unified argument" and that the very inconsistencies in it "express its particular truth: its fluctuations are the fluctuations of the experience which it defines" (p. 95).

᪵§ 659. TOKSON, ELLIOT H. "The Image of the Negro in Four Seventeenth-Century Poems." *MLQ* 30:508–22.
Discusses the image of the Negro in Herbert's "Aethiopissa ambit Cestum Diversi Coloris Virum," Henry Rainold's "A Blackmore Mayd Wooing a fair Boy," Henry King's "The Boy's answer to the Blackmore," and John Cleveland's "A Faire Nimph scorning a Black Boy Courting her." Compares and contrasts the poems to show how they dramatize certain major attitudes toward Negroes: "The attitudes suggested by the sympathetic treatment in the poems of Herbert and Rainolds tend to

stand out clearly against the popular tendency to view the Negro solely in derogatory terms as unfeeling, ugly, inferior, savage and subhuman; the speakers in the King and Cleveland poems, on the other hand, add to the texture of conceptions that divided the races then, and still to some degree keep them apart today" (p. 522). Says that Herbert's poem rises above mere cleverness and "sympathizes imaginatively with its subject, producing a sensitively realized scene" (p. 509): "To be the only poem about secular love written by a religious poet would make this poem unique; to be written in a period in which the very nature of the Negro as a human being was considered questionable makes it remarkable" (p. 510).

୶§ 660. Tonkin, Humphrey. "A Bibliography of George Herbert 1960–1967: Addenda." *SCN* 27:29.
Addenda to "George Herbert: A Recent Bibliography, 1960–1967" compiled by Harry B. Caldwell, Edward E. Samaha, Jr., and Donna G. Fricke (entry 615). Lists eighteen items.

୶§ 661. Untermeyer, Louis. "The Oddities of Poetry." In *The Pursuit of Poetry: A Guide to Its Understanding and Appreciation with an Explanation of Its Forms and a Dictionary of Poetic Terms*, pp. 124–37. New York: Simon and Shuster.
Discusses briefly Herbert's highly experimental forms, his anagrams, acrostics, echo verses, shaped poems: "Never has there been a poetry so pious and yet so playful" (p. 124). Brief critical commentary on "Anagram of the Virgin Marie," "Paradise," "Heaven," and "The Altar."

1970

୶§ 662. Carpenter, Margaret. "From Herbert to Marvell: Poetics in 'A Wreath' and 'The Coronet.'" *JEGP* 69:50–62.
Presents a close reading of Herbert's "A Wreath" and Marvell's "The Coronet" in order to show that, although both poems are similar in a number of respects, they greatly differ and suggests that a study of their dissimilarities reveals a great deal about each poet's achievement. Although both poems deal with "the problem of writing a poem felt by its author to be not truly worthy of God" (p. 51), Herbert asks God to substitute a more fitting poem for his unworthy one, whereas Marvell seeks annihilation of both his poem and his body. Two major differences emerge: (1) Marvell "makes more explicit than Herbert the double subject of his poem: the poet-artist in particular and man in general as a creative being and for whom, therefore, the specific poet-artist can be a metaphor" and (2) Marvell "operates primarily by the indirection of ironic implication and suggestion" (p. 61).

◄§ 663. DIECKMANN, LISELOTTE. "Poetic Hieroglyphics." In *Hieroglyph-ics: The History of a Literary Symbol*, pp. 86–96. St. Louis: Wash-ington University Press.

Maintains that Joseph Summers's chapter 6, "The Poem as Hieroglyph" in *George Herbert: His Religion and Art* (entry 369) is "the most inter-esting study of the term hieroglyphic in the metaphysical poets" (p. 94). Shows how the term is used metaphorically in the seventeenth century and "has lost its connection with Egypt" (p. 95): "Neither the *Altar* nor the *Wings* by Herbert are Egyptian hieroglyphics, nor did the Egyptians write poetry to explain a visual image or to be considered, formally, as a symbol" (p. 95). Distinguishes between hieroglyph and emblem.

◄§ 664. EL-GABALAWY, SAAD. "George Herbert's Affinities with the Homiletical Mode." *HAB* 21:38–48.

Discusses a number of relationships and common features between Herbert's theory and practice of poetry and the homiletic literature of his day, maintaining, "There is no division in Herbert's consciousness be-tween his career as a poet who communicates his religious experience and his vocation as a priest who conveys the Word of God to man" (p. 47). Points out that both the preacher and the poet shared similar assumptions about the purpose and function of their respective arts; that they em-ployed similar uses of rhetoric, diction, and imagery; that they attempted to convey a conversational tone and a sense of spontaneous thought; and that they held similar views on the employment of humor, irony, sarcasm, and mimicry and shared a fondness for proverbs.

◄§ 665. ———. "The Pilgrimage: George Herbert's Favourite Allegori-cal Technique." *CLAJ* 13:408–19.

Comments on a number of Herbert's allegorical poems, especially "The Pilgrimage," "Peace," "Redemption," "Christmas," and "The Bag," "with the intention of showing that the pilgrimage is the poet's favourite allegorical form, demonstrating how he revitalizes this traditional meth-od, with a didactic purpose, to make it a dynamic vehicle freshly available to serious poetry" (p. 408).

◄§ 666. ELLRODT, ROBERT. "George Herbert and the Religious Lyric." In *English Poetry and Prose, 1540–1674*, edited by Christopher Ricks, pp. 173–205. History of Literature in the English Language, vol 2. London: Barrie & Jenkins. Paperback ed., Sphere Books, 1970.

Discusses the particular nature of Herbert's extraordinary achievement in the religious lyric, contrasting his achievement with that of Donne, Crashaw, Vaughan, and Traherne. Maintains, "A strong flavour of in-dividuality is the distinguishing mark and excellence of the religious lyric in seventeenth-century England, as compared with earlier devotional verse or with the Baroque lyric of the Continent" (p. 173). Recognizes the various currents of philosophical and theological thought that shaped Herbert's vision and admits the influence of Donne, the liturgy, the emblem tradition, etc., but stresses the individuality of Herbert's imagination and style. Discusses Herbert's particular intuition of space and time as reflected in his poetry, his individual religious sensibility and mode of devotion, and his unique sense of form.

⋙§ 667. FARMER, NORMAN K., JR. "A Theory of Genre for Seventeenth-Century Poetry." *Genre* 3:293–317.
Points out that most critical discussion of seventeenth-century poetry is devoted to the lyric and that other genres tend to be neglected. Presents a theory of genre as a way of laying "the aesthetic foundation for an understanding of seventeenth-century poetry that is based on something other than whether a poem is 'metaphysical' or 'cavalier,' 'classical,' or 'Jonsonian'" (p. 312) and "offers an explanation for the richness of seventeenth century poetry by showing how the lyric stood in relation to other more public genres commonly practiced at the time and how poets were able to develop the 'I' of the lyric poem with greater facility than their predecessors by virtue of cutting across generic lines and developing the rhetorics of various other modes as well" (p. 312). Maintains also that "our awareness of the relative referentiality and contextuality of the various genres and subgenres of seventeenth-century poetry serves to remind us of some very important cultural factors that led to the development of the lyric" (p. 312). Discusses the nondidactic sacred lyric as one of the specific genres of the seventeenth century and distinguishes it from the secular lyric. Argues that, although the sacred lyric "*is* a self-enclosed form which invites full play of the reader's critical imagination within the construct of the poem," the "very fact that it is sacred rather than secular poses a problem for the critic who would nonetheless make fine distinctions regarding referentiality" (p. 310). Suggests that Herbert's poems, which primarily deal with the problem of belief, "continually invite their readers to make the referential leap between poem and belief . . . or between the poem and the liturgy" (p. 310). Suggests that both Rosemond Tuve's *A Reading of George Herbert* (entry 344) and Arnold Stein's *George Herbert's Lyrics* (entry 629) may mislead the reader into thinking that in order to understand and appreciate Herbert's poems one need only master the various contexts of belief (Tuve) or only focus on the interiorized contexts (Stein).

⋙§ 668. FISH, STANLEY E. "Letting Go: The Reader in Herbert's Poetry." *ELH* 37:495–516.
Expanded version, "Letting Go: The Dialectic of the Self in Herbert's Poetry," in *Self-Consuming Artifacts: The Experience of Seventeenth-Century Literature* (entry 729), pp. 156–223.
Maintains that the reader is very much a part of the drama and the

process in Herbert's poems. Argues that "those problems which engage Herbert's protagonists engage his reader also" and that the poems "are structured so as both to describe an experience and give one, and that experience is, in a very special sense, self-diminishing" (p. 476). Demonstrates that characteristically Herbert asserts in his poems that God is everything and that thus "the claims of other entities to a separate existence, including the claims of the speakers and readers of these poems, must be relinquished" (p. 478). In other words, the fundamental insight that "God's word is all is *self*-destructive, since acquiring it involves abandoning the perceptual and conceptual categories within which the self moves and by means of which it separately exists" (p. 478). Shows then how Herbert consciously "writes himself out of his poems" so that they become, "quite literally, *God's* word" (p. 479) and how as readers of the poems we are required "to let go first of the terms in which we think (and say), and then of thinking, and finally of (separate) being, in all its manifestations, including Herbert's poetry" (p. 480). Illustrates this thesis through a close reading of "Clasping of hands," "Even-song," "The Hold-fast," "A true Hymne," and especially "The Altar."

⋖§ 669. GALLAGER, MICHAEL P. "Rhetoric, Style, and George Herbert." *ELH* 37:495–516.
Discusses Herbert's poetry "in the light of his professional expertise in the arts of style and language" (p. 495) and attempts "to clarify what the plain style meant in the rhetoric that Herbert knew, examining his own views on style and poetry insofar as we know them, and finally looking at the rhetoric of some of his poems" (p. 496). Maintains that Herbert endorses the classical plain style as it was adapted to Christian rhetoric by St. Augustine in his *De Doctrina Christiana* and shows that for Herbert the plain style "was clearly more than a matter of figures or language or logical structure; it involved moral values and attitudes to experience" (p. 512).

⋖§ 670. HALEWOOD, WILLIAM H. "Herbert." In *The Poetry of Grace: Reformation Themes and Structures in English Seventeenth-Century Poetry*, pp. 88–111. New Haven and London: Yale University Press.
Shows how certain Reformation ideas, interests, and attitudes shape not only Herbert's theology and preoccupations but also influence the characteristic forms of his poetry. Suggests, for instance, that the basic situation that Herbert depicts in "The Collar" has striking similarities to Calvin's theology. Desires to place Herbert, therefore, in his proper historical context: "By appealing to a Reformation reading of life instead of the medieval one that Miss Tuve suggests (though not denying continuities), we secure the double benefit of restoring to Herbert an appropriate intellectual background (a guard against random moderniza-

tions) and preserving the modern critic's perception that there is a special element of shock in the poem" (p. 96). Shows how a Reformation reading of life contains the elements of shock, surprise, and paradox. Discusses the specifically Protestant and Augustinian nature of Herbert's poetry, finds a number of elements that could be called "enthusiastic," and thus accounts for Herbert's appeal among the Nonconformists: "His account of the religious life, though attentive to church feasts and occasions and to the Church as an institution . . . , is mainly cast in terms of vivid personal experiences which practitioners of individual religion would recognize and appreciate" (p. 102). Suggests that Herbert's Christology, his stress on the importance of the will, and his strong and precise sense of humility are fully in accord with and informed by Protestant teaching. Calls Herbert's poetry "the poetry of reconciliation" and argues, "The gap between ostensible truth and the truth of God is Herbert's constant theme and is the conceptual basis for a poetic form in which opposites clash violently and subside in reconciliations which are in fact victories for one voice in the dialectic and defeats for the other" (p. 98). Relates Herbert's plain style to his theological views.

⊷§ 671. HANDSCOMBE, R. J. "George Herbert's 'The Collar': A Study in Frustration." *Lang&S* 3:29–37.
A reading of "The Collar" that employs interpretative stylistics. Sees the poem *"as a linguistic event which demands developing response"* (p. 29). Suggests that in the poem Herbert represents "by way of reflection in language the pain of a crisis in religious conviction through an assault on the reader's faith in his own linguistic competence, a crisis almost as important and painful" (p. 37).

⊷§ 672. HERBERT, GEORGE. *Herbert's Remains. Or Sundry Pieces of that Sweet Singer of The Temple, Mr George Herbert* (1652). A Scolar Press Facsimile. Menston, Eng.: Scolar Press. 168, 194p.
Facsimile (original size) of the 1652 *Remains* (Wing H 1515). Contains "A Prefatory View of the Life of Mr. Geo. Herbert" (later claimed by Barnbas Oley as his own), *A Priest to the Temple, Jacula Prudentum*, two prayers, "Mr. G. Herbert to Master N. F.," three Latin poems, and "An Addition to Apothegmes by Severall Authors" (none of which is by Herbert). Bibliographical note on the volume and on items included.

⊷§ 673. HINMAN, ROBERT B. "The Apotheosis of Faust: Poetry and New Philosophy in the Seventeenth Century." In *Metaphysical Poetry*, edited by Malcolm Bradbury and David Palmer, pp. 149–79. New York: St. Martin's Press; London: Edward Arnold.
Rejects the generally accepted twentieth-century view that during the seventeenth century art and science were fundamentally opposed to each other and that the new science had a generally bad effect on the poetry

of the period. Maintains that actually the artists and the new philosophers were "spiritual allies, even if they were not always aware of the alliance, and that despite individual and occasional antagonisms—the total effect of each group on the other was salubrious" (p. 149). Suggests that "the same ordering, synthesizing, all encompassing, imaginative surge toward 'reality,' towards as much truth as man can grasp or express, seems evident in such diverse achievements as *The Temple* and *Principia Mathematica*" (p. 156). Shows that Herbert in *The Temple* "is just as much concerned with demonstrating or discovering a pattern where none seems to be as Newton is" and that Herbert's poems "express a kind of spiritual topology in which inside and outside are seen to be one, just as Newton's mathematics express an unseen connection between falling bodies and planetary motions" (p. 157).

⊷§ 674. HUNTLEY, FRANK L. "A Crux in George Herbert's *The Temple*." *ELN* 8:13–17.

Suggests on the basis of history, manuscript evidence, and close literary analysis that "the poem now so awkwardly entitled 'Church-lock and key' be called what Herbert once called it, 'Prayer,' and that it be read not with 'Church-Monuments' and 'Church-Windows' but in the position where Herbert once placed it, next to that masterful sonnet, 'Prayer the church's banquet . . . something understood' " (p. 17).

⊷§ 675. LAMBA, B. P., and LAMBA, R. JEET. "Herbert's 'The Agonie' 9–10." *Expl* 28:item 51.

Suggests that lines 9–10 of "The Agonie" ("A man so wrung with pains, that all his hair, / His skinne, his garments bloudie be") refer to David, not to Christ, as suggested by Rosemond Tuve in *A Reading of George Herbert* (entry 344). For a reply, see Edgar F. Daniels and René Rapin, entry 695.

⊷§ 676. LEIMBERG, INGE. "George Herbert 'The Sinner' der Tempel als Memoria-Gebäude." *Archiv* 206:241–50.

Presents an explication of "The Sinner" in terms of its architectural imagery, especially in terms of Herbert's use of images of stone, engraving, and quarries. Maintains, "Das Thema des Gedichte ist der Verlust und die Wiederherstellung der Ebenbeldlickeit" (p. 243). Also comments on the architectural imagery in *The Temple* in general.

⊷§ 677. McGRATH, F. C. "Herbert's 'The Bunch of Grapes.' " *Expl* 29:item 15.

Explicates "The Bunch of Grapes" to show that in the poem Herbert "has concisely and effectively woven his personal emotional experience and individual destiny with that of all men for all time and has resolved these mutual destinies in the blood of Christ." Through its intricate uses of imagery and diction, the poem distinguishes between the "pre-Christian promise of everlasting joy and the Christian promise of salvation in the crucified and resurrected Christ."

✥§ 678. MAHOOD, M. M. "Something Understood: The Nature of Herbert's Wit." In *Metaphysical Poetry*, edited by Malcolm Bradbury and David Palmer, pp. 123–47. Stratford-Upon-Avon Studies, 11. New York: St. Martin's Press; London: Edward Arnold.

Surveys the range, complexity, and variety of Herbert's wit and shows that a "concern for dramatic form, with ordered movement towards a timely conclusion, guides Herbert in his choice and use of all the technical resources of his poetry: diction, imagery, sentence-structure, stanza forms, rhyme and rhythm" (p. 125). Illustrates generic points with detailed examples drawn from many of the poems, especially "Prayer (I)," "Constancie," "The Pearl," "Love unknown," "Vertue," and "Love (III)."

✥§ 679. MANGELSDORF, SANDRA R. "Donne, Herbert, and Vaughan: Some Baroque Features." *Northeast Modern Language Association Newsletter* 2:14–23.

Discusses certain baroque features in Donne's "The Canonization," Herbert's "Easter-wings," and Vaughan's "Corruption." Uses the terminology of Wölfflin and Sypher to find the following baroque qualities in "Easter-wings": its "exploration of an idea in the variance from man's fall in the first stanza and the speaker's own in the second, organic unity, use of images to reinforce ideas, nearseeing, molding, openness, and dynamism," and especially its "total merging of form with content" (p. 20).

✥§ 680. MARTZ, LOUIS L. "The Action of the Self: Devotional Poetry in the Seventeenth Century." In *Metaphysical Poetry*, edited by Malcolm Bradbury and David Palmer, pp. 101–21. Stratford-Upon-Avon Studies, 11. New York: St. Martin's Press; London: Edward Arnold.

Points out that seventeenth-century devotion involved "an active, creative state of mind, a 'poetical' condition . . . in which the mind works at high intensity" and that thus devotional poetry "should not . . . be taken to indicate verse of rather limited range, 'merely pious' pieces without much poetic energy" (p. 103). Argues that devotional poetry is the result of "a state of mind created by the 'powers of the soul' in an intense dramatic action, focused upon one central issue" (p. 103). Warns against overestimating the influence of Donne on the development of English devotional poetry and contrasts the instability, tension, and even querulous action of Donne's *Holy Sonnets* with the deeply achieved sense of security and familiar confidence that pervades *The Temple*. Presents analyses of "Vertue," "Conscience," and other selections from Herbert to contrast the states of mind and resulting poetical techniques of the two poets. Comments in particular on the technique of repetition found throughout *The Temple*: "Upon the fabric established by these repetitions, Herbert weaves an astonishing variety of designs, including some of the boldest familiarity with God found anywhere in literature" (p. 111). Shows that Vaughan's poetry, though often in direct imitation of Herbert's, fails to achieve the same stability and architectural neatness.

⊷§ 681. REITER, ROBERT E. "George Herbert and His Biographer." *Cithara* 9:18–31.

Discusses the formation and development of the biographical tradition surrounding Herbert and surveys various biographical accounts published since 1633, specifically those of Nicholas Ferrar (1633), Barnabas Oley (1652), Walton (1670), George L. Duyckinck (1858), J. J. Daniell (1893), George Herbert Palmer (1905, entry 1), A. G. Hyde (1906, entry 8), F. E. Hutchinson (1941, entry 223), Joseph H. Summers (1954, entry 369), and Marchette Chute (1959, entry 425). Points out that, although various biographers have corrected certain details and minor facts in Walton's biography, in fact, "it was really not until 1954 that Joseph Summers radically reinterpreted the life of Herbert and showed that Walton's understanding of Herbert could be wrong" (p. 31). Points out a number of serious lacunae in our present information and suggests that "about his activities from his late twenties to about 1633 we still know relatively little" (p. 31).

⊷§ 682. STANWOOD, P. G. "Poetry Manuscripts of the Seventeenth Century in the Durham Cathedral Library." *DUJ* 31:81–90.

Describes Durham MS Hunter 27, which contains a translation of Herbert's *The Church Militant* into Latin hexameters and also a Latin verse translation of "Good Friday" by James Leeke (1605–1654), a fellow of Peterhouse. Suggests that since Leeke probably completed his translation soon after 1633, he is Herbert's first translator. Reproduces the first sixty-six lines of the translation.

⊷§ 683. STRZETELSKI, JERZY. *The English Sonnet: Syntax and Style.* Krakow, Poland: Jagellonian University. 149p.

A study in descriptive linguistics that examines the contribution of syntax to the style of the English sonnet. Attempts "to find out what describable formal syntactical features of the sonnets differentiates the style of the English sonneteers from one another" (p. 12). Mentions Herbert in several places (pp. 25, 26–27, 82, 119, 127, 143). In particular, comments on "Prayer (I)," the only example found among the 278 sonnets considered that does not contain a finite verb. Suggests that Herbert's style is more involved and complex than Donne's. Several illustrative tables.

⸲§ 684. SUMMERS, JOSEPH H. "Gentlemen at Home and at Chu⸲⸲
Henry King and George Herbert." In *The Heirs of Donne and Jonson*, pp. 76–101. New York and London: Oxford University Press.

Calls *The Temple* "the best and wittiest collection of religious lyrics in English" (p. 88). Comments on *The Church-Porch* and explains its inherent relationship to *The Church*, which is more readily recognized as great poetry. Suggests that *The Church-Porch* is an effective and necessary presentation of the moral life as totally rational and that one of its chief pleasures is in recognizing "memorable formulations of traditional wisdom" (p. 91). Contrasts *The Church-Porch* and *The Church* and sees the latter as introducing the reader to "an almost completely different world of thought and discourse" (p. 96), in which instead of being told about religion the reader finds poems that are "the reflections and creations of a religious life: the hymns, complaints, cries, laments, examinations, quarrels, rejoicings, and promises of a talented poet who was most concerned with the relation of his experience to God's work and Word" (p. 97). Comments on Herbert's effective use of monosyllabic lines, his playfulness and diverse experimentation with form, his rhetorical skill, and his profound simplicity, which often conceals his art. Cites "Love (III)" as a prime example of Herbert's use of rhetoric and Christian persuasion.

⸲§ 685. ————. "The Heritage of Donne and Jonson." *UTQ* 39.107–26.
Distrusts the term *metaphysical poets* because it "inevitably results in and emphasis on the influence of Donne and one kind of poetry at the expense of other influences and kinds" (p. 108) and suggests that *heirs of Donne and Jonson* is preferable, "not with the implication that later poets had any familial or natural rights or that either Donne or Jonson intended that they should inherit, but in simple recognition that they came to occupy a good deal of the literary estate of their two great predecessors" (p. 108). Suggests that the inheritance "was less important as a fabulously rich collection of specific models than as a suggestion of the possibilities available for individual poets who were willing to explore varying, and even contrasting, speakers, genres, and literary ideals" (p. 126). Outlines the major features of Donne's and Jonson's art, showing the differences as well as the similarities between the two. No specific mention of Herbert.

⸲§ 686. VENDLER, HELEN. "George Herbert's 'Vertue.' " *ArielE* 1:54–70.
Reprinted as chapter 1 of *The Poetry of George Herbert* (Cambridge, Mass.: Harvard University Press, 1975), pp. 9–24.

Detailed analysis of "Vertue." Shows that the surface simplicity and ease of the poem are deceptive and fully accounts for the complex, often surprising, and interrelated conceits that lie beneath its surface: "Almost every line in it surprises expectation, though few poems in English seem to unfold themselves with more impersonality, simplicity, and plainness" (p. 55). In order to illustrate the artistic excellence and precision of the poem, the author often rewrites individual lines and stanzas and also compares the poem with Wesley's adaptation of it: "The distinction between the hymn writer, versifying doctrine, and the poet, expressing feeling, is nowhere clearer than in Wesley's revisions of Herbert" (p. 70).

৶§ 687. ———. "The Re-Invented Poem: George Herbert's Alternatives." In *Forms of Lyric: Selected Papers from the English Institute*,
    edited by Reuben A. Brower, pp. 19–45. New York and London:
    Columbia University Press.
    Reprinted as chapter 2 of *The Poetry of George Herbert* (Cambridge,
Mass.: Harvard University Press, 1975), pp. 25–56.
    Discusses and demonstrates how "a poem by Herbert can repudiate itself, correct itself, rephrase itself, rethink its experience, re-invent its topic" (p. 45). Argues that Herbert's poems are "constantly self-critical poems, which so often reject premises as soon as they are established" (p. 20). Shows that Herbert often uses a traditional image or concept but then frequently "re-invents the poem afresh as he goes along: he is constantly criticizing what he had already written down, and finding the original conception inadequate, whether the original conception be the Church's, the Bible's, or his own" (p. 24). Illustrates the complexity and pervasiveness of this principle, especially in "The Invitation," "Doomsday," "Prayer (I)," "The Temper (I)," "The Forerunners," "Affliction (I)," "The Flower," and "Love (III)." Concludes, "It is in this free play of ideas that at least part of Herbert's true originality lies" (p. 45).

৶§ 688. VICKERS, BRIAN. *Classical Rhetoric in English Poetry*. London:
    Macmillan and Co., St. Martin's Press. 180p.
    Mentions Herbert throughout this concise history of rhetoric. Gives evamples of Herbert's uses of certain rhetorical figures: (1) *anadiplosis* in "Love (III)," (2) *anaphora* in "Longing," (3) *antanaclasis* in "Church-monuments," (4) *antimetabole* in "Affliction (I)" and in "Hope," (5) *asyndeton* in "Good Friday," (6) *auxesis* in "Church-monuments," (7) *epanalepsis* in "Love (I)," (8) *gradatio* in "Justice," "Confession," and "Sinnes round," (9) *paronomasia* in "The Temper (II)," (10) *polyptoton* in "The Forerunners," and (11) *syllepsis* in "Time." Presents a rhetorical analysis of "A Wreath" (pp. 161–63) to show how Herbert "makes a fresh and imaginative use of rhetoric" (p. 164).

৶§ 689. WATSON, GEORGE. "The Language of the Metaphysicals." In
    Literary English Since Shakespeare, edited by George Watson, pp.
    156–74. London, Oxford, New York: Oxford University Press.
    Argues that "there is no strictly linguistic way to take intellectual pos-

session of metaphysical poetry, and that this judgment must apply, though in differing measure, to Renaissance and to modern methods of linguistic analyses" (p. 162). Chooses Donne's "Negative Love" and Herbert's "Vertue" to test certain "ancient and accepted assumptions about the ways that language works in them" (p. 162). Comments on a number of common (though not universal) aspects of metaphysical poems: the narrative quality, the use of dramatic monologue, the sense that the poet and the reader share an experience, the coterie nature of much of the language, the uses of argumentation, etc. Argues, "The brief history of metaphysical poetry, from the 1590's down to the Restoration, seems to be a progress toward public status. This is a language that begins in relative secrecy among friends, and turns decisively towards public utterance with Herbert's *The Temple*" (p. 170). Comments on a number of literary, philosophical, and moral reasons for the virtual demise of metaphysical poetry after 1660.

◄§ 690. WILLIAMS, R. DARBY. "Two Baroque Poems on Grace: Herbert's 'Paradise' and Milton's 'On Time.'" *Criticism* 12:180–94.

Explicates Herbert's "Paradise" and Milton's "On Time" as "game poems," as "exercises in poetic fancy that intentionally riddle the imagination and challenge the reader to match wits with the poet" (p. 180). Characterizes the "game poet" by "his attempt to transcend ordinary poetic conventions (and often, verbal conventions as well), his intensely self-conscious playfulness, and his willingness to be deliberately obscure for wit's sake." (p. 181) Calls "Paradise" a "cryptic *technopaignion*, an art-plaything with a crossword puzzle-like riddle for the reader to unknit" (p. 182). Shows how the poem operates on two levels: one the clever celebration of the conventional *hortus conclusus* theme and the other an elaborate puzzle developed within the poem that allows the reader to pare certain of the capitalized letters and end up with the statement: I GROW CHRISTS FRIEND.

◄§ 691. WINNY, JAMES. "A Critical Examination of Some Metaphysical Poems." In *A Preface to Donne*, pp. 120–52. Preface Books, edited by Maurice Hussey. New York: Charles Scribner's Sons; London: Longman Group.

Presents a close reading of Herbert's "Conscience" (pp. 144–45). Primarily contrasts Herbert with Donne, suggesting that, whatever Herbert may have learned from Donne, "he was much closer in feeling and outlook to the writer of the twenty-third Psalm" (p. 145).

1971

◄§ 692. BLAU, SHERIDAN D. "The Poet as Casuist: Herbert's 'Church-Porch.'" *Genre* 4:142–52.

Discusses the relationship between *The Church-Porch* and *The*

Church, accounting for the moral, stylistic, and structural differences between the two by relating the former to the seventeenth-century Anglican practice of case-divinity or casuistry. In *The Church-Porch* Herbert attempts to define holiness in terms of moral conduct; it is directed "not to the polluted but the perplexed, and it serves as a living guide to the everyday questions of what is right and lawful in particular actions" (p. 145). Suggests that Herbert considered *The Church-Porch* "as a sort of sermon based on practical divinity or casuistry and that its purpose, like that of all sermons, was to prepare its audience for the prayers of 'The Church'" (p. 150).

◦§ 693. BOTTRALL, MARGARET. "Herbert, 1593–1633." In *English Poetry: Select Bibliographical Guides,* edited by A. E. Dyson, pp. 60–75. London and New York: Oxford University Press.

Evaluative bibliographical essay on Herbert divided into five major sections: (1) texts, (2) critical studies and commentary, (3) biographies and letters, (4) bibliographies, and (5) background reading, followed by a selective listing of items according to the above categories.

◦§ 694. CHOSSONNERY, PAUL. "La composition et la signification de *The Temple* de George Herbert." *EA* 24:113–25.

Reinterprets the meaning of "The Altar" in the light of two of Herbert's Latin poems in *Lucus* and argues that the poem does not refer to a physical altar upon which the remainder of the poems are offered, as suggested by Joseph H. Summers, but rather refers to the fallen condition of man before he embarks on his Christian voyage. Sees "The Sacrifice" as a presentation of Christ, who redeemed fallen man and made his Christian life in the Church possible. Traces out in other poems this symbolic journey to show that the main theme of *The Temple* is the problem of salvation: Herbert "allait démontrer à ses lecteurs comment chacun d'eux pouvait faire de son âme un Temple où Dieu pourrait venir habiter" (p. 123). *The Church-Porch* thus is seen as simply a moral treatise that shows those limited virtues that man can achieve without the help of the Church.

◦§ 695. DANIELS, EDGAR F., and RAPIN, RENÉ. "Herbert's 'The Agonie.'" *Expl* 30:item 16.

Two separate replies that argue that the man mentioned in the second stanza of "The Agonie" is Christ, not David, as is suggested by B. P. Lamba and R. Jeet Lamba, entry 675.

◦§ 696. EL-GABALAWY, SAAD. "George Herbert and the *Ars Amatoria.*" *XUS* 10:28–33.

Suggests that some modern critics tend to overemphasize the impact of secular love poetry on Herbert's religious lyrics and that "to lay too much stress on it may lead us to disregard the spiritual and ethical connotations of the poet's tears, sighs and complaints, which are, in fact, an integral part of his religious sensibility" (pp. 32–33). Maintains that Herbert would probably have scorned the notion that he was indebted to the love poets and would have argued that "these poets had derived their style and devices from the Hebrew religion" (p. 29). Points out various amatory elements found in the psalms; in the works of St. Augustine, St. Bernard, St. Anselm, and St. Bonaventure; and in much medieval religious verse, all of which are more likely sources and models for Herbert than are the secular love poets.

⊷§ 697. ———. "A Seventeenth-Century Reading of George Herbert." *PLL* 7:159–67.

Suggests that the "Alphabeticall Table," a kind of subject index, composed by an anonymous compiler and found in the 1656 edition of *The Temple* and all subsequent editions up to 1709, provides "a window, or perhaps a loophole, however narrow, through which one may see how the poet was read by a seventeenth-century man attempting to guide the reader of his day" (p. 159). Shows that the index is important because "it classifies systematically some fundamental conceptions and motifs of the poet, provides a key to certain passages and poems, and suggests the age's understanding of *The Temple* as a whole" (p. 159). Maintains that the primary concern of the indexer was "to indicate the universal significance of *The Temple*" and that he "shows little interest in its poetry as a private statement expressing the author's individual experience" but rather sees *The Temple* "as an objective record of religious thought and feeling, valid for all Christians whatever their persuasions may be" (p. 167).

⊷§ 698. ERICSON, EDWARD E., JR. "The Holy Mr. Herbert." *Christianity Today* 15 (10 September):7–11.

Discusses Herbert as "one of the finest exemplars of wholeness and balance in the spiritual life; and as "the devotional poet par excellence" (p. 7). Maintains that, like St. Paul, Herbert recognizes the limitations of human reason and knowledge even though he is a very learned poet and writes poetry informed by learned images: "He felt no need to deny his mind in order to exercise his spirit" (p. 10). Argues that Herbert's devotion is not mindless emotionalism: "It is the quality of his intellect . . . that refines his devotion and makes his poetry, not a superficial emoting, but a power force for the promoting of truly spiritual living" (p. 11).

⊷§ 699. FENS, K. "Terzijde Liturgische teksten." *Streven* 24: 1068–73.

Uses Herbert's "The Holy Scriptures (II)" as an example of the proper attitude for a religious poet and takes to task the contemporary Dutch religious poets for their views. Ridicules the widespread notion in Holland that contemporary readers cannot understand Scripture and require that it be rewritten in a contemporary idiom, using modern imagery. Concludes his argument by quoting the first stanza of "Church-musick" and maintaining that, although the past is indeed past, the present makes a mistake by responding hostilely to it.

◄§ 700. FESTUGIÈRE, A. J., O. P. *George Herbert, poète, saint, anglican (1593–1633). Études de théologie et d'histoire de la spiritualité, 18.* Paris: Librarie philosophique J. Vrin. 349p.

Primarily sees Herbert as an Anglican saint and stresses the various religious influences on his sensibility and art, especially the influence of Calvinism and *The Imitation of Christ.* Says that *The Temple* "est l'*Imitation* mise en vers" (p. 11). Chapter 1, "Le cadre politique" (pp. 15–28), discusses the reigns of Elizabeth I, James I, and Charles II. Chapter 2, "Le cadre de la vie temporelle" (pp. 29–43), describes daily life in Herbert's time. Chapter 3, "Le cadre de la vie spirituelle" (pp. 45–145), is divided into three main sections: (1) "The Church-Porche" (pp. 45–62) presents a prose translation of the poem into French with commentary and concludes that the poem was written before 1627, (2) "Le Service Divin du Prayer Book et ses parallèles" (pp. 63–101) compares the Catholic Mass with the Anglican service and comments on the attitudes toward the Mass in Calvin's writings and in *The Imitation,* and (3) "Sources de la spiritualité de Herbert" (pp. 102–45) discusses the role of the sacraments in Herbert's spirituality and concludes, "Sa vie spirituelle n'est pas essentiellement sacramentelle" (p. 102). Also comments on the influence of *The Imitation* and the Prayer Book and outlines the relationship between Herbert and the Anglican Church, especially the influence of the liturgical year. Chapter 4, "Vie de George Herbert" (pp. 147–84). Chapter 5, "The Country Parson" (pp. 185–216), describes country life and parish life in Herbert's time and presents a French translation of parts of *The Country Parson.* Chapter 6, "Les crises spirituelles de George Herbert" (pp. 263–304), outlines Herbert's conversion, his obsession with sin, and his various spiritual vacillations, exemplified by translations of a number of Herbert's poems. Appendix 1, *Le Complete Gentleman* de Henry Peacham" (pp. 305–18), discusses the influence of Peacham on Herbert's work, especially on *The Country Parson.* Appendix 2, "L «Autobiographie» d'Edward, Lord Herbert of Cherbury" (pp. 319–35), points out certain parallels between the *Autobiography* and *The Church-Porch* and *The Country Parson.* Appendix 3, "Le yeoman anglais sous Élisabeth et Jacques Ier" (pp. 337–49), describes the yeomen of Herbert's parish, their social background, financial status, religious faith, etc.

◄§ 701. GARDNER, HELEN. "Religious Poetry." In *Religion and Literature,* pp. 121–94. New York: Oxford University Press.

Series of three lectures delivered at the University of California at Los Angeles in March 1966: (1) "Religious Poetry: A Definition" (pp. 121–

42), (2) "Secular and Divine Poetry" (pp. 143–70), and (3) "Seventeenth-Century Religious Poetry" (pp. 171–94). Herbert is mentioned only briefly in the first essay, which attempts to define the nature of religious poetry and to discuss various forms available to the religious poet at different periods. The third essay surveys English religious verse of the seventeenth century and attempts to account for the fact that this period, perhaps more than any other, was propitious for religious poetry. Denies the assumption that Herbert was greatly influenced by Donne: "There are very few even possible borrowings from Donne in Herbert's poetry and none that are unquestionable" (p. 173) and suggests that the most important bond among the religious poets of the time was the common religious tradition that they shared, especially the practice of discursive meditation. Contrasts Herbert's "The Sacrifice" with the late fifteenth-century "Woefully arrayed" (wrongly attributed to Skelton) and Herbert's "Dialogue" with the medieval "Quia Amore Langueo" to show the marked differences in the religious sensibilities and approaches of the two periods, especially commenting on Herbert's wit. Contrasts also Herbert's "Deniall" with Hopkins's sonnet "I wake and feel the fell of dark, not day" and briefly comments on "Redemption" and "Love (III)." Agrees with Huxley that the majority of Herbert's religious poems are poems of "inner weather." Suggests three things that make seventeenth-century religious poetry appeal to readers of various persuasions: (1) the "poems are made poems, not effusions of feeling" (p. 192); (2) the poetry is highly intellectual, "though full of feeling, emotion, strength of devotion and personal faith, [it] is laced by, and built upon, a scheme of thought, and a universe of discourse that is not the poet's own invention, but has the toughness of systems that have been debated and argued over for centuries" (p. 193); and (3) the poetry reflects "the unembarrassed boldness and naturalness with which these poets approach their subject, and the freedom with which they bring the experience of daily life, their experience of art, their native powers of mind, their skill in argument and their wit, to play over religious doctrine, religious experience, and religious imperative" (p. 193).

◄§ 702. GEORGE, ARAPARA G. "Metaphysical Poetry." In *Studies in Poetry*, pp. 37–59. New Delhi and London: Heinemann.
Handbook for students and the general reader. Contains a brief introduction to metaphysical poetry, especially to Donne's poems. Herbert is mentioned only in passing. Calls Herbert's poems "short lyrics full of pious aspirations and admirable pictures of nature" (p. 42).

◄§ 703. HERBERT, GEORGE. *Selected Poems of George Herbert*. Edited with an introduction, commentary, and notes by Gareth Reeves. Poetry Bookshelf. London: Heinemann Educational Books; New York: Barnes and Noble. ix, 171p.

Introduction (pp. 1–31); selective bibliography (p. 32); seventy-two poems selected from *The Temple* and from Walton's *Lives* (pp. 33–109); extracts from *The Country Parson* (pp. 110–18); commentary and notes (pp. 119–66); and index of titles and first lines of poems (pp. 167–71). The introduction contains a biographical sketch and presents a general discussion of the major characteristics of Herbert's art. Comments on the influences on his poetry, especially the Bible, and on the particular religious sensibility reflected in the poems. Detailed comments on "The Flower" as an example of Herbert's poetic technique and as it compares with Donne's "Loves growth." Also examines in some detail "The Collar," which is called "the supreme example of Herbert's powers of organization and perfection" (p. 29).

704. HOYLES, JOHN. *The Waning of the Renaissance, 1640–1740: Studies in the Thought and Poetry of Henry More, John Norris, and Isaac Watts.* International Archives of the History of Ideas, 39. The Hague: Martinus Nijhoff. xvii, 265p.
Briefly compares Herbert with John Norris (sometimes called "the last of the metaphysicals") and with Isaac Watts. Comments on *Select Hymnes taken out of Mr Herbert's Temple* (1697), a volume published by the Dissenters for private and family devotions. Suggests that this volume "must have helped crystallise the influence of Herbert into a tradition" (p. 215).

705. HUGHES, RICHARD E. "Metaphysical Poetry as Event." *HSL* 3:191–96.
Argues for the development of a "mythico-religious poetics" so that the twentieth-century reader might better understand and appreciate metaphysical poetry: "Writing in a time of anxiety amenable to myth; nurtured by a faith supportive of a sacramental response to reality; accepting the world as a panorama of symbol-saturated events rather than neuter objects: the poets of the earlier seventeenth century were involved in poem, myth and religious insight all at once" (p. 196). Mentions Herbert several times by way of illustration.

706. JOHNSON, LEE ANN. "The Relationship of 'The Church Militant' to *The Temple*." *SP* 68:200–206.
Surveys attempts of various modern critics to explain the exact relationship of *The Church Militant* to the total design of *The Temple* and finds all of them unconvincing. Maintains that the content and the formal and stylistic characteristics of *The Church Militant* and especially its positioning in the early folios suggest that it should be considered as a separate entity and not as an organic part of the three-part structure of *The Temple*.

⛛§ 707. KEAST, WILLIAM R., ed. *Seventeenth Century English Poetry: Modern Essays in Criticism*. Rev. ed. A Galaxy Book, 89. London, Oxford, New York: Oxford University Press. x, 489p.

First published in 1962 (see entry 480).

Collection of previously published essays. There are five general essays on metaphysical poetry: (1) Herbert J. C. Grierson, "Metaphysical Poetry." From *Metaphysical Lyrics & Poems of the Seventeenth Century: Donne to Butler* (entry 58), pp. xiii–xxxviii; (2) T. S. Eliot, "The Metaphysical Poets" (entry 56); (3) Helen Gardner, "The Metaphysical Poets." From *The Metaphysical Poets* (entry 400), pp. xix–xxxiv; (4) Earl Miner, "Wit: Definition and Dialectic." From *The Metaphysical Mode from Donne to Cowley* (entry 653), pp. 118–58; (5) Joseph Anthony Mazzeo, "A Critique of Some Modern Theories of Metaphysical Poetry" (entry 339). There are three items specifically on Herbert: (1) Joseph H. Summers, "The Poem as Hieroglyph." From *George Herbert: His Religion and Art* (entry 369), pp. 123–46; (2) Jeffrey Hart, "Herbert's *The Collar* Re-Read" (entry 456); and (3) Arnold Stein, "George Herbert: The Art of Plainness" (entry 630).

⛛§ 708. KUSUNOSE, TOSHIHIKO. "George Herbert." In *Shi to Shi-Donne o Meguru Shijin tachi* [*Poetry and Faith: Poets Surrounding Donne*], pp. 75–105. Tokyo: Keibunsha.

General biographical sketch that suggests, among other things, that Herbert's various illnesses and diseases are clearly reflected in the poems. Stresses the fact that Herbert is neither a mystic nor a nature poet but rather sees nature as God's second book of revelation. Comments on the tension between Herbert's sincere desire for simplicity and his rhetorical skill and the tension between the worldly and the sacred as reflected in his poetry. Discusses briefly the religious situation in England during the early seventeenth century and comments on Herbert's religious attitudes. Finds that the poems are characterized by a keen intellectual awareness and an equally fervent faith in God.

⛛§ 709. LEA, KATHLEEN. "The Poetic Powers of Repetition." *PBA* (for 1969) 55:51–76.

Discusses the variety, delicacy, and force of the rhetorical device of repetition in English poetry. Points out Herbert's skillful use of the device in "The Quip," "The Pearl," "The Bag," "Aaron," "Sinnes round," "Clasping of hands," "A Wreath," "Sighs and Grones," and "The Call."

⛛§ 710. MOLLENKOTT, VIRGINIA R. "Experimental Freedom in Herbert's Sonnets." *CSR* 1:109–16.

Disagrees with the idea that Herbert's use of the sonnet is characterized by an unexpected conservatism. Shows that "the sonnets are typical of Herbert's poetic output in their experimental freedom" (p. 116). Points out that they exhibit a broad range of subject matter and are highly innovative in technique. Discusses the technical aspects of "Love (I)," "The Holdfast," "Josephs coat," and "The Answer."

◄§ 711. ORGEL, STEPHEN. "Affecting the Metaphysics." In *Twentieth-Century Literature in Retrospect*, edited by Reuben A. Brower, pp. 225–45. Harvard English Studies, 2. Cambridge, Mass.: Harvard University Press.

Points out that the label *metaphysical* is largely the creation of critics, not of the poets themselves; yet "from the time 'metaphysical' was first formulated as a critical term its definition has remained relatively constant, but the list of poets whom critics regarded as metaphysical has varied wildly from generation to generation" (p. 226). Presents a brief history of the term and considers how a seventeenth-century reader would have regarded poetry such as Donne's. Shows that "no theory of metaphysical poetry has proved adequate" because " 'metaphysical' refers really not to poetry, but to our sensibilities in response to it" (p. 245). Discusses in particular Renaissance concepts of poetic images, especially emblems, stressing that even in emblem books the verbal element is basic: "Renaissance poets tended to think of images as tropes or rhetorical figures, that is, as verbal structures" whereas twentieth-century critics "think of them as *visual* structures" (p. 238). Concludes, "What we find as critics in works of art is largely determined by what we are looking for, and it is one of the functions of criticism to make us look again and again at works of art in ways that are valid but untried," but warns that "we must beware of taking our responses for historical data" (p. 245). Herbert is mentioned throughout by way of illustration.

◄§ 712. POWELL, W. ALLEN. "The Nature of George Herbert's audience as revealed by method and tone in 'The Country Parson' and 'The Temple.' " *CCTE* 36:33–36.

Maintains that the unsophisticated nature of his congregation at Bemerton influenced the method and tone of Herbert's sermons and that, therefore, he consciously avoided both theological controversy and the use of a witty and erudite style. Suggests that the reaction of Herbert's audience is revealed in the method and tone of many passages in *The Temple* and primarily in *The Country Parson*: "The simplicity and homeliness of style, the directness of tone, the diplomatic method of reprimanding all wrongdoing, and the uses of images which unmistakably present a spiritual truth all combine to depict the simple faith and devout spirit of George Herbert's humble audience" (p. 36).

⋙ 713. RAUBER, D. F. "Critics and Collars." *PCP* 6:50–54.

Reply to P. M. Levitt and K. G. Johnston, "Herbert's 'The Collar': A Nautical Metaphor," entry 648. Completely rejects the notion that nautical imagery is dominant in "The Collar" and argues that, in fact, "when we examine the actual operation of the nautical imagery as presented by Levitt and Johnston, we find that it distorts rather than clarifies, destroys rather than organizes" (p. 51). Calls such criticism free, loose, fragmentary, highly limiting, and inhibiting.

⋙ 714. TOLIVER, HAROLD E. "Poetry as Sacred Conveyance in Herbert and Marvell." In *Pastoral Forms and Attitudes*, pp. 116–50. Berkeley, Los Angeles, London: University of California Press.

Contrasts Herbert and Marvell as poets who employ poetry as a sacred conveyance for bringing God to man and man to God. Whereas Marvell typically employs persons, places, nature symbols, and specific historical events as the means for achieving this end, Herbert uses the Christian temple. Suggests that in *The Temple* the poet, the sinner, and the priest "approach communion [with God] in separate ways—through words, cleansing of the heart, and sacraments—but their methods often overlap and reinforce one another" (p. 116). Shows how each of these three "seeks conveyances to bring the mind to Christ and Christ into visible form where his Real Presence may be experienced" (p. 116). Discusses how Herbert transforms various secular forms and modes (the sonnet, the song, and the pastoral) into sacred conveyances and argues, "Discovery of an appropriate mode of praise depends upon the poem's receptivity to renewal; as for the sinner, capacity to render praise depends upon the heart's preparation for sanctification and for the priest, upon the validity of the rites he administers" (p. 118). But when "each of these conveyances succeed, Christ, the original of paradise, is rejoined to nature in them" (p. 118). Discusses the various means that Herbert employs to make "poetry an enclosed epitome of the world and an incarnation of paradise" and examines some of the "theoretical and practical matters that a concept of sacred poetic and pastoral enclosures involves" (p. 119).

⋙ 715. WEINBERGER, G. J. "George Herbert's 'The Church Militant.'" *ConnR* 4:49–57.

Argues that *The Church Militant* is not simply a continuation of the two preceding parts of *The Temple* but rather should be viewed as a companion poem to them. *The Church-Porch* is an exhortation to seek salvation; *The Church* records the individual's struggles for salvation; and *The Church Militant* "is the same record but is presented as mankind's progress towards salvation through the ages (i.e. historically)" (p. 49).

Suggests that the chief protagonist of *The Church Militant* is religion (the Church) and that the principal antagonist is sin. Presents a reading of the poem from this point of view and attempts to account for the differences between it and the two preceding parts of *The Temple*.

◄§ 716. WEST, MICHAEL. "Ecclesiastical Controversy in George Herbert's 'Peace.'" *RES* 22:445–51.

Rejects the notion that "Peace" is an allegory of human experience or of religious conversion and argues that "it draws upon thoroughly traditional symbolism to comment on ecclesiastical controversies of growing prominence in early seventeenth-century England" (p. 446). Suggests that stanza 1 attacks enthusiastic sects, especially the Seekers; stanza 2 is directed against the Puritans and the Congregationalists; stanza 3 challenges the Erastian position in the Anglican establishment; and the last four stanzas defend orthodoxy and serve as an invitation to participate in the Eucharist of the Anglican Church.

◄§ 717. WILLY, MARGARET, ed. *The Metaphysical Poets*. English Library. London: Edward Arnold; Columbia, S.C.: University of South Carolina Press. x, 149p.

An anthology of metaphysical poems that contains a general introduction to metaphysical poetry (pp. 1–11) and seven of Herbert's poems: "Affliction (I)," "The Collar," "The Flower," "The Pulley," "Man," "Redemption," and "Love (III)," with a brief critical introduction and explanatory notes for each (pp. 87–105). Selective bibliography.

1972

◄§ 718. BEER, PATRICIA. *An Introduction to the Metaphysical Poets*. London and Basingstoke: Macmillan Press; Totowa, N.J.: Rowman & Littlefield. 115p.

General introduction to metaphysical poetry designed primarily for students in their first year of reading for an English honors degree. Divided into seven chapters: (1) The Term "Metaphysical," (2) The Chief Characteristics of Metaphysical Poetry, (3) John Donne, (4) George Herbert, (5) Henry Vaughan, (6) Andrew Marvell, and (7) The Metaphysical Poets and the Twentieth Century. The chapter on Herbert (pp. 55–70) presents a brief biographical sketch, comments on general features of Herbert's poetry, and suggests ways that modern students might approach the poetry. Also gives a brief critical reading of "Redemption," "Jordan (I)," and "Death."

◄§ 719. BROWN, C. C., and INGOLDSBY, W. P. "George Herbert's 'Easter Wings.'" *HLQ* 35:131–42.

Presents a detailed reading of "Easter-wings," commenting on the artistic integrity of the complex, sophisticated, and precise symbolism of the two wing-shaped stanzas and arguing that the poem "will not yield its meaning unless one reads the visual shape as part of its carefully controlled symbolic language" (p. 131). Maintains that, although the general shape of the poem is Greek in origin, "the precise dimensions [are] Hebrew, so that in writing 'Easter Wings' Herbert opened for himself the problem of defining an attitude toward the pagan and Hebraic sources from which the wings drew some of their meaning" (p. 131). Points out how Herbert skillfully transformed his sources: Simmias's form in *The Greek Anthology*, various Old Testament types, and Plato's metaphor of the winged soul in the *Phaedrus*. Suggests that the primary and controlling text that stands behind the poem is the messianic text found in Mal. 4:2. Shows how the metrical and thematic decline and growth of the first stanza enact the fall of mankind and how the metrical and thematic decline and growth of the second stanza enact the speaker's personal experience. Argues that "Easter-wings" may be seen, in fact, as a model of the kind of precise artistic wholeness that Herbert strove for in all his poems.

◄§ 720. BRUMM, URSULA. "Edward Taylor and the Poetic Use of Religious Typology." In *Typology and Early American Literature*, edited by Sacvan Bercovitch, pp. 191–206. Amherst: University of Massachusetts Press.

Compares and contrasts Edward Taylor's and Herbert's uses of biblical typology in their poetry: "Herbert's case is indeed relevant: his use of typology, although often more disguised and more integrated esthetically, is comparable to Taylor's and can perhaps help us to a fuller exploration of the problem" (p. 193). Comments specifically on "The Agonie," "Whitsunday," and "The Bunch of Grapes."

◄§ 721. CARRIVE, LUCIEN. *La Poésie religieuse anglaise entre 1625 et 1640: Contributions à l'étude de la sensibilité religieuse à l'âge d'or de l'anglicanisme*. Vol. 1. Caen: Assoc. des Pubs. de la Faculté des Lettres et Sciences Humainies de l'Université de Caen. 546p.

Divided into four major sections. (1) "Les poètes religieux et la société" (pp. 15–49) discusses the social background of English religious poets from 1625 to 1640 and maintains that Herbert's poetry "ne se comprend pas si nous ne savons pas que le poète fut éminemment et jusqu'en ses dernières années un homme de cour" (p. 25). (2) "Les principales variétés" (pp. 53–259) comments on such matters as biblical imagery, paraphrases of the psalms, emblems, prayer, spiritual exercises, and mysticism and discusses Herbert's poetry in the light of each of these topics. States, "La plus doué des écrivains de ce temps et ce pays aussi bien par la ferveur de sa foi et l'intensité des sentiments qu'il avait de la présence de Dieu que par l'habileté à utiliser les ressources du style et de la prosodie, ce prêtre au tempéramment mystique, ce grand poète «métaphysique» qu'est George Herbert, se sent tenu lui aussi par cette idée de la prière" (p. 169). Nevertheless denies that Herbert is a mystic: "Pour Herbert, comme pour Luther, comme pour Bunyan, la paix et la joie ne viennent pas d'une illumination de la présence de Dieu, mais de la certitude du pardon et de l'amour gratuit de Dieu, cet amour qui ne met point de condition et ne fait pas acception de personne" (p. 248). Disagrees with Louis Martz concerning the dominance of the meditative mode in the period. (3) "Caractères de cette poésie" (pp. 263–339) discusses various intellectual and moral aspects of the poetry of the period in general and of Herbert's poetry in particular. Suggests that Herbert, strictly speaking, should perhaps not be considered a "metaphysical" poet: "Il préfère l'affirmation des vérités de sa foi à l'exploration, même poétique, des subtilités et des contradictions de sa doctrine" (p. 267). (4) "Dieu et ses exigences" (pp. 343–513) comments on various theological themes and attitudes reflected in the poetry of the period and specifically in Herbert's poetry: God, Christ, the Church, the sacraments, etc. Comments on the devotional aspects of the period and their shaping effects on the poets. Bibliography (pp. 515–30). Index.

◈§ 722. CHARLES, AMY. "The Williams Manuscript and *The Temple*." *RenP* (for 1971), pp. 59–77.
Doubts if anyone but Herbert can fully discern the exact reasons for the ordering of the poems in *The Temple*, "because, for one thing, they were not precise, but personal, intuitive, and allusive" (p. 60). Suggests that the Williams MS is "probably more important as a measure of Herbert's development than the more famous Bodleian Manuscript" (p. 59). Although the Williams MS contains less than half the poems in *The Temple*, it is important "for its earlier versions of many poems, the general three-part division, a scheme of order for the lyrics in 'The Church,' and Herbert's subsequent retention or rejection of some of its features" (p. 59). Compares the two manuscripts and finds the Williams "a skeletal version" of the Bodleian, with a number of significant variations, corrections, reorderings, and expansions. Shows that the final arrangement of the poems was thus carefully and subtly ordered by Herbert. Comments on how the Bodleian MS grew by accretions, points out that the title, *The Temple*, was probably added by Nicholas Ferrar, and comments on a number of individual revisions and changes. Concludes that at the time Herbert completed the Williams MS he was already an accomplished poet.

◈§ 723. CLARK, IRA. " 'Lord, in Thee the *Beauty* Lies in *Discovery*':
'Love Unknown' and Reading Herbert." *ELH* 39:560–84.
Maintains that Herbert is "a radically typological lyricist, whose poems are structured on personal neotypology" (p. 560). Argues that in many

of the poems of *The Church* Herbert creates a persona "who in contention against or in search of God discovers that he himself is a contemporary neotype of Christ akin to Old Testament types of Christ" (p. 560), that during the dramatic lyric the persona "discovers the beauty of God through situations Herbert has devised out of Christian recovery of types," and that thus the reader "reads through Herbert's persona and typological settings to discover the beauty of God" (p. 561). Presents a detailed reading of "Love unknown" as a model to demonstrate this technique and shows how Herbert typically "teaches us to read typological situations, emblems, and diction; his symbolic matrices in *The Church*; his local poetic structure" (p. 583). Sees "Love unknown" as Herbert's version of Psalm 51.

◆§ 724. DALY, PETER M. "Trends and Problems in the Study of Emblematic Literature." *Mosaic* 5:53–68.

Detailed discussion of the present state of scholarship in the study of emblematic literature, its major trends, and some of the remaining problems. Challenges certain assumptions in Rosemary Freeman's *English Emblem Books* (entry 284), especially her notion that "there is 'no necessary likeness' between an emblem image and its meaning" (pp. 56, 59). Brief references to Herbert.

◆§ 725. DESSNER, LAWRENCE J. "A Reading of George Herbert's 'Man.'" *CP* 5, no. 1:61–63.

Disagrees with those critics who see "Man" as one of Herbert's "expository and declaratory poems of praise" and argues that the poem is, in fact, "a dramatic monologue whose speaker's praise of God is criticized by the verbal actions of the poet" (p. 61). Suggests that the speaker's "faulty logic and the poem's diction expose him as one who has lost sight of *his* duty to that other 'world' which awaits *for* him, in exclusive contemplation of the world of Nature which waits *on* him" (p. 63). Comments on how the rhyme scheme and other technical features reinforce the meaning of the poem.

◆§ 726. DUNDAS, JUDITH. "Levity and Grace: The Poetry of Sacred Wit." *YES* 2:93–102.

Discusses the various inherent oppositions between wit and faith, attempts to identify those particular qualities "which distinguish poems that successfully marry wit and faith from those that merely yoke them together," and suggests "the possible form that sacred wit may take in poetry today" (p. 93). Argues that the tension between wit and faith "can be the very source of power in a poem by polarizing these opposites and then voluntarily sacrificing the cleverness of wit to the divine simplicity" (p. 96). Contrasts Christopher Harvey and Herbert in order to distinguish between true and false sacred wit. Comments specifically on

"Prayer (I)" and sees the poem as "a good example of sacred wit in its incongruities, its far-fetched metaphors, both conventional and novel, which are nevertheless controlled both formally and emotionally" (p. 97).

⊷§ 727. EL-GABALAWY, SAAD. "George Herbert's Christian Sensibility: A Resumé by El-Gabalawy." *Cithara* 11:16–22.

Shows how completely Herbert's literary insights and art are informed by Christian doctrine and his sensibility permeated by Christian values and awareness. Maintains that to understand the subtlety and uniqueness of Herbert's art it is essential "to see his deeply-rooted affinities with the Christian tradition" (p. 21). Points out that, although Herbert's ideas are not original, he has the "enormous ability to 'make new' the traditional material which is common to all" and to reshape "the shared and known so that it acquires the uniqueness and freshness of a new revelation never known before" (p. 21).

⊷§ 728. ENDE, FREDERICK VON. "George Herbert's 'The Sonne': In Defense of the English Language." *SEL* 12:173–82.

Argues that, although "The Sonne" may be seen as a celebration of Christ's resurrection, it "is more than just another religious lyric honoring Christ: it is an assertion and a demonstration, in a concentrated classical oration form, of the capacity and the adequacy of the English tongue for glorifying the Son of God" and, by extension, is in fact "a defense of the English language" (p. 173). Shows that Herbert's proof of the adequacy of the English language rests primarily on the *sun-son* homonym in the poem, a traditional Christian image and a conventional pun in Renaissance poetry. Suggests that lines 1–3 closely approximate the *exordium* and *narratio* of classical oration; line 4 is the *propositio*; lines 5–6 are the *partito*; lines 7–10 are the *confirmatio* and explain the many meanings of the *sun-son* homonym; and lines 11–14 approximate the *peroratio*, "applying the combined meanings of the *sun-son* to the Son of God and in so doing suggesting that any language which could say so much about both the humility and the glory of Christ in a single word could hardly be judged inadequate" (p. 173).

⊷§ 729. FISH, STANLEY E. "Letting Go: The Dialectic of the Self in Herbert's Poetry." In *Self-Consuming Artifacts: The Experience of Seventeenth-Century Literature*, pp. 156–223. Berkeley, Los Angeles, London: University of California Press.

Paperback ed., 1974.

Much expanded version of "Letting Go: The Reader in Herbert's Poetry," entry 668. Maintains that Herbert's is "a poetics of tension, reflecting a continuing dialectic between an egocentric vision which believes in, and is sustained by, the distinctions it creates, and the relentless pressure of a *resolving* and *dissolving* insight" (p. 157). Tries to show how

Herbert actually writes himself out of his poems and thus makes his poems a gift from God, not a gift to God. Argues that Herbert's poems "perform what they require of us, for as they undermine our reliance on discursive forms of thought, and urge us to rest in the immediate apprehension of God's all-effective omnipresence, they become the vehicles of their own abandonment" (p. 158). Thus, to read Herbert is "to experience the dissolution of the distinctions by which all other things are" (p. 158). Illustrates this concept by commenting on many more poems than in the earlier version. Discusses in some detail "The Temper (I)," "Even-song," "Church-monuments," "Sepulchre," "The Holdfast," "The Pearl," "Miserie," "The Thanksgiving," "The Crosse," "The Elixir," "Love (I) and (II)," "Jordan (I) and (II)," "A true Hymne," "Coloss. iii.3," "The Altar," "The Forerunners," and the two sonnets written to Herbert's mother.

730. FISHER, WILLIAM N. "*Occupatio* in Sixteenth- and Seventeenth-Century Verse." *TSLL* 14:203–22.

Discusses the rhetorical figure of *occupatio* (affirmation through denial) in various sixteenth- and seventeenth-century poems, "attempting to discover the essence of the figure, its thrust and its effects, the way it acts out a particular kind of felt experiential truth" (p. 207). Points out Herbert's use of *occupatio* in "Jordan (I)," "a poem that denies poetry the ability to say effectively what the poet wishes to say: 'My God, My King'" (p. 216). Of course, by denying that poetry is adequate, "the poet affirms, along with his extralogical, extraverbal meaning, the poem itself, for he weaves his compact phrase into the poetic structure even as he denies its poetic efficacy" (p. 216). Comments also on Herbert's subtle uses of *occupatio* in "A Wreath," in which the poet denies that his poem, "the poore wreathe," can succeed in praising God, yet the poem does praise God "because, while the wreath contains and restricts and the word 'wreath' is contained and restricted within the poem, the poem and its poet do not presume to be more than they can be"; thus "it is possible that the poet may, with grace, someday be able 'to give thee a crown of praise': and with this awareness of the contingencies on that possibility, the poet can already bestow praise, as poor as it is" (p. 219).

731. FREER, COBURN. *Music for a King: George Herbert's Style and the Metrical Psalms.* Baltimore and London: Johns Hopkins University Press. xiv, 252p.

Discusses the various affinities in both form and matter between Herbert's lyrics and the versified translations of the psalms. Chapter 1, "Introduction" (pp. 1–49), argues that the metrical psalms "offer helpful guides for reading a poet like Herbert who is concerned with religious praise and lament, expressed simultaneously through technical brilliance and homeliness" (p. 8); that by studying Herbert's relation to the versified psalms one can better understand "the role of humility in Herbert's religious thought and poetic" (p. 5); and that Herbert is inclined to "use the low style and offer (often by means of the high style) a critique of its poetic and its defense of poetic crudity in the translation of spiritual impulse" (p. 46). Presents a brief history of the development of the versified English translations of the psalms. Chapter 2, "Some Metrical Psalm Styles" (pp. 50–115), surveys and comments on various metrical psalm styles in Wyatt, the old version of the psalms (Sternhold and Hopkins, et al.), Sidney and the Countess of Pembroke, and George Wither. Chapter 3, "Orchestral Form" (pp. 116–93), discusses how Herbert's metrical structures, stanza forms, and patterns of sound and syntax "become integral parts of his poetic meaning" (p. 116), claiming that there is "an especially articulate orchestration in the way Herbert uses themes and conventions of the metrical psalm" (p. 116). Chapter 4, "Tentative Form" (pp. 194–241), argues that by studying Herbert's use of metrical psalm techniques one can see that "there is sometimes a discrepancy between the way a Herbert poem behaves and the way it says it behaves" (p. 194). For instance, the literal sense of a poem "may be assertive while the form is hesitant; or the sense may be uncertain and the form suggest an answer" (p. 194). Illustrates this concept by a detailed discussion of a number of individual poems, especially "The Collar," "Praise (II)," "Justice (II)," "Longing," "The Banquet," "Affliction (I)," "The Flower," "The Familie," "Vertue," "The Quidditie," and the two Jordan poems. Chapter 5, "Epilogue" (pp. 242–45), reemphasizes the notion that the psalm style "is not an ornamental trim with Herbert, much less a glue or adhesive; it is part of his character, his 'real' character and his poetic character" (p. 243). Index.

⤳§ 732. HILL, D. M. "Allusion and Meaning in Herbert's *Jordan I*." *Neophil* 56:344–52.

Argues that an informed response to "Jordan (I)" consists of two states: (1) initially the reader is encouraged to see the apparent simplicity and affirmative nature of the poem's argument, and (2) as the reader becomes progressively more aware of the many complex ambiguities, ambivalences, paradoxes, and allusions in the poem, he is asked to reevaluate and qualify his initial response. Maintains that these two states "exist together, in a manner which seems to represent a condition of mind recurring whenever Herbert meditated upon his art and its relationship to his religion, the simple surface argument representing a wished-for clarity and confidence of response, the unfolding intricacies and ambiguities then gradually vying with one another for more and more attention" (p. 351). Presents a detailed reading of the poem to demonstrate this theory and comments in some detail on the various subtle allusions to Plato's *Republic* contained in the poem. Concludes that "Jordan (I)" "is much more a portrayal of mind than an argument," a poem in which Herbert through his art reveals "all the contradictory detail of his inner being" (p. 351).

◄§ 733. HOLLANDER, JOHN. "The Poem in the Eye." *Shenandoah* 23, no. 3:3–32.

Discusses the importance and intricacies of the visual aspects of poetry and comments on the picturelike properties of much poetry. Discusses briefly the *technopaignia* (shaped verse) of Alexandrine poetry and comments on various Renaissance imitators and critics of the practice. Calls Herbert's "Easter-wings" "the most remarkable instance of sophisticated shaping in the seventeenth century" (p. 9), a poem that, even more than "The Altar," "seems to create the pattern of its picture, rather than being forced into shape by it" (p. 9). Comments briefly also on certain modern poets who employ shaped verse, notably Apollinaire, Dylan Thomas, Gregory Corso, and May Swenson.

◄§ 734. LEACH, ELSIE. "T. S. Eliot and the School of Donne." *Costerus* 3:163–80.

Summarizes the shifts in Eliot's critical position toward the metaphysical poets and argues that "the changing emphases of Eliot's criticism parallel developments in his own verse" (p. 163). Points out that "in nearly everything Eliot writes about Herbert he explains the poetry by reference to the personality of the poet" (p. 164). Shows how Eliot evidences an increasing enthusiasm for Herbert as his interest in Donne, Marvell, and Crashaw decreases: from 1931 on, Eliot's "evaluation of Donne is much less enthusiastic than earlier, and his evaluation of Herbert is more favorable" (p. 177). Summarizes Eliot's various critical comments on Herbert and accounts for his shifting attitudes. Notes that Eliot's study of Herbert for the British Council's Writers and Their Works Series (entry 477) is the longest essay he wrote on a single metaphysical poet.

◄§ 735. LEITCH, VINCENT B. "Herbert's Influence in Dylan Thomas's 'I See the Boys of Summer.'" *N&Q*, n.s. 19:341.

Points out a number of parallels between Herbert's "The Search" and Dylan Thomas's "I See the Boys of Summer," especially the image of the "kissing poles."

◄§ 736. LOW, ANTHONY. "Herbert's 'Jordan (I)' and the Court Masque." *Criticism* 14:109–18.

Argues that "Jordan (I)" is directed against court poetry (which would include much love poetry), and especially against the court masques of the Stuarts, those who wrote them, and the way of life that they represent" (p. 109). Presents a detailed reading of the poem to show that many of its difficulties, especially the ending, can be solved if it is read as an anticourt poem. Suggests that Herbert parodies or imitates the court masque in the poem and writes, in effect, "in miniature, a divine masque, designed as a compliment to God the King as the court masque compliments His human shadow" and that at the same time the poem is "a reduction of the courtly compliment from an elaborate masque and from fulsome flattery to a simple and direct statement of loyalty to God and to King" (p. 118).

◄§ 737. MARTIN, F. DAVID. "Literature and Immanent Recall." In *Art and the Religious Experience: The "Language" of the Sacred*, pp. 183–227. Lewisburg, Pa.: Bucknell University Press.

Briefly comments on "The Altar" and suggests that, although shaped verse has now fallen into general disuse, there is a revival of sorts in "concrete poetry."

◄§ 738. MOLESWORTH, CHARLES. "Herbert's 'The Elixir': Revision Towards Action." *CP* 5, no. 2:12–20.

Compares the two versions of "The Elixir" and discusses Herbert's changes in order to show that he "was more than a careful craftsman, or, rather that his care in craftmanship was matched by a deepened sense of the mystery of the Incarnation" (p. 19). Points out that through the rearrangement of stanzas, the development of thought, the subtle shifts in tone and figurative language, certain verbal substitutions, etc., Herbert fundamentally changes the whole emphasis and meaning of the poem: "The first states that man by adopting God's 'Light' dignifies his actions, but they still remain, in the context of the poem, fundamentally human actions. The later version speaks of a *transformation* (the stone 'turneth all to gold') and the actions themselves partake of the divine nature" (p. 13).

◄§ 739. MOLLENKOTT, VIRGINIA R. "George Herbert's Epithet-Sonnet." *Genre* 5:131–37.

Categorizes various kinds of sonnets on the basis of their mode of presentation or their controlling technique and comments in particular on the epithet-sonnet, "which defines and clarifies its subject by means of a series of brief descriptive phrases" (pp. 131–32). Presents a close reading of "The H. Scriptures (I)" and "Prayer (I)" as sacred parodies of the Elizabethan epithet-sonnets, especially those of such poets as Sidney, Constable, Daniel, and Bartholomew Griffin.

◄§ 740. MURAOKA, ISAMU. "Shakespeare and George Herbert." *ShStud* 11 (1972–1973):37–59.

Maintains that Herbert borrowed a number of images, especially simple and homely images of everyday and domestic life, from Shakespeare and attempts to account for this influence. Suggests that in part Herbert was consciously trying to displace the profane with the sacred and comments briefly on the influence of Dionysius the Areopagite on Herbert's attitude toward imagery and symbolism. Cites a number of possible specific borrowings.

◄§ 741. PARFITT, GEORGE A. E. "Donne, Herbert and the Matter of Schools." *EIC* 22:381–95.

While recognizing the influence of Donne on Herbert, especially on certain of Herbert's best poems, the author distrusts the label *School of Donne* and argues that it "conceals more than it reveals" (p. 395). Contrasts Herbert and Donne as religious poets and sees Donne primarily as "the great religious poet of self-dramatization" (p. 382), who objectifies his experience in order to come to a personal understanding of his relationship to God and who projects in his poetry a great lack of confidence and sense of uncertainty in his belief. States, "Donne is better as a poet of individual faith and doubt than as a celebrator of the communion of Christian belief and of the great occasions of the life of the Church" (p. 386). Herbert, on the other hand, has a much stronger sense of the public function of his poetry and works diligently to communicate with his audience. Concludes, therefore, that Herbert's poems are less egocentric than Donne's, less imbued with doubt and rebellion; Herbert sees his own experience as analogous to that of all Christians.

◄§ 742. PARKS, EDNA D. *Early English Hymns: An Index.* Metuchen, N.J.: Scarecrow Press. viii, 168p.

Presents an index of early English hymns, in part to challenge the assumption that English hymn writing dates from Isaac Watts (1674–1748). Includes much religious poetry of the seventeenth century, since "much which was suitable was soon adapted and joined with a tune" (p. iv), even though it was not originally designed for congregational singing. Poems that were never set to music are also included if they conform to the definition of the hymn. Arranges the hymns in alphabetical order by first line and also presents (1) the meter, (2) the number of lines or stanzas in the earliest publication of the poem, (3) the name of the author, (4) date of publication and page or line numbers where the hymn can be found, and, when possible, (5) information about the tune and composer. Lists sixty-eight items for Herbert. Contains a bibliography (pp. 143–54), author index (pp. 155–62), composer index (pp. 163–65), and tune index (pp. 166–68).

◄§ 743. PATRIDES, C. A. *The Great Design of God: The Literary Form of the Christian View of History.* London: Routledge & Kegan Paul; Toronto: University of Toronto Press. xvii, 157p.

Much amplified version of the author's earlier study, *The Phoenix and the Ladder: The Rise and Decline of the Christian View of History* (Berkeley, Los Angeles, London: University of California Press, 1964). Comments briefly on the influence that the Christian view of history had on the structure of Herbert's "The Collar," claiming that the poem "compresses within its thirty-six lines the broad circumference of the traditional vision of history" (p. 82).

◄§ 744. SANDLER, FLORENCE. " 'Solomon vbique regnat': Herbert's Uses of the Images of the New Covenant." *PLL* 8:147–58.

Maintains that, although most critics recognize the importance in *The Temple* of the New Testament notion that the functions of the Temple on Mount Sion have been replaced by the human heart, it has not been generally recognized that Herbert's images of the New Covenant fall consistently into three major categories—the temple, the altar, and the tablets of the Law—and that these categories correspond to the three traditional offices or roles of Christ—king, priest, and prophet. In the first category Christ is seen as taking up his abode in the temple or the palace of the human heart and conquering his enemies. In the second, the heart is seen as the altar upon which Christ exercises his priestly sacrifice. In the third, the heart is seen as the tablet upon which Christ as prophet inscribes the New Law. Maintains that Herbert's uses of New Testament typology are precise and consistent, that his typology is particularly Pauline, and that his concepts are consistent with Reformation teaching and reflect his own comments in *Briefe Notes on Valdesso's "Considerations."*

◄§ 745. STEADMAN, JOHN M. "Herbert's Platonic Lapidary: A Note on 'The Foil.' " *SCN* 30:59–62.

Maintains that "The Foil" is an intricate and complex poem that "combines Platonic and Christian allusions into a lapidary meditation on a variety of traditional themes: the contrast between visible and invisible beauty and sensuous and intellectual vision, the dignity and misery of man, the antithesis between the splendor of virtue and the foulness of sin, and perhaps . . . on the contrast between the church and the world and the problem of the priest in persuading men to virtue by concrete examples or similitudes that they can see and understand" (p. 59). Presents a detailed reading of the poem, commenting particularly on its rhetorical aspects, its Platonic and Christian allusions, and its central conceit of the jeweler's foil.

◄§ 746. WARNKE, FRANK J. *Versions of the Baroque: European Literature in the Seventeenth Century*. New Haven and London: Yale University Press. xi, 229p.

Uses the term *baroque* "to denote not a precisely definable style but a period complex made up of a whole cluster of more or less related styles—a complex which in its earlier phases (approximately 1580–1610), contains significant survivals of the preceding complex, or period style (i.e. the Renaissance), and, in its later phase (approximately 1650–90), anticipations of the subsequent complex (i.e. Neoclassicism)" (pp. 1–2). Maintains that a "literary period cannot be conceived of as a time span populated by authors expressing themselves in virtually identical styles, style itself being too individual a phenomenon to allow for such a conception. A literary period is, rather, a time span in which underlying shared spiritual preoccupations find expression in a variety of stylistic and thematic emphases" (p. 9). Isolates a number of emphases, preoccupations, and topoi of baroque literature in nine chapters: "Terms and Concepts," "Appearances and Reality," "The Experience of Contradiction," "The World as Theatre," "Art as Play," "Metaphysical and Meditative Devotion," "The Baroque Epic," "The Sacrificial Hero," and "The End of the World." The baroque characteristics of Herbert's art and sensibility are mentioned throughout. Chapter 5, "Art as Play" (pp. 90–129), discusses the playful spirit of much baroque literature. Specifically cites *The Temple* as a prime example of the play-aesthetic and suggests that many modern critics fail "to recognize just how funny much of the poetry is, and just how necessary an appreciation of its funniness is to an appreciation of its profound, personality-transforming seriousness" (p. 94). Specifically comments on the play-element in "The Collar," "Deniall," "Trinitie Sunday," "The Forerunners," and the shaped or pattern poems. Praises Herbert's wit and "his tricks with language": "his volume becomes, from one point of view, an offering like that of the jongleur of Notre Dame" (p. 96). Chapter 6, "Metaphysical and Meditative Devotion" (pp. 130–57), deals with the baroque religious and devotional lyric, both English and Continental. Outlines some of the major characteristics of the baroque devotional lyric, such as its private versus its public voice; its blend of levity and seriousness; its uses of sacred parody; its complex uses of paradox; its highly dramatic elements; its uses of a persona, specific setting, and implied audience; its capacity to simultaneously express individual emotion and complex thought; etc. Relates many of these characteristics to the art of discursive meditation and suggests reasons for the decline of baroque sensibility during the last half of the seventeenth century.

⋙§ 747. Waswo, Richard. "The True Believer." In *The Fatal Mirror: Themes and Techniques in the Poetry of Fulke Greville*, pp. 109–54. Charlottesville: University of Virginia Press.

Contrasts Herbert and Greville. Presents an analysis of "Love (III)" to illustrate Herbert's religious sensibility and poetic technique and contrasts the poem with Greville's sonnet 99, suggesting that the main difference between the two is Herbert's superior control and discipline, "the limitations of the possible connotation of the vehicle as such, the refusal to allow it to run away with the poem" (p. 140). Comments on Herbert's uses of dramatic narrative structure, simple diction, concrete and homely dialogue and metaphors, intimate tone, and extension of metaphors, all of which serve a precise theological function. Briefly contrasts Herbert's "Sinne (II)" with Greville's sonnet 100.

◄§ 748. YODER, R. A. "Toward the 'Titmouse Dimension': The Development of Emerson's Poetic Style." PMLA 87:255–70.

Comments on Herbert's influence on Emerson's poetic development, pointing out that Herbert provided Emerson with a model "not merely for simplicity of speech and imagery, but for combining simplicity with architectonic skill, with the concentrated and integrated organization that distinguishes the seventeenth-century meditative style" (p. 256). Points out that from Herbert and his contemporaries Emerson also learned "the art of 'neatness': the way to structure a poem on a single metaphor or situation . . . ; the smoothness of tone and rhythm, conventional but always melodic, never jagged but sufficiently pointed and varied to gain the quality of speech" (p. 257). Points out Emerson's borrowings from "Sinne" in "Grace," and from "The Elixir" in "Art," as well as noting the influence of "Man" on Nature.

1973

◄§ 749. ALLISON, A. F. Four Metaphysical Poets: George Herbert, Richard Crashaw, Henry Vaughan, Andrew Marvell: A Bibliographical Catalogue of the Early Editions of their Poetry and Prose (To the end of the 17th Century). Pall Mall Bibliographies, no. 3. Folkestone & London: Dawsons of Pall Mall. 134p.

Brief biographical sketch of Herbert and a chronological listing of the publication of Herbert's works to 1700 (pp. 13–14). Presents a bibliographical description of every separate edition and issue of Herbert's poetry and prose to 1700 (pp. 14–23). Reproduces facsimiles of each title page, which are keyed to the entries (pp. 61–85). Contains an index of printers and publishers, also keyed to the entries (pp. 133–34).

◄§ 750. ASALS, HEATHER. "The Tetragrammaton in The Temple." SCN 31:48–50.

Comments on the various forms of, and explicit references to, the Name of God in The Temple. Points out that from Old Testament times onward the Name of God was seen as a symbol and as an expression of God's very essence, not simply as a referent. Discusses how Herbert was aware of these subtleties in his precise use of God's name in The Church, defining and redefining his relationship with God by using various traditional forms of God's name.

◦§ 751. CHOSSONNERY, PAUL. "Les 'poèmes figurés' de George Herbert et ses prétendues fantaisies poétiques." *EA* 26:1–11.

Defends Herbert's shaped poems and uses of verbal ingenuity and reviews selected negative criticism of Herbert's practice by Hobbes, Dryden, Addison, Cowper, Coleridge, George Herbert Palmer, and Margaret Bottrall. Maintains that such displays of ingenuity and play are not fantastic nor mere virtuosity but are closely related to meaning: "Il y a une irréductible incompatibilité entre l'idée de fantaisie débridée et ce que nous savons du poète, de son caractère et de sa conception de la poésie" (p. 4). Challenges Joseph H. Summers's use of the term *hieroglyph* in describing Herbert's poetry and faults Summers for not noting important distinctions between much contemporary practice and Herbert's uses of shaped verse and verbal wit. Suggests that Herbert's uses of these devices reflect a theory of knowledge that was current at that time and maintained that man learns through the senses: "Ce que les critiques, depuis le milieu du XVIIᵉ siècle, ont pris pour un exemple du mauvais goût chez un poète de la Renaissance, pour une simple ingéniosité ou une recherche de la difficulté à seule fin de la surmonter, n'était donc, dans son esprit, que le moyen d'expression le plus direct qu'il avait pu trouver, puisqu'il appliquait tout bonnement la théorie de la connaissance de son temps" (p. 8).

◦§ 752. CLEMENTS, A. L. "Theme, Tone, and Tradition in George Herbert's Poetry." *ELR* 3:264–83.

In the light of disagreement among various critics concerning Herbert's mysticism, the author reexamines the meditative and contemplative elements and traditions that inform Herbert's poetry. Presents a detailed reading of "Artillerie" and then attempts "to relate this and other Herbert poems to the curiously well integrated and great speculative tradition of late medieval Christian mysticism" (p. 265). Recognizes the influence of Scupoli's *Spiritual Combat* in "Artillerie" but suggests that the radical difference in tone between Herbert's poem and Scupoli's treatise "signalizes the spiritual distance or progress between the early or meditative stages of the religious life and Herbert's own attainment of more advanced or contemplative stages" (p. 273). Accounts for the difference in tone by considering the late medieval contemplative concept of man's two-fold self, of "the phenomenal or finite ego, of which he is mainly conscious and which he tends mistakenly to regard as his true self, and an infinite and hence not wholly definable self, the inward man or image of divinity in him" (p. 275). Argues that *The Temple* "may very well be regarded as a various record of many spiritual conflicts, griefs, and joys, coordinated and made more coherent by the central theme of submission to God's will, particularly if this submission is understood as the major means for effecting the glorious changing of the fallen Adam into the Son of God" (p. 275).

Discusses this theme in such poems as "The Altar," "Love (III)," "Clasping of hands," "The Quip," "The Temper (I) and (II)," "Love (II)," "The Search," "Grief," "The Crosse," and "The Flower."

◄§ 753. COLIE, ROSALIE L. "Small Forms: *Multo in Parvo.*" In *The Resources of Kind: Genre-Theory in the Renaissance,* edited by Barbara K. Lewalski, pp. 32–75. Berkeley, Los Angeles, London: University of California Press.

Comments on the influence of emblem literature and the emblematic technique on Herbert's poetry. Maintains that, in spite of certain recognizable groups of poems in *The Temple,* the book as a whole "resists schemes to organize it into a consistent structure, although scholars have tried to fit it to one or another Procrustean bed" (pp. 51–52). Suggests, however, that as a whole *The Temple* has a major emblematic subtheme: "The collection is, among other things, a 'school of the heart' much like continental devotional emblem books" (pp. 53, 57). Comments on the various heart images and concludes, "The true temple of God is not a temple, but the human heart—for all its architectural poems, Herbert's book *The Temple* is written out of and for that metaphor: it is a school for the heart, teaching it to become a temple fit for God's dwelling" (p. 67).

◄§ 754. EAKER, J. GORDON. "The Spirit of Seventeenth-Century Anglicanism." *SCB* 33:194–96.

Comments on some of the beliefs and on the emerging spirit of seventeenth-century Anglicanism as they are reflected in the literature of the period and maintains that the "literary divines illustrate how the Anglican Church of the seventeenth century, by its 'gentle authority,' cultivated spiritual freedom in its adherents, never compelling, always persuading" (p. 196). Calls Herbert "the finest poet of the Church of England" (p. 195) and surveys some of his major ethical and moral beliefs as they appear in *A Priest to the Temple* and in *The Temple,* especially in *The Church-Porch.*

◄§ 755. EL-GABALAWY, SAAD. "George Herbert: The Preacher Poet." *N&Q,* n.s. 20:165.

Points out that lines 5–6 of *The Church-Porch,* in which Herbert asserts that the aims of poetry and preaching are the same, were frequently quoted in the seventeenth century by various writers of commendatory and devotional verse. Notes in particular Benlowes's *Theophilia* (1652), Thomas Washbourne's *Divine Poems* (1654), John Rawlet's *Poetick Miscellanies* (1687), Samuel Speed's *Prison Pietie: Or, Meditations Divine and Moral* (1677), Henry Delaune's *Patrikon doron. Or, a legacy to his sons* (1651), John Flavell's *Husbandry Spiritualized* (1669), and Edward Sparke's *Scintilla Altaris* (1660). Concludes that all of these writers, like Herbert, see a basic relationship between the didactic function of poetry and preaching and that they "apparently regard Herbert as a great model of the poet preacher using his art as a means of persuasion and 'delightful instruction.'"

◄§ 756. HEDGES, JAMES L. "Thomas Adams, Robert Burton, and Herbert's 'The Collar.'" *SCN* 31:47–48.

Comments on the proverbial nature of Herbert's phrase *rope of sands* in "The Collar." Tilley in his *Dictionary of Proverbs* (entry R174) traces it back through Jacobean drama and Bacon's commentaries to Erasmus's *Adagia*. Points out two other contemporary references: (1) Burton uses it in the 1624 edition of *The Anatomy of Melancholy* to describe a kind of melancholy arising from vain curiosity and to suggest needless industry about unprofitable things, and (2) Thomas Adams in 1625 refers to "a rope of sand" in his gloss on Jer. 5:22, stating that sand binds the sea (described as a "roaring monster"). Suggests that, although Adams's comment was not published until 1633 in his *Commentary on Second Peter*, Herbert "may well have known the verse in Jeremiah as possible gloss on the proverb" (p. 48).

◄§ 757. HERBERT, GEORGE. *George Herbert: Selected by W. H. Auden.* Poet to Poet Series. Harmondsworth, Eng.: Penguin Books; Baltimore: Penguin Books. 134p.

Brief biographical and critical introduction to Herbert (pp. 7–13) by W. H. Auden. Says that the two poets he would most like to have known are William Barnes and George Herbert. Maintains, "Since all of Herbert's poems are concerned with religious life, they cannot be judged by aesthetic standards alone" (p. 9). Calls Herbert's poetry "the counterpart of Jeremy Taylor's prose: together they are the finest expression we have of Anglican piety at its best" (p. 10). Comments on Herbert's religious sensibility and praises his poetry for its clever uses of antithesis and wit, its directness and ingenuity, and its technical excellence in securing musical effects. Suggests that "Prayer (I)" "seems to foreshadow Mallarmé" (p. 12). Selections from *The Temple* (pp. 15–126), from *A Priest to the Temple* (pp. 127–31), and from a letter to Mrs. Herbert (29 May 1622) from Walton's *Life*.

◄§ 758. JONES, ROGER STEPHENS. "Herbert's 'Vertue.'" *AWR* 22:116–23.

Reviews various critics on "Vertue" and concludes that the poem is "far more complex than any of the critics have imagined" (p. 121). Presents a detailed reading of the poem and calls it an "extremely ascetic statement of Christian truth" (p. 122). Argues that those critics "who view the first three stanzas as a wistful and beautiful lament for the passing of earthly glory are grossly mistaken and have fallen victim to

Herbert's deliberate deception of the reader" (p. 122). Herbert's uses of the lyric form, the refrain, and conventional carpe diem images "are all literary devices which lure the reader into a sensuous and sentimental attitude towards the mutability of earthly beauty" (p. 122), but because of the puns and the various kinds of wordplay the reader comes to recognize this aesthetic deception.

✎§ 759. KRANZ, GISBERT. "Beziehungen zwischen Malerei und Dichtung." In *Das Bildgedicht in Europa: Zur Theorie und Geschichte einer literarischen Gattung*, pp. 19–41. Paderborn, W. Ger.: Schöningh.

Historical and critical survey of the shaped poem with a brief discussion of Herbert's "Easter-wings" (with a German translation of the poem).

✎§ 760. LAWLER, THOMAS M. C. "Fruitful Business: Medieval and Renaissance Elements in the Devotional Method of St. John Fisher." *M&H* 4:145–59.

Analyzes the structure and religious sensibility of St. John Fisher's meditations and comments on "some possible sources which illustrate the continuity between medieval and Renaissance elements in his devotional method" (p. 145). Points out various parallels between the devotional method of Fisher and Herbert's *The Temple* and suggests that "Bitter-sweet" "distills the Cistercian tradition that inspired Fisher" (p. 156).

✎§ 761. McCANN, GARTH A. "Dryden and Poetic Continuity: A Comparative Study." *SAQ* 72:311–21.

Contrasts and compares Herbert with Donne and Dryden: "His images are midway between Donne's puzzling and Dryden's plain ones. But he is more careful than they to link the imagery with the ethical ideas they are intended to develop" (p. 313). Comments briefly on "Man" and concludes, "Like Donne, he uses concrete images; like Jonson, he makes moral mandates; like Dryden, he writes clearly" (p. 314). Compares Herbert's didacticism with that of Donne, Jonson, and Dryden and suggests that Herbert is more clearly didactic, his purpose being to teach men religion. Sees a link also between Dryden and his predecessors in that he attempts to couple generalizations with particular examples, as Herbert does, for example, in "Vanitie" and "Man."

✎§ 762. MOLLENKOTT, VIRGINIA R. "George Herbert's 'Redemption.' " *ELN* 10:262–67.

Presents a close examination of "Redemption." Argues that the speaker of the poem is not a mean-spirited materialist (as John R. Mulder suggests) nor a dim-witted petitioner (as Arnold Stein suggests) but is "the spiritual nature of Everyman, not thriving under the Old Testament covenant and finally seeking a New Testament one, with the smaller rent of grace taking the place of the old lease of the law" (p. 263). Sees the narrator as "that part of everyman's soul which desires peace with God, crystallized at the historical moment of Christ's incarnation and crucifixion" (p. 266). Finds the legalistic and business imagery appropriate to the allegory of the poem and well established in Christian tradition: it "is intended to point us to the real drama of God's relationship to man: He had 'dearly bought' the world long ago, by the act of creation, and because of the Fall must now 'take possession' by paying back—redeeming it—on the cross" (pp. 264–65). Views the poem as "an allegorical narrative in the first-person point of view" (p. 266) and comments on its dramatic elements.

◄§ 763. MULDER, JOHN R. "George Herbert's *The Temple*: Design and Methodology." *SCN* 31:37–45.
In part a reply to John M. Steadman, entry 745. Argues that *The Temple* is a consciously structured sequence, since the persona, or speaker, goes through a dramatic series of spiritual changes and emotions in his struggle to understand God and human experience. Suggests that at first the speaker is faulty in thinking that he can himself be an effective instrument in giving God glory and is actually sinful in assuming that the Bible, nature, and human experience can be understood from a more or less anthropocentric point of view, but then, as God tempers the speaker's pride by leading him through a series of spiritual fluctuations and trials, he gradually comes to recognize that his earlier perceptions were wrong and that the presence of Christ is central to everything. Once the persona sees Christ in a theologically correct way, his conflicts cease and his soul is filled with joy and peace. Suggests that by using capital letters and italics for design, Herbert has actually created two authors for the poems in *The Temple*: the poet who, though limited, can order and reorder his perceptions of God and human experience; and God, who constantly orders the poet's perceptions and thus offers him lessons in the great mystery of His dealings with His people.

◄§ 764. PATRICK, J. MAX. "Critical Problems in Editing George Herbert's *The Temple*." In *The Editor as Critic and the Critic as Editor*, with an introduction by Murray Krieger, pp. 3–40. Los Angeles: William Andrews Clark Memorial Library, University of California, Los Angeles.
Argues in the first part of the essay that the textual editor must make careful use of criticism and attacks F. E. Hutchinson's edition of Herbert (entry 223), claiming that much of Hutchinson's trouble results from his having been taken in by Walton's fictional account of how Nicholas Ferrar received the manuscript of Herbert's poems. Argues that the first edition of *The Temple* (1633) was set up from Herbert's own fair copy,

perhaps as early as 1632, and that thus the first edition is the authoritative source, rather than the Bodleian MS, which Hutchinson trusted
in preparing his eclectic edition. Comments in the second part of the
essay on the problems facing the editor of Herbert in making available to
the reader the numerous subtleties of the patterned poems and the significant stanza shapes of Herbert's poetry. Points out, for example, that
"The Agonie" is shaped to resemble not only a printing press and a wine-
press but also a well-known instrument of torture. Maintains that the
modern editor must make sure that these significant forms are adequately
reproduced.

765. PAYNTER, MARY. " 'Sinne and Love': Thematic Patterns in
George Herbert's Lyrics." YES 3:85–93.
Maintains that Herbert's religious consciousness and also the thematic
structure of *The Temple* are dominated by the notion of "the constructive force of God's love set in dynamic opposition to the destructive power of sin" (p. 93). Points out that throughout *The Church*
Herbert's primary image of love is that of the feast, the *sacrum con-
vivium*, with its eucharistic suggestions, while the primary images of sin
are the stony heart and the box. Shows that from "The Agonie" to
"Love (III)" "the Christian experience of divine love, seen in the
image of the feast, and the sense of personal sin, revealed in images of
the stony heart and the closed box, are portrayed in vital counterpoint"
(p. 93).

766. POLLOCK, JOHN J. "George Herbert's Enclosure Imagery." SCN
31:55.
Points out that Herbert employs the concept of enclosure as a structural basis for a number of his poems (for example, "The Pilgrimage")
and that he uses images of enclosure to render his notion of the Eucharist (in, for example, "The Priesthood").

767. RAMSARAN, JOHN A. "Divine Infatuation: Crashaw and Mīram
Baī; Herbert and Mīram Baī." In *English and Hindi Religious
Poetry: An Analogical Study*, pp. 89–108. Studies in the History
of Religions, 23. Leiden: E. J. Brill.
Compares and contrasts Herbert's poetry with that of Mīram Baī, a
late fifteenth- and early sixteenth-century Indian poetess. Suggests that,
although Herbert's poetry is more personal in tone and diction, more
intellectual and analytical, and more full of conflict and tension than
that of Mīram Baī, the two poets shared many resemblances, especially
their yearning for union with God. Compares several individual poems,
especially "Home," "The Search," "The Flower," "Love (III)," and
"Longing," with several of Mīram Baī's poems and concludes that those
poems that reveal the more intimate and personal experiences of Her-

bert the man, rather than those that announce the general spirit of Christian worship, show the most affinities with the Indian poetess.

◄§ 768. RICHMOND, H. M. *Renaissance Landscapes: English Lyrics in a European Tradition.* De Proprietatibus Litterarum, Series Practica, edited by C. H. Van Schooneveld, 52. The Hague: Mouton. 156p.

Discusses the evolution of the landscape lyric and briefly comments on Herbert's debt to *The Greek Anthology*, pointing out, however, that, unlike the Greeks, Herbert presents a "doctrinaire accommodation of landscape allusions to an exposition of Christian concepts" (p. 141). Briefly compares and contrasts Herbert with Alcman, Goethe, and Wordsworth.

◄§ 769. ROGERS, ROBERT. "A Gathering of Roses: An Essay on the Limits of Context." *HSL* 5:61–76.

Surveys the metaphorical uses of the rose and assesses "the potential range of thought and feeling of metaphoric beds of roses by glancing at a number of more or less unrelated contexts to discover what associations such images may have in common" (p. 62). Comments briefly on Herbert's use of the rose in stanza 3 of "Vertue" and discusses the wide-ranging symbolic value of the rose in "The Rose," concluding that the poem "produces endopsychic tension commensurate with the gravity of its subject by setting up a series of oppositions between conscious, conventional meanings and unconscious, psychosexual 'affective correlations' of the imagery" (p. 73).

◄§ 770. Røstvig, MAREN-SOFIE. "Idehistorie og litterær tekstanalyse." *Nordisk Tidsskrift For Litteraturforskning* 53:41–52.

Discusses the importance of cooperation between the history of ideas and close textual analysis, especially for an understanding of Renaissance poetry. Outlines certain trends in literary criticism since the First World War, evaluates their strengths and weaknesses, and insists that the history of ideas and a knowledge of tradition are necessary correctives to the excesses of "new" criticism and of psychological criticism. Specifically mentions William Empson's study of Herbert (entry 108) and sees Rosemond Tuve's *A Reading of George Herbert* (entry 344) as proof of the need to combine close reading with a knowledge of tradition. Presents a brief structural analysis of "Content" and "Deniall" to show that in order to understand the poems one must support textual analysis with the history of ideas and with a good grasp of informing traditions.

◄§ 771. ———. "Structural Images in Cowley and Herbert: A Comparison." *ES* 54:121–29.

Shows through a close structural analysis of Herbert's "The Deniall" and "Content" and Cowley's "The Resurrection," "Hymn to the Light," and "The Ecstasie" that "Cowley's structural manipulations, although sufficiently impressive as a *tour de force*, fail to move; they seem static rather than dynamic" and that "in Herbert alone is the poetic impact perceptively increased and the meaning substantially enriched, by observing the import of the structure" (p. 129). Argues, therefore, that poetic structure is just as useful as poetic images in determining poetic excellence and should be studied and classified as carefully as images.

৵§ 722. Schwartz, Helen J. "Herbert's 'Grief.' " *Expl* 31:item 43.
Suggests that "Grief" is an example of Herbert's technique of expressing the theme of a poem hieroglyphically: "The overflowing, immeasurable quality of the speaker's grief is the poem's subject; the overflowing of the sonnet form shows this idea in action."

৵§ 773. Stanwood, P. G. "The Liveliness of Flesh and Blood: Herbert's 'Prayer I' and 'Love III.' " *SCN* 31:52–53.
Comments on "Prayer (I)" and "Love (III)" as poems that, when read together, illustrate each other: " 'Love' demonstrates that prayer is possible, but Herbert's 'Prayer' is a poem of love" (p. 53). Suggests that the two poems represent in small a major pattern in *The Temple*: "They both characterize the external movement of the flesh and portray the sensitive and . . . wholly responsive answer of the spirit" (p. 52). Comments on the reciprocal movement between the poet and his desire in each poem: "a going forth in order to receive, and an offering that requires an acceptance" (p. 53).

৵§ 774. Treglown, Jeremy. "The Satirical Inversions of Some English Sources in Rochester's Poetry." *RES* 24:42–48.
Points out that the opening of Rochester's poem, "Woman's Honour" ("Love bade me hope, and I obeyed") inverts the sense of Herbert's opening line of "Love (III)" ("Love bade me welcome: yet my soul drew back"). Suggests that the speaker in Rochester's poem presents a sexual version of Herbert's submission to Love ("You must sit down, sayes Love, and taste my meat:/ So I did sit and eat").

৵§ 775. Ward, David. " 'The Fire and the Rose': *Four Quartets*." In *T. S. Eliot: Between Two Worlds*, pp. 223–88. London and Boston: Routledge & Kegan Paul.
Contrasts Eliot with Herbert and maintains that the major difference between the two poets is that Herbert is confident in his poetry whereas Eliot is racked with anguish and doubt. Briefly discusses how this fundamental attitude is reflected in the poetry of each.

◆§ 776. WILKINSON, JEAN. "Three Sets of Religious Poems." *HLQ* 36:203–26.

Compares and contrasts the religious and aesthetic sensibilities, the biases, and the views of experience of three Anglican poets—Herbert, Christopher Smart, and John Keble—who wrote series of poems dealing with the liturgical feasts of the Church and with certain doctrinal beliefs. Specifically contrasts the rhetorical elements, the uses of language, and attitudes toward art in three Christmas poems: Herbert's "Christmas," Smart's "Epiphany," and Keble's "Christmas Day." Argues that both Herbert and Smart are superior to Keble, who tends to sentimentalize; maintains that Smart, however, is Herbert's equal.

1974

◆§ 777. CAMPBELL, GORDON. "Words and Things: The Language of Metaphysical Poetry." *Language and Literature* (Copenhagen) 2, no. 3:3–15.

Challenges critics, such as Rosemond Tuve, who attempt "to experiment with the analytical tools of the Renaissance in an attempt to recreate the sixteenth- and seventeenth-century readers' understanding of poetry" and argues that "these methods, although historically justified, are ultimately destructive, and that an appreciation of Renaissance poetry, particularly metaphysical poetry, is predicated on a knowledge of the poets' ideas about the nature of poetry rather than an ability to implement the philosophers' ideas on how a poem should be analysed" (p. 3). Challenges the notion that Ramism accounts for metaphysical poetry and summarizes the long debate among poets and philosophers of the Renaissance about the primacy of words or things. Sees Herbert as a poet who clearly aligned himself "with those who thought words should take priority over things, that rime rather than reason should unify a poem" (p. 10). Concludes that metaphysical poetry "is primarily a poetry of words rather than things" and that "it is a glorification of the power of words as words, and we should be content to admire it at that level" (p. 11).

◆§ 778. CHARLES, AMY M. "Mrs. Herbert's Kitchen Booke." *ELR* 4: 164–73.

Discusses Magdalen Herbert's household account book kept by her steward, John Gorse, and frequently signed by her (now in the collection of the Earl of Powis at Powis Castle). Covers twenty-one weeks, from the day before Easter until early June 1601, soon after the Herbert household moved to London from Oxford. Records various interesting details about the daily life of the Herbert family, its many guests and visitors, and what the Herbert sons were reading and studying during this period. The article contains a reproduction of a portrait of Magdalen Herbert (perhaps the work of Sir William Segar) and facsimiles of folios 56ᵛ and 57 of the book.

◆§ 779. CRAVEN, ELIZABETH. "The Caldron of Affliction in the Journey Through *The Temple.*" *Graduate English Papers* (University of Arizona) 6, no. 1:2–5.

Maintains that *The Temple* "traces the journey of a soul from a blind acceptance of the letter of the Law to complete communion with the spirit of the Law," that from *The Church-Porch* to "Love (III)" "the soul is moving from what is essentially ignorance toward an intimate knowledge of the spirit of Christ," that the "journey between these two points is marked by a series of trials through which the soul eventually learns the way of Christ," and that the five "Affliction" poems "mark these trials with the lamentations and protestations of the soul" (p. 2). Analyzes the five "Affliction" poems to illustrate this progression and maintains, "What the five 'Affliction' poems suggest in subtle progression, 'Love Unknown' explains in allegory" (p. 4).

◆§ 780. DODGE, CAROLYN JUNE. "Kinaesthetic Effect in the Poetry of George Herbert." *RUO* 44:202–17.

Discusses Herbert's use of kinesthetic effects in his poetry and defines these effects as "the muscular, behavioral response to the sounds and rhythms of metrical structures" (p. 202). Argues that the rhythms of Herbert's poetry effect "an imitation of movement away from or toward God" and that thus the reader experiences "the physical, muscular sense or feeling which accompanies each spiritual act that constitutes the meaning experienced in the poetry" (p. 202). Suggests that Herbert may have known such a theory through certain medical tracts and poetic treatises of the Renaissance. Through a discussion of a number of specific poems, the author attempts to show that kinesthetic effect "is associated with metrically emblematic structures such as counterpoint, contract, and enjambment to express man's creatural relationship to God; with hieroglyphic forms; and with interrelated uses of sense imagery" (p. 217). Maintains, for example, that in "Easter-wings" the reader kinesthetically experiences spiritual flight and in "The Collar" kinesthetically experiences the sense of rebellion. Concludes that the kinesthetic effect is in fact "part of the unity of images and idea, form and substance, subject and style in *The Temple* where the act of creation by the poet and the re-creation by the reader is an act of worship" (p. 217).

◆§ 781. FISH, STANLEY. "Catechizing the Reader: Herbert's Socratean Rhetoric." In *The Rhetoric of Renaissance Poetry: From Wyatt to Milton,* edited by Thomas O. Sloan and Raymond B. Waddington, pp. 174–88. Berkeley, Los Angeles, London: University of California Press.

Argues that Herbert's poetic strategy is closely related to the method of catechizing discussed in chapter 21 of *A Priest to the Temple*. Suggests that the poet assumes the role of the questioner or catechist and that the reader becomes the one catechized and argues that such an approach accounts for the elements of order and surprise in Herbert's poetry: "The order belongs to the Questionist-poet who knows from the beginning where he is going" and the "surprise belongs to the reader who is 'driven' by 'questions well ordered' to discover for himself 'that which he knows not' " (p. 176). Shows how, for instance, Herbert often "strikes deliberately naive poses that are calculated to draw a critical or corrective response from an interlocutor; that is, he makes assertions which *function* as questions because they invite the reader to supply either what is missing or what is deficient" (p. 177). Demonstrates how this strategy functions in "Love-joy," "Love unknown," "The Holdfast," and especially "The Bunch of Grapes." Comments also on how this rhetorical strategy is consistent with Herbert's views on the moral purposes of poetry.

782. GRANT, PATRICK. *The Transformation of Sin: Studies in Donne, Herbert, Vaughan, and Traherne.* Montreal & London: McGill-Queen's University Press; Amherst: University of Massachusetts Press. xiii, 240p.

A study of Donne, Herbert, Vaughan, and Traherne that approaches these devotional poets "in terms of a hypothetical encounter between guilt culture and enlightenment" (p. 38), in other words, in terms of a conflict between traditional Augustinian theology and sensibility and a new ethical view of man. Argues, "The conflict of the old and the new in the seventeenth century is not simply between Protestantism and Catholicism, or between Renaissance and Reformation, but between two modes of regarding the ethical nature of man" (p. 38). Although Herbert is mentioned throughout this study, three chapters specifically discuss him. Chapter 3, "Augustinian Spirituality and George Herbert's *The Temple*" (pp. 73–99), contrasts Herbert and Donne, maintaining that, although both were Augustinian and medieval in the main, Herbert's "fascination with Calvinist predestination affords his poems those qualities which most readily distinguish them from Donne's" (p. 76). Outlines the influence of Augustinian tradition on Herbert and finds many similarities between his religious poems and the medieval religious lyric, which in turn was informed by Franciscan spirituality. Discusses the *Biblia Pauperum* and the *Speculum humanae salvationis*, two medieval handbooks of popular devotion imbued with Franciscan spirituality and concludes "The medieval tradition on which George Herbert's devotional poetry predominately draws is . . . primarily Augustinian, mediated to the Renaissance through a devotional tradition, mainly Franciscan" (p. 92). Chapter 4, "George Herbert and Juan de Valdés: The Franciscan Mode and Protestant Manner" (pp. 100–133), discusses the theology and spirituality of Juan de Valdés, pointing out important analogues between the Spanish writer and Herbert. Argues that Herbert's spirituality "is Franciscan in the manner that the spirituality of Valdés is also Franciscan" (p. 123) but notes, "We find in Herbert a traditional Augustinian piety modified by doctrines of justification by faith, election, and predestination, but modified in such a way that the opposing tendencies are sustained momentarily in harmony" (p. 123). Chapter 5, "Henry Vaughan and the Hermetic Philosophy" (pp. 134–69), although devoted primarily to Vaughan, contains a comparison of Herbert and Vaughan and points out a number of significant differences between the master and the disciple: "In their poetry of the fall and original sin, Herbert's object is behavior, Vaughan's is cosmology" (p. 144).

◄§ 783. HAMMOND, GERALD, ed. *The Metaphysical Poets: A Selection of Critical Essays.* Casebook Series, edited by A. E. Dyson. London and Basingstoke: Macmillan Press. 254p.

Contains an introduction to the metaphysical poets, including comments on Herbert (pp. 11–32) and selections from criticism from the seventeenth century to the modern period. Herbert is mentioned in the following: (1) Selections from Edward Phillip's *Theatrum Poetarum Anglicanorum* of 1674 (p. 37); (2) selection from *Select Hymns out of Mr Herbert's Temple* of 1697 (pp. 40–41); (3) selection from Addison, *The Spectator* of 1711 (pp. 42–46); (4) selections from Coleridge taken from *Coleridge on the Seventeenth Century*, edited by Roberta Florence Brinkley in 1955 (entry 374) (pp. 59–60); (5) selections from Emerson's *Notebooks* (1831–1845) (pp. 67–70); (6) selections from George Macdonald's *England's Antiphon* of 1868 (pp. 71–74); (7) selection from Rosemond Tuve's *Elizabethan and Metaphysical Imagery: Renaissance Poetic and Twentieth-Century Critics* of 1947 (entry 279) (pp. 91–115); (8) S. L. Bethell's "Gracián, Tesauro, and the Nature of Metaphysical Wit" of 1953 (entry 346) (pp. 129–56); (9) selection from Joseph H. Summers's *George Herbert: His Religion and Art* of 1954 (entry 369) (pp. 157–81); (10) selection from Josephine Miles and Hanan C. Selvin's "A Factor Analysis of the Vocabulary of Poetry in the Seventeenth Century" of 1966 (entry 579) (pp. 182–96); (11) selection from Earl Miner's *The Metaphysical Mode from Donne to Cowley* of 1969 (entry 653) (pp. 197–214). Select bibliography (pp. 243–45).

◄§ 784. HERBERT, GEORGE. *The English Poems of George Herbert,* edited by C. A. Patrides. London: J. M. Dent & Sons. 247p.
1st American ed., Totowa, N.J.: Rowman and Littlefield, 1975.

"To the Reader" (pp. 1–3) contains a note on abbreviations, a note on the text (except for six poems from the Williams MS and two from Walton's *Lives*, the primary authority is the first edition of 1633), and acknowledgments. "An Outline of Herbert's Life Within the Context of Contemporary Events" (pp. 4–5). A general critical introduction to Herbert's poetry, entitled "A Crown of Praise: The Poetry of Herbert" (pp. 6–25), stresses the grace, complex simplicity, and self-conscious plainness of Herbert's art and outlines major themes, techniques, and general characteristics of his poetry. Comments on the pervasive influence of the Bible, emblem books, wisdom literature, the parables, and music and discusses the structure of *The Temple*, commenting particularly on the importance of the Eucharist and of the concept of grace in Herbert's religious sensibility as reflected in his poems. "A Note on Typology" (pp. 26–27). *The Temple* (pp. 29–200) with notes. Appendix 1: "Poems not included in *The Temple*" (pp. 201–6). Appendix 2, "Three versions of a poem by Herbert" (pp. 207–8), gives three versions of "The Elixir." Appendix 3: "Some secular poems parodied by Herbert" (pp. 209–13). Extensive bibliography (pp. 214–38), index of titles (pp. 239–43), and index of first lines (pp. 244–47).

≈§ 785. HIGBIE, ROBERT. "Images of Enclosure in George Herbert's *The Temple*." *TSLL* 15:627–38.

Maintains that Herbert's extensive use of enclosure imagery (walls, locked doors, houses, boxes, cabinets, etc.) forms one of the major unifying elements in *The Temple*. Suggests several reasons for Herbert's choosing such images: "Accepting God for him seems to have meant accepting some sort of containment, some boundaries within which God would protect him" (p. 627). Notes, "A temple itself is a kind of enclosure, and Herbert seems to have chosen the enclosure image for its relation to his concept of the temple, which . . . represents for him God's perfect enclosure, the ideal of which his earlier enclosure images are imperfect reflections" (p. 627). Points out, therefore, that the imagery in *The Temple* progresses, though not directly, "from the earthly man-made enclosure, the house and the church, to the divine enclosure of the temple, the perfection that the church tries to embody on earth" (p. 627). Views the various conflicts, the contradictions, and the sense of constraint and limitation in *The Church* as Herbert's means of giving the reader "a sense of the straitness of our earthly dwelling-place, to make us feel imprisoned in it, and by doing so to make us want to transcend the earthly and seek the divine" (p. 628). Suggests that through his use of enclosure imagery and strict forms Herbert also intends to suggest that poetry itself, since it is man-made, is inadequate to lead us to God. Sees "Love (III)" with its eucharistic overtones as the climax of *The Church*: "It is for this final 'entrance' (l. 4) into God's enclosure that the enclosure imagery has been constructed, and this ritual act representing union with

God is what it is meant to enclose. It is not merely a physical but a spiritual enclosure, the place within which the union can be consummated. And this enclosure . . . is the temple to which Herbert's title refers—not an earthly temple, any more than the Eucharist taken inside it is earthly food, but rather an ideal, a temple raised in the heart" (pp. 635–36).

◄§ 786. HOLLOWAY, JOHN. "Poetic Analysis and the Idea of Transformation-Rule: Some Examples from Herbert, Wordsworth, Pope, and Shakespeare." In *Miscellanea Anglo-Americana: Festschrift für Helmut Viebrock*, edited by Kuno Schuhmann, Wilhelm Hortmann, and Armin Paul Frank, pp. 279–96. Munich: Karl Pressler.

Although he generally distrusts the application of linguistic theory to poetry as it is presently practiced by many linguists and literary critics, the author suggests that the literary critic "allow his mind to play freely over two general ideas, which indeed come from linguistics in the context of linguistic transformation-rules, as possible helps to poetic analysis in certain cases" (p. 283). The two ideas are "first, simply the idea of a rule itself; and then, the idea that the kind of rule he may find is operative will be a rule whereby sentences of one form are transformed systematically into sentences of another" (p. 283). Applies this notion to a number of poems and poetic passages. Comments on the inversion of normal word order in Herbert's "The Windows" and contrasts it with the inversions found in Wordsworth's "Anecdote for Fathers." Comments also on certain structural features in "Mortification."

◄§ 787. KELLIHER, W. HILTON. "The Latin Poetry of George Herbert." In *The Latin Poetry of English Poets*, edited by J. W. Binns, pp. 26–57. London and Boston: Routledge & Kegan Paul.

Presents a detailed historical and critical survey of Herbert's Latin verse. Calls *Memoriae Matris Sacrum* "the masterpiece of Herbert's Latin poetry" (p. 47) and says that it clearly "illustrates by its highly personal tone no less than by the Metaphysical spirit that is evident in individual poems how Herbert's mastery of classical idioms was made to serve his own immediate needs rather than merely to fulfill a literary ideal" (p. 54).

◄§ 788. LINDEN, STANTON J. "The Breaking of the Alembic: Patterns in Alchemical Imagery in English Renaissance Poetry." *WascanaR* 9: 105–13.

Contrasts two literary uses of alchemy during the Renaissance. Points out that from Chaucer onward to Donne and Jonson, alchemy was presented with a satirical intent; it became synonymous with greed, deceit, self-delusion, and all kinds of moral depravity. However, before this satirical tradition died out, there also developed (between 1580 and 1630) a new and different pattern of alchemic usage, one in which alchemy was used metaphorically to suggest growth, change, and even regeneration.

Maintains that the poetry of Donne and Herbert gives us the best examples of the way that alchemy was utilized during the transitional period, since they "tend to use alchemy with an awareness and understanding of its full range of denotations, connotations, and associational nuances" (p. 109). Cites Herbert's "The Elixir" as an example.

◄§ 789. McFarland, Ronald E. "Thanksgiving in Seventeenth Century Poetry." *Albion* (Washington State University Press) 6:294–306.

Surveys the background and tradition of Christian poems of thanksgiving and comments on a number of representative thanksgiving poems written during the seventeenth century in England. Contrasts Herbert's "The Thanksgiving" with thanksgiving poems by Herrick and Marvell and points out that Herbert's emphasis is "upon the *response* to God's most important gift—the possibility of salvation through Christ" (p. 304). Presents an analysis of the poem and shows how its positioning in *The Temple* informs its full meaning. Suggests that Herbert's poem is "not in fact a thankful response, but rather a consideration of possible responses; it is not a poem *of* thanksgiving so much as it is a poem *about* thanksgiving" (p. 305) and maintains that other poems, such as "Gratefulnesse" and "Praise (II)" more closely resemble the typical thanksgiving poems of the age. Concludes that the issue of the proper response to redemption "is fittingly resolved in" "Love (III)" (p. 306).

◄§ 790. McGuire, Philip C. "Private Prayer and English Poetry in the Early Seventeenth Century." *SEL* 14:63–77.

Discusses the influences of private prayer, as opposed to formal discursive meditation, on poetic practice in the early seventeenth century as reflected in six poems by Donne, Jonson, and Herbert. Outlines various contemporary attitudes toward, and definitions of, prayer and points out that Renaissance devotionalists "divided private prayer into a preface (which could also be a conclusion) and three major components—confession, invocation, and thanksgiving—which were organized either to praise God or, more frequently, to persuade him" (p. 65). Analyzes Herbert's "The Altar" as a prayer of praise and petition in which the speaker's act of framing his prayer as a poem heightens his praise and the persuasiveness of his petitions" (p. 75).

◄§ 791. Mambrino, Jean. "Simone Weil and George Herbert." *Etudes* 340:247–62.

Argues that the poetry of Herbert was a decisive influence on the life of Simone Weil, who was first introduced to the poetry in 1938. Reproduces Weil's comments on Herbert and points out that she especially liked "Discipline," "Bitter-sweet," and "Love (III)," which she called "le plus beau poème du monde" (p. 250). Outlines certain affinities between the life, faith, and death of Herbert and those of Weil and presents French translations of "The Collar," "Discipline," "Bitter-sweet," "Vertue," and "Love (III)."

◆§ 792. MILWARD, PETER, S.J. "Anglican and Catholic in the Religious Poetry of the XVIIth Century." *ELLS* 11:1–12.

Suggests that had the Civil War and the resultant triumph of Puritanism not occurred, the Anglican Church might have been reunited to the Catholic Church by the end of the seventeenth century. Sees the poetry of Herbert and Crashaw as representative of two successive and continuous stages in the development of Anglicanism. Recognizes Herbert's negative attitudes toward the Papacy and the fundamentally Protestant temper of much of his theology but maintains that in his poems he "expresses an ideal of the Church and Christian worship which is fundamentally at one with Catholic tradition" (p. 6). Suggests that the merits and defects in the poetry of both Herbert and Crashaw "correspond in varying degrees to the merits and defects of the Anglican and Catholic communions of their period" (p. 10). Views Herbert as perhaps more parochial and more English than Crashaw, who was more open to the Continental, baroque expression of Christianity.

◆§ 793. MORILLO, MARVIN. "Herbert's Chairs: Notes to *The Temple*." *ELN* 11:271–75.

Considers Herbert's various references to chairs in *The Temple* and disagrees with F. E. Hutchinson's gloss on the chairs in "Mortification" and "The Pilgrimage." Points out that in "The Temper (II)," "Jordan (I)," and "Church-rents and schismes," Herbert uses *chair* primarily in its etymological sense as "a seat of authority" or "throne," but that in both "Mortification" and "The Pilgrimage" he is referring to portable chairs, "conveyances in a stage of the allegorical journey rather than stationary places of repose" and that "though indeed emblematic of old age, [the chairs] point specifically to old age in progress, not in repose" (p. 273). Suggests that "since journeys provide the allegorical terms in both poems and since abundant evidence indicates that 'chair' in that context would be readily understood as designating a conveyance for royalty, the sick, wounded, or the feeble aged, Hutchinson's note summons an image of the hearthside chair that is inconsistent with the controlling conceit of both poems" (p. 275).

◆§ 794. OSMOND, ROSALIE. "Body and Soul Dialogues in the Seventeenth Century." *ELR* 4:364–403.

Discusses the revival of interest in body-soul dialogues in the first half of the seventeenth century and presents a number of reasons for "this apparently anachronistic literary form" making "a sudden and brief appearance between 1602 and 1651 only to die out completely after that date" (p. 364). Suggests, "Careful examination of the characteristics of both the form and content of the medieval debates makes it clear that they have much more in common with at least certain aspects of early seventeenth century thought and literature than one might suppose" (p. 364). Briefly comments on Herbert's uses of personification in his presentation of the soul in his poetry and shows that, although Herbert and his contemporaries "did not consciously believe the soul to be visible, they just as certainly did imagine it to be so" (p. 379) in their poems. Thus, although poetic images "cannot be taken at face value as literal statements of belief" (p. 379), they do subtly help to form certain theological attitudes and influence the general understanding of certain theological concepts.

✎§ 795. SEGEL, HAROLD B. *The Baroque Poem: A Comparative Survey.* New York: E. P. Dutton & Co. xx, 328p.

The purpose of this study is two-fold: (1) "to present a comprehensive survey of the Baroque: the state of scholarship in the field, problems in the definition and use of Baroque as a term and concept, the relationship of mannerism to Baroque, the political, religious, scientific, and philosophical background of the age, the possible impact of nonliterary events on the evolution of the Baroque taste, art, and outlook, the various types of Baroque poetry and aspects of Baroque poetic style" (pp. xix–xx) and (2) "to illustrate points made in the first, or survey, part of the book by giving a broad selection of representative poems, mostly lyrics, in the original languages and accompanying English translations" (p. xx). Contains 150 poems from the following literatures: English, American, Dutch, German, French, Italian, Spanish, Mexican, Portuguese, Polish, Modern Latin, Czech, Croatian, and Russian. Mentions Herbert throughout and sees him as a baroque poet. Includes eleven poems by Herbert.

✎§ 796. SHARP, NICHOLAS. "Herbert's 'Love (III).'" *Expl* 33:item 26.

Points out that the word *host* refers not only to a person who gives a banquet but also to the communion wafer. Suggests that "Love (III)" is "a prayerful interchange between the modest communicant (the guest) and Christ really present in the communion host." Maintains that on a literal level, "with allegorical or anagogical exegesis, the poem concerns the Communion banquet which, as the structural ambiguity insists, is truly a feast of love." Suggests that to miss this literal level is also to miss "the distinction between Herbert's metaphysical piety and the similar but distinct piety of medieval religious verse."

✎§ 797. SUMMERS, JOSEPH H. "Stanley Fish's Reading of Seventeenth-Century Literature." *MLQ* 35:403–17.

Essentially a review-article of Stanley E. Fish's *Self-Consuming Arti-*

facts: The Experience of Seventeenth-Century Literature (entry 729).
Suggests that "the chief virtues of Fish's book derive from his recognition
that the basic data of any literary criticism are the *experiences* of an
alert, intelligent, and sensitive reader as he reads the text within time"
(p. 417) but distrusts Fish's assumption "that admirable literary designs
on the reader should always be antagonistic, tricky, or evangelical; that
the ultimate recognition the best seventeenth-century works provide is
the distrust of any sort of reliance on the 'self' or human reason; and
that what they bring the reader to, again and again, is the recognition
both of their own and the readers' inadequacies before divine revelation
and the inexplicable will of God" (p. 406). States, "I think that while he
observes numbers of important happenings which we need to notice,
he omits or misinterprets a good deal by attempting to stick so closely to
one perspective on the reading process" (p. 405). Points out that "with
Herbert's marvellously artful poems, the major limitations of Fish's
principal metaphor are most evident" (p. 411) and rejects Fish's notion
that Herbert is primarily a dialectician unconcerned with beauty: "Any
reading of Herbert's poems which ignores *any* notions of the beautiful is
likely to be at best partial, if not peculiar" (p. 411). Challenges a number of Fish's interpretations of Herbert: for example, "it is Fish rather
than Herbert who assumes that poetry per se is 'presumptuous' or
suspect" (p. 412).

&§ 798. Taylor, Mark. *The Soul in Paraphrase: George Herbert's Poetics*. De Proprietatibus Litterarum: Series Practica, 92. The Hague
and Paris: Mouton. 127p.
Argues that *The Temple* "demonstrates Herbert's total poetic and
linguistic involvement in the Christian experience" (p. 2). Chapter 1,
"Poetry and Silence: Herbert's Art of Poetry" (pp. 9–52), discusses
Herbert's theory of poetry and shows that "it is a theory of words,
deriving from a sense of the inability of traditional scholastic rhetoric
or the language of secular poetry to express the truth" (p. 2). Chapter
2, "Poetry and Time: Herbert's Image of Time" (pp. 53–84), comments
on "the way in which verse can enable the poet to transcend the limitations of temporal mortality and enter into eternity, a movement that
Herbert presents metaphorically as the subservience of the human
words of poetic composition to the poem's God-given truth" (pp. 2–3).
Chapter 3, "Poetry and Light: Herbert's Synaesthetic Imagery" (pp. 85–
115), argues that a study of Herbert's synesthetic imagery "will show
that, as God is both the Word and the Light, so can human words
reflect the revealed light in which they have their origin; there is a
sense in which visual and verbal transmission and perception are one"
(p. 3). Maintains that all of these informing notions are unified by
Herbert's personal, yet totally orthodox Christian experience and by

his imaginative uses of certain concepts derived from St. Augustine. Selected bibliography (pp. 118–22).

◆§ 799. THEKLA, SISTER MARIA. *George Herbert: Idea and Image.* Buckinghamshire, Eng.: Greek Orthodox Monastery of the Assumption, Filgrave, Newport Pagnell. 308p.

Detailed discussion of the theological and spiritual dimensions of Herbert's poetry. Sees a double, simultaneous movement in *The Temple* and suggests that, although on one level *The Temple* can be seen as an exposition of Anglican theology and dogma in verse, on another level it is a record of Herbert's own mystical thinking: "It is this double movement which I have tried to lean towards in my exploration of *The Temple*, that is, the reality of Herbert's allegiance to his Church, the Church of England, on earth, with all the consequences, and, then, the reality of the love which can not be contained in the Church on earth, or indeed within the confines of the created world" (p. 14). Part 1: "The Works of Faith" (pp. 19–116) is divided into four chapters. Chapter 1, "Priest of the Church of England" (pp. 21–39), comments on Herbert's attitudes on, and love of, the Church and his attitudes on the priesthood. Chapter 2, "World of Grace and World of Nature" (pp. 39–69), discusses Herbert's theology of redemption and comments on such matters as redemption, faith, grace, and the imputation of righteousness. Chapter 3, "Theology in Practice" (pp. 70–96), discusses Herbert's attitudes on the saints, the Bible, the Eucharist, and the meaning of suffering in the Christian life. Chapter 4, "The Angry God" (pp. 96–116), traces "how, in the uncertainty of any assurance of continued Grace, in the no-knowledge of success, and, with a seemingly inherent distaste for an absolute doctrine of the imputation of Righteousness, Herbert found his path by a creative submission of *the Angry God*" (p. 116). Part 2: "The Work of Love" (pp. 117–205) is divided into three chapters. Chapter 1, "The Person of Christ" (pp. 119–51), outlines Herbert's Christology. Chapter 2, "Participation in Christ" (pp. 152–77), discusses Herbert's attitudes on sin, repentance, mortality, and death. Chapter 3, "The Offering of Praise" (pp. 178–205), comments on how Herbert sees all his work as a form of praise and views his poetry primarily as a medium of devotion. Part 3: "Key Poems of the Mystery" (pp. 207–46) presents a discussion of poems in which Herbert "explicitly gives the hint of his conviction of the Mystery, which, within him, transcends all systems of theology" (p. 209): "Divinitie," "The Flower," "The Answer," "The Collar," "Miserie," "Jordan (II)," "Josephs coat," "Love unknown," "The Pulley," "Mans medley," "Home," "The Pilgrimage," and "Hope." Part 4: "Synopsis of the Imagery" (pp. 247–75) presents a detailed discussion of Herbert's imagery illustrated by diagrams of the complexity of the interrelationships of the imagery. Conclusion: "A Note on the Place of Literature in Understanding Between the Churches" (pp. 277–78). Appended is Sister Maria's essay, "George Herbert: Aspects of His Theology" (pp. 279–305), first published in 1972, which, in a sense, presents a microcosmic summary of the theological discussion of her book. Index of poems (pp. 306–7).

No Date

⊷§ 800. HERBERT, GEORGE. "Sweet day so cool; trio for two sopranos & bass with piano forte accompaniment (ad lib). Words by The Reverend George Herbert; music by Brinley Richards." Boston: Russell & Fuller. 5p.
  Musical setting for "Vertue."

Author Index

Subject Index

(The following is an index of subjects mentioned in the annotations in this bibliography. The reader is advised to check all general studies related to a specific topic.)

Index of Herbert's Works
Mentioned in Annotations